D0216314

MAGAZINES
OF THE
AMERICAN SOUTH

Recent Titles of
Historical Guides to the World's Periodicals and Newspapers

This series provides historically focused narrative and analytical profiles of periodicals and newpapers with accompanying bibliographical data.

Black Journals of the United States
Walter C. Daniel

Mystery, Detective, and Espionage Magazines
Michael L. Cook

American Indian and Alaskan Native Newspapers and Periodicals, 1826–1924
Daniel F. Littlefield, Jr., and James W. Parins

British Literary Magazines: The Augustan Age and the Age of Johnson, 1698–1788
Alvin Sullivan, editor

British Literary Magazines: The Romantic Age, 1789–1836
Alvin Sullivan, editor

British Literary Magazines: The Victorian and Edwardian Age, 1837–1913
Alvin Sullivan, editor

Children's Periodicals of the United States
R. Gordon Kelly, editor

International Film, Radio, and Television Journals
Anthony Slide, editor

Science Fiction, Fantasy, and Weird Fiction Magazines
Marshall B. Tymn and Mike Ashley, editors

American Indian and Alaskan Native Newspapers and Periodicals, 1925–1970
Daniel F. Littlefield, Jr., and James W. Parins, editors

MAGAZINES OF THE AMERICAN SOUTH

Sam G. Riley

Historical Guides to the World's Periodicals and Newspapers

Greenwood Press
New York • Westport, Connecticut • London

PUBLIC LIBRARY OF PINE BLUFF
AND JEFFERSON COUNTY

Library of Congress Cataloging in Publication Data

Riley, Sam G.
  Magazines of the American South.

  (Historical guides to the world's periodicals and
newspapers, ISSN 0742-5538)
  Bibliography: p.
  Includes indexes.
  1. American periodicals—Southern States—History.
I. Title. II. Series.
PN4893.R54   1986   051   85-8012
ISBN 0-313-24337-9 (lib. bdg.: alk. paper)

Copyright © 1986 by Sam G. Riley

All rights reserved. No portion of this book may be
reproduced, by any process or technique,
without the express written consent of the publisher.

Library of Congress Catalog Card Number: 85-8012
ISBN: 0-313-24337-9
ISSN: 0742-5538

First published in 1986

Greenwood Press, Inc.
88 Post Road West
Westport, Connecticut 06881

202785

Printed in the United States of America

The paper used in this book complies with the
Permanent Paper Standard issued by the National
Information Standards Organization (Z39.48-1984).

10   9   8   7   6   5   4   3   2   1

FOR THOSE I LOVE

3-28-81

Contents

Preface

Of all the media of mass communications, magazines have received the least attention from scholars or from commentators of any kind. Excepting the largest national magazines and the best literary magazines, few have been chronicled or criticized. If one accepts the contention that the South had been and remains one of America's most distinctive regions, it is especially regrettable that so little has been written about this region's magazines.

Some information on Southern magazines may be found in Frank Luther Mott's monumental five-volume work, *A History of American Magazines* (1930–1968), which includes magazines published from 1741 to 1930. Chapters on the magazines of the nineteenth-century and early twentieth-century South are to be found in such books as W. T. Couch's *Culture in the South* (1934) or Edwin Mims' *The South in the Building of the Nation*, vol. VII (1909), and portions of chapters in other histories: R. S. Cotterell's *The Old South* (1936), T. D. Clark and A. D. Kirwan's *The South Since Appomattox* (1967), and F. B. Simkins' *The South Old and New* (1947).

Only a handful of books have been written about specific Southern magazines or their editors and publishers, whereas innumerable books have been published on Southern *belles lettres* and at least a modest number on Southern newspapers and newspapermen. Only scant contributions to scholarly journals have dealt with Southern magazines and their history.

Writing in *Culture in the South* (1934), Professor Jay B. Hubbell of Duke University observed:

The Southern magazines—probably the best expression of the mind of the South—were never adequately supported in their day, and all but a handful have been forgotten. We have seldom cared enough about them to collect their back files, and as a result the literature of the South is better studied in Northern libraries. It was impossible to complete this essay without going to Northern libraries for much of my material . . . it was only in the New York Public Library that I found nearly complete files of certain important magazines of the twentieth century: *The Double Dealer*, *The Reviewer*, *The Fugitive*, and *Uncle Remus's Magazine*. The literature of the South is of considerable importance, at least to us who live there, but we shall never know much about it until we stop boasting of our literary achievements and *study* them.

It is likewise true that Southern magazines of today receive little attention from the national periodicals that carry articles on the American magazine publishing scene: *Forbes*, *Business Week*, *Advertising Age*, *The Wall Street Journal*, *The New York Times*, *Dun's Media Decisions*, *Saturday Review*.

In writing this book and in compiling a companion volume entitled *Index to Southern Periodicals*, which is a reasonably complete list of the region's magazines and other nonnewspaper periodicals from 1764 to 1984, I hope to make a start in supplying a missing chapter in the cultural history of the South. A further hope is that other writer-researchers will be stimulated to provide more descriptive, and eventually integrative, work on the subject.

As the South becomes ever more urbanized and industrialized, the contrast between the region's old and new becomes decidedly more dramatic. Further work in this area should be of use in assessing the mind of the South—the region's consciousness, experience, and folkways—as it has existed and altered through time. Today far more nationally circulated magazines are being published in the Southern states than was the case a few decades ago, which indicates that the region's magazine industry is not as parochial or inward-directed as it once was. One might be surprised to learn that the nation's only magazine for atheists, *American Atheist*, is published in Texas; that America's largest pets magazine, *Cats*, is published in Florida; or that the nation's highest circulation magazine for the home computer trade, *Compute!*, is based in North Carolina. This work, however, focuses on magazines that are "Southern" in terms of regional content and anticipated audience. Magazines designed to appeal to a national audience or to specialized groups are included in other volumes in the series Historical Guides to the World's Periodicals and Newspapers.

One usually speaks of "The South" as though it were a region of exact boundaries, which is not really the case. For the purpose of this book, the South has been operationally defined as the states of the Confederacy—Alabama, Arkansas, Florida, Georgia, Louisiana, Mississippi, North Carolina, South Carolina, Tennessee, and Texas—plus Kentucky, long considered a predominantly Southern state. The most difficult question was what to do with Maryland. In the early years covered by this work, Maryland was clearly Southern. Even into the first decade of the 1900s magazines were being founded in Baltimore bearing the designation "Southern" in their titles, yet today Baltimore has more in common with the cities of the Northeastern seaboard than with the small towns grown large that pass for cities farther south. To be conservative, I have chosen to include Baltimore as a Southern city, and Maryland as a Southern state, until the Civil War.

Why has the Southern magazine been the subject of so little attention in the past? I am not certain of the answer, even after much reflection, but it is possible that magazine history has simply fallen between disciplinary cracks. Professors of English have been interererested in magazines only for their literary content, but of all the thousands of magazines the region has spawned, only a relative few have been devoted to *belles lettres*. Historians, on the other hand, have likely avoided research in this area because of the alien necessity of dealing, at least to some degree, with the literary merit of magazines' copy. My colleague Marshall Fishwick once wrote that magazines have received little scholarly analysis because they are too derivative and "popular" for scholars in general and too diffuse and secondary for the historian in particular. In a casual conversation, this same Fishwick also lamented the fate of that which is written for periodicals, saying that it soon becomes "lost in the Great Storm," in other words, here today and gone tomorrow. In most cases this has been true enough.

Another consideration is the inconvenience and expense of doing this kind of project. There is no one magazine center to which the researcher can go, no one library that holds files of most Southern magazines. The Library of Congress and the New York Public Library have the best collections, and some of the earliest of these periodicals have been made far more accessible by having been put on film by University Microfilms of Ann Arbor, Michigan, in their American Periodicals Series. Still, holdings are widely scattered. Some of the South's libraries having magazine collections worthy of special note are those at Duke, the University of North Carolina at Chapel Hill, the University of South Carolina, Tulane, and the University of Texas, though the researcher who wished to examine a great many titles would have to travel to many, many other collections as well.

In making my selections for the profiles herein, I have tried to choose periodicals that would be of relatively general appeal, avoiding specialized scholarly journals, trade magazines, technical periodicals, and any other category that would presumably be of interest to only a small group of readers. In no way should these titles be thought of as "the best Southern magazines," though some of the very finest have been included—*Niles' Weekly Register*, *The Southern Literary Messenger*, and *DeBow's Commercial Review*, to name a few. Others were selected in an attempt to counter the overwhelming impression the author received in his literature review for this project: that Southern magazines, so often poorly supported and short-lived, were the stuff of penultimate dullness. Here I might be faulted by some readers for possibly overemphasizing humor periodicals and the humorous content of other more general magazines.

Some magazines were chosen because they are graphically beautiful, others because they provide good examples of how very specialized, even atomized, magazine publishing has become. A few were picked because they do not seem to square with the image most "outlanders," or even those of us born and bred here, have of the South. One category that has been intentionally short-changed is the religious magazine, although the South has produced hundreds. Religious periodicals will be covered in another book in this series, *ReligiousPeriodicals of the United States*, edited by Charles H. Lippy. By like token, Southern magazines published by and for blacks do not appear here because they have been covered in an earlier book in the series, Walter C. Daniel's *Black Journals of the United States*.

The English Department scholar who peruses a copy of this book may be horrified and repulsed when he or she finds a magazine of real literary merit cheek to jowl with a farm magazine, a sports periodical, or a journal of society tittle-tattle. Here I wish to stress that literary criticism is not my main intent. The focus of this book is not on the magazine as literature, but simply on magazines as magazines, admitting that peoples' literary needs are only one area of a magazine's usefulness, and that practical information or amusement are also important components of the total picture.

Put somewhat facetiously, I see myself falling somewhere between an Agrarian and a Rotarian—not as indifferent to literary merit as the average businessman, perhaps, but not as enamored of literary niceties as would have been the Agrarian, or the Transcendentalist, or the Tractarian, or the Pre-Raphaelite, or whatever.

Thought was given in the selection process to providing some balance as to time periods in which the magazines were founded, and to a lesser extent to achieving balance by geographic location. It should come as no surprise, of course, that important early publishing centers such as Baltimore, Charleston, and New Orleans are well represented here and that Arkansas and Mississippi are more sparsely represented.

More quotations have been included from early than from current magazines in an effort to impart the flavor of unfamiliar times, inasmuch as eighteenth and nineteenth-century writing styles differ considerably from those to which today's reader is accustomed. Quotations from a magazine within the article on that magazine are cited in parentheses in the text. For example (4, 8: 35–37) indicates volume 4, number 8, pages 35–37. Shortened references may be used if some of the information is clear from context, or if the magazine in question does not use volume or number designations. For example (4: 35–37) indicates volume 4, pages 35–37, and (no. 8: 35–37) indicates number 8, pages 35–37. Pages given alone will be preceded by p. or pp.

As is the case with the other volumes in this series, titles are arranged alphabetically to facilitate access. An asterisk (*) is used in each profile to denote the first appearance of the title of any other magazine profiled in this volume. Cross-references have been provided alphabetically for magazines having had substantial changes in their titles.

Each entry includes a historical essay on the magazine's development, editorial policies, and content. Entries also include two sections that provide data on Information Sources and Publication History, arranged in tabular form for ready reference. The Information Sources section lists bibliographic information, index sources, and location sources. The section on Publication History lists title and any title changes, volume and issue data, publishers and places of publication, editors, and circulation figures. Circulation figures for the older magazines were often unobtainable; those figures reported here represent peak circulation unless otherwise identified.

The book also includes two appendixes that list the titles profiled by date founded and geographical location.

Finally, it would seem that the 1980s are an auspicious time to begin serious work in this area. Magazine publishing in the region has undergone considerable growth in recent decades, a fact not widely recognized. Since World War II the total number of Southern nonnewspaper periodicals has more than doubled. I hope that I have done justice to providing a representative sample of Southern magazines and that the current editors and publishers who have been so helpful in providing information for this volume will feel their magazines were dealt with accurately and fairly.

Acknowledgments

Thanks are due to librarians at the Library of Congress; the New York Public Library; the libraries of Duke University, the University of North Carolina, and the University of Illinois; and especially to Joanne Eustis and the other Humanities librarians at Virginia Polytechnic Institute and State University where the author is a professor/administrator. The photocopying efforts of staff at Yale University's Beinecke Library and the South Carolina Historial Society are also appreciated.

For material on current magazines the author extends his gratitude to the editors and publishers who expressed interest and provided information by mail and by telephone.

Thanks also to those who did the typing for this manuscript: Norma Montgomery, Bernice Born, Karen Smith, Kathy Stone, and Peggy Price.

Finally, thanks are due the College of Arts and Sciences at Virginia Polytechnic Institute and State University for having provided grant monies to fund travel to the libraries named above and many other expenses of the project.

Profiles of Magazines of the American South

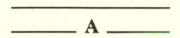

A

THE AMERICAN FARMER

Though articles on agricultural topics appeared earlier in miscellanies, the first farm periodical both in the South and the nation appears to have been the weekly *Farmer's Library; or, Ohio Intelligencer* published in Louisville, Kentucky, from 1801 to 1808 by Thomas Vail.[1] Second among America's farm periodicals was the *Agricultural Museum*, founded in 1810 by the Rev. David Wiley at Georgetown in the District of Columbia.

Third in the subject field, and second in the South, was the *American Farmer* of Baltimore, a slim but viable periodical established in 1819 by postmaster John S. Skinner, who later edited or published at least four more periodicals.[2] Running under a succession of editors and publishers until 1897, the *American Farmer* enjoyed the greatest longevity of any periodical of its day—seventy-four years— allowing for the Civil War period in which it was suspended (July 1861-June 1866).

Instead of the usual introductory address to readers, Skinner began page 1 of his eight-page first number (April 2, 1819) with a treatise by William Cobbett ("Peter Porcupine") extolling the virutes of the Ruta Baga, also known in those days as the Swedish turnip. On page 3 is a woodblock of a resentful-lookingDelaware ox, with his various parts (sirloin, rump, flank, brisket, etc.) outlined for meat cutting. The eclectic nature of the magazine, and that it was edited for *gentlemen* farmers, can be seen in an article on page 5 regarding differences between the familiarity shown servants by the French as contrasted to the more distant English. The following page contains witty tidbits, most borrowed from English periodicals, and the editor's address to his public. In it Skinner promises that for $4 per annum, in advance, the subscriber will receive practical farm information, "original and selected essays and extracts calculated for amusement," and current market price information.

Skinner's *Farmer* was urbane and witty and even included poetry, such as this brief impromptu on the romantic nature of Greenland:

O happy Greenland! Happy Swains!
    Who ne'er the deadly war-trump hear;
Where gentle love triumphant reigns,
    And every night is—*half a year.* [1, 1:7]

It is difficult to imagine that many readers of today's farm magazines would be moved to submit, or many of these magazines accept, such a contribution as "The Leaf of Tobacco," an anonymous three-verse poem that began:

Let the Irishmen boast, they're the lads for the ladies,
That fighting and loving their own native trade is—
    While the Shamrock so green shades the bosoms so bold:
But the Shamrock, when gather'd, will quickly decay,
'Tis honor'd one moment, the next thrown away:
Now the plant on Patuxent, we rear as our boast,
When the most of it is faded, we honor it most—
    'Tis the leaf of Tobacco, as yellow as gold! [1, 23: 184]

The *American Farmer*'s pages provided an outlet for many "agriculturalists" who offered advice on every conceivable aspect of farm life: crop rotation, hedging, use of lime, use of barley as a fallow crop, the fattening of lambs, stump removal techniques, use as a manure of oyster shells burnt with marsh mud, cheese making, and the like. In one issue a letter from Thomas Jefferson offered the master of Monticello's observations on the making of parmesan cheese in Europe (1, 52: 410).

The transactions of agricultural and horticultural societies at home and abroad were printed, as were descriptions of agricultural fairs, cattle shows, and other exhibits. Current price information was regularly listed for such commodities as bacon, beef, brandy, butter, cheese, feathers, flax, flour, rice, soap, sugar, tea, tobacco, and wool. Wood engravings of farm implements and engines were occasionally used.

An intensely practical magazine, the *Farmer* still made room for items that justified their inclusion primarily as entertainment, such as the aforementioned Cobbett's feisty defense of field sports against those who criticized them as a form of cruelty to animals (2, 2:11). From an anonymous contributor came a humorous account of a traveler's experience with bedbugs at a turnpike inn. Attacked by "files, phalanxes and legions" of the hideous enemy, the weary traveler was forced to spend his night in a chair. The writer occupies an entire three-column page with an essay on the history of "Cimex Lectuarius" and various means of its eradication, an example of which is to "take corrosive sublimate mercury one ounce, crude salammoniac half an ounce, water one quart, let it stand a few days and lay it on the joints of the bedstead with a brush every week until it forms a small crystallization'' (1, 50: 398).

The *American Farmer* began as a monthly but was at various times during its long life a weekly and a semimonthly. After several changes of title, ownership, and editorship, the magazine came into the possession of Samuel Sands, whose family either owned or edited it until 1891. In 1892 the magazine moved to Washington, D.C., where it ceased publication in 1897.

Notes

1. See Frank McLean, ''Periodicals Published in the South before 1880'' (Ph.D. diss., University of Virginia, 1928), p. 100. Files of this magazine are unavailable.

2. See the entry on the *American Turf Register and Sporting Magazine* in this volume.

Information Sources

BIBLIOGRAPHY:

Edgar, Neal L. *A History and Bibliography of American Magazines, 1810–1820*. Metuchen, N.J., 1975. P. 94,

McLean, Frank. ''Periodicals Published in the South before 1880.'' Ph.D. dissertation, University of Virginia, 1928.

Mott, Frank Luther. *A History of American Magazines, 1741–1850*. New York, 1930. I: 153.

INDEX SOURCES: None.

LOCATION SOURCES: American Periodical Series microfilm, Library of Congress.

Publication History

MAGAZINE TITLE AND TITLE CHANGES: *The American Farmer* (April 2, 1819-March 7, 1834); *The Farmer and Gardener, and Live-Stock Breeder and Manager* (May 9, 1834-April 28, 1835); *The Farmer and Gardener* (May 5, 1835-May 22, 1839); *The American Farmer and Spirit of the Agricultural Journals of the Day* (May 29, 1839-June 1850); *The American Farmer* (July 1850-June 1861 and July 1866-December 1871); *The American Farmer and Rural Register* (January 1872-December 1873); *The American Farmer* (January 1874-December 1880); *American Farmer; Devoted to Agriculture* (January 1881-February 1897).

VOLUME AND ISSUE DATA: Series 1–12 (April 2, 1819-February 1897); monthly (1819; 1832-April 1834; July, 1845–1888; 1894–1897), weekly (1820–1831; May 9, 1834-June 1845), semimonthly (1889–1893).

PUBLISHER AND PLACE OF PUBLICATION: John S. Skinner (1819–1829); Gideon B. Smith (1830–1834); J. Irvine Hitchcock (1834–1835); Sinclair and Moore (1835); E. P. Roberts and Samuel Sands (1836–1840); Samuel Sands (1840–1853); Sands and Worthington (1854–1857); N. B. Worthington and Company (1858–1859); Worthington and Lewis (1860–1869); Samuel Sands and Son (1872–1891); William B. Sands (1891); Farmer Publishing Company (Middletown, Md., January-February 1, 1892); American Farmer Company (Washington, D.C., 1892–1897). Until 1892 in Baltimore, Maryland.

EDITORS: John S. Skinner (1819–1829); Gideon B. Smith (1830–1834); J. Irvine Hitchcock (1834–1835); Edward P. Roberts (1835–1840); Samuel Sands (1840–1871);

Samuel Sands and William B. Sands (1872–1891); William B. Sands (1891). CIRCULATION: Unknown.

THE AMERICAN GLEANER AND VIRGINIA MAGAZINE

When University Microfilms of Ann Arbor filmed the *American Gleaner and Virginia Magazine* for its American Periodicals Series, the only file that could be located was at the Virginia State Library in Richmond. This slender literary miscellany was intended to be a weekly but was published irregularly in Richmond between January 24 and December 26, 1807. The only extant copies are numbers 1, 7,[1] 9,[2] and 10–18.

One of Virginia's early attempts at magazine publication,[3] the *Gleaner* was edited and published anonymously. The magazine was done in a rather primitive-looking two-column format with a double rule between columns, and it was sixteen pages long. The nameplate bore the Latin motto *Cum Utile Dulci*, "The Useful along with the Pleasurable."

The initial number began with "Memoirs of the Late George Wythe, Esquire," who was referred to by some as "the Virginian Socrates." The memoir was unsigned in number 1 but was continued in later issues, which are unavailable. Following in the first number was a reflective essay on the progress of America over the past 200 years. The point of view of the anonymous writer, very likely the editor, can be seen in this quotation: "It was only 200 years since, that the present populous and wealthy states of America, were one entire wilderness, thinly inhabited by savages almost incapable of civilization; men of rude minds and violent passions, restrained by no principle of humanity or reason" (no. 1: 4). This essay was in turn followed by a humorous piece signed "Honestus" and titled "On Fashionable Manners" (pp. 5–7). The "varnish of town vices" that gave a man social polish was nicely held up to the light.

The remaining pages (13–16) were taken up by original poetry, some of which is too sentimental to have enduring value. More pleasing were lighter-hearted offerings, such as "The Origin and Formation of An old Bachelor," which began:

> What sullen old mortal is that,
> > Who sits in his hut all alone,
> Excepting his dog and his cat,
> > That grey with their master have grown. [P. 14]

or "Ode to the Virtues" by Peter Pindar, Esq. (p. 16).

The next available issue, number 7, began with the didactic "Letters to a Young Lady on a Course of English Poetry" (pp. 97–99), a continuing feature, and also contained a letter written by Benjamin Franklin on August 9, 1768, to John Alleyne, Esq., on the topic of early marriage (pp. 100–101).

In succeeding numbers, the *Gleaner*'s prose became progressively more lack-luster, but of some interest in number 9 was a brief essay contrasting sullenness and gentleness. In the same issue is "To Miss J. L., 16 Years Old," a poem of tribute to Southern womanhood, typical of the period. It began:

> Dear J——lovely child of May,
>   Fairest of all her progeny
> Young, tender, innocent and gay,
>   The season breathes delight in thee. [P. 141]

Far the best poem in number 9, however, is "Answer to a Challenge" by H. H. Brackenridge, a delightful devil's advocate of "chivalry." Its first verse read:

> A challenge comes. A challenge? Mercy
>   From one as hot as Hotspur Piercy—
> A challenge! what? to fight a duel?
>   I'd live ten years on water gruel,
> Rather than stand up to be shot at,
>   Like a racoon that can't be got at. [P. 142]

Another witty poetical contribution in this number came from a Dr. Young:

> As in smooth oil, the razor best is whet,
> So wit is by politeness sharpest set:
> Their want of edge from their offense is seen,
> Both pain us least when exquisitely keen. [P. 144]

Though the essays, speeches, anecdotes, and more serious poetry displayed in the *Gleaner* did little to enhance the magazine's literary reputation, the editor continued to show a definite flair for light-hearted verse. In number 10 appeared a poem written after hearing a young man boast that he would never dance with a plain woman:

> Young Damon vows, nay, hear him swear,
>   He'll dance with none but what are fair,
> Suppose we girls a law decree,
> To dance with none but *men of sense*.
> Suppose you should, pray, Ma'am what then?
> *Why Sir, you'd never dance again.* [P. 160]

Another example, this one from number 12, is "The Odds":

> The bright, bewitching Fanny's eyes,
>   A thousand hearts have won,

> Whilst she regardless of the prize,
>   Securely keeps her own.
> Ah! what a dreadful girl are you,
>   Who if you e'er design
> To make me happy, must undo
>   999! [P. 192]

Among the tedious essays signed with such pen names as Eusebius and Vidua appear memoirs of General Nathaniel Green (no. 12: 177–81), a rather nice sonnet by Anna Seward (no. 16: 254–56) and a portrait of George Washington (no. 17: 259–61). Late in the year the editor bowed to the worsening political situation in "Peace or War?" (no. 17: 271–72).

Apparently unwilling to carry on publication in the face of the gathering political storm, the publisher let the *Gleaner* die after the eighteenth number. A suitable ending to this summary of what little is known about the magazine is an extract from "The Carrier's Address," of which the editor remarked, "The following lines have little merit to originality, but are very appropriate to the present crisis."

> When God from chaos gave this world to be,
> Man then he form'd, & form'd him to be free,
> In his own image stampt the favourite race—
> How dar'st thou, Tyrants, the fair stamp deface!
> When on mankind you fix your abject chains,
> No more the image of that God remains;
> O'er a dark scene a darker shade is drawn,
> His work dishonour'd, and our glory gone!
>
>   From Europe's realms fair freedom has retir'd
> And even in Britain has the spark expir'd—
> Mark well the change that haughty empire feels,
> Sigh for her doom that no disguise conceals. [P. 287]

Notes

1. Incomplete, pp. 97–104 only.
2. Incomplete, pp. 137–44 only.
3. Earlier titles, none of which have available files, were the *Press* (one issue only, January 6, 1800); the *Recorder, or, Lady's and Gentlemen's Miscellany* (1801–3?); *Minerva, or Lady's and Gentlemen's Magazine* (1804-?); and *Amoenitates Graphicae* (1805).

Information Sources

INDEX SOURCES: None.
LOCATION SOURCES: American Periodical Series microfilm, Virginia State Library (Richmond).

Publication History

MAGAZINE TITLE AND TITLE CHANGES: *The American Gleaner and Virginia Magazine.*

VOLUME AND ISSUE DATA: Vol. 1, nos. 1–18 (January 24-December 26, 1807), irregular.

PUBLISHER AND PLACE OF PUBLICATION: Publisher unknown, Richmond, Virginia.

EDITOR: Unknown.

CIRCULATION: Unknown.

AMERICAN TURF REGISTER AND SPORTING MAGAZINE

The first sports magazine in the South, and in the nation, was the *American Turf Register and Sporting Magazine* of Baltimore. It was founded by John S. Skinner, a Baltimore postmaster who had earlier founded the *American Farmer** (1819) in that same city. The *Register* was far more successful than most of its contemporaries, enjoying a sixteen-year life from 1829 to 1844.

Given the longevity of this pioneer sports magazine and the Southern male's passion for the sporting life, it is surprising that the genre failed to catch on in the South until well into the 1900s. The only other nineteenth-century Southern sports magazines were the *Southern Sportsman* of New Orleans (March 18-June 4, 1843); *Young's Spirit of South and Central America. A Chronicle of the Turf, Field, Sports, Literature, and the Stage* published first in Nashville in 1858, then in Louisville; *Southern Pit Games* of Blakely, Georgia (1894–1909?); and *Grit and Steel*, a cock-fighting periodical that appeared in Gaffney, South Carolina, in 1899.

The *Register* was a far more interesting periodical than one might imagine. Its length, originally fifty-six pages, was later increased to sixty-four; and it was illustrated with engravings of superior quality, most of them depicting thoroughbred horses. The *Register*'s *raison d'être* was to provide an unbiased record of the performances and pedigrees of thoroughbred horses in the same manner that this need was served by the *Sporting Magazine* in England. Without such a repository, it was difficult to trace the pedigree and calculate the value of bred horses—a minor matter to most Americans but of major import to serious horse people. The magazine also ran copy dealing with racing, trotting, shooting, hunting, fishing, the natural history and habits of American game of all kinds, and veterinary articles, such as "Cure of Lockjaw in Horses" (4, 1: 13) or "On the Inflammatory Complaints of Horses" (10, 1: 39).

In his first number the editor, Skinner, seems at great pains to head off the criticism of the somber and righteous. His very first page begins with a quotation from a minister, the Rev. W. B. Daniel:

PUBLIC LIBRARY OF PINE BLUFF
AND JEFFERSON COUNTY

There are intervals when the studious and the grave must suspend their inquiries, and descend from the regions of science; and to excel in those innocent amusements which require our activity, is often one of the best preservations of health, and no inconsiderable guard against immoral relaxation.

Less than a page into his introduction, Skinner brings up reinforcements in the person of a Rev. Dr. Parr, presumably known to many of the *Register*'s readers, who is also quoted to the effect that the relaxing influence of sport and other social entertainments are helpful in promoting good will among men. Skinner quotes scripture ("a time to weep and a time to laugh," etc.) and notes in his own words that "the elasticity of the bow is maintained by frequent relaxation."

The editor then solicits material from any interested party who might have outdoor anecdotes or observations to share, saying, "The misfortune is, that most people are too apt to consider what they observe of the habits of various animals, birds, fishes, etc., as being either already known, or of too little importance to be put in print. The fact is far otherwise—it is to the plainest men in the ordinary walks of life, that we owe the most authentic materials of natural history." Secretaries of sporting clubs were asked for copies of their minutes, and jockey clubs for their rules, club histories, and track statistics.

Today's sports magazine afficianado would doubtless be suprised by the poetry that appeared in the *Register*, two sample excerpts of which follow:

Of fishes next, my friends, I would inquire;
How the mute race engender, or respire.
How all with careful knowledge are endued,
To choose their proper bed, and wave, and food;
To guard their spawn, and educate their brood? [1, 1: 35]

Come thou harmless recreation,
    Holding out the angler's reed;
Nurse of pleasing contemplation.
    By the stream my wanderings lead. . . .
Yea, when autumn's russet mantle
    Saddens the decaying year,
I will fish, and I will chant, 'till
    Feeble age shall change my cheer. [1, 1: 37]

Odd, intriguing tidbits occasionally appeared in the *Register*'s pages, such as "The Richmond Barbecue Club," the editor's account of his visit to one of the South's oldest social clubs, which reportedly drew up its constitution in 1788 after more than forty years of less formal existence. The club consisted, Skinner said, of judges, lawyers, doctors, and merchants and boasted some highly prominent members. Every second Saturday they met at Buchanan's Spring, about a mile from the city, for convivial dining, quoits, and backgammon.

After completing the sixth volume, Skinner retired to edit a new periodical, the *Journal of the American Silk Society and Rural Economist* (1839–1840).[1] Gideon Smith became publisher and Allen J. Davie editor of the *Register*. Davie's connection was brief, and Smith assumed the magazine's editorial duties for its eighth and ninth volumes, after which William T. Porter[2] became editor and publisher (1839) and the magazine moved to New York City, where it expired in 1844. In buying the *Register*, Porter became one of the earliest U.S. magazine publishers to buy out his competition, as he was already propietor of the *Spirit of the Times: A Chronicle of the Turf, Agriculture, Field Sports, Literature, and the Stage*, a lively New York magazine.

Notes

1. Still later, Skinner edited the *Journal of Agriculture* in Baltimore (1845–48) and the *Plough, the Loom, and the Anvil* in Philadelphia, later in New York (1848–59).
2. See Francis Brinley, *Life of William T. Porter* (New York, 1860).

Information Sources

BIBLIOGRAPHY:
Brinley, Francis. *Life of William T. Porter*. New York, 1860.
Mott, Frank Luther. *A History of American Magazines, 1741–1850*. New York, 1930. I: 479.
INDEX SOURCES: None.
LOCATION SOURCES: American Periodical Series microfilm, Library of Congress, New York Public Library, University of North Carolina Library (Chapel Hill), University of Texas Library (Austin).

Publication History

MAGAZINE TITLE AND TITLE CHANGES: *American Turf Register and Sporting Magazine*.
VOLUME AND ISSUE DATA: Vols. 1–15 (September 1829-December 1844), monthly.
PUBLISHER AND PLACE OF PUBLICATION: John S. Skinner (September 1829–1835); Gideon B. Smith (1835-January 1839); William T. Porter (February 1839-December 1844). Baltimore (1829–1838); New York City (1839–1844).
EDITORS: J. S. Skinner (September 1829–1835); Allen J. Davie (1835-August 1836); Gideon B. Smith (September 1836-January 1839); William T. Porter (February 1839-December 1844).
CIRCULATION: Unknown.

ANTIQUE MONTHLY

A current Southern periodical that has attracted national attention, partially because of its attractive editor/publisher, is *Antique Monthly*, which was begun in November 1967 as *Antique Quarterly* and was converted to monthly publication in May 1969. The magazine's founder is Martha Gray Davis Boone, a Baytown, Texas, native who at the time her antiques magazine was founded was married to Jim Boone, now a prominent newspaper publisher in Alabama and Mississippi. Gray Boone's father-in-law, Buford Boone, then publisher of the *Tuscaloosa News*, gave the new sheet an ad in *Southern Living** in August 1968, which provided a significant stimulus to its circulation.

In 1969 Mrs. Boone still did much of the writing for her growing periodical; her editorial page listed only herself, an advertising manager, and a circulation manager. Today, except for her brief editorials, she is more apt to be written about than to write. The list of staff members has grown to almost a full column, including Editorial Director Kellee Reinhart, Associate Publisher Anita Giani Mason, a senior editor, associate editor, Washington editor, New York editor, California editor, London editor, specialty editor for silver, two contributing editors, a five-person editorial staff, librarian, and a sizable business staff. *Antique Monthly* has grown from its eight-page beginnings to a three-section tabloid that averages about sixty pages.

The periodical is richly laden with display ads for dealers, auctioneers, and appraisers from all over the nation and a few from abroad. Readers familiar with the fine antique auction and appraisal scene will recognize the names of these advertisers: Richard A. Bourne, Inc., of Hyannis, Massachusetts; Samuel T. Friedman & Co. and The Fine Arts Company of Philadelphia; Wechler's and C. G. Sloan & Company of Washington, D.C.; Du Mouchelles of Detroit; Hart Galleries of Houston; Mortons of New Orleans; and Christie's and Sotheby's of New York City.

Prominent dealers advertising in *Antique Monthly* include Israel Sack and Levy Inc. of New York; Childs of Boston and New York; H & R Sandor of New Hope, Pennsylvania; Gerald R. Brown and The Gables of Atlanta; Lake Silver of Lake Providence, Louisiana; the Tudor Gallery and Janet Brady Yancey of Richmond, Virginia; Laws in Manassas, Virginia; and Arthur H. Danielson in Raleigh, North Carolina.

Asked what other antiques periodical was considered *Antique Monthly*'s primary competitor, Editorial Assistant Donna Callahan replied the *Antiques Magazine* of New York City, circulation 61,000, a slick monthly founded in 1922;[1] that the two periodicals share so many advertisers tends to confirm this judgment. Other competitors are *Collectors Mart*[2] of Wichita, Kansas (circulation 106,000); *American Collector* of San Antonio and Kermit, Texas (100,000); *Antique Trader Weekly* of Dubuque, Iowa (90,000); *Collectors News*, Grundy Center, Iowa (28,000); the *Collector Investor* of Chicago (20,000 non-paid, 2,500 paid); *Antique Market Tabloid*, Silver Spring, Maryland (15,000); and the *Antiquarian*, Huntington, New York (15,000).

Antique Monthly's own circulation is now 70,000, winnowed from over 100,000 several years earlier, said Ms. Callahan, as a management effort to optimize the mix of quality circulation and adveristing rates. The magazine's entry in the

1983 *Writer's Market* indicates that 27 percent of subscribers have postgraduate degrees, that more than half have annual incomes of $35,000 or more, and that the "average reader" has been an antique collector for more than twenty years. One can only reflect that given the quality antiques pictured in *Antique Monthly*'s pages, a person who even remotely qualifies as a "collector" needs an income *greatly* in excess of $35,000. The cover page of the January 1981 number, to cite one mind-boggling example, pictures a block-and-shell carved chest of drawers that sold at Sotheby Parke Bernet's for $360,000 (14, 2: 1A). In a later number the sale of a weathervane for $75,000 is reported (15, 7: 1A). One wonders how many subscribers to this and other antiques periodicals are mere spectators or admirers, as opposed to actual buyers.

Still, there is undeniable pleasure for the armchair collector in marveling at Armand Hammer's successful bid of $5.2 million for the thirty-six-page illustrated manuscript known as the Da Vinci Codex (14, 2: 4A) or an article on "the most important piece of English furniture" ever auctioned on the West Coast—a 1710 Queen Anne green Japanned bureau bookcase that brought (antique buffs prefer "fetched") $125,000 (17, 5: 1C).

Feature articles on antique shopping are often used, some on shopping as far away from the magazine's home base of Tuscaloosa, Alabama, as New Zealand (14, 2: 10C); exhibits of antiques and art objects, sometimes at such an unexpected location as Walt Disney's *Epcot* Center, are written up (17, 5: 10C); and occasionally readers are introduced to the lesser-known terminology of the trade, as in a piece on "Vetting," or judging antiques to verify their value (15, 7: 3A).

Articles on public places furnished in antiques are used, as in a feature on the Locke-Ober Cafe in Boston—an eating place of Victorian magnificence (14, 2: 3B)—and pieces on auctions of the property of famous people are popular. Sales of portions of Bing Crosby's and Jack Benny's estates appeared in 1982 and 1984 (15, 7: 8B and 17, 5: 1C), and an article on a Butterfield's auction of Hollywood props, which included some fine antiques, was doubtless well read (16, 11: 4B and 10B). Another feature with show-biz connections was on BBC's series on Lady Nancy Astor and its producer's difficulties in locating appropriate antiques for props (17, 5: 4 and 5B).

Mrs. Boone's magazine also offers a book review section, listings of "Interesting Places" and "Interesting Shops," classified ads, and a directory of professional services which lists appraisers, furniture restorers, silversmiths, antiques packers and shippers, and specialists in the restoration of porcelain, dolls, barometers, and the like. "Furniture Forum" and "Potpourri Opinions" are departments to which readers may send snapshots of their antiques and questions about the pieces' age or value. "On the Block" is yet another department, this one providing photos of articles recently sold at auction with summary descriptions and prices.

In its eighteen-year life *Antique Monthly* has made an impressive success of appealing to a wide audience of dealers, collectors, and admirers. Mrs. Boone has expanded her operation in several directions, writing a syndicated newspaper column on antiques,[3] publishing a weekly antiques newsletter called the *Gray Letter*, and going partners with British Viscount De L'Isle to form De L'Isle-Gray Journeys, a series of tours through English houses. Her most recent project was her 1978 purchase of *Horizon Magazine*[4] from the American Heritage Publishing Company; expenses were cut 65 percent by moving the magazine from Manhattan to Tuscaloosa, where it and *Antique Monthly* are jointly headquartered in a restored Italianate villa, a fit setting for magazines that deal in beauty.

Notes

1. Telephone conversation between the author and Donna Callahan of *Antique Monthly*, May 14, 1984.

2. Formerly *Antique & Collectors Mart*.

3. Mrs. Boone's column appears in Arizona, California, Florida, Massachusetts, Missouri, Pennsylvania, New Jersey, New York, and West Virginia.

4. *Horizon*'s circulation is 62,200.

Information Sources

BIBLIOGRAPHY:
Brown, Elizabeth. "Quality of Life Preserved through Heritage." *Memphis Press-Scim-itar*, April 2, 1979.
Conroy, Sarah. "What's Happening in the 19th Century." *Washington Post*, February 26, 1978.
Dougherty, Philip. "Mrs. Boone Revitalizes Horizon." *New York Times*, April 24, 1979.
East, Cammie. "Antiques Are News to Gray Boone." *Mobile Press-Register*, September 30, 1978.
Elebash, Camille. "First Lady of Antiques." *Sky Magazine*, August 1978.
Ewing, Betty. "Texan Adds Horizon Magazine to String of Publications." *Houston Chronicle*, October 8, 1978.
Jackson, Lily. "Modern Pioneer Launches Her Own Antiques Newspaper." *New Orleans Times-Picayune*, September 12, 1978.
Kelley, Margaret. "Queen of America's Antiques Scene." *Chattanooga News Free Press*, June 1, 1980.
Leviton, Joyce. "Gray Boone Is One American Woman Who Is Flattered to Be Anointed the 'Antique Queen.' " *People Magazine*, November 6, 1979.
INDEX SOURCES: None.
LOCATION SOURCES: Library of Congress, Virginia Polytechnic Institute and State University Library.

Publication History

MAGAZINE TITLE AND TITLE CHANGES: *Antique Quarterly* (November 1967-February 1969); *Antique Monthly* (May 1969-present).

VOLUME AND ISSUE DATA: Vols. 1–18 (November 1967–1984); quarterly (1967–1969), monthly (1969-present).

PUBLISHER AND PLACE OF PUBLICATION: Gray Davis Boone. Tuscaloosa, Alabama.

EDITOR: Gray Davis Boone.

CIRCULATION: 70,000.

ANTIQUE QUARTERLY. *See* ANTIQUE MONTHLY

ARKANSAS TIMES

In a state not noted for magazine publishing, the monthly regional magazine *Arkansas Times* is an example of what *can* be done. The burgeoning of U.S. city and regional magazines in the 1960s and 1970s has been a mixed bag of impressive successes and abysmal failures. Well-written, well-edited city magazines in large enough population centers have usually found a "natural selection" of advertisers—local hotels, restaurants, shops, etc. Many regional magazines of equal quality that have tried to cover a wider geographical area have run into problems attracting advertisers. Starting without competition from similar periodicals, the *Times* has managed to operate as a state magazine and build enough of an advertising base to become profitable; since 1982 the magazine has grossed over $1 million annually.

At its birth in 1974 the magazine was not the full-color slick it is today. Its original title was the *Union Station Times*, named for the building in which it was published. Its founder was Alan Leveritt, at the time a twenty-two-year-old dropout from the University of Arkansas at Little Rock, where he had edited an independent student newspaper, *Essence*, in competition with the official campus paper, the *Forum*. After dropping out of college, Leveritt wrote obituaries and club notices for the *Arkansas Gazette*, then decided to start a periodical of his own that would feature investigative journalism. He wrote to journalism schools around the country, advertising for idealistic young writers who might be willing to join him, *sans* salary, in his venture. Two writers were attracted; one remained.

Though the early issues of the *Union Station Times* did indeed contain serious investigative pieces, the little magazine, done on newsprint and selling for a $4 a year or 35¢ an issue, was aimed at a young, not-so-affluent audience. Many of its ads were for health food stores, pizza restaurants, music stores, sellers of house plants, and the like. In the typical issue a hard-news story such as "Little Rock's Most Crucial Election," about the politics of urban growth, appeared alongside the likes of "Teeny Boppers, Raunchy Rock and the Barton Rumble" (3, 2: 8–15, 26–30; 20–21, 24–25). In this way the magazine survived its most difficult period, publishing twice monthly and establishing a split but distinctive personality.

Bill Terry, formerly the wire editor of the *Arkansas Democrat*, became the *Times*' editor in January 1975, allowing Leveritt to devote more attention to the business side of the enterprise. Terry, a product of Exeter and Yale who had worked for United Press International in San Francisco and had written for the *Washington Post*, brought needed experience to the *Times* and remained until early 1983, when he sold his equity in the magazine and moved to scenic Berryville, Arkansas. Under his editorship the *Times* won an award in 1976 from the Society of Professional Journalists, Sigma Delta Chi, for a series on the University of Arkansas Medical School.

In August 1978 Leveritt and Terry risked their magazine's future by converting to slick format. An earlier step in this direction had come in 1977 when the *Times'* newsprint pages were dressed up with a slick, full-color cover. The considerable improvement in the magazine's appearance attracted more subscribers and more advertisers, and finally Leveritt was able to pay his staff token salaries.

Like many other city and regional magazines, the *Times* quickly discovered the popularity of listing coming events. "Culcha," a "catfish calendar of current cultural events," became a regular feature, listing craft shows, films, bicycle rides, canoe races, rock concerts, and other attractions of interest to its predominantly young readers. Also like other regional magazines, its contents were a potpourri of fiction and nonfiction, the only common thread being a definite Arkansas angle. Roughly half of the magazine's column inches are devoted to editorial copy, a far cry from *Southern Living** and *Texas Monthly** in which one must search diligently among the myriad advertisements to find an article to read.

The *Times'* content was probably influenced somewhat by the competition it was given during 1979 and early 1980 by the *Arkansan*, another glossy monthly published in Little Rock by newspaperman Ralph K. Patrick, former publisher of the *Arkansas Democrat* and the *North Little Rock Times*. The *Arkansan's* appeal was to an older, more affluent audience, and like the majority of regional magazines, its editorial policy was to shy away from investigative pieces in favor of articles that described what was *right* in Arkansas. Patrick arranged for a column by Paul Greenberg, a Pulitzer Prize winner and editorial writer for the *Pine Bluff Commercial*, an outstanding small daily paper. Other *Arkansan* writers with regional reputations were Gene Lyons and Crescent Dragonwagon. Brought in as associate editor was Bob Lancaster, a native of Grant County, Arkansas, who had written for the *Pine Bluff Commercial* and both the *Gazette* and *Democrat* in Little Rock and had written a superb column for the *Philadelphia Inquirer* during the Nixon years. He was quoted in the *Arkansas Gazette* as saying he returned to his native state from Philadelphia because he "was tired of living in a police state,"[1] a reference to the flamboyant, tough-guy mayoral reign of Frank Rizzo.

The *Arkansan* gave up the ghost in mid–1980, and Lancaster replaced Terry as the *Times'* editor in March of 1983. He now directs an editorial staff of three full-timers and three part-timers.

Today's *Arkansas Times* lists Robert L. Brown, Bob Cochran, Paul Greenberg, B. C. Hall, and James Whitehead as contributing editors and graphically holds its own among other regional magazines. As the publisher and his staff have edged into middle age, the audience at which they aim has also become older, though the *Times* has not lost its tone of good-natured irreverence. Assessing the best and worst aspects of Arkansas for 1983, a feature popularized much earlier by such older city magazines as *Philadelphia* and *Washingtonian*, the *Times* writes, "Maybe the worst feature of the year was that the state legislature met twice. Maybe its best feature was that the state legislature didn't meet three times" (10, 8: 57).

The best political suggestion for 1984, said the same article, was that the state's constitution be amended to provide for elections every four years, but that two-year terms of office be continued. The state's "best kept secret" was that more than 366,000 Arkansans over age twenty-five cannot read, a 27 percent illiteracy rate.

Inserted in the April 1984 issue was a delightfully tasteless April Fools Day spoof on Little Rock's daily newspapers, done on newsprint as the *Arkansas Regrette* and the *Arkansas Demagogue*. The *Times* has been called a self-made magazine that "still has dirt under its fingernails," a jaunty periodical that is slick enough in appearance to compete anywhere but still "has the smell of possum about it."[2]

The magazine now is less investigative than in its earlier years, and according to Editor Lancaster, its most popular features are its restaurant guide, food articles, and tips on where to find bargains. Though the *Times*'brief restaurant reviews might appear to be quite gentle, the magazine is, according to Lancaster, being boycotted by the Arkansas Hospitality Association.[3]

Leveritt's company, the Arkansas Writers' Project, Inc., has furthered its prosperity by publishing city and area guides for Central Arkansas, the El Dorado-Camden area, Northwest Arkansas,and Hot Springs, plus Austin, Texas. As of April, 1984, another guide for Raleigh, North Carolina, is being assembled. A twice-monthly tabloid called *Arkansas Business* has also been started by Leveritt, and a collection of local restaurant menus entitled *Little Rock Menus* is in the works.

Notes

1. Doug Smith, "Two Magazines in Game of One-Upsmanship," *Arkansas Gazette*, August 12, 1979, p. 12F.
2. Smith, "Two Magazines."
3. Telephone conversation with the author, April 19, 1984.

Information Sources

BIBLIOGRAPHY:
"Arkansas Times Magazine: Covering the State from Corner to Corner." *Inside Arkansas*, Winter 1983, pp. 21–23.
Donald, Leroy. "After Lean Years, Magazine Has Arrived." *Arkansas Gazette*, April 10, 1983.
Smith, Doug. "Two Magazines in Game of One-Upsmanship." *Arkansas Gazette*, August 12, 1979.
INDEX SOURCES: None.
LOCATION SOURCES: None located.

Publication History

MAGAZINE TITLE AND TITLE CHANGES: *Union Station Times* (September 1974-
    February 1975); *Arkansas' Union Station Times* (March-December 1975); *Arkansas Times* (January 1976-present).
VOLUME AND ISSUE DATA: Vols. 1–10; twice monthly (September 1974-February
    1975), monthly (March 1975-present).
PUBLISHER AND PLACE OF PUBLICATION: Alan Leveritt. Little Rock, Arkansas.
EDITORS: Alan Leveritt and Vernon Tucker (1974-January 1975); Bill Terry (January
    1975-March 1983); Bob Lancaster (March 1983-present).
CIRCULATION: 30,000 in 1984.

ARKANSAS' UNION STATION TIMES. *See* ARKANSAS TIMES

THE ARKANSAW TRAVELER

A noteworthy Southwestern humor periodical of the late 1800s was the *Arkansaw Traveler*, first published in Little Rock on June 4, 1882. The *Traveler* had the physical appearance of a newspaper, but its editor never made any pretense of covering the news. The eight-page sheet appeared weekly in a six-column format under a wild-looking nameplate employing an ornate typeface through which ran a musical score. Nestled among the lettering and its accompanying vine motif were two horseback scenes depicting Col. Sandy Faulkner, a fiddle-playing cotton planter who left Kentucky for Arkansas in 1829 and became the original "Arkansas Traveler."

Proprietors of the new humor sheet were Little Rock businessman Philo D. Benham, who managed the periodical's business affairs and journalist Opie P. Read,[1] its editor. Read's skill as a storyteller and dialect writer enabled him to tickle readers' funny bones at the expense of Arkansas' blacks and poor backwoods whites. Thanks to Read's distinctive style, the proprietors made good on the claim appearing in their salutatory that circulation would be extensive and nationwide (1, 1: 4). By the tenth number the proprietors were proclaiming the largest circulation of any daily or weekly periodical in the state, and by their third year the figure had climbed to an impressive 85,000.[2]

Read's introduction to journalism had been a job setting type for the Franklin (Kentucky) *Patriot*. After studying at Neophegen College in Gallatin, Tennessee, he returned to the *Patriot* as a reporter, later published the Scottsville (Kentucky) *Argus*, founded an unsuccessful paper called the *Prairie Flower*, edited the Bowling Green (Kentucky) *Pantagraph*, wrote for Henry Watterson's *Courier-Journal* in Louisville, was city editor of the Little Rock *Democrat*, did a special assignment for the *New York Herald*[3] and in 1878 became city editor of the Little Rock *Daily Arkansas Gazette*. Here he made a reputation as a wit and as he put it, "had been embalmed in the patent insides and had otherwise accumulated fame" (1, 1: 4). When the *Gazette*'s owner demanded more straight news and fewer sketches, Read left for a job on the Cleveland *Leader* but returned to Little Rock in less than a year and, with Benham, bought out a newspaper, the *Arkansaw Traveler*. Their own *Traveler* was to be considered an entirely new periodical, the new owners told their readers in their initial issue.

Page 1 of the newly constituted *Traveler* contained Read's brief humorous items and sketches, the first of which was "Graley and His Sister." For the next five years the front page was almost exclusively Read's own work. Inside appeared a considerable amount of material selected from such sources as *Texas Siftings*,* the *Saturday Review*, *Laramie Boomerang*, *New Haven Palladium*, *New York Mercury*, and *Pall Mall Gazette*.

Under the standing head "Plantation Philosophy" appeared Read's homespun dialect wisdom:

> Life is like ridin' backwards on de hine end ob a car: yer doan see nuthin till yer's passed it.

> De rattlesnake is de alarm clock ob nature.

> De eel is de politician among fish.

> My idea of de better worl is whar dar is a election goin on all de time, case den de white folks is allers perlight.

An idea of Read's peculiarly zany imagination can be drawn from "A War Reminiscence" (1, 1:4), in which the editor sets history straight about Hannibal's great Italian campaign. When a messenger arrived with dire news, wrote Read, "Hannibal's eyes blazed and he was so agitated that he struck three matches before he could light his pipe, then exclaimed in blank verse, which was all he spoke:

> I'm hounded like the weary fox that
> Runs for miles and miles and then is forced
> To turn and face the rabid hounds that yelp
> Along the course which fleetly he has traversed.

> Old man, you've been a kind and gen'rous friend,
> You've loaned me shirts when mine were in the wash,
> And by my side at table, man, you've fought
> Devouring beef that case knives could not cut.

> Old man, upon whose brow the name of slouch
> Has ne'er been written by a mortal hand,
> Good-bye, for here I end my wearied life."

The messenger, himself a "blank verser," replied:

Hold, hold, my master, brave and strong,
Do not with weapon take your glorious life . . .

In my grip I have a black chunk bottle
Filled with deadly whiskey from St. Louis,
Three drinks, and then beyond the human sea
Your great soul will be swiftly wafted.

For their $2 yearly or 5¢ a copy, Opie Read's readers also got the editor's
pick of short jokes and witticisms:

A western man told his daughter that if she learned to work he would
suprise her. She learned and he surprised her by discharging the hired girl.

What is philosophy? It is something that enables a rich man to say there
is no disgrace in being poor.

What becomes a stout woman? Anybody can answer that question. The
slim, giggling girl becomes a stout woman.

In Read's hands, a news story was apt to be treated in the following manner:

The editor, born of woman, is of few days and full of trouble. The other
day John B. Gaines, editor of the Louisville *World* and Col. Sears, editor
of the *Evening Post*, met on the streets and emptied their revolvers at each
other. Now if they had met on a revolver and emptied a street at each
other, the result (would) have been more satisfactory. Col. Sears was shot
in the foot, and a disinterested man, who stood a short distance away,
suddenly became interested by receiving a shot in the arm. . . . Probably
the size of Col. Sears' foot suggested the slaughterhouse and prompted
Mr. Gaines to shoot at it, impressed with the idea that he was killing a
beef. . . . [1, 7: 4]

The continuing misadventures of a fictitious character called the Rev. Mr.
Mulkittle appeared on page 1 for many weeks, alongside other Read sketches
with titles like "A Mule's Story" and "Why an Arkansas Man Struck a Professor
for Selling His Wife a Picture." In busy weeks he filled in with his own earlier
material that had appeared in *Louisville Home & Farm*, the Little Rock *Gazette*,
TidBits, the *New York Mercury*, the *Chicago Rambler*, and other publications.
Many issues also contained the borrowed work of other popular funnymen of
the day: Mark Twain, M. Quad, Bill Nye, Eugene Field, Bob Burdette, Carl
Pretzel, George Ade, and Brick Pomeroy.

Despite the *Traveler*'s popularity, some Arkansas locals began to feel that
Read was laughing at, rather than with them. As Frank Luther Mott so aptly put
it, "when a man was elected to the legislature for having said he would like to

tie a rope around the editor's neck and lead a mule out from under him, Read decided to make the *Traveler* justify its title and moved to Chicago."[4] There, such bucholic backwoods archetypes as Thick Lip Anderson, Flat-nose Phil, Web-foot Bob, and Knock-kneeded Alf would be written about at a safer distance. From Chicago, it would be easier, and safer, to portray Old Squire Huggleson, in Little Rock from the hinterlands, being taken to a performance of "Il Trovatore":

> "Lawd a massy, look at that woman with the fine duds. My lawd, how she hollers. They call that singin', don't they?"
> "Oh, yes, that's singing. It is grand opera."
> "Yes, but when air we goin' to have some musuc?" [6, 17: 1]

As time went by, Read had been able to use less selected material, and in its place had appeared contributions done expressly for the *Traveler* by Alex E. Sweet,[5] Ned Buntline, H. S. Keller, Ike Philkins, D. W. Curtis, Phil Farraday, Guy Transom, Luther G. Riggs, Lock Malone, Jennie Porter Arnold, Charles Blackburn, Dick Steele, and many other writers. Good examples of humor verse written for the *Traveler* were "I Want My Tail Again" (7, 14: 5), a lament to Charles Darwin penned by Fred Shelley Hyman of New York City, and Thomas Burke's efforts, such as "Tale of a She-Epicure" (14, 4: 4), "Ye Coffee Bean" (14, 5: 5), and "Beware" (14, 6: 5), which began,

> It was a modern millionaire,
>   Of Congress an ex-member,
> Who had a young wife of the age
>   Denominated 'tender'.

In October 1888 Read and Benham formed a stock company after having bought out the *Illustrated Graphic News*, a Chicago paper noted for its illustrations. The Arkansaw Traveler Publishing Company announced its plans to increase its length to sixteen pages and to use more art. These changes were effected with the December 1, 1888, issue. Page 1 was filled with a single engraving or line drawing, a larger typeface was used for text, and a greater amount of nonoriginal, sentimental, nonhumorous verse appeared.

Benham, now Read's brother-in-law, left for St. Louis to publish a religious magazine, and Read had tired of the constant demands of producing original copy for the *Traveler*. At the end of 1891 Read severed his ties with the magazine and thereafter concentrated on writing fiction, eventually producing fifty-two books, some of the earliest of which had been serialized in the *Traveler*.[6]

Under the ownership of the Review Publishing Company, the *Traveler* went monthly; began using more cartoons; reverted to the heavy use of one-liners, which had the sorry look of filler; and created a department called "The Metropolitan Stage" to satisfy the public's interest in the likes of Jack and Ethel Barrymore, George M. Cohan, Billie Burke, and Fritzi Schaff. A number of the large cartoons were reused in later issues, a sure sign of failing revenues. Without Opie Read, the magazine's soul had fled, yet the *Traveler* managed to limp on until 1916.

Notes

1. Standard works of reference disagree as to Read's middle name. The *Dictionary of American Biography*, for instance, lists him as Opie Pope Read, *Southern Writers: A Biographical Dictionary* as Opie Percival Read. Others list him, as did the *Arkansaw Traveler* itself, as Opie P. Read; still others, such as the *Dictionary of Literary Biography*, merely have him as Opie Read. Read's obituary in the November 3, 1939, *New York Times* sheds no light on the mystery. More information on Read is available in two biographies: Maurice Elfer's *Opie Read* (Detroit, 1940), and Robert L. Morris' *Opie Read, American Humorist* (New York, 1965).

2. Opie Read, *I Remember* (New York, 1930), p. 182.

3. Read covered a yellow fever epidemic in Memphis for the *Herald*.

4. *A History of American Magazines, 1865–1885* (Cambridge, 1938), III: 270.

5. Editor of *Texas Siftings*.

6. Examples are *Mrs. Annie Green*, *Len Ganset*, and *A Kentucky Colonel*.

Information Sources

BIBLIOGRAPHY:

Mott, Frank Luther. *A History of American Magazines, 1865–1885*. Cambridge, 1938. III: 270.

Mundt, Shirley M. "Opie Read." In *Dictionary of Literary Biography*. Detroit, 1983. XXIII: 284–92.

Thompson, Lawrence S. "Opie Perceival Read." In *Southern Writers: A Biographical Dictionary*. Baton Rouge and London, 1979. Pp. 374–375.

INDEX SOURCES: None.

LOCATION SOURCES: American Antiquarian Society (Worchester, Massachusetts), Library of Congress, University of Illinois Library.

Publication History

MAGAZINE TITLE AND TITLE CHANGES: *The Arkansaw Traveler*.

VOLUME AND ISSUE DATA: Vols. 1–43 (June 4, 1882–1916); weekly (1882-at least 1889), monthly (1906 or earlier–1916?).

PUBLISHER AND PLACE OF PUBLICATION: Read and Benham (1882–1888); The Arkansaw Traveler Publishing Company (October 20, 1888–1891); The Review Publishing Company (January 1892–1916). Thomas Deveraux, publisher (1892-?); A. J. Gontier, publisher (?–1916). Little Rock, Arkansas (1882-May 7, 1887); Chicago, Illinois (May 14, 1887–1916).

EDITORS: Opie P. Read (1882-December 1891); Harry Stephen Keeler (1892–1916?).

CIRCULATION: At least 100,000.

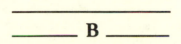

B

THE BALTIMORE LITERARY MONUMENT. *See* THE
BALTIMORE MONUMENT

THE BALTIMORE MONUMENT

One of the better Baltimore literary magazines of the 1830s was the *Baltimore Monument: A Weekly Journal, Devoted to Polite Literature, Science, and the Fine Arts*, published for two years as an eight-page weekly (1836–1838) and continued for an additional year (1838–1839) under different ownership as a fifty-page monthly.

Regarding the weekly's subtitle, of science there was little beyond an occasional "pop-science" selection, such as "Natural Curiosities in Texas," "Physical Properties of the Sun's Light," and the like. Similarly, with the exception of publishing a modest amount of music, scant attention was paid the fine arts beyond the sphere of the literary. The magazine, published on Saturdays at No. 2 Calvert Street and edited by J. N. M'Jilton and David Creamer, was predominantly a literary periodical.

In his first editorial message, headlined "The Corner Stone," Creamer wrote:

We have laid the corner stone of our 'Monument,' and with pleasure, do we anticipate rearing thereon a firm foundation, and a high and healthy superstructure. . . . Our city has long boasted her monuments of marble. They lift their lofty summits in exalted sublimity. . . . They, like the chain of history, link the present with the past. . . . Our aim is to erect a fabric in Literature that shall not deteriorate from the high honors of the 'Monumental City.' It is not meet that all our boast should be in marble, while the glory of other cities, is in the volumes they send forth bearing enlightenment upon their wings, and diffusing knowledge in their flight. [1, 1]

Boston, Creamer noted, with its population of 80,000 to 90,000, could boast six or seven literary periodicals in 1836; Baltimore, with 100,000 inhabitants, should be able to sustain two. "We have already been encouraged beyond our most sanguine expectations," he wrote in the first issue, and the venture began with a respectable number of charter subscribers. Creamer dreamed of the dawning of a better age for literature, as opposed to "this age of show and shallowness, when flimsy fictions assume the ascendancy, and superficial scribblers pamper a vitiated taste, that is polluting the public mind, and leading it away from morality." He singled out the *American Monthly* and the *Knickerbocker Magazine* as examples of current magazines that had defied the trend and were helping "purify the waters" of U.S. periodical literature.

The *Monument* exhibited concern with the public morality, running essays on such religious topics as the Sabbath, the Apostle Paul, and the Savior, plus other moral pieces on infidelity, swearing, and oaths. Creamer's editorial comments often dealt with education: the importance of education in a democratic society, expressions of concern over Baltimore's public schools, and the like. The women of his city, said the editor, were generally acknowledged as beautiful but had been slighted in their educational opportunities:

> Some unjust, ungenerous, and exceedingly arbitrary spirit, seems to have fixed the sphere of women, and with all the impudence and audacity imaginable, it has said, 'thus far shalt thou go.' . . . Custom, however, not man, is the tyrant, and it may be that woman's emancipation from this mental thraldom will be effected of itself. [1, 1: 14]

Another Creamer editorial dealt with liberty of the press and its vital importance in a free society, yet the editor decried the press' degenerative partisanship, commenting about "how unfortunate it was that many public journals which otherwise are of eminent utility . . . should descend to the abyss of degradation to which we find their party columns reduced" (1, 21: 166). Yet another editorial criticized the federal government for failing to take adequate steps to preserve "a minute and faithful history of the North American Indians" (1, 21: 166).

The substantial amount of original poetry that appeared in the *Monument* was interspersed among the prose content rather than being gathered into a separate poetry department. A number of selections, notably the contributions of Giles M'Quiggin, combined poetry and prose, as in the case of a humorous piece headlined "Mike Von Grover, The Loafer" that began in verse:

> Loafers of low and high degreee
> Denizen this land of liberty:
> There are statesman loafers with meaning blinks,

Who wait the lobby loafers' winks;
The merchant loafers who seek with care,
To find where the pedling loafers are;
The poet loafers who hunt a name,
Beyond the world of loafer fame,
There are loafers young and loafers old
Loafers backward and loafers bold
And of hosts that answer the loafers' call
The *bar room* loafer's the Satan of all. [1, 8: 57]

Another example of the *Monument*'s humor poetry is a piece entitled "Faux Pas":

Two gentlemen were at a ball one night,
Said one to t'other, "Pray, who's yonder fright?"
"What! that pale lady?" "Yes." "O, that's my mother."
"Not her,—you must be looking at another,—
I mean that the one in blue—that time you missed her,"
"The azure dress?" "Yes." "Why—she sir, is my sister."
"Not her—not her, the next one, on my life
I think a horrid fright—who's she?" "MY WIFE." [1, 10: 80]

Like most other magazines of the day, the *Monument* was troubled by subscribers who were slow to pay. Instead of weedling or grumbling about it in the usual pedestrian fashion, the editors chose a more subtle approach—verse set to the tune of "John Anderson, My Joe" ("Joe" being Scottish for "sweetheart"). Its first two stanzas read:

John Neverpay my Joe, John, why don't you pay my bill?
It's long been due, you know 'tis true, but unpaid is it still.
You surely ought to know John, 'tis wrong to treat me so,
And for my trust you should be just, John Neverpay my Joe.

John Neverpay my, Joe, John, with debts my ledger groans,
And times are hard, still no regard is paid unto my moans;
The folio I forget John, but figures there will show
A claim long due that stands 'gainst you, John Neverpay my Joe.
   [1, 18:40]

The editors also had an eye for witty prose contributions, as in "Traits of the Esophagus," signed by "Umph," whose thesis was that a person's character could be discerned by his or her table manners. An excerpt reads:

Just for a moment observe that juvenile plying his knife and fork with a
dexterity so barbarous in his unintermitted onslaughts upon that unoffend-

ing steak. See! he fairly pitches at it! How his huge head wags and rolls from side to side with infinite satisfaction, as his ponderous mandibles close and crunch upon the evanishing morsels. His eyes rove to and fro over the table with a flesh-searching gaze, absolutely awful. [1, 2: 11]

In sum, the quality of the weekly *Monument*'s content was most respectable. In the last number of his second volume Creamer announced that the magazine would be continued as a monthly and that "a gentleman of known literary attainments" would henceforth be associated with its editorial management. This gentleman was T. S. Arthur, who assumed the office of publisher and co-edited the monthly version with J. N. M'Jilton; the magazine's title was changed to the *Baltimore Literary Monument*. With the departure of Creamer, content quality declined. Gone were the wit and the pungent editorial comments. Supplanting these were sentimental fiction that descended to the sorry level of romantic drivel about heroines with "soft hazel eyes and rich brown curls . . . bounding airiness of step, exquisitely rounded figures, musical voices," etc. The quantity of the poetry remained about the same, but quality declined here, too, as the new management showed a fondness for the precious, as in "A Lady's Lament on the Death of Her Pet Kitten, Bell Tracy"; "To a Sleeping Child"; and "To My Flowers."

The mawkish and the precious were occasionally interrupted by the somber, as in "The Power of Education" by John L. Yeatts, M.D. One item worth noting positively is a series of biographical sketches of contemporary female poets run in volume 1, number 2, of the monthly.[1] Also of better than average quality was the continued poetry and short prose of Giles M'Quiggin, who was honored in volume 1, number 2 (page 68) with "To Giles M'Quiggin," a poem of tribute. This writer's wit and flair can be seen in the first verse of his "To a Musquito":

> Begone you starveling—illstarred creature,
> So lank of limb and gaunt of feature,
> You luckless, witless, foolish thing!
> How dare you enter one's upstairs,
> And get upon his ears to sting?
> And whether he's at books or prayers,
> You come with your eternal song,
> Whu-u-u-whut, and who can read
> Or pray with any kind of speed,
> You spider-legged imp! —go long! [1, 1: 27]

As in the weekly *Monument*, issues contained a small amount of original music, and most issues were embellished with a single engraving.

No editorial message announced the monthly's end in its final issue (October 1839). Timothy Shay Arthur later moved to Philadelphia, where in 1844 he became editor of the *Ladies' Magazine of Literature, Fashion and the Fine Arts*. Still later he wrote for *Godey's Lady's Book*, the *Christian Parlor Magazine*, and the *Union Magazine*.

Note

1. Selections included are on Lydia Huntley Sigourney (pp. 72–74), Hannah F. Gould (pp. 74–75), Emma C. Embury (p. 75), Anna Maria Wells (p. 76), Sarah Louisa P. Smith (pp. 76–77), Frances Sargent Osgood (pp. 77–78), Caroline Gilman (p. 79), Elizabeth F. Ellet (pp. 79–80), Sarah Josepa Hale (pp. 80–82), and Anna Peyre Dinnies (pp. 82–83).

Information Sources

BIBLIOGRAPHY:
Mott, Frank Luther. *A History of American Magazines, 1741–1850*. New York, 1930. I: 381.
INDEX SOURCES: None.
LOCATION SOURCES: American Periodical Series microfilm, Library of Congress, Peabody Institute Library (Baltimore), State Historical Society of Wisconsin (Madison).

Publication History

MAGAZINE TITLE AND TITLE CHANGES: *The Baltimore Monument: A Weekly Journal, Devoted to Polite Literature, Science, and the Fine Arts* (October 8, 1836-September 29, 1838); *The Baltimore Literary Monument* (October 1838-October 1839).
VOLUME AND ISSUE DATA: Vols. 1–2 (October 8, 1836-September 29, 1838), weekly; Vols. 1–2 (October 1838-October 1839), monthly.
PUBLISHER AND PLACE OF PUBLICATION: David Creamer (October 8, 1836-September 29, 1838); T. S. Arthur (October 1838-October 1839). Baltimore, Maryland.
EDITORS: David Creamer and J. N. M'Jilton (1836-September 1838); T. S. Arthur and J. N. M'Jilton (October 1838-October 1839).
CIRCULATION: Unknown.

THE BIVOUAC. *See* THE SOUTHERN BIVOUAC

BOB TAYLOR'S MAGAZINE

A turn-of-the-century champion of New South ideals was *Bob Taylor's Magazine* of Nashville, Tennessee, published under this title from April 1905 until December 1906 and thereafter until December 1910 as the *Taylor-Trotwood Magazine*, the result of its merger with *Trotwood's Monthly* (1905–1906), also of Nashville.

The magazine's original namesake, Robert Love Taylor, had been governor of Tennessee from 1887 to 1891 and again from 1897 to 1899 and had become a popular platform figure, often speaking in 1905 on "The Funny Side of Politics." A photographic portrait of the splendidly mustachioed Gov. Taylor appeared on page 120 of his magazine's initial number; a second portrait was run in volume 3, number 1 (p. 353).

A tone was set in the first issue that was maintained throughout the monthly's entire run. The magazine was good humored and had a literary quality of the light, popular sort, yet an underpinning of solid, conservative business values was always present. In the first issue this aspect of the Taylor "formula" was made manifest in Austin P. Foster's article "Sources of Southern Wealth" (pp. 62–65) and in the regular department "Men of Affairs" (pp. 17–22), which in volume 1, number 1, provided a mug shot and brief biographical information on business executive Samuel Spencer; jurist James C. M'Reynolds; the Rev. Thomas Dixon, Jr.; and dapper Atlanta journalist John Temple Graves.

Lighter copy in number 1 included a Southern humor article, "Tildy Binford's Advertisement" (pp. 46–53), by Holland Wright; "Society of the Forest" (pp. 66–79), a children's tale by M. W. Connolly; and a short-lived department entitled "Lyrical and Satirical" (pp. 87–89) conducted by "Vermouth." Beginning this department's offerings was an unattributed piece of doggerel, "The Rural Sheet," which began:

> The rural paper is a peach without a single
>   doubt,
> It is patent on the inside, patent medicine
>   without;
> Yet it giveth information both select and
>   wide of reach
> From a card of thanks for kindness to a
>   double column preach;
> It tells about the infant at the home of Bill
>   and wife,
> And it gives a thrilling storiette replete with
>   love and strife;
> It says the roads are passable though slightly
>   out of shape,
> An obituary notice names survivors wearing
>   crepe . . . [1, 1: 87]

Another poem in this issue was "The Old Order Passeth" by Grace McGowan Cooke, which depicted in dialect what Taylor and his readers deemed the "right kind of Negro." A photograph above the poem showed an ancient black man whose earthly cares appeared very nearly over; his daughter read to him from the Bible. He asks her to sing his favorite hymn—about the wicked ceasing their trouble and the weary going on to their rest. The final verse read:

De wicked—dat's dese new style folks,
  Pleased wid de things dey see,
Wid ruffled cape an' uppish ways,—
  And de weary—dat is me! [P. 61]

The Southern whites' nostalgia at the passing of the docile, servile Negro surfaces again, this time in prose, in "The Passing of the Old Negro" by Rosa Naomi Scott (1, 4: 405–9).

From the first issue the magazine contained a "Lyceum" department in which can be found photographs of such luminaries as Opie Read and Capt. Jack Crawford (The Poet-Scout) and a column called "Books and Authors," first conducted by Genella Fitzgerald Nye.

The monthly was of a respectable length, usually 116 pages, and enjoyed an enviable volume of advertising of all sorts—furniture, factories, hotels, insurance companies, buggy makers, schools, theaters, cigar stores, suspenders, garters, long underwear, pianos, engravers, Maxwell House Coffee, nostrums, and even a company that manufactured the machines for making cotton candy.

Covers were in color and were modestly attractive at first, though the cover design was not changed for each issue. Taylor opted for a plainer cover style with no art in October 1906, no doubt as a cost-cutting measure, though more interesting covers were later restored, including in 1909 a few featuring photographs. Also in 1909 the magazine's yearly subscription rate of $1.00 was raised to $1.50.

Old Southern favorites were resurrected, such as the poem "The Conquered Banner" (1, 4: 462–63) by Father Ryan. Familiar literary figures of the region were recalled, as in "Paul Hamilton Hayne" (1, 3: 321–23) by Harriet Hobson Dougherty. An especially interesting piece on a then contemporary writer was Hattie Parks Miller's "How Bill Arp Got His Name" (4, 1: 100–106).

Gov. Taylor offered his reflections under the standing head "Sunshine and Moonshine," and after the January 1907 merger with *Trotwood's Monthly*, Co-editor John Trotwood Moore conducted a department entitled "Historic Highways of the South."

To balance the regular feature, "Men of Affairs," the title of which was altered in 1910 to "Prominent Southerners," the recurrent feature "Some Beautiful Women of the South" was created. Many lived up to their billing; others appearing here might more honestly have been tagged "Some Wealthy Women of the South." A third similar department was "Little Citizens of the South"—cute photos of the sons and daughters of affluence. Other departments were added: "Familiar Faces behind the Footlights," a stage column, and "Laugh and the World Laughs with You," a department of original but wan humor conducted by Walter Pulitzer.

Travel articles appeared on such diverse destinations as Lookout Mountain (11, 1: 13–20),[1] the Shenandoah Valley (6, 4: 391–98), and the Yosemite Valley (1, 4: 396–404; 10, 5: 376–83). Some interesting articles on miscellaneous topics were Gibson Willets' "A New Yorker in Texas" (2, 4: 449–58); William R. Stewart's "The Trade of the World in Furs" (2, 6: 700–8); "When Men Wore Lace," on 16th-century court attire (3, 1: 99–107); and Grantland Rice's "Baseball's Boom in Dixie" (11, 1: 97–104). John Trotwood Moore's "The Gift of the Grass," the story of a race horse cast in first-person as though it were the animal's autobiography, was serialized endlessly in volumes 7 through 10.

Throughout its five years and nine months of life, this monthly retained the same page size, page length, periodicity, and tone, expiring without previous notice after the December 10, 1910, number.

Note

1. The article was written by Elizabeth Fry Page, who in May 1910 became the magazine's associate editor. Her full-length photo appears on page 12.

Information Sources

INDEX SOURCES: None.
LOCATION SOURCES: Library of Congress, New York Public Library, Oberlin College
     Library, University of Michigan Library, University of Tennessee Library.

Publication History

MAGAZINE TITLE AND TITLE CHANGES: *Bob Taylor's Magazine* (April 1905-
     December 1906); *The Taylor-Trotwood Magazine* (January 1907-December 1910).
VOLUME AND ISSUE DATA: Vols. 1–12 (April 1905-December 1910), monthly.
PUBLISHER AND PLACE OF PUBLICATION: The Taylor Publishing Company (April
     1905-December 1906); The Taylor-Trotwood Publishing Company (January 1907-
     December 1910). Nashville, Tennessee.
EDITORS: Robert L. Taylor (April 1905-December 1906); R. L. Taylor and John Trot-
     wood Moore (January 1907-December 1910).
CIRCULATION: Unknown.

BROWN'S GUIDE TO GEORGIA

A substantial part of all city and regional magazines' function is utilitarian—informing readers as to what to do, where to go for cultural opportunities or entertainment, where to shop, where to dine, and so on. One of the most useful of this genre was *Brown's Guide to Georgia*, founded in December 1972 and published for a decade thereafter. Not only was *Brown's Guide* unusually serious about its role as an information provider, but it was different in another respect. Whereas most city and regional books are written for the person who will go by car to the places described in the magazine, *Brown's Guide* tried to get their readers out of their automobiles for a more intimate look at Georgia. Much emphasis was placed on walks and hikes and on getting the reader to see the state from a canoe or a bicycle.

The magazine began as a quarterly, became a bimonthly in 1974, and went monthly in 1976. Format changed from 7″ by 10″ to 8 1/4 ″ by 11″ in March 1977. Giving the magazine its name was publisher Alfred Brown, who had edited his college newspaper at LaGrange College, worked as a newspaper reporter in Massachusetts and South Carolina, and had been a Public Relations man before starting his magazine. His associate publisher was the late James L. Townsend, earlier the founder of *Atlanta Magazine*. Townsend worked with Brown for about a year, then resigned for health reasons.

Brown's Guide was also unusual in that it was almost entirely staff written, whereas most city and regionals depend heavily upon freelancers for their article copy. The magazine's staff was unusually large for a magazine whose circulation peaked in the early 1980s at 63,000. Out of a total staff of twenty-four, eight were editorial staffers.

Of these, Bill Cutler, who became Brown's associate editor, specialized in bike trips, such as "A 30-mile Autumn Pedal through Pike County, Georgia's Next Boom Area. Or Is It?" (9, 10: 36–37), which was followed by Cutler's tips on proper bike equipment and where to buy it. Cutler's bike trip suggestions were always accompanied by carefully drawn maps for the cyclist.

Tom Patterson contributed similar articles for the hiker, such as "Secret Trails: Walking through the Mountains That Nobody Knows" (9, 8: 48–50) on the Armuchee District of Georgia's Chattahoochee National Forest. Maps were also provided with these articles.

Specializing in canoeing articles was Reece Turrentine. An example of his work was "One Bang Mulberry: If This Is a Four-Foot Drop, Mustn't This Be North Georgia?" (7, 6: 43–49), a piece on Mulberry Creek.

More diverse in their contributions were staffers Malcolm Mackenzie and Susan McDonald. Mackenzie's work included a long article on the state of old-house restorations in Georgia and where to find the architectural antiques, period hardware, specialty millwork, ironwork, period lighting, consultants and contractors necessary to this work (9, 8: 22–36, 38), and a guide to Georgia's private colleges (8, 2: 58–66, 68–69). Susan McDonald specialized in extensive "super sections," such as her guide to the Low Country lying between Savannah and Charleston (9, 10: 50–62), and wrote other long features, such as a look at Georgia's interior designers (9, 8: 40–46) and a piece on a really serious hiker entitled "Bill Foster's Long Walk: What to Pack for a 13-Year Hike" (7, 6: 32–39).

Possibly the longest special section *Brown's Guide* ever ran was Tom Patterson's guide to Atlanta (9, 1: 34–38, 40–41, 43–46, 51, 73–78, 80, 82, 84–86, 88, 90, 93–94, 96), which not only did a thorough job of listing and describing the usual attractions but gloried in the distinctive elements of city life that make Atlanta stand out from other Southern municipalities, most of which are more nearly overgrown small towns despite their swollen populations. An example was Patterson's account of a sidewalk preacher bawling at passersby in his peculiar, Southern-born idiom:

You gonna hafta face God-a yo' own selves-a, praise Jeeezus-a. . . . You ain't gonna have no excuses-a! Naw! They ain't gonna be No excuses when that day come-a! Just look at the shape the world is in-a! . . . But ever' man's gonna reap what he gonna sow-a! Thankya Jeeezus-a! [9, 1: 36]

A pleasant feature in *Brown's Guide* was the one-page, non-by-lined human interest profile of interesting Georgians. In one issue appeared Capn'n Sam Stevens, skipper of *The Waving Girl*, Savannah's tour vessel, and John Inger, a Chamblee-based collector and restorer of player pianos (7, 6: 50). In another appeared Albany (pronounced locally as "All-benny"), Georgia's Lamar "Bubba" Ross, maker of rattlesnake-proof leather boots (9, 1: 99).

Far more rare was *Brown's Guide*'s "Eating Out" section. Whereas most city and regional magazines contain such a department, few are more candid than a vote-hungry politician; most read as though they were written by the restaurant owners themselves. The reason is simple: pan a restaurant, lose an advertiser. *Brown's Guide* was never timid. Fred Brown and staff pulled no punches in their reviews. A North Georgia restaurant's fare was once described, for example, as follows:

Dreary salad fixings came with a cloyingly sweet house dressing and a thumpingly heavy blue-cheese topping. An entree labeled 'Veal Florentine' consisted of a thin escalape inside a giant eggy envelope, on the side of which hulked a great clump of spinach that resembled high-tide leavings on a hurricane-battered beach. [9, 1: 105]

Longer restaurant features went well beyond what one normally finds in magazines of this type. Articles like "Hotel Food, Indeed!" (7, 6: 56–59) about Hugo's, a posh restaurant in Atlanta's Hyatt Regency, made good reading and went into considerable detail. Surprises were often unearthed, as in a review of the Surf Motel and Restaurant of Fernandina Beach entitled "Just Your Average Motel Restaurant. . . . With a Little Ol' 16-Page Wine List" (8, 2: 76–77).

In 1979 the magazine took on a feistier edge, due to Fred Brown's desire to explain what really makes Georgia tick and Bill Cutler's affinity for trenchant prose. A letter to the editor in June of that year read in part, "All right, Bill Cutler. Describing someone's eyebrows as ' . . . like pearl grey kittens jerked in midleap sideways by worms in their intestines . . . ' is not only terrible writing, it's disgusting as well" (7, 6: 3).[1] The Cutler article from which this quotation was taken raised many eyebrows in and near the tiny community of Springfield near Savannah. Other eyebrows, and even hackles, were raised by other controversial Cutler pieces on Macon and especially Waynesboro, the town that seems to generate more controversy per capita than any other Georgia community.

Despite its very strong editorial content, *Brown's Guide* could never attract the advertising it needed. The ad/editorial ratio was about 40:60, and only 10 percent of ads were national. Major ad categories were restaurants, hotels, resorts, sellers of second homes, and other local or regional advertisers. Editorial color work was hardly ever used because of cost.

Due to the expense of maintaining a sizable staff and inability to attract quality advertising, the magazine expired in October 1982. It deserves to be remembered as one of the best statewide regional magazines ever published.

Note

1. The article in question was "The Legacy of Abner Graham," which had run in the April 1979 number.

Information Sources

INDEX SOURCES: Access: The Supplementary Index to Periodicals.
LOCATION SOURCES: Emory University Library, University of Georgia Library.

Publication History

MAGAZINE TITLE AND TITLE CHANGES: *Brown's Guide to Georgia.*
VOLUME AND ISSUE DATA: Vols. 1–10 (December 1972-October 1982); quarterly
    (1972–1974), bimonthly (1974–1976), monthly (1976–1982).
PUBLISHER AND PLACE OF PUBLICATION: Alfred Brown Publishing Company;
    Alfred Brown, Publisher. College Park, Georgia.
EDITOR: Alfred Brown.
CIRCULATION: 63,000.

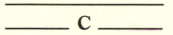

C

CAROLINA LIFESTYLE

Carolina Lifestyle, a short-lived, two-state regional magazine, had a rather complicated lineage. It was the 1982 product of the merger of two earlier state magazines: *Sandlapper: The Magazine of South Carolina* (1968–1982) and *Tar Heel: The Magazine of North Carolina* (1977–1982). *Tar Heel* itself was a continuation of the *New East* (1973–1977), a North Carolina regional published in Greenville, located in what Tar Heels customarily refer to as "the eastern part of the state."

Longest lasting of all these various incarnations was the *Sandlapper*, published in Columbia, South Carolina, as a monthly from its inception through 1970, in ten numbers yearly from 1971 to 1972, and again as a monthly from 1973 to March 1982. Its founding editor and publisher was Robert Pearce Wilkins, whose associate editor was Delmar L. Roberts. Subsequent editors were Roberts (1970–1973), Bob W. Rowland (1974–1978), Gerald Drucker (1978–1980), Harry Hope (1980–1981), and Robert L. Craft (1981–1982). Its first publishing company was Sandlapper Press, Inc., which was followed by Greystone Publishing (1977–1980), then by Cygnet Communications, the publishing concern of Norfolk-based Leonard A. Swann, Jr. *Sandlapper*'s appearance improved steadily over its fifteen volumes, and it grew into a truly attractive regional with lovely nature photography and entirely respectable article content. Perhaps the most scenic feature ever to appear in *Sandlapper* was a photo-laden interview with Rita Jenrette, who later became better known via another picture spread in a far more revealing magazine.[1]

The New East was published during 1973–1974 by Eden Press Inc, and during 1975–1977 by New East Inc., both of Greenville, North Carolina. A modest fifty-two-page monthly with all black and white on the inside and art work that left much to be desired, the magazine excited little interest outside its own part of the state. On one occasion Editor Thomas A. Williams received a new sub-scription with an attached letter to the editor from well-known North Carolinian H. F. "Chub" Seawell of Carthage, who allowed that he was subscribing since the *New East* couldn't possibly be any worse than the Near East or the Far East.

Operating under the aegis of the New East Inc. from 1977 to December 1980, the magazine, rechristened *Tar Heel*, took on an improved appearance and achieved more interesting content. Varying from fifty-two to eighty-four pages, it used a modest amount of editorial color. Among its best contents were stories by Guy Owen: "The Fighting Rooster,"[2] "A Christmas Tale,"[3] and "The Man at the Still."[4]

In January 1981 *Tar Heel* was taken over by Leonard Swann's Cygnet Com-munications, which had purchased *Sandlapper* in October 1980. The two mag-azines were merged in February 1982 under the new title *Carolina Lifestyle*. Swann was publisher, and Cole C. Campbell and Robert L. Craft were co-editors of volume 1, number 1. In the new monthly's next number, Susan Spence was editor, with Robert Craft and Ann A. Allen as regional editors. Spence became senior editor with the July 1983 issue, and Steven M. Adams became editor, though the magazine lasted for only one additional issue.

Peak circulation was 36,280 paid, 675 nonpaid, with an almost even split between the two Carolinas. Readership was 60 percent male, 40 percent female, 80 percent maried, 20 percent single. Sixty-four percent of subscribers were either professionals or business executives, according to information furnished by Leonard Swann.[5]

Personality profiles were better than those in most regional magazines; ex-amples introduced the reader to Carolina astronaut turned businessman, born-again Christian Charles Duke (1, 1: 40–41, 43, 64–65); Charlottte's journalistic storyteller Kays Gary (2, 4: 28–32, 56–58, 60); former *Greenville News* editorial cartoonist Kate Salley Palmer (2, 2: 34–39); and Hugh Morton, owner of Grand-father Mountain (1, 4: 42–51). Also of special interest were pieces on the seafood towns of Calabash and Murrells Inlet, South Carolina (1, 3: 46–47), and the R. J. Reynolds Company (2, 1: 34–44, 57–58).

Carolina Lifestyle's final issue in August 1983 contained articles on country music's Doc Watson; LaGrange, Tennessee's Lucy Pickens, whose face appeared on the Confederate $100 bill; the gypsy-like residents of Murphy Village, South Carolina; and six families who had broken away from the traditional lifestyle.

Carolina Lifestyle is presented here as a latter-day example of the many Southern magazines that are the result of mergers or continuations. According to Leonard Swann, who also publishes *Commonwealth Magazine*, it is possible that *Carolina Lifestyle* will be revived.

Notes

1. *Sandlapper*, 14, 1:32–43.
2. *Tar Heel*, 7, 4: 25–26, 37, 55.
3. Ibid., 7, 7: 31–32, 56.

4. Ibid., 8, 9: 33–36.
5. Letter dated September 21, 1984.

Information Sources

INDEX SOURCES: None.
LOCATION SOURCES: Duke University Library, North Carolina State University Library, University of North Carolina Library (Chapel Hill), University of South Carolina Library.

Publication History

MAGAZINE TITLE AND TITLE CHANGES: *Carolina Lifestyle* (April 1982-August 1983); the result of the merger of *Tar Heel: The Magazine of North Carolina* (September 1977-February 1982) and *Sandlapper: The Magazine of South Carolina* (January 1968- March 1982).
VOLUME AND ISSUE DATA: Vols. 1–3 (April 1982-August 1983), monthly.
PUBLISHER AND PLACE OF PUBLICATION: Leonard A. Swann, Jr. Norfolk, Virginia.
EDITORS: Cole C. Campbell and Robert L. Craft (April 1982); Susan L. Spence (May 1982-June 1983); Steven M. Adams (July-August 1983).
CIRCULATION: 36,280 paid, 675 nonpaid.

THE COMMERCIAL REVIEW OF THE SOUTH AND WEST. *See* DEBOW'S REVIEW

COSMOPOLITAN MONTHLY. *See* SCOTT'S MONTHLY MAGAZINE

COUNTRY MAGAZINE

In appearance, *Country Magazine* of Alexandria, Virginia, which began publication in 1980, is quite like dozens of other upscale regional magazines. It is unique, however, in the regional niche it has carved out for its "beat." Located in the Virginia suburbs of Washington, D.C. (where the Civil War memorials begin to face south), *Country* qualifies as a Southern magazine, but its real regional identity is Eastern.

In the mid–1970s Walter Nicklin recognized the similarities in the countrysides of Pennsylvania, Maryland, Delaware, Virginia, and West Virginia and thought he could convince advertisers that this region constituted a unified magazine market. Nicklin, a 1967 English/philosophy graduate of Washington and Lee, with a master's degree in foreign affairs from the University of Virginia,[1] published a pilot issue in 1977 but could not raise sufficient capital to continue. Over the following two years Nicklin and partner Wilson Morris, presently House Budget Committee information director, lined up support for the venture, which began anew in October 1980 and has since expanded its territory to New Jersey and North Carolina.

On the inside cover of volume 1, number 1, appeared Nicklin's statement of purpose, which staked out the magazine's territory and told the reader that the new magazine would be published for those who "seek a sense of time and place." By this he referred to urban or suburban dwellers who had grown nostalgic about their rural roots and wanted to know or even experience something of this heritage. Writing in the "Style" section of the *Washington Post*, Stephanie Mansfield called *Country* "America's mellowest monthly—devoted to pumpkin picking, Blue Ridge ballooning, Appalachian heel stomping, auctions, antiques, fox hunting and hearth fires."[2] The same writer reports that the magazine's subscription list includes Jacqueline Kennedy Onassis, Roger Mudd, Eugene McCarthy, James J. Kilpatrick, and Sen. John Warner.

Overall, the magazine's subscribers are a prosperous lot in early middle age, with a mean income of $54,188 and a median age of forty-six. Subscribers are evenly split between men and women, with 90 percent of its 70,000 paid circulation coming from subscriptions as opposed to newsstand sales.

When *Country* began in 1980, Nicklin was publisher and Wilson Morris was editor. A managing editor, art director, circulation and production managers, calendar editor, three contributing editors, and two advertising salespersons rounded out the staff, headquartered at 809 Cameron Street in Alexandria. The subscription rate was set at $15.00 a year, which remains unchanged; single-copy price was $1.50, now $1.95. The original full title was *Country Magazine: A Guide—From the Appalachians to the Atlantic*. In October 1983 the title was altered to *Country Magazine: The Guide to Eastern Living, From the Appalachians to the Atlantic*—long, perhaps, but providing further definition of the magazine's unique territory.

Like many other regional magazines, *Country* has from the start provided its readers a calendar of coming events. An ad in the first number solicited charter subscribers and enumerated the magazine's interest in real estate, camping, fishing, hunting, antiques, homesteading, hiking and backpacking, skiing, sailing, canoeing, country music, horses, second homes, wood stoves, folklore, history, nature, rock climbing, solar energy, arts and crafts, restaurants, inns, and gardening. Articles in number 1 told the reader about woodstove safety and how to select a woodstove; wilderness areas in the Shenandoah National Park; environmental problems of the Chesapeake Bay; endurance riding—the marathon for horseback riders; country auctions; Tom Davenport's filmmaking in Delaplane, Virginia; and how to plant hedges that will serve in place of a fence. A "Country Place" profile described Fan Hill, a lovely Georgian house near Fredericksburg, Virginia, and another article profiled historic Frederick, Maryland.

From its first issue *Country* has featured each month one fine old house that is on the market. The first was Seven Springs, a brick house built in the early 1700s—asking price, $350,000, with ninety-two acres included. This profile is accompanied each month by several pages of ads for other historic properties ranging in price from $100,000 to $2 million. In April 1982 what came to be one of the most highly publicized houses of recent years was advertised in this section: Poplar Forest, Thomas Jefferson's 1806 octagonal house, offered with fifty acres for $1,150,000 (3, 4: 51).

Real estate and travel are *Country*'s biggest advertising categories. Other ads are for log homes; companies that salvage and resell old heart pine flooring, chestnut paneling and oak beams; sellers of ceiling fans and wood stoves; antique dealers; and purveyors of preppy clothing.

That *Country* is aimed at the prosperous and at those who dream of prosperity can be seen in articles on steeplechasing, coaching, tailgating, and fox hunting. The disenchanted urbanite with money to invest was instructed in "How to Buy Country Property," a three-part series by Promotion Director Pat Bland (vol. 4, nos. 9, 10, 11).

In the October 1981 number was a whimsical exchange of articles on the groundhog, the first by former senator Eugene McCarthy, the second by his Rappahannock County, Virginia, neighbor, conservative columnist James J. Kilpatrick, whose animal-loving instincts do not extend to the groundhog. Like other residents of Virginia hunt country, Kilpatrick believes that the only good groundhog is a dead groundhog because of the little animal's habit of digging pasture holes into which horses step and break their expensive legs. Kilpatrick's contribution was followed by recipes for Sherried Groundhog and Groundhog Chasseur. Several months later McCarthy and Kilpatrick's efforts were expanded in a feature on the Slumbering Groundhog Lodge of Lancaster County, Pennsylvania, a group of part-time eccentrics who mount a colorful vigil each February 2 to determine whether the celebrated furry weatherman sees its shadow.

The magazine's proclivity for running occasional articles by famous persons may also be seen in "The Politics of Trout" by former president Jimmy Carter, with photos of Carter and wife Rosalynn fly casting (3, 4: 22–25).

Nicklin's ability to put together neat editorial "packages" was seen again in September 1983 in his treatment of Philadelphia (4, 9: 26–35). The first article was a more or less standard travel writer's treatment of the city, the second a humorous look at Philadelphia by an area columnist, the third a detailed "Brotherly Guide" providing tourist information. The writing was augmented by splendid photography; a tourist map of "Philadelphia, the city surrounding the Liberty Bell" drawn for *Country* by Elizabeth Luallen; and a masterful full-page Ben Franklin cartoon by the *Philadelphia Inquirer*'s Tony Auth.

An especially interesting food-related article was on Mary Randolph (5, 3: 71–72), author of the first Southern cookbook, *The Virginia House-wife, Method Is the Soul of Management*, 225 pages bound in leather and published in 1824. In another issue appeared a brace of articles on Virginia's lost treasures: $20 million in gold, silver, and jewels reportedly buried in the early 1800s by Thomas Jefferson Beale, and a cache of gold hidden in 1775 by England's General Braddock (3, 2: 30–34).

Staff at *Country* has increased only modestly. Nicklin became both editor and publisher following the magazine's purchase in 1982 by the Baltimore Sunpapers, whose publisher, Reg Murphy,[3] is now Nicklin's boss. A marketing director and a traffic coordinator have been added, the ad staff increased to four, and the list of contributing editors bumped up to eleven.

Niklin aims for an advertising/editorial mix somewhere between 40:60 and 45:55. Around 90 percent of *Country*'s feature articles, which average from 1,500 to 2,000 words in length, are from freelancers, and the magazine is nicely illustrated with artwork and photographs that are about half color, half black and white. The renewal rate for subscribers is a most satisfactory 70 percent. Articles are less outdoors-oriented than in the first two years; more attention is being paid to house and garden copy—with a slightly bucolic flavor, of course. With its quality editorial product, strong backing from the Sunpapers, and with the populous Baltimore–D.C.–Richmond market area to draw from, *Country*'s future looks bright.

Notes

1. Nicklin has written for UPI and Scripps–Howard newspapers, was editor of *Europe Magazine* for the Common Market, and was a correspondent for the *London Economist*.
2. "Country Chic: Bucks in the Backwoods," December 15, 1983.
3. Murphy, a Georgian, was a reporter for the *Macon Telegraph* and *News* and was editor of the *Atlanta Constitution* when he was kidnapped in 1974. Ransomed and released unharmed, Murphy became editor and publisher of the *San Francisco Examiner*, where he remained until his move to Baltimore in 1983.

Information Sources

BIBLIOGRAPHY:
Cohen, Stanley E. "How Bright Will the Sun—and Murphy—Shine?" *Advertising Age*, May 9, 1983, pp. M4–5.
Fannin, Rebecca. "Regional Magazines Gain National Impact." *Marketing & Media Decisions*, 17, 9: 64–66, 135.
Mansfield, Stephanie. "Country Chic: Bucks in the Backwoods." *Washington Post*, December 15, 1983.
INDEX SOURCES: None.
LOCATION SOURCES: Library of Congress.

Publication History

MAGAZINE TITLE AND TITLE CHANGES: *Country Magazine: A Guide—From the Appalachians to the Atlantic* (October 1980-September 1983); *Country Magazine: The Guide to Eastern Living, From the Appalachians to the Atlantic* (October 1983-present).
VOLUME AND ISSUE DATA: Vols. 1–5 (October 1980-present).
PUBLISHER AND PLACE OF PUBLICATION: Walter Nicklin (1980-present). Alexandria, Virginia.
EDITORS: Wilson Morris (1980–1982); Walter Nicklin (1983-present).
CIRCULATION: 70,000 paid, 4,000 nonpaid.

THE COUNTRYMAN

A delightful and apparently unique periodical of the Civil War–era South was the *Countryman* (1862–1865), an essay paper published on a remote Georgia plantation. This *Countryman* was patterned after the justly famous essay papers so successful in England a century earlier. Though the benign influence of Addison and Steele had been reflected in many magazines of the American South,[1] seldom was the influence so direct as in the case of this plantation journal, edited and published by a man with a singularly appropriate name—Joseph Addison Turner. In a letter to an Augusta, Georgia, businessman in 1861, Turner said, "I am indulging a quixotic freak to publish a [sic] Essayist—not a newspaper—on my plantation, to be devoted to—everything generally."[2]

This Georgia planter, who earlier had published four other periodicals (discussed later in this volume under the third of these, the *Plantation**), acquired a used Washington hand press, had it moved to Turnwold Plantation, and on March 4, 1862, ran off the first copy of the *Countryman*,[3] an eight-page weekly that bore the motto "Brevity Is the Soul of Wit." In it were some of Turner's own poetry, news articles of local interest, agricultural pieces, and editorials supporting the defense of the Confederacy. Also in this first number was an advertisement for a printer's devil; it was soon answered, and the job filled by thirteen-year-old Joel Chandler Harris, who worked under Turner's tutelage for the next four years.

In April, Turner reduced his periodical's page size and issued a new prospectus, saying:

> My aim is to model my journal after Addison's Little Paper, *The Spectator*, Steele's Little Paper, *The Tatler*, Johnson's Little Papers, *The Rambler* and *The Adventurer*, and Goldsmith's Little Paper, *The Bee*. . . . It is my aim to fill my Little Paper with Wit, Humor, Anecdote, Essays, Poems, Sketches, Agricultural Articles, and Short Tales. I do not intend to publish any thing that is dull, didactic, or prosy. I wish to make a neatly printed, select Little Paper—a pleasant companion for the leisure hour, and to relieve the minds of our people somewhat from the engrossing topic of war news.[4]

In a September number Turner urged his subscribers to preserve their copies of the *Countryman* for the sake of posterity. A file of old periodicals, he said, "brings up the past age with all its bustle and everyday affairs, and marks its genius and its spirit more than the most labored description of the historian" (September 29, 1862, p. 8). His own father, he added, was an "indefatigable preserver of newspapers," which gave J. A. Turner a ready source of filler for the *Countryman*.

By the following April, Turner was claiming subscribers in every state of the Confederacy and said his journal had "almost too many subscribers for the present unfavorable times, and its list is steadily increasing" (April 7, 1863, p. 2), a real success story in view of his start twelve months earlier with only one paid subscriber. The *Countryman* was far and away the most successful of Turner's five periodicals. Its success was remarkable in that the magazine began and managed to prosper during the war years.

Before war had been declared, Turner had made himself unpopular by speaking out against secession, but upon the outbreak of hostilities, he became steadfast, and as overly optimistic, as any supporter of the Confederacy. He used his pages to whip up enthusiasm for the cause, not only in editorials but with patriotic songs and poems, such as "The Southern National Anthem"[5] and "Away from Yankee Land."[6]

The *Countryman* often contained tips on how to improvise during wartime shortages, as in a short item headlined "Cheap Light," which advised readers to "take a cup of grease of any kind (lard or tallow) and into it put a sycamore ball, saturate in the same, and then light it. You will have a light superior to two candles. One ball will last three or four nights" (July 14, 1863, p. 15). The first time Joel Chandler Harris ventured into print was in just such an article in the *Countryman*, this one offering a recipe for homemade ink (December 1, 1862).

Turner was never afraid to speak his mind, even on the tenderest of subjects. He frequently wrote on religion, opposing the hellfire-and-damnation dogma so frequently preached, then and now, in rural Georgia. Speaking of himself as "The Countryman," he wrote:

> In his view of religion, he endeavors to look *up* instead of *down*. Could man be induced to cast their eyes more upon the Sun of Righteousness, and less upon the Blackness of Diabolism, The Countryman thinks it would be much better for the human family. . . . The Countryman will continue to oppose religious bigotry and intolerance, whether it comes from Methodists, Baptists, Presbyterians, Infidels, Jews, Episcopalians, Universalists, Unitarians, Catholics, or what not. . . . When there is perfect toleration of differences in religious faith, then and only then will there be that "peace on earth." [April 7, 1863, p. 2]

Though ever faithful to the Confederacy, Turner had less faith in the judgment of President Jefferson Davis. An example is his editorial decrying Davis' request that he be given censorship power over the Southern press (January 10, 1865, p. 8). Another is his assessment later the same year of two widely differing versions of Sherman's march through Georgia. Sherman himself said of his "retreat" that it was "very agreeable," but President Davis reportedly said that it would be more disastrous than Bonaparte's retreat from Moscow. "Both parties," Turner said, "are wrong. The truth probably lies between them, but nearer to Sherman than to Davis." Sherman, Turner noted, had passed through the state from one end to the other with hardly a scratch. "This should mantle with the blush of shame," wrote Turner, "the cheek of every Georgian, and every Confederate. We, for one, feel deeply mortified—humbled—chagrined— even degraded" (January 10, 1865, p. 10).

On the *Countryman* ran, with worthy copy of considerable variety: Southern poetry, travel pieces, articles on field sports, and humor copy. Turner was not above lifting a clever item from a Northern publication, as in the case of this epigram, taken from an old New York newspaper:

> Adam in Paradise to sleep was laid,
> Then was there from his side a woman made;
> Poor Father Adam! much it grieveth me
> That thy first sleep thy last repose should be. [September 29, 1862]

Turner himself contributed a mildly humorous series in dialect, the "Sally Poke letters," *à la* Major Jack Downing. His three-act play *West Point*, based on the sorry story of Benedict Arnold, was serialized in the *Countryman*, and of all his own poetry that appeared in its pages, "The Old Plantation" was the best. This 1,346-line effort was also serialized (October 27-December 15, 1862).

Though Turnwold Plantation sustained some damage from Sherman's troops, Turner's press and type were spared. His outspokenness began causing him trouble with the federal authorities in June of 1865, resulting in a six-month suspension of the *Countryman* until January 30, 1866. The plantation economy Turner had espoused was gone, however, and the postwar role of his journal was less than clear to him. Consequently, Turner ended his Addisonian efforts with the May 8, 1866, number. The master of Turnwold died in February 1868 at age forty-one. His *Countryman* is worthy of remembrance both for its intrinsic value and because it was the initial training ground for an even more outstanding Southern journalist and literary figure, Joel Chandler Harris.

Notes

1. See Guy A. Cardwell, Jr., "The Influence of Addison on Charleston Periodicals, 1795–1860," *Studies in Philology*, 35 (1938): 456–70.

2. Quoted by Paul Cousins in *Joel Chandler Harris* (Baton Rouge, 1968), pp. 56–57.

3. Turner had earlier used "The Countryman" as a pen name when writing for Georgia newspapers.

4. *Countryman*, September 29, 1862, p. 8.

5. September 29, 1862, p. 5. This song was sung in Kentucky, the article says, as the Confederate National Anthem. Its first and last verses follow:

> God save the South!
> God save the South!
> Her Altars and Firesides!
> God save the South!
>   Now that the war is nigh,
>   Now that we're armed to die,

Chanting our battle cry,
   Freedom or Death!

War to the hilt,
Theirs be the guilt,
Who fetter the Freeman,
To ransom the slave.
   Then still be undismayed,
   Sheathe not the battle-blade,
   Till the last foe is laid
      Low in the grave!

6. This air, to be sung to "Dixie," begins:

Oh! southern men, awake to glory,
Heed no more the Union story,
But away!—but away!—away from yankee land!
Valiant sons of the old plantation,
Bow no more to the yankee nation,
But away!—but away!—away from yankee land!

Information Sources

BIBLIOGRAPHY:
Cousins, Paul. *Joel Chandler Harris*. Baton Rouge, 1968.
Huff, Lawrence. "The Literary Publications of Joseph Addison Turner." *Georgia Historical Quarterly*, 46 (1962): 223–36.
INDEX SOURCES: None.
LOCATION SOURCES: Emory University Library, University of North Carolina Library (Chapel Hill).

Publication History

MAGAZINE TITLE AND TITLE CHANGES: *The Countryman*.
VOLUME AND ISSUE DATA: Vols. 1–21 (March 4, 1862-May 8, 1866), weekly.
PUBLISHER AND PLACE OF PUBLICATION: Joseph Addison Turner. Turnwold Plantation, Putnam County, Georgia.
EDITOR: Joseph Addison Turner.
CIRCULATION: Unknown.

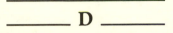

D

DEBOW'S REVIEW

In January of 1846 a young man with the imposing name of James Dunwoody Brownson DeBow commenced publication of a ninety-six-page magazine with the equally imposing title of the *Commercial Review of the South and West: A Monthly Journal of Trade, Commerce, Commercial Polity, Agriculture, Manufacture, Internal Improvements, and General Literature*. His original intention was to publish it in Charleston, but the first number appeared instead in New Orleans.

The designation "Commercial Review," said DeBow, was meant in the broadest sense. "You cannot touch a practical interest," he wrote, "which does not, to a greater or less extent, trench upon commerce. . . . Touch agriculture, touch the arts, the professions, fortifications, defenses, transportation, legislation of a country, and the chances are a thousand to one you touch commerce somewhere."[1] This kind of magazine, he continued, had never been attempted in the South or West, and in the North only by *Hunt's Merchant's Magazine*, which he took as his model. DeBow had in mind to serve, as he put it, "the humble tradesman, or the extensive merchant, the commercial jurist, the farmer and the planter, the manufacturer, as well as providing articles of interest and instruction for the general reader."[2] This "positioning" scheme was to make DeBow's *Review* the approximate equivalent in the South of today's *Wall Street Journal*, in that both have tried to promote themselves as indispensable to the practical man of affairs.

Prior to this ambitious venture, DeBow had read for the law and had assisted Daniel K. Whitaker in editing the *Southern Quarterly Review** in Charleston. Supposing that the South might be hospitable to a quality magazine of a more practical, less intellectual nature, DeBow decided to risk a magazine venture of his own. From the beginning he preached the need of the South to emulate the

PUBLIC LIBRARY OF PINE BLUFF
AND JEFFERSON COUNTY

industrial development taking place in the North. He gave his readers hard facts and considerable statistical information regarding a wide variety of trade and commercial subjects and market information. "Commerce is King," a line from Carlyle, was the *Review*'s motto, and of all the varieties of commerce discussed in its papers, cotton was king. Much attention was also paid to transportation topics—canals, plank roads, railroads, river transport—and to education in the South. Literature would not be entirely neglected, wrote DeBow, but *belles lettres* were not to have a significant place in the *Review* for many years. Usually DeBow devoted his space to the strictly serious and practical, and only on occasion did he permit a bit of whimsy, as was the case in volume 1 with "Humbugiana" (no. 1: 444–48) by Dr. D. Maccaulay of New Orleans, who discoursed at some length on what he saw as the prevalance of humbug, trickery, and quackery, concentrating his remarks on medical humbugs and quack advertising. The final twenty-four pages of the first number, however, contained a department set in small type and entitled "Southern and Western Statistics, Commerce, Agriculture, &c," a miscellany crammed with statistical data.

The last number of volume 1 found DeBow boasting of success beyond his anticipation. "Not a breath of complaint has yet been made. We have been cheered onward by the warmest plaudits from every quarter. A great proportion of the leading and prominent men of the city and state, are on our list" (1, 6:546). At the conclusion of his second year, DeBow claimed to have gained a larger circulation than any other Southern magazine, and the strongest influence. This success had not yet brought prosperity, however. In November 1848 the *Review* began a six-month suspension but was rescued from financial ruin by Maunsell White, a Louisiana sugar planter.

At this juncture DeBow was thirty years old; Frank Luther Mott offers a vivid description: "a tall, gaunt man . . . with a great shock of black hair and a rather wild-looking black beard, out of the midst of which stared keen eyes . . . while a large beaked nose thrust out belligerently."[3] The title page of volume 5 (1848) lists DeBow as professor of political economy, commerce, and statistics at the University of Louisiana, New Orleans.

A change of printers and the hiring of two successful subscription solicitors brought a happy change in DeBow's fortunes, and in 1851 his brother, Benjamin Franklin DeBow, joined his staff on the business side.

Though the *Review*'s attention to the West dated from its first number with an article on the commercial promise of Oregon and California, the South was its primary focus, and in 1853 *West* was dropped from the magazine's masthead. A department for literature had been added in 1850 with "The Sciote Lovers," a poem by Paul Hamilton Hayne (vol. 9, July-December 1850, pp. 344–45), followed by an English translation of the Marseilles Hymn, provided by "Z," a contributor from near Natchez, Mississippi. Some travel copy appeared, as did a very small amount of minor-league literary criticism and a fair amount of material on historical topics.[4]

Politics was taboo in DeBow's magazine until slavery and the quarrel with the North became unavoidable issues toward the end of the 1840s. An examination of the splendid index of the *Review* compiled by Willis Duke Weatherford and Don L. Moore, available on reel 855, American Periodical Series microfilm, will show the heavy attention DeBow paid the slavery issue, which accounts for roughly 1,000 of the 15,000 references in the index. *DeBow's Review* contains probably the most extensive single treatment of this issue to appear in any magazine of the nineteenth century, and DeBow himself became one of the South's most influential exponents of the slavery system. He was elected president of the 1857 Southern Convention in Knoxville, where he advocated reopening the African slave trade, the practice of which had been prohibited for the past forty years. Later, at the 1859 Vicksburg Convention, he was named president of the African Labor Supply Association.[5] In the *Review* of April 1860 appeared "The Secession of the South," a long essay by "Python" calling for secession and a new confederation of the Southern states, Texas, Mexico, Central America, and the West Indies (28: 367–92).

At the Vicksburg Convention, a delegate from Mississippi argued that God would not permit the Union to be dissolved, to which DeBow replied that there was "a God of battles as well as a God of submission" and reminded the delegate of a remark he attributed to one of Oliver Cromwell's generals: "Put your trust in God, but keep your powder dry" (vol. 27, September 1859, p. 469).

When the war began, DeBow became the Confederacy's cotton-purchasing agent. The editorial office went with DeBow to Richmond, and B. F. DeBow removed the business office to Charleston. The magazine's predominant focus changed from economic to political during the war. Publication became irregular, and following the combined May-August 1862 issue, the *Review* was suspended. But for a single issue, the combined July-August 1864 number, which was published in Columbia, South Carolina, the magazine remained dormant until January 1866.

DeBow's books and records were buried for the duration of the war but survived in reasonably good condition. By late 1865 he was hard at work attempting to collect old accounts receivable and soliciting new subscribers and advertisers. His "After the War Series," he said, would have a national character but would place particular emphasis on reestablishing the prosperity of the vanquished South. The search for new subscribers was aided by a number of good subscription agents, the most effective of whom seems to have been R. G. Barnwell, who had been with the magazine before the war.[6]

DeBow's headquarters were in Nashville due to his having been made president of a new railroad, the Tennessee & Pacific; the business office was at 40 Broadway in New York City in the care of B. F. DeBow, whose health by this time was failing. In December 1865 the editor was in position to print an issue; the magazine's new title was *DeBow's Review: Devoted to the Restoration of the Southern States, and the Development of the Wealth and Resources of the Country*. The new rate was $6 annually, up from the original $5, though combination rates were also offered as inducements. Some of the magazine's prewar contributors reappeared in the new series—W. M. Burwell, Josiah Nott, George Fitzhugh, and William Elliott. New writers appeared, among them Charles Gayarré, George Frederick Holmes, W. W. Boyce, and W. A. Benthuysen. Percy Roberts and William Sherwood wrote on Europe; engineer Albert Stein on rivers and streams; Holmes, Gayarré, and James Noyes on history; and DeBow himself on trade, travel, and reconstruction. More selected, as opposed to original, material was used than before the war. Cotton trade continued to receive as much attention as ever, though DeBow argued that the South needed to diversify. His editorials also urged Northern investments in the South, offering mountains of statistical data to back up his arguments. A new education department encouraged language study and supported public education, and another department was devoted to concerns centering on the former slaves of the South.

DeBow died on February 27, 1867, and his brother shortly thereafter. The *Review* was published by Mrs. J. D. B. DeBow and co-edited by R. G. Barnwell and Edwin Q. Bell, a DeBow in-law, until its sale in March 1868 to William MacCreary Burwell, who moved it back to New Orleans. Here the magazine continued the downhill slide that had been going on since DeBow's death, and finally it was suspended after the July 1870 issue. Almost a decade later L. Graham and Company bought the remnants of the magazine and revived it for the brief period of October 1879 to June 1880. After another long suspension—almost four years—the *Agricultural Review* of New York City bought what was left of *DeBow's Review* but itself went out of business soon thereafter.

The files of this sensible, practical magazine contain the most complete single source on the economic life of the pre–Civil War South. Its importance lies not in its literary worth but in its informational value.

Notes

1. *Commercial Review*, 1, 1: 4.
2. Ibid.
3. *A History of American Magazines, 1741–1850* (New York, 1930), I: 341.
4. DeBow was a founder of the Louisiana Historical Society.
5. See vol. 27 (August 1859), pp. 205–20, for the edited text of two speeches regarding reopening slave trade.
6. For what is probably the most thorough account of the difficulties of resuming publication of a Southern magazine after the Civil War, see Ottis C. Skipper, " 'DeBow's Review' after the Civil War," *Louisiana Historical Quarterly*, 29 (April 1946): 355–93.

Information Sources

BIBLIOGRAPHY:
Mott, Frank Luther. *A History of American Magazines, 1741–1840*. New York, 1930. I: 338–48.
Nixon, Herman Clarence. "DeBow's Review." *Sewanee Review*, 39 (January-March 1931): 54–61.
Rogers, Edward Reinhold. *Four Southern Magazines*. Studies in Southern Literature, Second Series. University of Virginia, 1902.

Skipper, Ottis C. " 'DeBow's Review' after the Civil War." *Louisiana Historical Quarterly*, 19 (April 1946): 355–93.

INDEX SOURCES: ALA Portrait, Poole's Index to Periodical Literature.

LOCATION SOURCES: American Periodical Series microfilm, Brown University Library, Detroit Public Library, Howard-Tilton Library (Tulane University, New Orleans), Louisville (Kentucky) Free Public Library, Mississippi Department of Archives and History (Jackson).

Publication History

MAGAZINE TITLE AND TITLE CHANGES: *The Commercial Review of the South and West: A Monthly Journal of Trade, Commerce, Commercial Polity, Agriculture, Manufactures, Internal Improvements, and General Literature* (January 1846-June 1850) [cover titles: *DeBow's Commercial Review of the South and West* (1847–50); *DeBow's Review of the Southern and Western States: Devoted to Commerce, Agriculture, Manufactures* (1850–52); *DeBow's Review and Industrial Resources, Statistics, etc.: Devoted to Commerce, Agriculture, Manufactures* (1853–64)]; *DeBow's Review: Devoted to the Restoration of the Southern States and the Development of the Wealth and Resources of the Country* (1865–1867); *DeBow's Review . . . Agricultural, Commercial, Industrial Progress & Resources* (1868–1880) [cover title: *DeBow's New Orleans Monthly Review* (1869–70)].

VOLUME AND ISSUE DATA: Vols. 1–34 (January 1846-June 1880), monthly.

PUBLISHER AND PLACE OF PUBLICATION: James Dunwoody Brownson DeBow (1846–1867); Mrs. J. D. B. DeBow (1867–1868); William M. Burwell (1868–1870); L. Graham & Company (1879–1880). New Orleans (1846–1852, 1859–1861, 1868–1870, 1879–1880), Washington, D.C. (1853–1858), Charleston (1861–1862), Columbia, South Carolina (1864), Nashville, Tennessee (1866–1868).

EDITORS: J. D. B. DeBow (1846–1867), R. G. Barnwell and Edwin Q. Bell (1867–1868); William MacCreary Burwell (1868–1870, 1880).

CIRCULATION: Unknown.

DELTA SCENE MAGAZINE

Delta Scene is probably the only regional magazine in America to be edited by a professor of Latin. Dr. Curt Lamar, who teaches both Latin and history at Delta State University in Cleveland, Mississippi, has edited this thirty-page quarterly since 1976, when it was donated to the university by former editor and publisher Edward A. Phillips. Phillips had purchased *Delta Scene* in early 1975 from founder Linda White, who had begun publishing the magazine in November 1973. Under Phillips the magazine turned a modest profit, but when he saw that revenues would not be sufficient to support his family, Phillips made a gift of *Delta Scene* and took a newspaper job with the Clarksdale *Press-Register*. Now the magazine is subsidized by Delta State University, which views it as part of its service role to the region and as an outlet for faculty, student, and alumni creativity. According to a statement by *Delta Scene* Business Manager Sherry Van Liew, the magazine's purpose is "to reflect the life and thought of the Delta region through articles that dealt with the history, literature, folklore, works of art, social institutions, education, and other facets of life, both past and present, in the Mississippi Delta.''[1]

Located in a state that publishes fewer magazines than any other in the South save Arkansas, *Delta Scene* is Mississippi's oldest general interest regional periodical. Two more recent contemporaries are *Persons*, a combination city/regional magazine for Hattiesburg and South Mississippi (January 1982-present) and *Mainstream* (Spring 1981-present), published quarterly in Jackson by the Mississippi Department of Economic Development.

Delta Scene's circulation is modest: 1,781 paid and 385 nonpaid. At least 75 percent of circulation is within Mississippi; most in the remaining 25 percent are university alumni. The subscription price and single-copy price have changed but once. With the Summer 1982 number, the single-copy price increased from $1.00 to $1.50, and the annual subscription price rose from $3.50 to $5.00. Ninety percent of circulation is by subscription, the remainder by newstand sales within Mississippi. Details on subscriber demographics were unavailable, but according to Van Liew, readers are typically college graduates of above-average income.

The Delta is a region of clear demarcation in its state. In her introductory message in volume 1, number 1, founder Linda White wrote:

> You know, if you were in Egypt, and met a man from New York City, he would tell you he lives in New York City. . . . A man from Biloxi would tell you he lives in Biloxi. But a man from Clarksdale (where *Delta Scene* originated) would probably say, 'I'm from the Delta.' [P. 1]

This is the kind of clearly defined area that makes sense for a regional magazine, and if this region were one of greater prosperity, university subsidization might not be needed.

As it is, advertising in *Delta Scene* is sparse, with car dealers, gift shops, insurance agencies, banks, restaurants, and furniture companies taking out small display ads and only occasionally springing for a full page, which sells for a modest $170 for a one-time insertion.

Like most in academe, *Delta Scene* must try to do a lot with very limited resources. Aside from the attractive color covers, little full-color work appears on the inside. The predominantly black-and-white illustrations are livened up here and there with one-color treatments. Drawn illustrations usually are only fair.

Feature articles, almost entirely from freelancers, many of whom are from outside Mississippi, must have a state or regional angle. Payments for the articles are of the token variety; no one writes for *Delta Scene* for the money. The magazine is most unusual for a regional book in that it strives for a 50:50 mix of fiction and nonfiction. Most regional magazines today run only a very limited amount of fiction, and Business Manager Van Liew reports that some *Delta*

Scene readers complain of too much fiction content, a symptom of businesslike American contempt for the world of letters, hardly atypical of any region of the country. A particularly pleasant example of *Delta Scene*'s brand of 1,000- to 2,000-word fiction is "The Ugliest Man" by Tom Dowling, a California free-lancer (10, 4: 8–9).

More or less regular features are the obligatory calendar of regional events and "Book Mark," a book review ably conducted of late by Rebecca Hood-Adams, who has also contributed verse, restaurant reviews, and feature articles for the magazine. Nonfiction features vary from accounts of regional curiosities (Layton Parker's highjumping mules [2, 4: 5], for example) to humor pieces with a Delta flair ("Of Grammar, Grits, and Good Ole Boys," a short treatise on how to tawk Suthun: "Hc like to died when I told him to go to hale" [7, 3: 14–15]) to standard travel articles (such as a piece on the *Mississippi Queen* and the *Delta Queen* riverboats [7, 3: 12–13]).

Stand-out nonfiction features in *Delta Scene* have been its historical articles. Noteworthy examples have been a piece on Briarfield, Jefferson Davis' plantation fifteen miles south of Vicksburg (9, 2: 16–19); an account of the sinking of the coal-fed side-wheeler *Sultana* in 1865, which resulted in the loss of roughly 1,700 lives, far more than were lost when the *Titanic* went down (10, 3: 21–23, 28); and a vignette by and about Sam Vick, a young Mississippi baseball player who went with the New York Yankees in 1918 and gained instant fame by hitting a bases-loaded triple when suddenly substituted for an injured Babe Ruth (2, 4: 8–9).

Though it is a modest regional magazine that depends upon subsidization in an era when city and regional books in richer markets are making a killing, *Delta Scene* has represented its state in this genre for over a decade and has certainly succeeded in reflecting the life and thought of the region.

Note

1. Telephone conversation with the author, June 21, 1984.

Information Sources

INDEX SOURCES: None.
LOCATION SOURCES: Delta State University Library, Mississippi State University Library.

Publication History

MAGAZINE TITLE AND TITLE CHANGES: *Delta Scene Magazine.*
VOLUME AND ISSUE DATA: Vols. 1–11 (November 1973-present), quarterly.
PUBLISHER AND PLACE OF PUBLICATION: Linda White (November 1973-January 1975); Edward A. Phillips (February 1975–1976); Delta Scene Corporation at Delta State University (1976-present). Clarksdale, Mississippi (1973–1976); Cleveland, Mississippi (1976-present).

EDITORS: Linda White (November 1973-January 1975); Edward Phillips (February
      1975–1976); Dr. Curt Lamar (1976-present).
CIRCULATION: 1,781 paid, 385 nonpaid.

DIXIE

A turn-of-the-century commercial magazine that originated in 1885 Atlanta
was *Dixie: A Monthly Record of Southern Industrial Possibility and Development*, first published by the Dixie Company and edited by Charles E. Wells. A
publisher's notice in the initial number promised that it would be a journal "of
the South, for the South, and by the South" and that it would serve no interests
but those of the whole South and of the publisher. "It will be as handsome as
money and artistic skill can make it," read the publisher's notice, "and as
reliable as watchful and persistent investigation can encompass" (1, 1: 36). A
year's subscription was $2 in advance, a single copy 20¢.

The editor's salutatory praised Southern progress of the past decade, writing
of a people devastated by war, "broken in purse and compelled to adopt new
methods in the conduct of affairs. . . . Who but a churl would censure their honest
pride in the measure of their success? . . . They have surmounted seemingly
impregnable obstacles" (1, 1: 36). Wells predicted a brilliant future for the
South, noting that the world had scarce knowledge of recent improvements in
the region's schools, transportation facilities, and broadening business structure;
"it too generally believes our natural products are confined to cotton, niggers
and mules." This last quote betrays the magazine's most noticeable shortcoming—bigotry.

Material of more general interest was promised: travel pieces about the South,
serial tales, and humor copy. The editor promised that "nothing in the form of
a 'puff' or advertisement will, under any circumstances, be admitted to our
reading columns" (1, 1: 36), and in discussing management's choice of a name
for the new monthly, Editor Wells pointed out that the North had no single word
to serve as their equivalent of "Dixie," which denotes "the whole southland."
Dixie, he promised, "is a journal of today, tomorrow, and the future, not of
yesterday and the sorrowful past."

In a column of miscellany headed "Current Notes," the editor notified his
readers that *Dixie* would regularly carry the cartoons of South Carolina's Charles
A. David, who had earlier cartooned for *Texas Siftings** and *Harper's Weekly*.
David had few equals and no superiors, the editor noted, as "a delineator of the
peculiar types of people to be found in the Carolinas" (1, 1: 39). In the main,
this meant that David had a knack for drawing blacks in such a way as to make
them look as simple and comical as possible. An example in the first number
(p. 44) showed an elderly, near-sighted gentleman of color politely tapping his
hat to the image in the full-length mirror of a clothing store and saying, "Morning' sah! I'se got a little trading' to do, an' I am gwine to buy my truck right

here whar de has culled gem'ens for clerks, I is. Pears like I has seed you some whar before dis time previously any how.''

Another David cartoon, this one in the second number, showed a barefoot Negro boy eating a purloined watermelon in a no-trespassing watermelon patch. A steel trap has clamped shut on his left foot, and the miscreant is saying to an unseen accomplice, ''Mus' be pizen in dis watermillion, fur I feels awful pains er shootin' up from my foot an' leg, an' dats' a sure sign ob pizenin!'' (1, 2: 94).

Such cartoons fit in perfectly with management's orientation toward the Negro. Years later, in 1903, *Dixie* editor T. H. Martin poo-pooed a politician's suggestion that all Negroes be deported to the Philippines, saying the Negro ''is a blessing to the South and the Southern people would not consent to his removal; this notwithstanding the very general impression to the contrary.'' Race relations in the South were not marked by antagonism, Martin wrote. Trouble was invariably the result of ''outside influences.'' Reading further, one finds that Editor Martin sees the Negro as innately inferior. He writes:

Let alone, the negro will share in the general progress. If false prophets shall lead him away from the white man, his fate is sealed. The white man can do without the negro but the negro is too near the jungle to stand alone; barbarism is only a few generations behind him, and it would be still fewer generations ahead of him without the white man's uplifting influence. [19, 1: 20]

Martin saw the Negro as desirable for the South mainly as a source of labor, secondarily as a partial guarantee against organized labor, inasmuch as he considered blacks too simple and lacking in ambition to be interested.

The first editor's fascination with the Negro could be seen in volume 1, number 2, in Donald Aylesworth Baine's long article ''A Negro Campmeeting,'' which was profusely illustrated with David cartoons. Four years later it was seen again in William Perry Brown's dialect story, ''Married by Santa Claus'' (5, 12: 1004–06), and Joel Chandler Harris' ''Mr. Crow and Brother Buzzard'' (5, 12: 1009–10), both written expressly for the 1889 Christmas issue of *Dixie*.

The Negro was also a favorite subject of the humor department, conducted by Atlantan Ed Wood, whose *nom de plume* was ''Fitzgoober.'' Wood also liked one-liners and humorous definitions: ''Egotism—Talkin' by th' yard, an' thinkin' by th' inch,'' ''Hotels—Great inn-conveniences,'' ''Lawsuits—A swimming pool filled with sharks'' (1, 1: 44). In this department appeared a marvelous cartoon of the editor, with the caption, ''Thoughts that breathe and words that burn,' said the editor as he assisted a 'poem on spring' into the stove'' (1, 1: 46).

Editor Wells did not entirely scorn verse, however. The second number featured Paul Hamilton Hayne's ''To the New South,'' which appeared in facsimile in the poet's own hand (1, 2: 51).

It is perhaps worth noting that *Dixie* began with attractive covers and a more literary quality, then moved to plain, busy covers and all-business content, whereas the region's most famous early magazine of commerce, *DeBow's Review** of New Orleans, started as all business and eventually became more literary. In any case, *Dixie* soon turned away from general interest-copy in favor of articles on iron, milling, lumber, cotton, electricity, textiles, and other business topics. Gone were the David cartoons. In their place appeared countless engravings of machines. The magazine grew fat with advertisements for engines, band saws, boilers, gears, turbines, dredges, steam shovels and lathes. Following page 20 of volume 5, number 1, is an insert—a beautiful color lithograph of a Saint Bernard dog in an Alpine setting, placed here to show the capabilities of the Rochester Lithography and Printing Company, the same kind of ad that appears today in *Advertising Age*.

Looking back at *Dixie* from today's vantage point, one can say that the magazine's editors often backed the wrong horse. In "Can Man Fly?" Jonathan Mills, inventor and mechanical engineer, took the ill-timed stand that probably man never will make much of a success at flying until he becomes an angel" (4, 1: 33).

By 1902 the magazine was taking positions that today seem quite thoroughly reactionary. Editor T. H. Martin came out against the eight-hour work day, saying that "good steady work never harmed any one. . . . The eight-hour day was a joint invention of the walking delegate and a lazy workman—one is hunting trouble and the other is trying to get rid of it. So the idea appeals strongly to both" (18, 12: 19). In the same issue Martin backed child labor in Southern cotton mills, saying that "child labor is productive of vastly more good than evil, if any evil at all" (18, 12: 34). Letters from mill owners and superintendents are printed which, not surprisingly, agree with the editor. A picture of a group of smiling young girls at a mill in Lindale, Georgia, appears. The caption identifies them as mill workers of at least six years experience and asks, "Is there need for legislation here?" (18, 12: 36).

The Southern Industrial Publishing Company took over as publisher, which continued through October 1903, when the magazine was bought by R. M. Martin, a Savannah newspaperman, and moved to that city. It changed hands again the following year and was moved back to Atlanta by the Southern States Publishing Company, where it was edited by Benjamin F. Ulmer. Under this ownership the magazine became more and more specialized, and with the February 1905 issue the subtitle was changed from *A Journal Devoted to Southern Industrial Interests* to *Devoted to the Technical Features of Sawmilling and Woodworking*. A further title change occurred with the September 1905 number; the magazine was retitled the *Dixie Wood-worker*. An announcement by Ulmer explained that management felt a magazine devoted solely to one industry can better serve both readers and advertisers. It became, he claimed, the first journal of its kind in the South.

Despite its many mistakes and its view of the Negro that would be unsettling to readers black and white today, *Dixie* provided much good coverage of New South industrialization. A fitting close for this selection is a verse from ''The Land of Dixie,'' a poem that appeared in the magazine's first issue:

> Gone the paralyzing deadness of the old disfranchised days,
>> Gone the haughty Southern languor, for the industry
>>> that pays,
>> Recognizing now the power, and the
>>> dignity of toil,
>> Fearing not that honest labor might
>>> some gentle fingers soil. [1, 1: 3]

Information Sources

INDEX SOURCES: None.
LOCATION SOURCES: Duke University Library, Library of Congress, New York Public Library, University of Texas Library (Austin).

Publication History

MAGAZINE TITLE AND TITLE CHANGES: *Dixie: A Monthly Record of Southern Industrial Possibility and Development* (1885-?); *Dixie: A Journal Devoted to Southern Industrial Interests* (?-January 1905); *Dixie: Devoted to the Technical Features of Sawmilling and Woodworking* (February 1905-August 1905); *Dixie Wood-worker* (September 1905-December 1907).
VOLUME AND ISSUE DATA: Vols. 1–23 (August 1885-December 1907), monthly.
PUBLISHER AND PLACE OF PUBLICATION: The Dixie Company (Atlanta, Georgia, 1885-?); The Southern Industrial Publishing Company (Atlanta, ?-October 1903); R. M. Martin (Savannah, Georgia, November 1903-May 1904); Southern States Publishing Company (Atlanta, June 1904-December 1907).
EDITORS: Charles H. Wells (1885–1891); T. H. Martin (1891-May 1904); Benjamin F. Ulmer (June 1904-March 1907); H. F. Reils (April-December 1907).
CIRCULATION: Unknown.

DIXIE WOODWORKER. *See* DIXIE

D MAGAZINE

One of the South's slickest city magazines, typically Texan in the attention it pays to money and power, is *D Magazine*, published in Dallas since October 1974 by the Southwest Media Corporation. A typical issue runs 200 pages and like its contemporaries *Southern Living** and *Texas Monthly,** *D* is fat with advertisements. An *Advertising Age* poll of forty-two magazine editors placed *D* at seventh-best among U.S. city and regional books and ninth in total ad pages.[1] Aiming at high-income readers, the monthly's average paid circulation was 79,049 in 1983.

A 1982 *Ad Age* interiew with then editor Rowland Stiteler reported that *D* was launched with a flurry of investigative reporting in the 1970s, then was switched to a lighter format after the local newspaper press began expending more effort on reporting social issues. For their part, the *Dallas Morning News* has called *D*'s writing uneven, saying that some of its more informative pieces "read like a Biology 101 term paper" or are "as bland as milk-soaked white bread."[2] The real success story of *D Magazine*, continues *Morning News* writer Lloyd Grove, is not in their editorial fare but in the volume of advertising they have been able to generate.

Ad prices are on the high side for a magazine of just under 80,000 circulation: $4,185 for a one-time full page ad in full color, for example, yet its pages are filled to overflowing with the accoutrements of the good life. Ad categories, in descending order of importance, are fashion/jewelry/accessories, restaurants/clubs/entertainment, real estate, travel/resorts/hotels, department stores/shopping centers, liquor/wine/beer/smoking requisites, housewares, automobiles, and health and beauty products. According to rough calculations, the ad/editorial ratio was about 60:40 in 1983.

Subscribers are 45 percent male, 55 percent female, and 71 percent of them are between the ages of 25 and 54, with a median age of 37.8. Married subscribers account for 67 percent of the total, singles for 21 percent, with the remainder listed as "other." Fifty-nine percent are college graduates; 31 percent have done postgraduate work. Median household income was $55,130 in 1983, mean income $81, 816, and 24 percent were on at least one board of directors. Median net worth of subscribers was $203,968, mean net worth $310,762.

Sales of *D Magazine* average 76 percent by subscription ($15.00 yearly), 24 percent from single-copy purchases ($1.95), and the magazine sells in all fifty states, though Texas subscribers account for all but about 5,500 of the total.

The magazine's founder and first publisher was Wick Allison, a 1970 American studies graduate of the University of Texas who convinced Dallas business magnate Ray Hunt to bankroll the venture. Hunt, then thirty-four years old, founded the Southwest Media Corporation for this purpose; in 1977 the parent corporation also began publishing the successful regional house book *Texas Homes*.* Allison left *D* in 1981 and was replaced by Bernard Kraft, who is now listed as president. Current Publisher Terry Murphy was previously in ad sales with *Sports Illustrated* and was associated with the Dallas Market Center, a merchandise mart. Editor as of 1984 is Lee Cullum, who had earlier spent eleven years as producer and moderator of the show "Newsroom" on Channel 13, Dallas' public television station.

Local newspaper critics to the contrary, *D Magazine* does indeed contain some very good writing. In placing Robert A. Wilson's column "Insights" on the final page, *D* is often saving its best for last. As the column name implies, Wilson is insightful, delightfully so, whether writing on tough issues, such as privacy versus the right to know (11, 6: 216) or musing about the pros and cons of committee work (11, 5: 248).

Another steady contributor who writes eminently readable copy is Contributing Editor Jo Brans, whose reflections were the brightest spot in a recent issue featuring "Summer Pleasures" (11, 7: 142–45, 148–49). Many of the heavy pieces are undertaken by Contributing Editor Richard West, who recently did articles on problems of West Dallas housing projects (11, 7: 158–61, 171–72) and the provocative story of a Dallas family's heartbreaking experiences with a schizophrenic son (11, 5: 98–101, 204–06), or Associate Editor Ruth M. Fitzgibbons, whose 1984 contributions included pieces on divorced fathers seeking child custody (11, 6: 78–79, 82–83, 158, 160, 162–63, 165–66) and "Nice Girls Do. Young Girls Do. Most Girls Do" on teenage pregnancy in Dallas, which leads the nation in this regard (11, 8: 140–43).

Typical city magazine pieces to appear have been features on the ten toughest bosses in the city (11, 6, 106, 111–12, 114) and in the same issue "A Muckraker's Tour of Dallas" (pp. 86–89). Also typical were "Dallas' Best Restaurants" (11, 8: 72–76, 184–85) and an instruction manual on how to complain about practically everything (11, 5: 88–95, 197–98, 200, 203), the last of which provided inspiration for a delightful cover that depicted a dapper, pinstriped gentleman with a huge fly in his soup.

Among regular departments are "Inside Dallas," a collection of news notes often, but not always concerned with money, beauty, and power; "Insiders," consisting of personality profiles (more money/beauty/power); a listing of Dallas-Fort Worth's top 10 companies (still more money and power, if not beauty); a calendar of arts and entertainment; a dining guide—revised to list restaurants by neighborhood instead of by type of food; a one-page listing of current art gallery offerings; and "The City," which reported that in 1983, Dallas hosted nearly 2,000 conventions, bringing more than 2 million visitors to the city (11, 6: 67).

True, the good-life copy serves the not-so-important function of allowing wealthy people to read about other wealthy people and get a comfortable feeling that all's right with the world, and true, the reader of *D* feature articles is tortured with endless jumps ("continued on page——"). Yet one can find truly creditable reading matter here and can learn a great deal about one of the South's most dynamic cities from the magazine's pages.

Notes

1. *Advertising Age*, April 5, 1982, pp. M–26 and M–27.
2. *Dallas Morning News*, October 1, 1978.

Information Sources

BIBLIOGRAPHY:

Gilliam, Linda. "City Publications Pop Up All Over Texas." *Advertising Age*, April 5, 1982.

Grove, Lloyd. "D: Slick, Fat and Prosperous." *Dallas Morning News*, October 1, 1978.

INDEX SOURCES: Access: The Supplementary Index to Periodicals.
LOCATION SOURCES: Southern Methodist University Library.

Publication History

MAGAZINE TITLE AND TITLE CHANGES: *D Magazine*.
VOLUME AND ISSUE DATA: Vols. 1–11 (October 1974-present), monthly.
PUBLISHER AND PLACE OF PUBLICATION: Southwest Media Corporation: Wick
     Allison (October 1974–1981); Bernard R. Kraft (1981-April 1983); Terry Murphy
     (May 1983-present). Dallas, Texas.
EDITORS: Jim Adkinson (October 1974–1976); Wick Allison (1976–1980); David Legge
     (1980–1981); Rowland Stiteler (1981-March 1982); Lee Cullum (April 1982-
     present).
CIRCULATION: 79,049 (average paid circulation duirng 1983), 7,391 nonpaid.

THE DOUBLE DEALER

The decade of the 1920s brought with it a surge in Southern literary efforts,
particularly in response to H. L. Mencken's characterization of the literary South
as "The Sahara of the Bozart."[1] It was a memorable time in the region's letters,
marked by the appearance of several literary magazines of greater or lesser
importance that offered their modest-sized audiences reading of a kind not being
supplied by the more popularly oriented magazines of the day.

Best financed of the lot was the *Fugitive** (1922–1925), brainchild of the
Vanderbilt University English Department. In Richmond, Virginia, appeared the
Reviewer (1921–1925), which merged in 1926 with the *Southwest Review* (1924-
present), itself a continuation of the *Texas Review* (1915–1924). *All's Well; or,
the Mirror Repolished* (1920–1935) was published in Fayetteville, Arkansas,
Phoenix at Emory University in Atlanta, the *Carolina Magazine* at Chapel Hill,
Archive at Trinity College (Duke University after 1925), *Cracker* at the Uni-
versity of Georgia in Athens, *Lyric* in Norfolk, and *Bozart* in Atlanta.

In New Orleans two young men named Julius Weis Friend and Albert Goldstein, each in his twenties, began in 1921 a literary magazine having the curious
title the *Double Dealer*, which they more or less explained in their slogan: "I
can deceive them both by speaking the truth." The two men had originally
intended to publish a spicier magazine of humor and scandal modeled after the
Mascot* (1882–1895). Reacting to Mencken, however, they opted for a more
dignified format and enlisted the aid of John McClure, who had recently edited
another New Orleans literary magazine, the *Southerner*, and the rather more
established writer Basil Thompson.

Friend and Thompson were co-editors; Goldstein and Paul L. Godchaux, Jr.,
were listed in the first number as associate editors. Vincent Starrett was their
Chicago correspondent, Louis Bernheimer their New York City correspondent.
Their editorial plan was to publish one short story a month, plus essays, reviews,

sketches, epigrams, and "sundry observations on the human animal as celestial aspirant and strap-hanger" (1, 1: 4).

The magazine began with a playfulness and youthful bravado that gradually mellowed as time and effort affected its editors. Indicative of the *Double Dealer*'s early inclination to be clever was the following characterization of the professions:

Law:	Justice bound in calf.
Medicine:	A ballyhoo man in a Mortuary Chapel.
Journalism:	Michelangelo painting a house.
Ministry:	The Song of Songs on a Victrola—God holding office hours.
Politics:	Socrates playing the stock market—Simon Legree joshing the slaves. [1, 2: 78]

In a similar vein the editors tweaked the ladies in "The Ephemeral Sex":

As a sex you are a delight and a necessity. As mothers, wives and mistresses, you are beyond compare, but, as creative artists, we reaffirm, complete failures, pathetic nonentities. . . . Find us a female Dante, Shakespeare, Beethoven, Bach, Leonardo, Michelangelo, Phidias, Rodin, Cervantes, Dean Swift, etc., etc. (space being shy) and, forthwith, we recant and apologize. [1, 3: 85]

In "College 'Education' " the editors again attempted to out-Mencken Mencken:

The American college of today has become in actuality more a country club than a place of learning, a country club with a few hours of recitation and lecture thrown in. . . . The fault, of course, lies with . . . the old traditionals: Harvard, Yale, Princeton, Cornell. They have become schools for manners. So you can tell a Harvard man by his affected quasi-English accent, and general attitude of omniscience; a Yale man by the cut of his clothes and his immobile features. . . . It is probable that both are mimicking the English—and the more recent colleges are mimicking them. [1, 5: 170]

The August 1921 *All's Well* carried a delightful plug for the *Double Dealer*, quoting the great Mencken himself:

The Double Dealer has the right air. It struts a bit, it doesn't give a damn for the old gods. I have read all of its issues diligently, and haven't found a single reference direct or indirect, to the charm and virtue of Southern womanhood, or to the mad way in which slaves used to love their masters, or to the strategy of General Stonewall Jackson, or to the lamentable event of April 9, 1865.[2]

Assessing their first year's experience, the *Double Dealer*'s editors already showed their mellowing: "For some we were too flippant, for others too high-brow. Where one reader found us 'up in the air,' another protests us 'of the earth, earthy.' Convicted on various counts by sundry judges we could but carry on with Chaplinesque nonchalance" (2, 7: 2). Still, the editors announced that from "a magazine for the discriminating," they had decided to become a "national magazine from the South"—a national medium for the encouragement of young writers of the region.

Writer Sherwood Anderson saw the *Double Dealer* and the movement of which it was a part as an attempt to reopen channels of individual expression in an America whose newspapers and magazines had become corporate, standardized, and advertiser oriented ("New Orleans, the Double Dealer, and the Modern Movement in America," 3, 15: 119–26). Certainly the little magazine, never once in the slightest danger of showing a profit, did its part in accomplishing this purpose. Only for the first year were contributors paid on a regular basis, and in the early issues the editors themselves had to provide most of the copy, covering up this weakness by the frequent use of pseudonyms.[3] Yet the magazine's quest for quality and originality gradually attracted contributions from not only the well-known Sherwood Anderson and Ezra Pound but from a variety of talented younger writers whose stars had not yet risen: Ernest Hemingway, William Faulkner, Hart Crane, Robert Penn Warren, John Crowe Ransom, and others.

In their sixth volume the editors declared that they were "sick to death of the treacly sentimentalities with which our lady fictioners regale us." They decried dialect writing as a thing of the past and begged for the emergence of an original penman "from the sodden marshes of Southern literature." The people of the North and East are made, added the editors; those of the Middle West and West are in the making; and the young people of the South "are being remade. It is this remaking that should arrest the literary eye" (6, 35: 84). In this, Mencken, who followed the magazine closely though he did not contribute to it, felt the *Double Dealer* had failed. It had not attracted enough new writers of its own to please Mencken, who came to consider its contents uneven and insufficiently Southern.

The magazine suffered a considerable loss when poet/editor Basil Thompson died in 1924 at age thirty-one. Thompson is reputed to have been the collegial hub around which the other writer/editors revolved. The latter part of the monthly's five-year, five-month life saw some irregularity of publishing. Gradually the fun, the iconoclasm, and the spirit went out of the enterprise. No longer did the *Double Dealer* strut, or "stalk Bozartian Sahara in jaunty unconcern" (editorial, 3, 13: 2). The unannounced end came with the May 1926 number.

Notes

1. "The Sahara of the Bozart," New York *Evening Mail*, November 13, 1917.
2. *All's Well*, 1, 9.
3. For details see Frances Jean Bowen, "The New Orleans *Double Dealer*, 1921–1926," *Louisiana Historical Quarterly*, 39 (1956): 451–52.

Information Sources

BIBLIOGRAPHY:
Bowen, Frances Jean. "The New Orleans *Double Dealer*, 1921–1926." *Louisiana Historical Quarterly*, 39 (1956): 443–56.
Durrett, Frances Bowen. "The New Orleans *Double Dealer*." In *Reality and Myth: Essays in American Literature in Memory of Richard Croom Beatty*, edited by William E. Walker and Robert L. Welker. Nashville, Tenn., 1964. Pp. 212–36.
Holson, Fred C., Jr. *Serpent in Eden: H. L. Mencken and the South*. Chapel Hill, 1974. Pp. 33–56.
Hubbell, Jay B. "Southern Magazines." In *Culture in the South*, edited by W. T. Couch. Chapel Hill, N.C., 1934. Pp. 174–77.
INDEX SOURCES: Index to American Little Magazines.
LOCATION SOURCES: Duke University Library, Library of Congress, Louisiana State University Library, New York Public Library, Princeton University Library, University of North Carolina Library (Chapel Hill), University of Texas Library (Austin), University of Virginia Library.

Publication History

MAGAZINE TITLE AND TITLE CHANGES: *The Double Dealer*.
VOLUME AND ISSUE DATA: Vols. 1–8 (January 1921-May 1926); monthly (1921-July 1925), bi-monthly (November 1925-May 1926).
PUBLISHER AND PLACE OF PUBLICATION: The Double Dealer Publishing Company. New Orleans, Louisiana.
EDITORS: Julius Weis Friend and Basil Thompson (1921-April 1923); Julius Weis Friend and John McClure (May 1923-May 1926).
CIRCULATION: 18,000.

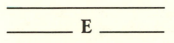

THE EMERALD

An early Baltimore "vehicle for the amusement of the ladies" was the *Emerald*, a sixteen-page weekly of 1810–1811. This light-hearted miscellany was published by Benjamin Edes, son of the Massachusetts newspaperman of the same name who is well-remembered today for his pre-Revolutionary War co-proprietorship (with John Gill) of the important patriot newpaper the *Boston Gazette*. The *Emerald* was edited by "Peter Pleasant and Co."; its masthead bore the motto:

> . . . . With Modest Skill,
> To Raise the Virtues, Animate the Bliss,
> And Sweeten All the Toils of Human Life:
> This be the EMERALD's Dignity and Praise.

Sold for $3 yearly, payable at the expiration of every four months, this magazine appeared on Saturdays and, according to its prospectus, was intended to cherish Baltimore's fair inhabitants' "taste for the effusions of genius, their regard for the moral pleasures of social and domestic life, and to hand them the weekly occurrences of this busy world, unalloyed by the intrusion of political debates, and unembittered by the asperities of party rancor."

While most magazines of this period contained no advertisements, number 1 of the *Emerald* devoted half a page to Mr. Edes' offer to do book and job printing ("Executed with Neatness, Accuracy & Dispatch"), and the lower half of the same page advertised Mrs. Edes' bonnet and millinary business.

The *Emerald*'s pages were filled with happy little items, some borrowed from English sources, such as this marriage notice for the union of John Rose and Mercy Bower:

Oft to the Bower shall John repair,
And, on a bed a Roses there,
Shall vows of love and friendship make,
And prostrate bend for Mercy's sake. [No. 1: 15]

or this epigram, taken from a Northern publication:

To view Passaic Falls, one day
A *Priest* and *Taylor* took their way:
"Thy wonders, Lord," the Parson cries,
"Amaze our souls—delight our eyes."
The Taylor only made this note—
"Lord, what a place—*to sponge a coat.*" [No. 2: 26]

Many of its items were original, however, and varied from the witty epigram:

Jack says that females all are fill'd
    With vanity and vain desire;
Jack never told the truth but once,
    And then he own'd himself a liar. [No. 3: 36]

to articles and verse that tugged at the fair readers' heart strings, as in "Sonnet to a Chimney Sweeper," which began:

Poor shiv'ring wight in tatter'd garb array'd
How much I pity thee; for, by my soul
Misfortune hangs around thy sooty form
As if she claim'd a kindred title there. [No. 3: 36]

The *Emerald*'s editor kept prose contributions far briefer than did most of his competitors, and though most of the poetry "Peter Pleasant" ran was original, much of the prose was selected. A hint as to the reason for the shortage of locally written prose appears in number 4 in the form of remarkably, perhaps suicidally, frank advice to would-be contributors:

We have found in our Letter-Box this week diverse communications; few of them reach *mediocrity*—many of them fall far below it. Averse as we may feel to offend our correspondents, we cannot, in honour to ourselves, or justice to the public, insert promiscuously, *the heap which surrounds us.* . . . The author of "an attempt at the obscure," has so far succeeded in his "attempt" as to incapacitate us from giving it an insertion." [No. 4: 50]

Selections in the *Emerald* were unswervingly light: a biographical sketch of John Hanbury Dwyer, a stage comedian from Dublin, Ireland; "The Mountress," a tale of marital infidelity; "Mary, A True Story," a serialized story of seduction and regret; and a brief essay entitled "On Friendship." An original contribution titled "Conjugal Celibacy" was intended to show the ladies why some men might choose to remain bachelors (no. 2: 18–22). A reader who signed himself "Timothy" applied to the *Emerald* for advice on his own souring marriage (no. 4: 43–45). Like modern advice columnists, the editor suggested that man and wife talk things out, though he added that "being as yet unfettered by chains of matrimony," he was ill-equipped to advise on marital strife. In the next number appeared what purported to be the wife's side of the matter, signed "Amelia" (no. 5: 51–52).

On page 1 of number 8 is a selected item that surely must have sparked criticism from the more pious segment of Baltimore society: "Petition of the Genteel and Fashionable for the Repeal of the Ten Commandments," which, tongue in cheek, suggests that the Commandments are old fashioned and "might do very well for the Jews, who were a sinful race, but is really too bad for us Christians" (no. 8: 87–89).

Marriages were occasionally announced, some without comment, others with puckish wit, as in the union of Capt. Thomas Lee and Miss Wilhelmina Helm:

'Twas Saturday nght, the twinkling stars
   Shone on the rippling sea,
No duty called the jovial tar—
   The *Helm* was lash'd a *Lee*. [No. 2: 26]

After four months, the *Emerald* gave up the ghost and sparkled no more until 1828, when it was revived for one more year's life as the *Emerald and Baltimore Literary Gazette*, also published by Benjamin Edes but edited this time by the poet Rufus Dawes.

Information Sources

BIBLIOGRAPHY:
Edgar, Neal L. *A History and Bibliography of American Magazines*. Metuchen, N.J., 1975. Pp. 139–40.
Mott, Frank Luther. *History of American Magazines, 1741–1850*. New York, 1930. I: 381.
INDEX SOURCES: None.
LOCATION SOURCES: American Periodical Series microfilm, Peabody Institute Library (Baltimore).

Publication History

MAGAZINE TITLE AND TITLE CHANGES: *The Emerald* (November 1810-March 1811); revived as *The Emerald and Baltimore Literary Gazette* (March 1828-April 1829).

VOLUME AND ISSUE DATA: Vol. 1, nos. 1–18 (November 3, 1810-March 2, 1811),
    weekly; Vol. 1–2, nos. 1–52 (March 29, 1828-April 11, 1829), weekly.
PUBLISHER AND PLACE OF PUBLICATION: Benjamin Edes. Corner of Market and
    South Streets, Baltimore, Maryland.
EDITORS: "Peter Pleasant, & Co." (1810–1811); Rufus Dawes (1828–1829).
CIRCULATION: Unknown.

THE EMERALD AND BALTIMORE LITERARY
GAZETTE. *See* THE EMERALD

THE EVANGELICAL AND LITERARY MAGAZINE
AND MISSIONARY CHRONICLE. *See* THE LITERARY
AND EVANGELICAL MAGAZINE

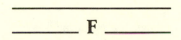

THE FARMER AND GARDENER. *See* THE AMERICAN FARMER

FETTER'S SOUTHERN MAGAZINE

"In one sense, the Southern writers who have been most successful have been lost to their people. Nearly all of them have gravitated toward the literary centers of the North" (1, 1: 66). So wrote the co-editors of a new Louisville, Kentucky, monthly in 1892. The periodical was *Fetter's Southern Magazine: A Popular Journal of Literature, Poetry, Romance, Art*; its editors were poet George Fetter and short story writer Charles Shober. In the same editorial the two noted that the better Southern writers who had not physically changed residence had undergone a mental change that had made them more cosmopolitan but detracted from their force as writers. In becoming less provincial they had become less original, and their work had "lost some of its freshness—a little of its rustic charm has vanished like the dissolving dew of morning. It is nearer to the Concord standard, but not so distinctively Southern. The critics like it better, the people like it less."

The new magazine, its editors promised, would "represent the new and catholic South . . . a South which is progressive without ceasing to be reminiscent, which is teeming with unwritten legends and songs which the great world has never heard, and whose mental wealth is developed only here and there, as sparsely as her mines and quarries" (1, 1: 66). A new literary life had been breathed into the South, the editors said, by the likes of Charles Egbert Craddock, George Washington Cable, Thomas Nelson Page, and James Lane Allen, yet Craddock had written only of the Tennessee hills, Cable of New Orleans, Page of Virginia, and Allen of Kentucky. The remainder of the region awaited similar

writers, which the new monthly hoped to foster. Reminiscence would be the
magazine's main stock in trade, though articles illustrative of the South's material
progress would also receive space. Louisville, standing between East and West,
"in touch with all the South and thoroughly *en rapport* with the central Northern
states" (1, 1: 68), the editors deemed an ideal location for such a project.

Granting the North's leading magazines the respect they were due, Fetter and
Shober adopted an "if you can't beat 'em join 'em" business philosophy and
made immediate arrangements to club subscriptions with *Lippincott's Monthly*,
Scribner's, *Cosmopolitan*, *Century Magazine*, *Harper's New Monthly*, *Harper's
Weekly*, *Harper's Bazaar*, *New England Magazine*, *Atlantic Monthly*, *Puck*,
Judge, and *Frank Leslie's*. Subscribed to alone, *Fetter's* ninety-four-page assortment of stories, essays, poems, humor, book reviews, and a woman's department sold for $2.50 annually. The magazine was well illustrated with drawings
by Robert Burns Wilson, Frederick Cawein, Carolus Brenner, J. Proctor Knott,
W. Benneville Rhodes, C. Grunwald, Elizabeth Chase, and other artists. The
engraving work was done by the Columbian Engraving Company of Chicago.

Examples of Southern reminiscence copy from volume 1 were "An Hour at
the Hermitage" by W. J. Lisle and Witherspoon Erwin's "Reminiscences of
William Gilmore Simms," which was just the sort of copy that gave H. L.
Mencken apoplexy, to wit:

> in his pages he has shown us . . . this mother in her widowhood, when the
> brave man of the house had fallen, without a tear or a tremor girding his
> father's sword upon her yet beardless son, and sending him forth to conquer
> for his country or to die in its defense. . . . What a promise for the future
> of the country that its statesmen, its soldiers and its citizens are to be raised
> up at the feet of these high-bred women whose bosoms are sanctuaries of
> all the higher virtues. [1, 1: 53]

The featured article in the first number was M. Kaufman's "Jew or Pariah—
Which?" (1, 1: 32–37), a plea for more favorable recognition of "a race much
maligned and greatly misunderstood" (1, 1: 74). To titillate the popular taste,
but in a dignified way, appeared "Eroticism in Fiction" (1, 1: 1–4) by J. Soule
Smith. Humor copy at the expense of the Negro included " 'Postle Paul's
Ruminatin' " (1, 3: 224), prose by Sam Stone Bush, and the dialect verse feature
"The New South" by "Falcon" (1, 1: 38–39), the following extracts from
which shows that the editors held blacks in low esteem. The poem was illustrated
with a photograph of a smiling Negro boy sitting astride a bicycle. Five of the
poem's ten verses are reproduced here with apologies to black readers and in
hopes that they will regard this copy in its historical context:

> Times, it seems to me, is changin'
>   Fer the wuss, with every day;
> White men in the fields a-rangin'
>   While the niggers is at play.

> Goin' ter town, to-day a nigger
> Passed me on a two-wheeled thing,
> Cuttin' up a fancy figger,
> Like the worl' was in er sling.

The white farmer, from whose point of view the poem is being related, unsuccessfully urges his horse to catch the boy, who from the rear looked, he said, like a bowlegged kettle riding on a pewter spoon:

> But the nigger kept agoin'—
> O'nery little lamp-black cuss!—
> Turnin' now an' then, an' crowin'
> Like a chicken. Wuss an' wuss.

> Then the blasted nigger, grinnin'
> Turned, an' crowed at me agin;
> An' went down the hill a-spinnin',
> Like old Satan chasin' sin.

> In the good ole times of slav'ry
> White men wuz the nigger's boss;
> Now—dad burn their sassy knavy'ry!—
> Niggers kin outrun a hoss.

Eleven months after the magazine's founding, Charles Shober's place as co-publisher was taken by Sam Stone Bush, whose infusion of new capital improved the monthly's looks. At the same time the editorship was assumed by Gen. Basil Duke, formerly editor of the *Southern Bivouac*.* Duke contributed an interesting piece on Audubon, which began on page 3 of volume 3, and in his department "The Editor's Table" held forth on such diverse topics as the fecundity of writers, morality in fiction, America's treatment of the Chinese, and the relationship of public servants and the people. In volume 3 the woman's department, still conducted by Angele Crippen, had its title changed to "My Lady's Escritoire," and Opie Read, former editor of the *Arkansaw Traveler*,* first in Little Rock, then in Chicago, edited a column called "Salmagundi." A "Books and Writers" department was also added.

The magazine's title was changed in August 1893, to the *Southern Magazine*. Despite its attractive appearance and middle-brow appeal, the monthly failed to prosper. The number for November-December 1894 did not appear, and the venture went into bankruptcy toward the end of that year. The property was bought by F. C. Nunemacher, who rechristened it the *Mid-Continent Magazine*, hoping to erase its Southern reputation, but its life was extended only from May to August of 1895.

Information Sources

BIBLIOGRAPHY:
Mott, Frank Luther. *A History of American Magazines, 1885–1905*. Cambridge, 1957. IV: 93.
INDEX SOURCES: None.
LOCATION SOURCES: Duke University Library, Library of Congress, Louisville (Kentucky) Free Public Library, New York Public Library, University of Chicago Library, University of North Carolina Library (Chapel Hill).

Publication History

MAGAZINE TITLE AND TITLE CHANGES: *Fetter's Southern Magazine: A Popular Journal of Literature, Poetry, Romance, Art* (1892-July 1893); *The Southern Magazine* (August 1893-March 1895); *The Mid-Continent Magazine* (May-August 1895).
VOLUME AND ISSUE DATA: Vols. 1–6 (August 1892-August 1895), monthly.
PUBLISHER AND PLACE OF PUBLICATION: Fetter and Shober (August 1892-July 1893); Fetter-Bush Publishing Company (August 1893-January 1894); The Southern Magazine Corporation (February-December 1894); The Southern Magazine Press (January-March 1895); Louisville, Kentucky. The Mid-Continent Press (May-August 1895); Chicago, Illinois, and Louisville, Kentucky.
EDITORS: George Griffith Fetter and Charles Ernest Shober (August 1892-July 1893); Basil W. Duke and T. E. Spencer (August 1893-?); Basil W. Duke (February-October 1894); F. C. Nunemacher (May-August 1895).
CIRCULATION: Unknown.

FOXFIRE®

Unique among American magazines is *Foxfire®*, written and published quarterly since 1967 by the students of Rabun County High School in Clayton, Georgia. *Foxfire®* is the brainchild of Eliot Wigginton, a Cornell M.A. who saw the desirability of preserving Georgia mountain folk knowledge after coming to teach in the Rabun Gap Nacoochi school district. Locals contributed article ideas, and Wigginton's students did the interviewing, writing, and editing in an educational process that can only be described as magnificently innovative. Where so many innovations in public school teaching are trendy creatures of brief duration, the Foxfire® program has not only continued, but has been improved and diversified.

As of the fall of 1983, the average print run for *Foxfire®* was 5,115, of which 3,638 were paid. Of the 3,638, 3,342 were sold by subscription and 296 on newsstands. Some of the copy from issues of the magazine has been supplemented by other material and published in book form. The first such volume, in 1972, was titled, *The Foxfire Book*, the other seven as *Foxfire 2*, *Foxfire 3*, and so forth. The most recent of these books, *Foxfire 8*, was published by Doubleday in 100,000 copies and distributed internationally. Today the eight books are available in softback for $7.95 to $9.95 or in hardback from $15.95 to $19.95 per volume.

Other publications from the Foxfire Press are *Aunt Arie: A Foxfire Portrait*, the folkloric biography of a mountain woman featured in early issues of the magazine; "The Foxfire Calendar"; and a 115-page oral history of the Tallulah Falls Railroad titled *Memories of a Mountain Shortline*. A cookbook was published in Autumn 1984, and a manuscript is in press (June 1985) for a book on traditional mountain toys and games. Mountain music has been preserved in two albums, "North Georgia Mountains" and "It Still Lives," and in a forty-five-minute cassette tape called "The Foxfire String Band." Foxfire® has even made Broadway in a stage production that ran from November 1982 until May 1983. The play, about an elderly Appalachian woman modeled after Aunt Arie, was written by Hume Cronyn and Susan Cooper and starred Cronyn and his wife Jessica Tandy, who got a Tony award for the performance.

Through the challenge grant program of the National Endowment for the Humanities, Wigginton has moved to ensure the continued ability of the Foxfire® organization to go on collecting bits and pieces of a disappearing way of life. For every $3 contributed by friends of the program, the Endowment pledged $1 toward the Foxfire® endowment. Among the patron, supporting, sustaining, and lifetime subscribers are not only locals but interested parties from such diverse and faraway places as Houston, Texas; Tacoma, Washington; Las Cruces, New Mexico; Winchester, Massachusetts; Danbury, Connecticut; Lee's Summit, Missouri; and Frostproof, Florida. Wigginton's goal is $900,000 from private donations, about 70 percent of which had been reached by August 1984.

These readers were touched, one suspects, not only by descriptions of vanishing skills and crafts but by glimpses of a kind of American once described in a popular song title as "dear hearts and gentle people." One such subject was Aunt Bessie Miller of Scaly Mountain, North Carolina, who had recently celebrated her ninety-third birthday at the Scaly Mountain Church of God. The interview, by Foxfire® student Adam Wilburn, gave Aunt Bessie's account of "just living to be ninety-three" (17, 4: 264–70). Others were Will Byrd of Blairsville, Georgia, who regaled student writer Chet Welch with his stories of the hobo life (18, 1: 32–39), and Cherokee woodcarver Goingback Chiltoskey, who lives by the Oconaluftee River near the Smokey Mountains National Park (17, 3: 166–77).

Sheriff Luther Rickman recalls the August 26, 1936, robbery of the Bank of Clayton (18, 1: 29–31), and student Curtis Weaver photographed and wrote about "praying rock," a boulder located deep in the woods to which his preacher grandfather, Charlie Bry Phillips, would repair to pray when troubled. Small pebbles placed on the rock in piles represented those for whom he had prayed. The pebbles, in two piles—those who had been saved and those who had not— had remained untouched since preacher Phillips' death in 1975 (18, 1: 46–51).

How the kind of oral history work done by Wigginton's students can bring to transitive life what might otherwise appear to history classes as a bone-dry corner of the nation and region's past is made clear in an extensive project on the Civil Conservation Corps (CCC) in the 1930s. In an introduction, Wigginton quoted the seventy-nine words in one U.S. history text that described the CCC's providing jobs for 250,000 unemployed men between the ages of eighteen and twenty-five. The *Foxfire®* interviews, many of them conducted by the grand-children of the interviewees, said Wigginton, allowed "one dead paragraph in a history text" to "come to life in a unique and powerful way" (16, 4: 226). The recollections of Oakley Justice, Minyard Conner, Ernest Gragg, Buck Carver, Alton Story, Carlton English, and others who worked in Rabun County's CCC camps told of the specific jobs they did and described in a personal way the camp messhalls, recreation programs, accidents, and discipline. Two issues of the magazine were devoted to the project (16, 4; 17, 1).

Other articles typical of *Foxfire®* trace the creation of Black Rock Mountain State Park near Clayton (17, 3: 185–205); a long piece entitled "Cleater Meaders Builds a Kiln" (17, 3: 147–65), in which the student writers methodically document and diagram all the steps in constructing a pottery kiln; "Searching for Antique Quilts in Rabun County" (18, 1: 52–61); and "Nicholson House" (18, 1: 17–23) on one of the county's old inns.

According to Administrative Assistant Joyce Colburn,[1] there are roughly 200 other high school magazines scattered throughout the United States; a number of these have benefitted from how-to workshops conducted by *Foxfire®* staffers. Surely few of the 200 have operations remotely as extensive as the one at Rabun Gap.

A recent readership study shows a nearly equal split between male and female subscribers. *Foxfire®* has an old audience, more than half of whom are fifty-five or older. Most are married, many have grown children, and most are in white-collar jobs. The largest group of subscribers falls into the $25,000 to $40,000 category in household income, and most have subscribed for at least nine years.

Foxfire® has subscribers in every state. About 20 percent of the total are in Georgia, and other states with high subscribership are Florida, North Carolina, Tennessee, Virginia, Ohio, New York, and California. The magazine has done nothing to solicit subscriptions, and most subscribers from other parts of the country have found out about the magazine through the eight *Foxfire®* books, which enjoy a wide circulation. Asked why they subscribe, readers replied that they liked the accurate portrayal of mountain life and that they found the *"Foxfire®* spirit" unique, which indeed it may be.

Note

1. Telephone conversation with the author, August 24, 1984.

Information Sources

BIBLIOGRAPHY:
Cornelison, Jimmy. "Foxfire: The Big Business of Back to Basics." *Greenville* (S.C.) *News*, February 27, 1983.

Handcock, Nicholas. "Foxfire Students Prove Kids Are Competent." Marshall (N.C.)
    News Record, September 3, 1981.
Wolfe, Bill. "Foxfire's Flame Grows Brighter." *Atlanta Journal*, April 3, 1983.
INDEX SOURCES: Access: The Supplementary Index to Periodicals.
LOCATION SOURCES: Bluefield State College Library (West Virginia), Brooks Mem-
    orial Library, (Brattleboro, Vermont), George Washington University Library
    (District of Columbia), Wake Forest University Library (North Carolina).

Publication History

MAGAZINE TITLE AND TITLE CHANGES: *Foxfire®*.
VOLUME AND ISSUE DATA: Vols. 1–18 (March 1967-present), quarterly.
PUBLISHER AND PLACE OF PUBLICATION: Foxfire Fund, Inc. Clayton, Georgia.
EDITORS: Eliot Wigginton, advisor (1967-May 1972); Eliot Wigginton and Margie
    Bennett, co-advisors (June 1972-present).
CIRCULATION: 3,638 paid, 1,477 nonpaid.

THE FUGITIVE

Not since the Charleston bookstore gatherings that led William Gilmore Simms,
Paul Hamilton Hayne, John Russell, and other literary gentlemen of that city to
found *Russell's Magazine** (1857–1860) had there been so interesting and congenial a group of literati as began to meet in 1914 Nashville and who later began
to refer to their little coterie as the Fugitives. Most of the original group were
either faculty or students at Vanderbilt University; their usual meeting place was
the home of wealthy, traveled Sidney Mttron[1] Hirsh. World War I scattered the
group, but at war's end all returned safe to Nashville and in 1920 resumed
meeting twice monthly, this time at the home of Hirsh's brother-in-law, James
M. Frank, a clothing manufacturer with literary interests. Meetings were presided
over by Hirsh, an imposing figure though then an invalid. Eventually their
discussions came to center on poetry, its reading and criticism, and at length
Hirsh suggested the creation of a poetry journal to showcase the group's work.
As such, the *Fugitive* began in 1922.

The eight original Fugitives who constituted the thirty-two-page periodical's
board of editors were Hirsh, Frank, Walter Clyde Curry, Donald Davidson,
Stanley Johnson, John Crowe Ransom, Alec B. Stevenson, and Allen Tate. It
was decided that the group would edit the new journal by committee, and a
foreword in the initial issue alerted readers that the Fugitives considered "Southern literature" a dead term. "The Fugitive," read the foreword, "flees from
nothing faster than from the high-caste Brahmins of the Old South. Without
raising the question of whether the blood in the veins of its editors runs red,
they at any rate are not advertising it as blue; indeed, as to pedigree, they
cheerfully invite the most unfavorable inference from the circumstances of their
anonymity" (1, 1: 2). The anonymity referred to here was the group's decision
to sign only pen names to their poems. Each pen name had whimsical signifi-

cance. The playful Davidson, who loved travel, styled himself "Robin Galli-vant"; Tate, admittedly vain, was "Henry Feathertop." "Roger Prim" was the pseudonym chosen by the proper Mr. Ransom.[2] After the first two issues, the policy of anonymity was discontinued and earlier pseudonyms identified in an editorial in number 3. One reason for the change was that a critic had suggested that perhaps all the verse in the first two issues was in reality the work of one author, probably John Crowe Ransom.

When the *Fugitive* first appeared, its editor-publishers were not at all sure about its publication interval. The foreword in number 1 indicated intervals of "one month or more, till three to five numbers have been issued." By the second issue the group had more or less decided upon quarterly publication, though they converted the journal to a bimonthly for 1923 and 1924 before returning to quarterly status for 1925, the magazine's final year.

Probably the title the *Fugitive* was suggested by Hirsh, and according to Tate[3] the term simply denoted a poet, one who flees the mundane for the contemplative. As Frederick Hoffman, Charles Allen, and Carolyn Ulrich point out in *The Little Magazine: A History and a Bibliography*,[4] it is easy to surmise that these Fugitives also fled the sentimental verse of the day, professional Southernism, and cheap-ening influences in literature in general.

The primary purpose of the *Fugitive* was to provide a suitable outlet for the small group's own work, but after finding that they could defray "the grim tolls of Mammon" at $1 per subscription and after receiving contributions from other poets all over the country, the group announced in number 3 that visitors' work would occasionally appear. The first visitors' copy appeared in number 4, best of which probably was Witter Brynner's "The Great Iron Cat," about Carl Sandburg (1, 4: 110–11). Among the guests who subsequently published here were Hart Crane of New York; poet/critic/anthologist Louis Untermeyer; imagist John Gould Fletcher; English poet/critic Robert Graves; *Double Dealer** As-sociate Editor Louis Gilmore; and Joseph T. Shipley, translator of *Poems in Prose* by Baudelaire and an organizer of *Folio*, a New York magazine of art and verse. Five new Fugitives were added to the group in 1922: the ultra-prolific sonneteer Merril Moore,[5] William Yandell Elliott, William Frierson, Ridley Wills, and Jesse Ely Wills. Only two other individuals became members of the *Fugitive's* editorial board: gifted Vanderbilt undergraduate Robert Penn Warren and mathematician Alfred Starr, the last to join the group. Editorialist Alec Stevenson, writing in the last number of 1922, described the group's setting off on their literary adventure as wanderers in the Sahara of the Bozart, whereas after a year's experience they now can "gloat over many a sudden oasis." "It has been more than gratifying," Stevenson continued, "to receive our modest dollar from Canada, California, London and Berlin" (1, 4: 98), as well as from subscribers of closer proximity.

In the April/May 1923 number the *Fugitive*'s editors announced a poetry competition for which they had received a $100 prize from the Associated Retailers of Nashville; competition for the prize was limited to poets who had not yet published a book of verse. A $50 prize was offered by Ward-Belmont College; eligible were women undergraduates only. The competition attracted hundreds of entries from all over the nation and was a public relations coup for the *Fugitive*. The $100 award was split between Rose Henderson of New York for "A Song of Death" and Cambridge, Massachusetts' Joseph Auslander for "Berceuse for Birds." The $50 prize went to Louise Guyol of Smith College for "Chart Showing Rain, Winds, Isothermal Lines and Ocean Currents."

The contest was repeated in 1924. This time the $100 Nashville Prize went to Laura Riding Gottshalk, who thereafter was voted to membership as the only woman Fugitive. A third prize of $25 was added, which went to Louis Gilmore of the *Double Dealer* in New Orleans.

The *Fugitive* quickly drew attention among poets, but circulation remained very, very small. In January of 1923 the journal had fewer than fifty subscribers but by a subscription increase to $1.50 and a mail campaign seeking financial contributors raised enough to meet expenses. During 1923 all business risks were assumed by Nashville advertising man Jacques Back. Circulation increased to perhaps 500, and with gifts from printer Simon Ghertner and others, the magazine remained on solid financial footing for the remaining two years of its life.

Time became a greater problem than money. As the editorialist in the final number put it, "The Fugitives are busy people, for the most part enslaved to Mammon. Not one of them is in a position to offer himself on the altar of sacrifice" (4, 4: 125) to do the business and editorial work necessary to keep the magazine going. The inability of the full group to deal with detail had earlier caused the *Fugitive* to name Donald Davidson editor and Allen Tate associate editor (1923 and 1924). With the June 1924 number Jesse Wills took over Tate's duties, then for 1925 John Crowe Ransom served as editor and Robert Penn Warren as his associate editor. Two Fugitives, Tate and Elliott, moved to New York and California and had to withdraw from membership in mid–1925. According to Donald Davidson, another factor leading to the magazine's discontinuance after the December 1925 number was the embarassment caused Tennessee and the South by the Scopes trial in that same year.[6]

Of all the poets represented in the *Fugitive*, perhaps John Crowe Ransom was the most polished. Donald Davidson, too, was talented and capable of surprise. Among such tedious titles as "Lichas to Polydor," "Malidon," and "Polyphemus Views the End" suddenly appears "The Wolf," Davidson's wry comment on the greed and banality of man (2, 8: 119). Other fine works could only have been done by a younger man, as with Allen Tate's "The Date," (2, 5: 25).

Poetry critics in the 1920s detected the similarities of a "school" in the Fugitives' work. Others have characterized their poetry as "metaphysical," in other words marked by the juxtaposition of meaning and feeling so as to appeal to both emotion and intellect. Without attempting to analyze the group's work, one can say that the Fugitives represent an important concentration of talent in the early years of what is now called the Southern literary renascence, a decade in which Southern letters were also graced by the work of Stark Young, Elizabeth Madox Roberts, Julia Peterkin, DuBose Heyward, Paul Green, Cleanth Brooks, Carson McCullers, James Agee, Eudora Welty, Thomas Wolfe, and William Faulkner. It was a time of change in the South, change confronted by writers who were able to bring modern thinking to bear on their region's heritage.

Happily for today's reader, the Johnson Reprint Corporation of New York City in 1966 produced a complete run of the *Fugitive* bound in a single volume, making access to this body of work far easier than it had been.

Notes

1. Mttron is pronounced Me-tát-tron.
2. Other pen names in number 1 were "Marpha" (Walter Curry), "Jonathan David" (Stanley Johnson), and "Drimlonigher" (Alec Stevenson). In number 2 James Frank apeared as "Philora," Sidney Hirsh as "L. Oafer," Merrill Moore as "Dendric," and Alec Stevenson as "King Badger."
3. Allen Tate, "The Fugitive, 1922–25," *Princeton University Literary Chronicle*, April 1942, p. 79.
4. Frederick J. Hoffman, Charles Allen, and Carolyn F. Ulrich (Princeton, 1946), pp. 120–21.
5. Moore, in later years a Boston psychiatrist, wrote perhaps as many as 100,000 sonnets during his lifetime.
6. "The Thankless Muse and Her Fugitive Poets," *Sewanee Review*, Spring 1958, p. 228.

Information Sources

BIBLIOGRAPHY:
Bradbury, John M. *The Fugitives: A Critical Account*. Chapel Hill, N.C., 1958.
Clark, Thomas D., and Albert D. Kirwan. *The South since Appomattox: A Century of Regional Change*. New York, 1967. Pp. 202–28.
Cowan, Louise. *The Fugitive Group: A Literary History*. Baton Rouge, 1959.
Davidson, Donald. "The Thankless Muse and Her Fugitive Poets." *Sewanee Review* 66 (Spring 1958): 201–28.
Hoffman, Frederick J., Charles Allen, and Carolyn F. Ulrich. *The Little Magazine: A History and a Bibliography*. Princeton, N.J., 1946. Pp. 116–24.
Moore, Merrill, ed. *The Fugitive: Clippings and Comment*. Boston, 1939.
Mott, Frank Luther. *A History of American Magazines, 1905–1930*. Cambridge, 1968. V: 100–16.
Tate, Allen. "The Fugitive, 1922–25." *Princeton University Literary Chronicle*, 3 (April 1942): 75–84.
The Fugitive: A Journal of Poetry. Johnson Reprint Corporation, New York, 1966.
INDEX SOURCES: Contents indexed in Louise Cowan, *The Fugitive Group*.
LOCATION SOURCES: *The Fugitive: A Journal of Poetry*, Johnson Reprint Corporation, New York, 1966.

Publication History

MAGAZINE TITLE AND TITLE CHANGES: *The Fugitive* (April 1922-June/July 1923); *The Fugitive: A Journal of Poetry* (August/September 1923-December 1925).

VOLUME AND ISSUE DATA: Vols. 1–4 (April 1922-December 1925; quarterly (1922),
    bimonthly (1923–1924), quarterly (1925).
PUBLISHER AND PLACE OF PUBLICATION: Published by committee. Nashville,
    Tennessee.
EDITORS: Edited by committee (1922-June/July 1923); Donald Davidson (August/Sep-
    tember 1923-December 1924); John Crowe Ransom (March-December 1925).
CIRCULATION: Perhaps 500 maximum.

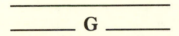

G

GAME AND FISH CONSERVATIONIST. *See* VIRGINIA WILDLIFE

THE GENIUS OF UNIVERSAL EMANCIPATION

It would not be quite accurate to call Editor/Publisher Benjamin Lundy one of the unsung heroes of the early abolition movement; he might better be termed one of its "semisung" heroes. In any case Lundy was a rare individual, a Quaker who began his crusading in the cause of temperance, then spent the rest of his life doing what he could to eradicate slavery.

Living in Mount Pleasant, Ohio, he had plans to establish an antislavery periodical but was beaten to the draw by Elisha Bates and his *Philanthropist* (1818–1822). Bates died soon after founding this organ, however, and in July 1821 Lundy promptly began publishing the *Genius of Universal Emancipation: Containing Original Essays and Selections on the Subject of African Slavery*, the first volume of which was thus dedicated:

To
The Rising Generation
Of the United States of America
On Whom Probably Depend
The Success and Prosperity, Or the Downfall and
Utter Ruin of the Republic

His address to the public that began volume 1, number 1 (July 1821), made his position clear: "That the abomination of abominations, the system of slavery, *must* be abolished, is as clear as the shining of the sun at noonday; the very nature of our government forbids its continuance, and the voice of the ETERNAL has decreed its annihilation.'' The relationship between master and slave was, Lundy quotes Thomas Jefferson, a matter of ''the most unremitting despotism on the one part, and the most degrading submission on the other.'' The nation must, Lundy continued, ''purge the land of this foul corruption'' and ''expel the insidious reptile which, by its siren charm, decoys the unwary, and tempts them to turn from the path of honest rectitude.'' His periodical, he promised, would be filled with well-written essays and letters from persons and societies interested in emancipation, plus short biographical sketches; reports of important law cases; details of unusual barbarity by slaveholders; and the constitutions, orations, reports, and proceedings of antislavery organizations. This sober copy, he said, would be lightened from time to time—especially for the ladies—with poetry[1] and amusing anecdotes. ''In short,'' Lundy concluded, ''the editor intends that this work shall be a true record of passing events, of the various transactions relative to the enslavement of the Africans; and he hopes it may eventually prove a faithful history of their final emancipation.''

Beginning with the barest handful of subscribers, Lundy offered an inducement to the effect that anyone who could procure six additional subscribers would receive a year's numbers gratis; the normal subscription price for the sixteen-page monthly was $1 a year, in advance.

In his biography of Lundy,[2] Thomas Earl reports that the *Genius'* proprietor was remarkable for walking great distances in connection with his work. He reportedly walked twenty miles to Steubenville, Ohio, to have his sheet printed, then carried the freshly printed issues home to Mount Pleasant.

In 1822 Lundy moved his periodical to Greenville, Tennessee, to take advantage of a press that had been purchased by the Manumission Society of that state. After losing an estimated 200 to 300 subscribers due to difficulties with the mails in this relatively isolated location, Lundy moved his magazine to Baltimore late in the summer of 1824. Another reason for the move was explained by the editor in his October 1824 number:

In conducting the 'Genius of Universal Emancipation,' it has ever been my steady aim to inculcate the opinion that Slavery is a *national* evil . . . , and consequently, that the exertions of the people in all parts of the United States will be requisite to effect its abolition. Hence it has been a leading object with me, to divest the paper of local or sectional features, that it might circulate generally, and partake of a national character. These motives have been duly appreciated by my fellow citizens, and its circulation has extended to nearly every State of the Union. [P. 191]

Circulation climbed, and Lundy's first year in Baltimore was a prosperous one. People were listening to his ominous warnings, which were later proved by events:

the storm is brewing; its dark and lowering clouds are congregating; and we occasionally hear the distant howlings of the tempest! Experience teaches us that the situation is critical, in the extreme. [4, 1: 1]

The magazine went weekly in July 1825, and its title was changed to *Genius of Universal Emancipation and Baltimore Courier*. The words *and Baltimore Courier* were dropped from the masthead beginning with the September 16, 1826, number, and the *Genius* returned to monthly publication in April 1830.

Despite his relatively moderate stand favoring gradual emancipation, his words were forceful and his depictions of the "market for human flesh" vivid. In 1827 a Baltimore slave trader beat Lundy, injuring him seriously, but he recovered and continued to speak as forcefully as before in his magazine and on his walking tours of other cities and states. On one of these jaunts he met the young William Lloyd Garrison and in 1829 hired Garrison as assistant editor of the *Genius*. After a year in this position, Garrison was jailed for criminally libeling the owner of a slave ship. Upon his release he returned to Boston and founded his own periodical, the *Liberator*. At this point Lundy moved the *Genius* to Washington, D.C. (1832–1833), and later moved again, this time to Philadelphia (1834–1839?). In 1839 Lundy made his final move, to Lowell, Illinois, where he died. His *Genius* died with him but was continued in Lowell by the *Genius of Liberty* (1840–1842), the *Western Citizen* of Chicago (1842–1853), and the *Free West*, also of Chicago (1853–1855).

During its nineteen-year, one-owner life, the *Genius* had many ups and downs, but the single-minded Quaker Benjamin Lundy never faltered, resolving, in his own words, "never to 'give up the ship,' while a plank remains to float upon" (September 5, 1825).

Notes

1. A delightful example of the *Genius*' wit is "Old Bachelors" (By A Lady), from page 32 in volume 1, number 2:

> Old Batchelors [*sic*] are hateful things,
> Which ought to be despis'd,
> With hearts like broken fiddle-strings,
> And just as highly priz'd . . .
>
> But, 'tis in vain for me to prate;
> I cannot make them clever,
> Old Bachelors I always hate,
> And must, and shall, forever.

Among the more serious poetry Lundy used were two quite respectable selections by Phillis Wheatly, who had been brought from Africa to Boston, where she was held as a slave by John Wheatly. (See vol. 1, no. 2, p. 31.) The quality of her poetry, Lundy said, "proves that genius is not exclusively the property of persons of a fair complexion, and furnishes an excellent commentary on the foolish opinion, entertained by some, that the Africans are of a species inferior to the rest of mankind."

2. *Life, Travels, and Opinions of Benjamin Lundy* (Philadelphia, 1847).

Information Sources

BIBLIOGRAPHY:
Earl, Thomas. *Life, Travels, and Opinions of Benjamin Lundy*. Philadelphia, 1847.
Mott, Frank Luther. *A History of American Magazines, 1741–1850*. New York, 1930.
    I: 162–65.
INDEX SOURCES: None.
LOCATION SOURCES: American Periodical Series microfilm, Boston Public Library,
    Library of Congress, New York Public Library, Oberlin College Library.

Publication History

MAGAZINE TITLE AND TITLE CHANGES: *The Genius of Universal Emancipation:
    Containing Original Essays and Selections on the Subject of African Slavery* (July
    1821-June 1825); *Genius of Universal Emancipation and Baltimore Courier* (July
    4, 1825-early September 1826; (used a variety of subtitles): *Genius of Universal
    Emancipation* (September 16, 1826–1839).
VOLUME AND ISSUE DATA: Vols. 1–16 (July 1821–1839); monthly (1821-June 1825),
    weekly (July 4, 1825-March 1930), monthly (April 1830–1839).
PUBLISHER AND PLACE OF PUBLICATION: Benjamin Lundy. Mount Pleasant, Ohio
    (1821); Greenville, Tennessee (1821-June 1824); Baltimore, Maryland (October
    1824–1830); Washington, D.C., and Baltimore, Maryland (April 1830-October
    ? 1832); Washington, D.C. (November 1832-December 1833); Philadelphia,
    Pennsylvania (January 1834–1839?); Lowell, Illinois (1839).
EDITOR: Benjamin Lundy.
CIRCULATION: Unknown.

---- **H** ----

THE HOUSTON GARGOYLE

A magazine of the Roaring Twenties and early 1930s that tried to be to Houston what the *New Yorker* was and is to New York City was the *Houston Gargoyle*, a standard-sized weekly published from January 1928 until September 1932 by the Mayflower Publishing Company. The company's president and editor of the *Gargoyle* was Allen V. Peden. Joining Peden as directors were Robert Neal, J. T. Scott, Jr., W. A. Kirkland, Joe J. Fox, and Roscoe E. Wright. Associate editors were Wright and Frank G. Ragsdale.

The first two numbers of the magazine appeared under the bland title *Houston's New Weekly*. The inside front cover of number 1 announced an unusual contest to find a permanent name for the new magazine. The prize for the winner would vary depending upon whether he or she had also sent in a subscription or subscriptions. The winner, announced in number 2, was Miss Vernice Vaughan of Houston, who suggested the *Houston Gargoyle*.

The two-color cover for the first number was typical of 1920-style smart sophistication; it depicted a mounted policeman trying to decide how to deal with an attractive young "flapper" who was holding up the traffic (and showing her legs).

The covers for numbers 3 through 12 featured a leering gargoyle; the cover design for those issues remained the same with only weekly changes in background color. After the twelfth issue the cover design changed weekly, and many covers were quite clever. The magazine's length began at thirty-two pages, dropped to twenty-four, then returned later to thirty-two. A single copy was 15¢, a yearly subscription $5.

In his introduction to the initial issue, Peden tried hard to let his readers know that the new arrival would be sprightly:

you will find us scurrying around to all the shows, trying frantically to make all the social functions, shinnying up a telegraph pole to watch the events of the week, scampering about on the playing fields, slipping back-stage in the business world, and generally dodging in and out, up and down the town from one week's end to the next. [1, 1: 12]

In preparing all this for its readers, Peden continued, the new weekly would "exercise all the care of a Ritz chef creating a culinary masterpiece." The introduction's close found Peden wishing his readers "no flat tires and no triplets during a year that opened so auspiciously a day or so ago" (1, 1: 12).

The *Gargoyle's* editorial content consisted for the most part of short items divided into numerous departments, or columns, such as "Through the Port-hole," a gossip column; "Show Business"; "Through the Lorgnon," society prattle and photos of the doyens of Houston society; "In Grandpop's Day," snippets from the city's raw past; "Those Ath-a-letic People," on the sports scene; "Lyres and Easels," on Houston culture; and "Junior League Notes." Clearly Peden was after the silk-stocking trade, and even the small pen-and-ink society figures sprinkled throughout his magazine are reminiscent of *Esquire* or *New Yorker*.

The first advertisers were a seller of Oriental rugs; a bank; the Houston Lighting and Power Company; the San Jacinto Inn; a portrait photographer; a florist; the Polar Wave Ice Palace (a skating rink); and the *Houston Post*, a Scripps-Howard newspaper.

Soon cartoons, also very much like those in *Esquire* and the *New Yorker*, began to appear. A few of them poked fun at the Irish, but most were concerned with the vagaries of the rich. One showed a lady of vast proportions eating chocolate and dictating a letter to her secretary while reclining luxuriantly in her bath. The caption read, "Er—Dear Cousin Clara: Just a hurried note before I catch my train" (1, 13: 3). In another, a society lady lay on her chaise, phoning a friend and saying, "Yes, it's going to be a real, old fashioned picnic. Can you bring your Dora along to serve?" (5, 13: 7). A third showed an old bowler-hatted bondholder at a cashier's window: "Have you any means of identifica-tion?" "I . . . er . . . have a small mole, sir" (1, 23: 2).

Another frequent feature was the poetry of Saul Mark, later revealed by Peden to be the pen name of Mrs. Marie Engle Johnson, who also worked in the magazine's business office.

Many, many photographs of Houston's fair upper crust appeared, including church-circle leaders, flower-show committees, and society brides. Society chil-dren also appeared frequently. Later issues began carrying a brief guide to the city's theaters, galleries, dancing establishments, and special events—standard offerings in today's city magazines.

After chronicling the swank and the posh of Houston for nearly five years, the *Gargoyle* expired without explanation after the September 25, 1932, number. On the inside back cover of that issue (5, 30) the *Gargoyle* was included as one of twelve city magazines aimed at "people of known buying power." The twelve were advertised as having a combined circulation of 125,000. Other titles on the list were Boston's *Beacon Hill*, Baltimore's the *Townsman*, Buffalo's *Town Tidings*, Cleveland's the *Bystander*, Kansas City's *Independent*, the *Philadelphian*, the *Spectator* of Portland (Oregon), the *Argonaut* of San Francisco, Washington's *Review*, Pittsburgh's *Bulletin Index*, and Minneapolis' the *Amateur Golfer and Sportsman*. These titles were the predecessors of today's upscale city/regional magazines. The only Southern magazine on the list, the *Gargoyle*, was an early attempt at Texas sophistication.

Information Sources

INDEX SOURCES: None.

LOCATION SOURCES: Houston Public Library, Library of Congress, New York Public Library, University of Texas Library, (Austin), University of Virginia Library.

Publication History

MAGAZINE TITLE AND TITLE CHANGES: *Houston's New Weekly* (January 3, 1928–January 10, 1928); *The Houston Gargoyle* (January 17, 1928–September 25, 1932).

VOLUME AND ISSUE DATA: Vols. 1–5 (January 3, 1928–September 25, 1932), weekly.

PUBLISHER AND PLACE OF PUBLICATION: The Mayflower Publishing Company. Houston, Texas.

EDITOR: Allen V. Peden.

CIRCULATION: Unknown.

HOUSTON'S NEW WEEKLY. *See* THE HOUSTON GARGOYLE

HUTTON & FRELIGH'S SOUTHERN MONTHLY. *See* THE SOUTHERN MONTHLY

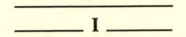

I

ICONOCLAST. *See* THE ROLLING STONE

───── J ─────

JOURNAL OF BELLES LETTRES

Most literary magazines, in the South and elsewhere, have been undertaken by their editors and publishers out of a laudatory desire to improve their readers' cultural opportunities but with an almost blind optimism that others will share their interest and subscribe. Most have been disappointed. Never was this more true than in the case of the *Journal of Belles Lettres*, which published its maiden issue in 1819 in Lexington, Kentucky, when this part of the country was still the frontier.

In their address to their readers in number 1, the editors speak of the "exquisite sensibility to pleasure with which the powers of Taste and Imagination are endowed" and say of their new periodical, "We presume, also, that the *utility* of these pursuits needs no defense. It appears to us, that if the world is ever to be united for the improvement of mankind, this great and glorious object is to be effected by means of the moral electricity of literature." One is glad that these scholarly, sensitive gentlemen, P. D. Mariano and John Everett, are not here today to see the *National Enquirer* and Harlequin romances. They were probably saddened sufficiently in their own time, when the average Kentuckian had little opportunity to reflect on the exquisite sensibilities while cutting logs for a cabin or while being chased by a bear.

This sixteen-page biweekly, published by Thomas Smith, was offered at 25¢ an issue or at $4 per annum, payable on delivery of the fourth number. It promised to provide its readers articles of political importance and essays on literature, both ancient and modern, with emphasis on the literature of foreign countries. "Accurate and liberal translations from ancient and foreign authors, philological and other critical matter, and in general all the varieties of elegant letters," said the editors, "will be received by us with satisfaction." Surely this was the most unlikely periodical ever to grace the rude frontier.

Perhaps the most interesting item in number 1 was a defense of Benjamin Franklin, who had been assailed a short time before in the *North American Review* of Boston as lacking in religious and moral character, vaccilating in politics, unimaginative as a writer, and second-class as a philosopher. The *Journal*'s four-page defense of Franklin, whom they termed "the pride and delight of human nature" and a man of "universal, god-like benevolence," ends by chiding the *Review*:

> Would not any one believe, that the review with its sneers, its spirit of detraction, and its damning with faint praise, was the production [not of an American, but] of some bitter Scotchman, who cannot conceive any merit to exist in the world, but what is centered in Robertson, Stewart and himself; or of some obscure Englishman, who lives upon the corruptions of a tottering government? [P. 7]

The lead article in number 3 is "German Literature: Parables"; introducing it the editor wrote:

> To enquire on Foreign literature—to make its genius familiar to our readers, is what our journal is chiefly intended to do. —If it be without contest, that all nations promoted the improvement of their languages by comparing with each other and studying the writings of the various inhabitants of the globe, of a greater and a more important nature, we think, would be the advantage resulting from this examination, to one which labours under the inconvenience of having no language of her own. [P. 33]

This process, the editors felt, would evolve an original, distinctive American language, "whose character and genius may be more precisely ascertained by a peculiar cost of ideas than by a new choice and sound of words." Their hope, of course, was to free Americans of what they considered a mental, linguistic servitude to England.

Also in number 3 appear "Ad Johannem Everett," a poem in Latin written by Editor Mariano and dedicated to his co-editor, and "Literature of the North of Europe: The Origin of Poetry," a tale from Scandinavian tradition, featuring forest dwarfs, enchanters, and the fair Teutonic maiden Gunloda. Ending the number is an enigma published in Latin.

Appearing in number 5 is "Gonnella," an Italian tale by Pietro Fortini. The editors compliment Fortini's "inventive powers and elegant style" and, though they were not partial to light literature, express the hope that this tale might "furnish an observer with sound reflections on the custom and the character" of the Italian. "Though deprived of the charm of its native language," the editors said, this tale should prove "acceptable through its ingenious *naivete*." In "Latin Literature: On Claudian" the editors present the work of a classical poet they considered to have been unjustly neglected in both Europe and America. Following this selection were two specimens of French poetry, the first a thirteenth-century celebration of knightly valor, the second a lighter piece of more recent but undetermined vintage. Both poems were published in French.

Ending the *Journal of Belles Lettre*'s final number (1, 5, February 26, 1820) were two enigmas published in Latin, followed by a brief notice to subscribers that "the publication of this work is suspended, for want of sufficient patronage, until further notice." That notice, of course, never came.

Information Sources

BIBLIOGRAPHY:

Edgar, Neal L. *A History and Bibliography of American Magazines, 1810–1820.* Metuchen, N.J., 1975. Pp. 164–65.

Mott, Frank Luther. *A History of American Magazines, 1741–1850.* New York, 1930. I: 207.

INDEX SOURCES: None.

LOCATION SOURCES: American Periodical Series microfilm, University of Chicago Library. [Only numbers 1, 3, and 5 located.]

Publication History

MAGAZINE TITLE AND TITLE CHANGES: *Journal of Belles Lettres.*

VOLUME AND ISSUE DATA: Vol. 1, nos. 1–5 (November 20, 1819-February 26, 1820), twice monthly.

PUBLISHER AND PLACE OF PUBLICATION: Thomas Smith. Lexington, Kentucky.

EDITORS: P. D. Mariano and John Everett.

CIRCULATION: Unknown.

A JOURNAL OF JUSTICE. *See* REED'S ISONOMY

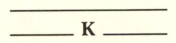

K

THE KEY

Maryland's earliest nonnewspaper periodical outside Baltimore was an eight-page weekly miscellany titled the *Key*, edited and published in 1798 by John D. Cary at the office of the *Federal Gazette* in Frederick Town. Cary began his first issue (January 13, 1798) with a rather charming disclaimer:

> The subscribers for the KEY are now presented with the first number, notwithstanding many circumstances hostile to the undertaking; and I trust, their candor and enlightened liberality of sentiment, will prevent them from criticising too harshly, especially when they consider there is an old proverb which says, 'Give not your opinion of a house at its threshhold, for fear that you may have occasion to retract when you come to visit its apartments.'

Also on page 1 was a letter to the editor addressing the subject of fashion. It began:

> Human invention has been in nothing more fertile than with respect to innovation in Fashion. In nothing, also, do mankind appear so much at a loss, how to establish a basis for a firm stability of principles. Mutability and variety mark its progression; a few wealthy citizens at the head of it lead the way, while the rest of the community are drawn heavily along.

On page 2 a brief item headlined "On Happiness" concludes that "happiness is all a vain pursuit, quite from the cradle to the grave. It is altogether an imaginary acquisition." A curious selection on pages 2 and 3 is "Soliloquy over a Dead Horse": "There lies my poor BALL! cut off in the prime of life by a fit of the staggers,'' etc., this followed by a jolly couplet borrowed from the *Hive*, a Lancaster, Pennsylvania, newspaper:

> 'Tis fashionable among men
> To relish nonsense now and then. [No. 1: 3]

This couplet might have provided the *Key* a good slogan, or motto, as the editor of this little periodical clearly took delight in amusement.

Also appearing in number 1 was "The Matrimonial Creed" (pp. 5–6), a bit of drollery that had appeared a year earlier in the *Weekly Museum** of Baltimore, and "A Description of a Good Wife, by an Unfortunate Husband" (p. 6) by a contributor who called himself Bobby Bohea and said that he had a sober, punctual, industrious, economical, organized wife who "is in every other respect the most disagreeable woman living." The one advertisement in the *Key*'s first number was for Charles Peale Polk, a Frederick Town portrait painter.

The lead article in number 2 is "Sketch of Frederick County,"[1] followed by "Female Patriotism," a brace of anecdotes about unsung American women who faced the British bravely in the late war, and a delightful account of a "gunpowder harvest," in which the Missouri Indians have the last laugh on a deceitful French fur trader.

Two more serious selections in number 2 are a table of Revolutionary War troops of the Continental Army and Militia provided by each state and "Influences of the American Revolution upon the Human Body" by the celebrated Benjamin Rush, M.D.[2] Seriousness, however, did not usually last long in the *Key*, and toward this number's end appear two poems, far more diverting than many of their day:

Lines Written on a Gambling Table

> To gild o'er avarice with a specious name.
> To suffer torment, while for sport you game;
> Time to reverse, and order to defy,
> To make your temper subject to a die;
> To curse your fate, for each unlucky throw,
> Your reason, sense, and prudence to forego;
> To call each aid infernal to your part,
> To sit with anxious eyes and aching heart,
> And fortune, time, and health to throw away;
> In what our modern men of taste call PLAY. [P. 15]

The Modest Wish of Susan, the Breeches Maker

> Beside a lamp, besmear'd with oil,
>   Sue toiling sat for riches;
> Her aching heart, a husband filled,
>   Her lap a pair of breeches.

"Ah me!" with feeble voice, she cry'd,
   While sighs oft rose with stitches,
"Ah me! and must I live a maid,
   And only *make* the breeches."

"Ye Gods!" then rais'd to heaven her eyes—
   "O! grant my wish, soon, which is,
A husband young, a kind, good man,
   And let me *wear* the breeches" [P. 15]

The origin of the magazine's title is explained in number 3 by an anonymous essayist in the first of many contributions under the running head "Observer." The "Key," he said is "to unlock the hidden treasure of the mind, and unbar the door which has hitherto obscured the radiant flame of reason" (p. 17). In earlier times, says the essayist, the world's fashionable vices have been treated by the *Spectator*, *Tatler*, and *Rambler*, yet—and here one sees the writer's interest in reaching women readers—"all their laboured efforts were not able to pluck one feather from a lady's head dress, or add one sentiment of virtue to her mind. —The lady remained as before, the giddy and gaudy object of her unbridled pursuits, and the midnight lamps of those authors have burned in vain" (p. 17).

Some other prose items of interest from the *Key*'s twenty-seven numbers include "Husbands at Home and Husbands Abroad, Compared" (no. 3: 19–20); "The Poor Man's Lot ("in the dark, dismal valley, at the foot of Mount Opulence"; no. 3: 22); "The Victim: An Indian History," an anecdote of pathetic heroism in a conflict between the Choctaws and the Collapissas (no. 4: 27); a truly marvelous anecdote about Gen. Harry Lee, a reputedly slovenly dresser, having been mistaken for a servant and having had to help in the kitchen before being fed (no. 4: 30–31); "Account of the Ugly Club in Charleston [South Carolina] and Their Mode of Procuring New Members" (no. 9: 67–69); "Proceedings in a Female Parliament: House of Ladies" (no. 12: 93–94); and "Advice to Females on the Management of a Lover" (no. 16: 126).

In number 5 appeared a series of witty poems addressed to various trades and professions; among the best is "To the Lawyers":

You, from others' brawls and strife,
Reap a quiet peaceful life;
Bread and butter, corn and peas,
Growing out of writs and pleas.
Pork and beef fly to their nations
At command of declarations.
While demurrers devious course,
Keeps the chaise, and feeds the horse. [P. 39]

Also in verse form was this admonition to the ladies who had sat in the gallery of the Maryland Assembly:

Dear daughters forbear
   To the house to repair
You know not what mischief you do,
   For when you appear
   My delegates here
Attend not to me, but to you.
   Four dollars per day
   Is sure too high pay
For services when you are night 'em.
   If you come here again,
And they do not refrain,I'll certainly clip their *per diem*. [No. 6: 46]

As the year wore on, later issues show that John Cary had used up his best material and that contributions of equal quality were difficult to obtain. This more than any other factor may well have led to the *Key*'s demise in July 1798 after its twenty-seventh number. Certainly no case can be made for the *Key* as a truly important early Southern magazine, yet this little miscellany was touched with the genius of humor and deserves to be remembered.

Notes

   1. P. 9. This piece is continued in no. 3, p. 18, and no. 5, p. 41.

   2. Pp. 14–15. This account is continued in no. 3, p. 20; no. 4, pp. 26–27; and no. 5, pp. 37–38.

Information Sources

INDEX SOURCES: None.

LOCATION SOURCES: American Periodical Services microfilm, Library of Congress.

Publication History

MAGAZINE TITLE AND TITLE CHANGES: *The Key.*

VOLUME AND ISSUE DATA: Vol. 1, nos. 1–27 (January 13-July 14, 1798), weekly.

PUBLISHER AND PLACE OF PUBLICATION: John D. Carey. Frederick Town, Maryland.

EDITOR: John D. Carey.

CIRCULATION: Unknown.

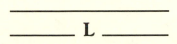

L

LADY'S EMPORIUM. *See* THE NATIONAL MAGAZINE (1830)

THE LAND WE LOVE

One of the earliest of the postbellum Southern magazines devoted to preserving memories of the Civil War and the Confederacy was the *Land We Love: A Monthly Magazine Devoted to Literature, Military History, and Agriculture,* founded in May 1866 by General Daniel Harvey Hill (1821–1889).[1] Hill edited the eighty-two page monthly and was co-publisher with James P. Irwin, who superintended the business side of the enterprise.

Hill was a graduate of West Point who, before the war, had taught at Washington College, Davidson College, and the North Carolina Military Institute in Charlotte. After the *Land We Love* folded in December 1869, Hill edited Charlotte's *Southern Home* and was president of the University of Arkansas (1877–1884) and Middle Georgia Military and Agricultural College (1885–1889).

In his editorials Hill adopted a reasonably conciliatory stance toward the North, with the exceptions of General Sherman, Reconstruction politicians, carpetbaggers, and scalawags. A portion of his editorial space was used to welcome new Southern magazines and to comment on older ones, paying particular attention to the agricultural magazines available to Southern farmers. The September 1866 number, for example, discussed the *Southern Cultivator** of Athens, Georgia (1843–1935), calling it ''a work of practical usefulness,'' and the *American Farmer** of Baltimore, one of the oldest agricultural magazines in the nation (1819–1897).

That General Hill was a very practical man can be seen clearly in his editorials. His disgust with Southern impracticality can be seen in the following example:

It is a curious illustration of the want of appreciation, by the South, of mechanical skill and inventive genius, that Wm. H. Wash, the inventor of the best percussion-cap machine in the country, probably the most ingenious man in the U.S., is without employment save as a mill-wright. In England honors would have been heaped upon him. At the North, wealth would have flowed upon him. But he is as poor and as neglected as was John Gill, of Newbern, N.C., the inventor of Colt's revolver. Dr. Read, of Tuscaloosa, Ala., the inventor of the Parrott gun, the best ordnance used in the war has fared a little better. But he had to carry his invention to Cold Spring, N.Y., and received but a pittance of the immense profits resulting from it. [October 1866, p. 446]

Hill spoke out for scientific farming and for a new emphasis in Southern education that would turn away from the classics and toward the study of science, business, and other applied concerns.

Hill's practicality carried over to his selection of war material for the magazine. He preferred manuscripts written by men who had fought in the battles they described. Battle accounts by generals Longstreet, Beauregard, Breckenridge, Hampton, and Cleburne were carried, and Stonewall Jackson's accidental wounding was described by an eyewitness (July 1866, pp. 179–82). A department headed "The Haversack" carried war memories written by soldiers of less exalted rank, a canny decision in that it produced a far more representative type of war coverage. Manuscripts by nonmilitary historians were spurned as the work of "pen-and-ink warriors."

Like many magazines of the period, the *Land We Love* was inundated with the work of amateur poets, most of which Hill rejected. In January 1868 he wrote of having his days of joy and days of sadness at the magazine. "The glad days," he said "are those in which no poetry comes to the office" (pp. 448–49). The work of established poets appeared, in the early issues under the head "Southern Lyrics." F. O. Ticknor's highly popular "Little Giffen" appeared (November 1867), as did poetry by Poe, Simms, Hayne, Ryan, J. R. Thompson, Ira Porter, Margaret Preston, and Fanny Downing.[2] Some anonymous verse also was published. In the unsigned poem that follows, the cloying sentimentality of the early verses is redeemed nicely at its conclusion:

Faded

She took the starry, blue-eyed flowers
   From her own shining hair:
"Sir Knight of mine," she gaily said.
   "Your Lady's colors wear!—
'Faithful'!—'tis as my love for you—
   The language that they bear"!

She fastened them upon my breast,
    Praising their azure hue,
While I, assenting, only saw
    Her eyes of sunny blue.
"Wilt guard them well?" On hand and flower
    I vowed:—a Knight most true!

'Twas years ago. I oped, by chance,
    A casket old, to-day,
O'er which, the dust of years forgot
    Had gathered, deep, and gray;
Within, a knot of wither'd flowers
    Were fondly laid away.

Her token! I had "kept them well,"
    Though lack of sun and showers
Had dimmed the brightness that they wore
    In those lost summer hours.
Fit emblem of *her love*, alas!
    That faded with the flowers!

I saw her yester-eve, the one
    So fair in memory.
Deceit dwelt in the brilliant eyes
    That won my heart from me,
And harsh lines marred the sunny mouth
    I loved when twenty-three!

I saw her 'mid the pomp and wealth.
    Which gild her false life o'er.
One glance, and, with a sigh, I turned
    Back to my books once more,
Thankful that love of *twenty-three*
    Sleeps well at *forty-four*. [March 1867, pp. 314–15]

Though literary criticism was not General Hill's forte, a "Book Notices" department appeared in the magazine. Often Hill was overly generous in his assessments.

A small amount of war-connected fiction was grudgingly included and a modest number of literary essays by established Southern writers appeared. The remainder of the magazine's editorial space was given over to agricultural articles, travel copy, and historical sketches of the ante bellum South.

Circulation probably never exceeded 12,000, and though some advertising space was sold, the magazine was never profitable. Aside from cover "embellishments," only six illustrations were ever published due to costs. Many of the publisher's subscribers failed to pay their $5 yearly ($3 if paid in advance), and after the March 1869 number, the *Land We Love* was absorbed by the *New Eclectic Magazine* of Baltimore and was discontinued. It should be noted that General Hill was one of only a handful of Southern publishers to pay his contributors, though the struggling magazine could ill afford his doing so.

Notes

1. A still earlier magazine of this genre was *Scott's Monthly Magazine** (Atlanta, Ga., 1865–70).

2. An interesting example of the poetry of reminiscence was Fanny Downing's "Dixie," run in the October 1866 number, p. 27. Its first, third, and fourth verses appear below:

> Created by a nation's glee
> With jest and song and revelry.
> We sang it in our early pride
> Throughout our Southern borders wide,
> While from ten thousand throats rang out
> A promise in one glorious shout
>   "To live or die for Dixie!"
>
> To die for Dixie!—Oh, how blest
> Are those who early went to rest.
> Nor knew the future's awful store,
> But deemed the cause they fought for sure
> As heaven itself, and so laid down
> The cross of earth for glory's crown.
>   And nobly died for Dixie.
>
> To live for Dixie—harder part!
> To stay the hand—to still the heart—
> To seal the lips, enshroud the past—
> To have no future—all o'ercast—
> To knit life's broken threads again,
> And keep her mem'ry pure from stain—
>   This is to live for Dixie.

Information Sources

BIBLIOGRAPHY:

Atchison, Ray M. "The Land We Love: A Southern Post-Bellum Magazine of Agriculture, Literature, and Military History." *North Carolina Historical Review*, 37 (January-October 1960): 506–15.

Mott, Frank Luther. *A History of American Magazines, 1865–1885*. Cambridge, 1938. III: 46.

INDEX SOURCES: Poole's Index to Periodical Literature.

LOCATION SOURCES: Library of Congress, New York Public Library, University of North Carolina Library (Chapel Hill), University of South Carolina Library, University of Texas Library (Austin).

Publication History

MAGAZINE TITLE AND TITLE CHANGES: *The Land We Love: A Monthly Magazine Devoted to Literature, Military History, and Agriculture* (May-October 1866);

The Land We Love: A New Monthly Magazine Devoted to Literature and the Fine Arts (November 1866–1869).
VOLUME AND ISSUE DATA: Vols. 1–6 (May 1866-March 1869), monthly.
PUBLISHER AND PLACE OF PUBLICATION: James P. Irwin and D. H. Hill (May-October 1866); Hill, Irwin, and Co. (November 1866-March 1869). Charlotte, North Carolina.
EDITOR: Daniel Harvey Hill.
CIRCULATION: 12,000.

LA SALLE'S ISONOMY. *See* REED'S ISONOMY

THE LITERARY AND EVANGELICAL MAGAZINE

Though not Richmond's first attempt at magazine publishing,[1] the *Virginia Literary and Evangelical Magazine*, as it was called upon its founding in 1818, was the only nonnewspaper periodical being published in the city. Its eleven-year life qualified it as the most successful Virginia magazine of that era.

In the editorial chair was the accomplished John Holt Rice, who had studied at Liberty Hall Academy (now Washington and Lee University), tutored at Hampden-Sidney College, and served as a Presbyterian pastor. In 1822 he was offered the presidency of Princeton University but remained in Virginia to organize and direct the Union Seminary in Prince Edward County, continuing all the while to edit his periodical, by now called the *Evangelical and Literary Magazine*. Assisting him in his editorial duties were Moses Hoge, president of Hampden-Sidney; George Baxter, president of Washington College in Lexington; the Rev. John Blair of Richmond; and others.[2] Their monthly magazine began with a length of forty-nine pages, done in one-column format, and sold either for $3 in advance or $4 at the end of the subscription year.

In a ponderous eight-page introduction in volume 1, number 1, Rice is careful to explain the choice of words in the magazine's title, paying particular attention to the selection of "evangelical" rather than "religious." He passed over "religious," he says, because it:

has been applied to the worship of Calves and Crocodiles, to the mythological fictions of Greece and Rome, to the brutal and fiendlike service of Juggernaut, to the bloody superstitions of Mahomet, to the pompous ritual of the Roman Catholics, and to the simple and unadorned observances of the various classes of Protestants. Hence it is obvious that a word more undefined and vague in its significance could hardly be used.

Then he attempts, but only *attempts*, to explain why "evangelical" is to him a term of more restricted latitude and goes on to note in true ecumenical spirit that "it is not truth of vital importance which, for the most part divides Christians; but questions about modes and forms." Quoting the words of Abraham to Lot, Rice writes to his non-Presbyterian readers, "Let there be no strife, I pray thee between me and thee, and between my herdmen and thy herdmen; for we are brethren."

His magazine, Rice says, would concern itself with worldly as well as spiritual matters; the magazine would be published "For God and our Country." He continues: "We rejoice that these are not inconsistent. Patriotism, as well as piety, makes us desirous to promote the interests of true religion. . . . By conducting a monthly journal consecreated to the interests of religion and learning, we hope in some measure to fulfill the duties which to us appear paramount."

The term "literary" in the masthead, Rice says, is used in its most general meaning. He promises articles on such topics as agriculture, inland navigation, road construction, and education, and he vows to avoid party politics. Also appearing in his pages are book reviews, obituaries, and a considerable amount of information on foreign countries. Much attention is also paid to Virginia interests and Virginia history.[3]

The first poetry to be featured in the magazine, other than short selections in book reviews, was one of the longest poems ever to appear in the Southern magazines of this era. The twenty-page, unsigned poem was "An Evening Walk." Following it was an editorial note in which Rice discusses his original intention *not* to use poetry for fear that short, amateurish poetic trifles would pour in upon him in a torrent but that he had changed his mind. He warns potential contributors, however, that "the hasty and crude effusions of conceited young men: odes to butterflies and to ladies' eyebrows, and fooleries of this sort cannot find a place in our poet's corner"(1, 9: 431).

By 1824 the monthly publication adopted its final title alteration and became the *Literary and Evangelical Magazine*. Despite the transposition of the terms "evangelical" and "literary," however, the great bulk of the magazine's content remained religious in orientation. Standing heads included "Short Discourses for Families," moralistic essays designed to check the progress of vice and stimulate more godly conduct; "Essays on Divinity," addressing topics such as the immortality of the soul; "Brief Expositions of Scripture"; and "Religious Intelligence," a department filled with church information from other parts of the world.

Among the more secular copy to appear here were biographical sketches, such as one on Patrick Henry written by William Wirt of Richmond; an article borrowed from the *Edinburgh Monthly Magazine* explaining the origin of the terms Whig and Tory;[4] and from the same source an essay on the usefulness of studying ancient and foreign languages.

An unusual item is "Hydrophobia" (1, 5: 190–92), a detailed account of the circumstances surrounding the death of twelve-year-old Edward Taylor of Richmond, who was bitten by a mad dog. The story was related in such detail to provide Rice a platform for inspiring his readers with the child's fervent deathbed prayers, which Rice said were expressed "in such terms as an experienced Christian might not have been ashamed to use."

An original essay entitled "On Reading to Excess" itself makes good reading because of Rice's candor:

> We bookish men are frequently complaining that the spirit of reading is too low among our neighbors, and trying to prevail with them to improve their minds and hearts by the use of good books. . . . Next to the gaining of a soul from the dominion of sin, it is delicious to thin the ranks of intellectual darkness and stupidity.
>
> But let it be remembered, in the meantime, that there is an opposite extreme, into which we are liable to ramble, namely that of reading too much. This takes place, when we lose sight of the main ends of reading . . . and sit gaping over our books, day after day. . . . To one who loves reading, and one who has a large library at hand, the temptation to sink gradually into this state is by no means a trifle. [1, 9: 394]

Few illustrations appeared in the magazine. The first, in an article entitled "Remarks on the Attempts Now Making to Christianize the World," was an engraving on pagan idols of the Pomare islanders that had been collected by missionaries and deposited in the British Museum (2, 5: 235).

By way of summary, one might say that the *Literary and Evangelical Magazine* was a quality product, consisting largely of original as opposed to "selected" copy; certainly it was a far more worldly, interesting periodical than most religious magazines of any era.

Notes

1. Earlier Richmond magazines were: the *National Magazine* (1799–1800)*; the *Press* (1800, one issue only); *Recorder; Or, Lady's and Gentlemen's Miscellany* (1801–13?); *Minerva; Or, Ladies and Gentlemen's Magazine* (1804); *Amoenitates Graphicae* (1805); the *American Gleaner and Virginia Magazine** (1807); the *Visitor* (1809–10); and the *Christian Monitor* (1815–17).

2. See Alfred J. Morrison, "The Virginia Literary and Evangelical Magazine, Richmond, 1818–1828," *William and Mary Quarterly Historical Magazine*, 19 (1911): 266.

3. Some sample titles are: "Churches Built in Lynchburg," "The Female Bible Society of Richmond," "The Female Cent Society of Richmond and Hanover," "The Necessity of a Better System of Instruction in Virginia," and "A Sketch of Lower Virginia."

4. "Whig," the article explains, is of Scottish origin and was first used to denote a sour milk drink. "Tory" is of Irish origin; its original meaning was "savage" or "robber."

Information Sources

BIBLIOGRAPHY:
Morrison, Alfred J. "The Virginia Literary and Evangelical Magazine, Richmond, 1818–1828." *William and Mary Quarterly Historical Magazine*, 19 (1911): 266–72.

Mott, Frank Luther. *A History of American Magazines, 1741–1850*. New York, 1930.
    I: 205.
INDEX SOURCES: None.
LOCATION SOURCES: American Periodical Series microfilm, Library of Congress.

Publication History

MAGAZINE TITLE AND TITLE CHANGES: *The Virginia Literary and Evangelical
    Magazine* (January 1818–1820); *The Evangelical and Literary Magazine and
    Missionary Chronicle* (1821); *The Evangelical and Literary Magazine* (1822–
    1823); *The Literary and Evangelical Magazine* (1824–1828).
VOLUME AND ISSUE DATA: Vols. 1–11 (January 1818-December 1828), monthly.
PUBLISHER AND PLACE OF PUBLICATION: Vol. 1 printed by William W. Gary;
    vol. 2 was designated "From the Franklin Press: W. W. Gray, Printer"; vols.
    3–6 printed by N. Pollard; vols. 7–11 printed by "Pollard and Goddard: at the
    Franklin Printing Office." Richmond, Virginia.
EDITOR: John Holt Rice.
CIRCULATION: Unknown.

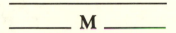

M

THE MAGNOLIA

One of the more peripatetic of Southern magazines, this sixty-four page monthly began its life in Macon, Georgia, as the *Southern Ladies' Book: A Magazine of Literature, Science and Arts*; moved to Savannah under the new title the *Magnolia; or, Southern Monthly*; and concluded its three-and-a-half-year life in Charleston as the *Magnolia; or, Southern Apalachian: A Literary Magazine and Monthly Review*. It was aimed primarily at women readers until its move to Charleston in the early summer of 1842.

Introducing their *Ladies' Book* in January 1840, Editors George F. Pierce,[1] and Philip C. Pendleton noted that with the exception of Richmond's *Southern Literary Messenger*,* ''signal failure has been the doom of every Literary enterprise of a similar character which has originated in the South,'' a situation that ''has seemed distinctly to indicate that some radical disability is inherent in our people.'' Announcing that theirs would be ''a magazine of sterling periodical literature,'' the editors remarked that:

> if the female mind has been wont to lavish itself upon trifles—to evaporate in idle exclamations—to hang enraptured upon the color of a ribbon—to tread with fantastic step the circle of fashion . . . it has been, and is the result not of native incapacity for weightier things, but of irrational education . . . nor yet will we cater to a vitiated taste with mawkish love tales and frothy sickly sentimentalism . . . and least of all shall we borrow from transatlantic folly, pictorial views of dress and fashion for a frontispiece, devoting columns and pages to notes and explanations. [1, 1: 2]

The *Ladies' Book* was sold for $5 per annum, payable upon receipt of the first number. Receipts were published in the magazine, revealing subscribers not only in the larger Georgia towns but in more out-of-the-way places as well, such as Talbotton, Vineville, and Cassville, Georgia. Each of the four Cotton sisters at Stallings Store, Georgia, subscribed. The editor's prospectus noted of the Southern press that:

> nearly all of the publications which issue from it are engaged in political discussions, and their columns teem with accusations, denials, abuse, and every other form of wordy warfare—carried up in language frequently unfit for 'ears polite,' and seldom suited to the delicacy and gentleness which belong so peculiarly to the Female character. [1: back cover]

The prospectus page also listed some of the magazine's contributors, including Caroline Gilman of Charleston; the Honorable A. B. Longstreet, then president of Emory College; S. T. Chapman, editor of the Columbus *Enquirer*; the Rev. Jesse Mercer of Washington, Georgia; Col. J. H. Lumpkin of Lexington, Georgia; and, most prolific of all the magazine's contributors, Charleston's William Gilmore Simms. Though he had prophesied the magazine's doom in no uncertain terms (3, 1: 1–3),[2] Simms became its associate editor in April 1842 and three months later, sole editor, partly out of his lifelong commitment to building a distinctive body of Southern letters and in part as a means of securing an income at a time when Simms was long on fame but short of cash.[3]

In December 1840, after the magazine's first six months, the editors printed a long, candid editorial apologizing for delays in printing. Even the embarrassment of having to borrow small sums to meet current obligations was detailed for their readers (2, 6: 346–48).

In January 1841 Pendleton became sole editor and moved his periodical to Savannah, filling his pages with the work of such writers as Miss Mary E. Lee of Charleston; Dr. J. E. Snodgrass of Baltimore; A. B. Meck of Tuscaloosa; Dr. W. A. Caruthers of Savannah; and, of course, the ever-productive Simms.

The move to Charleston and Simms' assuming the editorship came in July 1842. With this change the magazine took on not only a new name but a new importance, rivaling even Richmond's *Literary Messenger*, by this time off its peak but similar in appearance and content to the *Magnolia*.[4] Judge Longstreet published some of his "Georgia Scenes" in the *Magnolia*, and under Simms' influence the book review section increased in importance. Serialized fiction gave way to more informational articles, and the amount of poetry was increased, as was the space devoted to travel copy. Two articles of special importance were "Original Journals of the Siege of Charleston, S. C. in 1780" (n.s. 1, 6: 363–74) and "Original Letters and Papers Relating to the American Revolution" (n.s. 2, 6: 374–80).

Throughout Simms' association with the magazine, two of his more noteworthy contributions were the novellette "Castle Dismal, or, The Bachelor's Christmas," which he signed "G. B. Singleton of South Carolina," and a controversial short story, "The Loves of the Driver," which dealt with *amour* between a black slave and an Indian.

As editor of the *Magnolia*, Simms' usual policy was to run most prose contributions either unsigned or signed with pen names. Otherwise, he reasoned, the work of newer writers would be put at a disadvantage. It was preferable, he felt, to let the reader "guess out the authorship."[5] This policy was also useful in camouflaging the sometimes embarrassing amount of copy done by the editor himself.

The magazine's poetry tended toward the sentimental. Simms' own feature, entitled "Song and Sonnet; or, The Lays of the Early Days," offered the reader such selections as "Lonely, I Know Thy Heart" and "Woods, Waters Have a Voice" (4, 5: 275–76).

Even under Simms, the magazine was unable to pay its better writers more than nominally; most contributors received nothing at all. Revenues were never sufficient to support engravings, though one of Washington's Tomb was run in March 1842. The editor claimed that it was the first engraving by a native resident artist of the South to appear in a Southern magazine (4, 3),[6] a claim that depends upon one's definition of "The South."

In November 1842 the *Magnolia* absorbed another Charleston literary miscellany, the *Chicora; or, Messenger of the South*, adding several hundred new subscribers to their already impressive list. Having subscribers, however, did not equate with having paying subscribers, and, adding to the difficulties, publishers Pendleton and Burges could not agree on business policy. In May 1843 Simms announced his withdrawal from the venture, and after the June number the *Magnolia* wilted and died.

Notes

1. Pierce was president of Georgia Female College.

2. The first paragraph of this extended letter to the editor beautifully summarizes the fate of Southern literary magazines, written as it was out of personal experience.

3. In 1841 Simms had flirted with politics but had backed away from campaigning after the death of his daughter, Mary Derrille.

4. For a full discussion of the similarities between these two magazines, see John C. Guilds, "Simms as Editor and Prophet: The Flowering and Early Death of the Southern Magnolia," *Southern Literary Journal*, 4 (Spring 1972): 79–80.

5. See text of letter quoted in Guilds, ibid., pp. 81–82.

6. Opposite the title page. The engraving was done by W. Keenan of Charleston after a drawing by J. R. Smith.

Information Sources

BIBLIOGRAPHY:

Gilmer, Gertrude. "A Critique of Certain Georgia Ante Bellum Literary Magazines." *Georgia Historical Quarterly*, 18 (December 1934): 293–334.

Guilds, John C. "Simms as Editor and Prophet: The Flowering and Early Death of the Southern Magnolia." *Southern Literary Journal*, 4 (Spring 1972): 69–92.

Mott, Frank Luther. *A History of American Magazines, 1741–1850*. New York, 1930.
    I: 699–701.
INDEX SOURCES: None.
LOCATION SOURCES: American Periodical Series microfilm, Duke University Library,
    Library of Congress, Tennessee State Library (Nashville), University of Georgia
    Library.

Publication History

MAGAZINE TITLE AND TITLE CHANGES: *The Southern Ladies' Book: A Magazine
    of Literature, Science and Arts* (January-December 1840); *The Magnolia; or,
    Southern Monthly* (January 1841-June 1842); *The Magnolia; or, Southern Apa-
    lachian: A Literary Magazine and Monthly Review* (July 1842-June 1843).
VOLUME AND ISSUE DATA: Vols. 1–4 (January 1840-June 1842); new series, vols.
    1–2 (July 1842-June 1843), monthly.
PUBLISHER AND PLACE OF PUBLICATION: Philip C. Pendleton and George F.
    Pierce (Macon, Georgia, January-December 1840); Philip C. Pendleton (Savan-
    nah, Georgia, January 1841-June 1842); Philip C. Pendleton and Burgess & James
    (Charleston, South Carolina, July 1842-June 1843).
EDITORS: Philip C. Pendleton and George F. Pierce (January-December 1840); P. C.
    Pendleton (January 1841-June 1842); William Gilmore Simms (July 1842-June
    1843).
CIRCULATION: Unknown.

THE MASCOT

Stirring up hornets' nests in New Orleans for over a decade—1882–1895—
was an eight-page newsprint pictorial sheet called the *Mascot*. It was a humor
periodical with heavy political overtones but took equal delight in sensationalism,
glorying in accounts of local fistfights, hair-pulling matches between ladies of
the night, blackmail, marital infidelity, police brutality, "houdouism" (black
magic), and murder, all of which were accompanied by cartoon illustrations.

The *Mascot*'s nameplate showed a girl holding a cornucopia, a flock of turkeys
at her feet. Also appearing there was a large horseshoe and the slogan "As Soon
As She Will Be with You, Bad Luck Will Disppear."

Let two prominent citizens of the town disagree with one another in a physical
way, and they would soon find themselves displayed with corresponding prominence in the pages of this saucy weekly. The full-page cartoon cover of the
November 10, 1894, issue, for example, depicts a brawl between Democrat H.
Meletta and Republican Ambrose A. Maginnis. Inside, the fight was written up
with relish. An excerpt reads:

Mr. Meletta went to work in a business-like way to give Maginnis as
handsome a licking as he ever got, but not near as bad as he deserved.
Straight out from the shoulder flew Mr. Meletta's right, hitting Amby on

the konk and drawing the claret; Amby went head over heels over a garbage can, into the gutter. [P. 4]

The *Mascot* also passed along dangerous gossip, as in "Cuckolded: A Married Tchoupitoulas Street Woman Meets a Camp Street Clerk." The woman's initials, the article says, were C. T. Though the article ends, "The Mascot pities the woman's poor cuckolded spouse" (November 10, 1894: 4), one suspects the writer of being more filled with glee than pity.

In another article from the same issue, the *Mascot* ruminates over woman's power to ruin a good man. Multideck headlines read: "A Siren's Spell/Leads Richard Lyons to Dishonor. Others Have Been under the Same Spell/Lyons Passed a Worthless Check for $400 upon L. A. Gourdain/The Enchantress Fat, Fair and Forty" (November 10, 1894: 6).

In a recurrent feature headed "Society," the activities of the city's ladies of easy virtue are described. The *Mascot* refers to them collectively as the Independent Society of Venus and Bacchus; in one issue the editors complain of the injustices that local amateurs are doing to the profession. "Several amateurs have been enjoying quite a good time of late in the residence at the rear of a grocery store on Derbiguy Street" (November 17, 1894: 8), adds the editor, never content with mere generalization.

"Things Theatrical" was another regular feature—a summary of attractions at the St. Charles Theater, Academy of Music, Grand Opera House, French Opera, and the like.

Irish humor was big in the *Mascot*, which offered a weekly dialect feature entitled "Miss Bridget Magee's Society Notes," from which the following is a brief sample: "Wurra, wurra, there's a tale that cums to me from the naborhood au Bagatille and Derbiguy sthrates that is surproisin' in the ixtrame, as the hoigh-toned people do say" (December 22, 1894: 2). Another of "Bridget Magee" 's columns offered Irish humor doggerel on the subject of a top hat. The first two verses read:

It wuz 'way back in sixty-two,
  Yer gran'pa Casey bought that hat;
It wuz a beauty, bright and new,
  It costs three dollars, chape at that.

It wuz a bargin, sicond hand,
  So nate au brim, so high of crown;
Fur thirty yares, ye understand,
  That dicer has been handed down. [October 13, 1894: 2]

In the verse feature "Oh! Where Is the Proivates?" the magazine pokes fun at Civil War officers who "kept safe their hoides" while the lowly privates did the real fighting. The first verse reads:

O where is the proivate, the ex-Confed proivate,
  The ragged hoigh proivate, that wint thro' the war?
Though wid doins au Curnils, an' Ginrals the journals
  Are filled, as duirnal they fought battles o'er,
'Tis the bothered ould proivate, whose record oi stroive at
  The truth to arroive at, before he's no more. [April 11, 1883: 296]

In "Augustus Wellington De Snooks, Esq., of the Clubs" the *Mascot* pokes equal fun at the other end of New Orleans' social spectrum in a dialect fairly reminiscent of John F. Kennedy, with a touch of Barbara Walters thrown in:

Weally, you know, this city is, ah, in a most disgwaceful condition in many wespects compared to othah cities not possessing her beauties, and, ah, natuwal advantages. There is, ah, you know, a lacking ingwedient in every thing undertaken by our pwominent men, excepting the awangement of the, ah, ballot boxes. There I must, ah, acknowledge they shine, you know, for no mattah how unpopular the movement, ah, may be, and how few votes they may secuah, they have a wefweshing way of showing a victowy. [November 11, 1882: 87]

"Capt. Rouse of the Low Marines" was a humor poem that poked barbed fun at the city's legal establishment:

Oh! we're the flowr of the New Orleans Bar,
That is, myself and colleagues are;
But I, Mr. Rouse, am smarter far
  Than my partners, Miller and Gurley.
For I have a ponderous legal mind,
When with the other two combined.—
Depend upon us wrinkles to find
  To clear our clients burly.

Parts of the following three verses read:

'May it please the coort, those 'lection laws,
As all do know, are full of flaws,
And we'll challenge each juror called (for cause)
  If he reads the MASCOT paper . . .

We'll accept no juror who has a mind
Of his own; and who might be apt to find
A verdict to put our clients behind
  The bars of a prison dreary . . .

For we know 'E Pluribus Unum'
Is the motto of every hoodlum bum,
Who counts on that grand Palladium,
    A made-to-order jury . . . [April 11, 1883: 296]

The *Mascot*'s headline writing was lively, if not in propriety. A curious example is "Thou Shalt Not Love Your Neighbor's Wife, Not Remembered by an Insurance Agent" (February 2, 1895: 1); another is the rhyming head "Black and White Quarrel and Fight, And Are Made to Mind by All Being Fined" (May 14, 1892: 6).

Like the magazine's cover page, its back page was often a full-page cartoon. The two preceeding pages were filled with advertisements for theaters, lotteries, saloons, billiard halls, booksellers, dentists, and insurance companies.

A fitting close for this racy little periodical, which seems to represent New Orleans' "sportin' life," is this excerpt from "To Teetotalers":

Fools! To assert that mortals dare not quaff
The flowing bowl, in measure and in reason.
At your mad ravings wise men only laugh—
Ravings alike devoid of sense and reason.
Because some drink too deep, must all abstain?
Ridiculous! You might as well maintain
That since a glutton at a feast
Doth gormandize far worse than any beast,
That it were best that all men should not eat.
Some lavish all on dress, to heighten beauty,
Pray for that cause, is nakedness our duty? [February 2, 1895: 6]

Information Sources

INDEX SOURCES: None.
LOCATION SOURCES: Duke University Library, New York Public Library.

Publication History

MAGAZINE TITLE AND TITLE CHANGES: *The Mascot*.
VOLUME AND ISSUE DATA: Vols. 1–13 (1882–1895).
PUBLISHER AND PLACE OF PUBLICATION: A. Zenneck, W. M. Mack, and J. S. Bossier (1882–1890?); P. J. Kelly and F. Bildstein (1890–1895). New Orleans, Louisiana.
EDITORS: A. Zenneck, W. M. Mack, and J. S. Bossier (1882–1890?); P. J. Kelly and F. Bildstein (1890–1895?).
CIRCULATION: Unknown.

THE MEDLEY

Kentucky's first magazine was a twenty-page miscellany called the *Medley; or, Monthly Miscellany* published in Lexington in 1803. For $1 a year, or 75¢ if paid in advance, the reader received during the monthly's one-year life a total of eighty-eight prose selections and forty-six poems,[1] many of which were "selected" from English magazines. Its editor and publisher was Daniel Bradford, a bachelor, and therein lies some of the most lively copy to appear in the *Medley*. Shining through the rather forgettable verse and borrowed essays of number 4 was a short item penned by the editor and entitled "Hints to the Ladies," in which he takes to task the fashionable females of the city:

> I have seen . . . an assemblage of prudes, coquettes, and aged maidens, a melancholy proof of female degeneracy. . . . I have seen the most lovely of the fair, clothed in smiles, and resembling angels, prostitute their talents in murdering the reputation, and wounding the sensibility of those still more lovely. . . . I have seen the pert Miss affect the Matron, and smile when I saw the Matron assume the frivolities of youth. I have seen the giddy and thoughtless Maria give her hand to the aged but wealthy Florio. [P. 79]

In number 5 the editor expands upon this theme in "Advice to Married Ladies," a selected extract that directs the ladies to show forbearance when their liege lord returns home in the wee hours from "the tavern, or billiard table, or some other place equally dishonorable." He advises them never to "complain of his absence, but rejoice at his presence; convince him by ten thousand assiduities that he is all the world to you (p. 92)—advice that only an unmarried man could dare give.

This hopelessly chauvinistic advice continues in number 7 in a biographical article on "Catharina I, Empress of Russia," which begins:

> Women, it has been observed, are not naturally formed for great cares themselves, but to soften ours—their tenderness is the proper reward for the dangers we undergo for their preservation; and the ease and cheerfulness of their conversation, our desirable retreat from the fatigue of our intense application. They are confined within the narrow limits of domestic assiduity; and when they stray beyond the sphere, are consequently without grace. [P. 132]

Catharina, the editor tells his readers, rose from poverty to her exalted position without departing from grace as a woman.

This brand of copy aroused the ire of at least one reader who signs herself "Charlotte" and whose letter to the editor also appears in number 7. "If my suspicions are just," she writes, "you are an Old Bachelor, who can enjoy more pleasure in the tavern with a bottle, than in the company of the ladies . . . that you are . . . a woman hater" (pp. 121–22). In a show of the intensely personal magazine journalism that has long since passed us by, the editor replies that though he is indeed a bachelor, it is "not from inclination, but necessity; never having been able to make any impression on the heart of a female with whom I could spend my days in the connubial bliss which forms a 'Paradise below.' " In number 9 the unhappy bachelor editor tries to regain the favor of the fair with "Thoughts on the Word Woman," which seems rather to over-do it, gushing that the *W* stands for wisdom, the *O* for order, the *M* for modesty, and so on. This, too, sparked a response. The lead article in number 10, written by a lady who identified herself only as "Rolinda," countered with a similar explanation of the word *man*. The *M*, she wrote, might signify moderation or magnanimity, the *A* affection or attachment, the *N* nobleness. In some cases, however, needles Rolinda, the letters might more accurately stand for malignity, avarice, and nuisance (p. 182).

It must be admitted that a fair amount of the *Medley*'s prose content was trying—an interminable essay titled "On Commerce" that continued through several numbers, for example, and a liberal dose of tedious axioms and aphorisms: "By doing nothing men learn to do ill"; "A man never loses by doing good offices to others"; "Give no great credit to a great promiser." Moralistic Eastern tales, then in vogue, appeared: "Omar; or, The Punishment of Avarice" or "The Vision of Hamid."

The editor much admired Thomas Jefferson and ran a description of Monticello, which at the time of writing (1796) was under construction, and "Character of Thomas Jefferson" by Allan B. Magruder, Esq., who calls Jefferson a "true citizen of the world." Also chosen for the *Medley*'s pages was "History of the Virginia Mountains," from Jefferson's "Notes of the State of Virginia." At the time Jefferson wrote this, the elevation of these mountains had not been accurately measured; he thought the Blue Ridge "of the greater height, measured from their base, than any others in our country, and perhaps in North America."

Other items of some interest are a letter written by Christopher Columbus to the king of Spain; "Dr. Herschel's Account of Volcanos in the Moon"; a biographical sketch of Samuel Adams; and "Ambulator," a series of fiction pieces featuring "Aunt Biddy" and her niece Charlotte.

At the conclusion of the final number appears an index to the volume, followed by a forty-two-page supplement entitled "Selected Poetry." The first of these works was penned by that formidable Revolutionary wordsmith Thomas Paine and had been "sung at the anniversary celebration of the Boston Female Asylum," an orphanage for girls.[2] Editor Bradford was more sprightly in his choice of poetry than prose; sample titles are "On Seeing a Lady in a Decline from Ill Treatment in a Love Affair"; "On a Watch"; "The Atheist and the Acorn"; "An Ode to a Whip"; "Ode Addressed by a Physician to His Horse"; "The

Sparrow, Hawk, and Butterfly''; and "Ode Written during a Severe Fit of the Tooth-Ache,'' most of which were original. An original ode to President Jefferson appears in Latin. Virtually all these poems were unsigned.

Readers of this supplement were entertained with epigrams, such as "On the Newly Imported French Mode of Wearing Watches in the Bosom'':

> Among our Fashionable Bands,
>   No wonder now if time should linger;
> Allow'd to place his two rude hands
> Where others dare not lay a finger.

Of the humor verse, a favorite was "Profundity—An Epigram,'' a spoof of lawyers that read:

> Profoundest quibbler of the quibbling race,
> Quiblerus rose with most important face,
> Address'd the learned bench—and as he spoke,
> Out flew the texts, from Blackstone, Hale, and Coke
> "Your honors know me deeply skill'd in laws,
> "And clear as light I'll prove this weighty cause;
> "But stop—'tis fit your honors first should know,
> "The only living witness, died ten years ago.''

Notes

1. Willard Rouse Jillson, " 'The Medley'—Kentucky's First Magazine,'' *Kentucky Register*, May 1924, p. 191.

2. The poem reads:

> Shall man, stern man, 'gainst heaven's behest,
>   His cold, unfeeling pride oppose;
> To thankless wealth, unlock his breast,
>   Yet freeze his heart, to Orphans' woes?
> Weak Casuist! where your thunder broke,
>   Seest how the livid light'ning glares!
> Behold it rives the knotted Oak,
>   But still the humble Myrtle spares.
>
> Let stoic valour boldly brave
>   The wars and elements of life;
> But, more like Heaven, who stoops to save
>   A being, sinking in the strife:
> Poor Exiles! wandering o'er this sphere,
>   Thro' scenes of which you form no part;
> Lov'd Orphan Girls! come welcome, here,
>   Th' Asylum of the human heart.

Information Sources

BIBLIOGRAPHY:
Jillson, Willard Rouse. " 'The Medley'—Kentucky's First Magazine." *Kentucky Register* (May 1924): 191–94.
Mott, Frank Luther. *A History of American Magazines, 1741–1850*. New York, 1930). I: 32, 206.
INDEX SOURCES: None.
LOCATION SOURCES: American Periodical Series microfilm, Lexington (Kentucky) Public Library, Library of Congress, State Historical Society of Wisconsin (Madison).

Publication History

MAGAZINE TITLE AND TITLE CHANGES: *The Medley; or, Monthly Miscellany.*
VOLUME AND ISSUE DATA: Vol. 1 (January-December 1803), monthly.
PUBLISHER AND PLACE OF PUBLICATION: Daniel Bradford. Lexington, Kentucky.
EDITOR: Daniel Bradford.
CIRCULATION: Unknown.

THE MIAMIAN. *See* MIAMI/SOUTH FLORIDA MAGAZINE

MIAMI MAGAZINE. *See* MIAMI/SOUTH FLORIDA
MAGAZINE

MIAMI PICTORIAL. *See* MIAMI/SOUTH FLORIDA
MAGAZINE

MIAMI MENSUAL

The first Spanish-language city magazine to be published in the United States is *Miami Mensual* (Miami Monthly), which made its appearance in December 1980. A quality product whose target audience is the prosperous segment[1] of the roughly one million Hispanics living in South Florida, the new monthly has received good advertising support, began showing a profit after one year,[2] and in 1984 has a circulation of about 25,000.

According to information provided by *Miami Mensual*, the Hispanic population across the United States stood at 20 million in 1980, representing an annual gross purchasing power of $68 billion or more. Also, the Hispanic part of our population appears to be the fastest growing, climbing at a rate six and one-half times faster than the general population. Projections show 40 million Hispanics with an annual purchasing power of $200 billion living in the United States by the year 2000. The same projections show that at least 80 percent of this swelling market will speak Spanish as their first language and that this condition will create a need for a variety of communications media to reach them in their native language.

In the forefront of what may in Florida and the Southwest become a significant movement toward Spanish-language magazines is forty-year-old Frank Soler, who was born in Havana, Cuba, came to Miami in 1960, and joined the *Miami Herald* as a copyboy, steadily advancing to reporter, columnist, and foreign correspondent. In 1975 Soler helped develop and became executive editor of the *Herald*'s innovative Spanish-language daily edition, *El Herald*.

Leaving the *Herald*, Soler became editorial coordinator and advisor for Editorial America in Miami, publisher of *Vanidades* and other Spanish-language magazines, then decided to launch his own magazine, in part to counter the negative press being given Florida's Hispanic community by showing its best side. Virtually everything in the magazine is in Spanish with the exception of Soler's own monthly column, run in both Spanish and English, and a few national advertisements. A city magazine has little circulation outside its own geographical area, of course, but within South Florida *Miami Mensual* has no doubt been a unifying influence, showing off the upper echelons of Hispanic society with considerable style.

Soler has also carried the banner for his community in Miami civic affairs, sitting on the boards of South Florida's new Center for the Fine Arts, WPBT-TV, Greater Miami United, the International Center of Florida, the Children's International Fund (Fondo Internacional para Niños), FACE (Facts About Cuban Exiles), SALAD (Spanish-American League Against Discrimination), and the Inter-American Businessmen's Association. He was also appointed to the Governor's Task Force on Criminal Justice System Revision and the Supreme Court Judicial Nominating Commission for Florida.

Soler's wife, Ana Picaza Soler, also from Havana, serves as executive vice president of *Miami Mensual*'s parent corporation, Quintus Communications Group, Inc., and is likewise active in civic affairs. Before joining her husband in founding Quintus, Mrs. Soler had established the Miami public relations firm Picaza & Rosler, Inc., of which she was president.

A subscriber survey conducted in Summer 1982 by the University of Miami's Graduate School of Business showed *Miami Mensual*'s subscriber sex split to be 58 percent male, 42 percent female, and their median age forty-two. Median household income was $55,550, and 68.6 percent were year-round Miami residents. Just over 69 percent had attended college; 30 percent had done postgraduate work. Eighty percent of subscribers owned homes in South Florida, the median value of which was $153,000. A surprising 54 percent had traveled outside the United States during the previous year.

Roughly 57 percent of the magazine's subscribers also read Spanish-language newspapers, 47 percent watch Spanish television, 44 percent listen to Spanish radio, and 51 percent read other Spanish-language magazines, the most frequently reported of which were *Selecciones Reader's Digest*, *Hola*, *Vanidades*, *Ideal*, *GeoMundo*, *Réplica*, *Cosmopolitan*'s Spanish edition, *Américas*, and *Buenhogar*.

That the Hispanic audience is a rich potential market has not been lost on advertisers. *Miami Mensual*'s big ad categories are fashion, home furnishings and design, banks, beauty products, automobiles—including Rolls Royce, Porsche, and Volvo—jewelry, and tobacco products.

Most of the editorial contents of *Miami Mensual* appear in regular departments (*secciones fijas*), the remaining non-ad space going to fashion spreads (*modas*) and feature articles (*artículos especiales*). Department titles that appear in virtually every issue are letters to the editor ("*Correo*"), Soler's column ("*Perspectiva*"), brief news items from the Hispanic world ("*Pulso*"), a page or two of society items with small photos ("*Panache*"), and a restaurant guide ("*Restaurantes*"). Most recent issues have also contained travel pieces ("*Viajes*") and a humor piece by Ralph Rewes, sometimes in the form of columns, sometimes as feature articles.

Departments that appear somewhat less regularly are restaurant reviews ("*Gastronomiá*"), a guide to area entertainment ("*En Estes Mes*"), money-management advice ("*Dinero*"), advice on wines ("*Vinos*"), art reviews ("*Arte*"), book reviews ("*Libros*"), record reviews ("*Discos*"), health advice ("*Salud*"), profiles of South Florida business executives ("*Ejecutivo*"), sports items ("*Deportes*"), and theater reviews ("*Teatro*").

The "soul" of the magazine is in Soler's monthly "*Perspectiva*." In a recent issue's column, he likened Miami to an ugly duckling changing into a swan, which most Anglos, who have read only about the city's troubles, might view with skepticism. Soler acknowledges Miami's troubles, speaking of "years of pessimism and negativism, even of self-flagellation" when "Miami stood on the brink of social Armageddon" (4, 4: 10). Leaders he credits with helping ameliorate the city's unrest are Vice President George Bush, Knight-Ridder Newspapers Chairman Alvah Chapman, Burdines Chairman Dick McEwen, and others.

Examples of recent feature pieces are a political article on the future of Latin America (4, 4: 70–75); tips to Latinos on the fine art of drinking scotch whiskey (4, 4: 48–50); "How to Survive a Nuclear War" (4, 9: 68–71); a travel feature on Puerto Rico (4, 9: 40–41, 43–44, 46, 48–49, 51–52, 54); and an especially interesting account headlined "Armando Valladares and 22 Years of Solitude" (4, 5: 65–72), the story of a Cuban political writer imprisoned by Castro's forces and at one point denied food for forty-six days. Valladares' resulting partial paralysis and the poetry he published while imprisoned caused him to become known as the "poet in the wheelchair." The combined efforts of forty-seven U.S. senators, the former presidents of Venezuela and Mexico, the International Red Cross, and President Mitterrand of France finally effected Valladares' release, a story better known among Hispanics than among Americans at large.

Though one hesitates to regard Miami as a swan among cities, one cannot but admire what the Solers are doing with *Miami Mensual*.

Notes

1. *Miami Today* estimates this segment of the South Florida Hispanic community at 350,000 in Michael Hayes, "The Solers' Miami Mensual," January 12, 1984.

2. John F. Sugg, "Sky Falls on New Florida," *Advertising Age*, April 5, 1982, p. M–9.

Information Sources

BIBLIOGRAPHY:
"Common Causes." *Miami Magazine*, April 1981.
Hayes, Michael. "The Solers' Miami Mensual." *Miami Today*, January 12, 1984.
Sugg, John F. "Sky Falls on New Florida." *Advertising Age*, April 5, 1982, p. M–9.
INDEX SOURCES: None.
LOCATION SOURCES: Library of Congress.

Publication History

MAGAZINE TITLE AND TITLE CHANGES: *Miami Mensual.*
VOLUME AND ISSUE DATA: Vols. 1–4 (December 1980-present), monthly.
PUBLISHER AND PLACE OF PUBLICATION: The Quintas Communications Group, Inc., Frank Soler, publisher. Coral Gables, Florida.
EDITOR: Frank Soler.
CIRCULATION: 25,000.

MIAMI/SOUTH FLORIDA MAGAZINE

This regional magazine, now prospering nicely in a three-county area that forms the nation's fourteenth-largest retail market area, has an interesting history of change. It began in 1920 as the *Miamian* and like most city magazines in those days was a chamber of commerce periodical. It was published off and on until the mid–1960s, then regularly until 1970, when it became the property of the R. R. Donelly company. A group of former *Philadelphia* staffers and investors headed by Bernard McCormick bought the magazine in 1972 and renamed it the *Miami Pictorial*. The group also owned *Gold Coast Pictorial Magazine* in Ft. Lauderdale. Under Publisher McCormick and Editor Gaeton Fonzi, the *Miami Pictorial* concentrated on society, long a staple with the state's magazines (*Tatler of Society in Florida,** *Palm Beach Life*)* and exposé journalism, following the lead of *Gold Goast Pictorial*. The combination did not work well, and *Miami Pictorial* perished after the February 1975 issue.

The magazine's mortal remains were bought in Summer 1975 by Sylvan Meyer, who earlier had edited the Gainesville, Georgia, *Times* and the *Miami News* and in a brief career as a college professor had launched the journalism program at Florida International University. Meyer revived the periodical in city magazine format in November 1975 as *Miami Magazine*. Its first editor, for one issue only, was Stephen Golob, who was followed for a one-year hitch by James Kukar. His successor was Cliff Yudell, who was in turn succeeded by Ron Sachs, a former *Miami Herald* staffer. Sachs left to go into television, and later in 1983 Meyer's daughter, Erica Meyer Rauzin,[1] became editor.

When Sylvan Meyer began the venture in 1975, only 4,700 of his initial 24,000 press run were sales. The remainder were promotional copies distributed in a third-class mail giveaway campaign. According to information provided by Meyer, paid circulation had increased to roughly 7,000 of the same size press run by late 1977. By late 1978 the magazine's first ABC audit showed 13,000 paid circulation out of a slightly increased press run of 26,000. By late 1979 paid circulation had reached 10,000. In 1982 the magazine topped 1,000 pages of advertising for the first time and ranked tenth in paid ad pages among U.S. city and regional magazines.

In 1983 Meyer widened his sights and turned his city book into a regional magazine serving three counties at the southern tip of Florida: Dade, the county in which Miami and twenty-five municipalities are located;[2] Broward to the North, in which Ft. Lauderdale and Hollywood are the first- and second-largest cities and Boca Raton the most northerly;[3] and Monroe, made up of the Florida keys.[4] Combined, the three-county area has almost 3 million inhabitants, easily a large enough population base to support a regional magazine. Meyer's dual tasks have been to put out a *good* regional book and to convince advertisers that the area is, as his sales pamphlet terms it, "a genuinely interactive region." The move to regional orientation appears to be working; by the end of 1983, ABC circulation figures showed 25,100 paid and only 3,000 distributed free, with 1983 revenues (circulation plus advertising) exceeding $2 million.

Meyer's magazine is located in a most unusual market area. The population is made up of at least 395,000 blacks, 593,000 hispanics, white permanent residents, and "seasonal" residents. In addition, a great many residents of South Florida have moved there within the past decade. Few of Meyer's readers are black or hispanic, and only 9 percent of the magazine's subscribers are over age sixty-five. Like virtually all city and regional magazines, *Miami/South Florida* targets the affluent. Over 61 percent of its readership have annual household incomes in excess of $50,000.

Reader demographics show a mean income of $86,400, median value of readers' homes at $120,160, and that fifty-two percent are college graduates. The subscriber sex split is practically even—51.2 percent female, 48.8 percent male—and 27 percent of subscribers are on the board of directors of at least one company. Roughly 10 percent of subscribers are millionaires. Meyer's promotional brochure claims that in the three-county area, roughly 124,000 households have incomes of more than $35,000 a year, meaning that a lot of the spending in this market is done by a small proportion of the households. Assuming this figure is accurate, *Miami/South Florida Magazine* has achieved good market penetration with the part of the population it has tried to reach, promoting itself by campaigns via radio, television, newspapers, and direct mail.

As with other regional periodicals in good market areas, the kind of readership *Miami/South Florida Magazine* has built has succeeded in attracting an impressive array of advertisers: clothing from Saks, Lord & Taylor, Neiman-Marcus, Jordan Marsh, and Burdines; expensive house and condo developments: St. Andrews, Boca Pointe, Boca Grove, and Parkside in Boca Raton, or Indian River Plantation at Stuart; BMW automobiles; Karastan carpets; Sony audio equipment; The Helmsley Palace in New York City. Liquor advertising is big: Jack Daniels whiskey, Johnny Walker scotch (Black Label, of course), Stolichnaya vodka, Aalborg Akvavit. Banks are fairly heavy advertisers in *Miami/South Florida Magazine*, and there are a modest number of restaurant ads. Upscale ad appeal reached a new high (or low, depending upon one's predilections) in a full-page ad for the V.I.P. Wing of Doctors Hospital in Hollywood, Florida, which turns going to the hospital into an exercise in status seeking.

The magazine's management opts for a rather small number of feature articles per issue—either three or four; about 40 percent of these are by freelancers. Editor Rauzin tries to use one journalistic piece in each issue,[5] a recent example of which is an examination of alleged safety hazards at Pratt & Whitney's large rocket and jet development plant in Palm Beach County (Janis Johnson, "A Reasonable Doubt," 25, 12: 62–66, 70–72, 76, 80); one consumer-oriented article such as a story by Sylvan Meyer's wife Anne[6] on Italy's cameo and coral jewelry ("Sea Sculpture," 35, 5: 68–71, 82–83); and one essayish lifestyle piece, for example the editor's own recent article on bulimia, a neurotic behavior disorder linked to fear of gaining weight in today's slim-minded society ("Bulimia," 35, 5: 72–73, 87–89).

The larger part of *Miami/South Florida Magazine*'s editorial matter is in its regular departments, which include Sylvan Meyer's monthly column "For Starters"; "Calendar," an entertainment guide for art galleries and festivals, dance, music, theater, movies, museums, sports, clubs, bars, and even lectures; a books department showcasing the work of area writers; and a movie review column, done until mid–1984 by Meyer's son David, who is living in Sun Valley, Idaho, where he is doing a book on snow skiing. The magazine provides a lengthy restaurant guide (not really restaurant reviews but detailed enough to be useful), a Dining-Out column giving more complete information on one type of restaurant (Italian, Indian, children's, etc.) per issue, an innovative puzzle page by Don Rubin, and a miscellany called "The Big Orange" edited by Maureen Griess-Glabman.

Most editorial illustration work is in color in this attractive monthly slick, which varies in length from 116 to 190 pages. If the magazine has a graphic shortcoming, it is that parts of the book have rather a busy appearance due to the amount of "guide" material included. The positive side of this coin, of course, is that a lot of information is packed into *Miami/South Florida Magazine*. Editorially, criticism concerns a possible overemphasis on wealthiness—frequent success stories that allow wealthy subscribers to read about how someone else in South Florida became wealthy, too, and for another example, a recent article on how to set up a "great home bar" that was cloyingly *nouveau riche* in its appeal. These minor quibbles aside, Sylvan Meyer and family have built a most respectable regional magazine and have now attracted enough national advertising that greater national recognition should be just around the corner.

The magazine's success has enabled Meyer Publications, Inc., to begin a twice-monthly tabloid for New York City computer users in October 1983. This new venture, *Computer Living/NY*, was joined in October 1984 by *South Florida Home & Garden*, a Miami venture that Meyer hopes will be as well received as the recent Texas magazines of this genre.

Notes

1. Mrs. Rauzin holds an M.A. from the Columbia Graduate School of Journalism and has several years' experience as a reporter for the St. Petersburg *Times* and suburban papers owned by the *Miami Herald*.

2. Dade's population in 1980 was 1,625,000, and since that time roughly 120,000 Cubans and 40,000 Haitians have arrived there. Despite Miami's well-publicized troubles, the first three years of the 1980s saw about $2 billion go into new downtown construction in that city.

3. In a sales promotion pamphlet prepared for the magazine, Meyer says that Broward County grew 63 percent during the 1970s and that ten of its cities did not exist in 1960.

4. In 1980 the Keys had about 80,000 permanent residents.

5. Telephone conversation with the author, July 10, 1984.

6. Anne Meyer is also a radio personality of long standing.

Information Sources

INDEX SOURCES: Access: The Supplementary Index to Periodicals.
LOCATION SOURCES: University of Florida Library, University of Kansas Library.

Publication History

MAGAZINE TITLE AND TITLE CHANGES: *The Miamian* (1920–1972); *Miami Pictorial* (1972-February 1975); *Miami Magazine* (November 1975-April 1983); *Miami/South Florida Magazine* (May 1983-present).
VOLUME AND ISSUE DATA: Vols. 1–35 (1920–1984), monthly.
PUBLISHER AND PLACE OF PUBLICATION: Greater Miami Chamber of Commerce (1920–1970); R. R. Donelly (1970–1972); Bernard McCormick (1972–1975); Sylvan Meyer (November 1975-present). Miami, Florida.
EDITORS: Unknown (1920–1970); Stephen Golob, James Kukar, Cliff Yudell (1971–1978), exact dates unknown); Ron Sachs (October 1978-September 1980); Richard Covington (September 1980-August 1981); Erica Meyer Rauzin (September 1981-present).
CIRCULATION: 25,167 paid, 3,000 nonpaid (June 1984).

THE MID-CONTINENT MAGAZINE. *See* FETTER'S
SOUTHERN MAGAZINE

THE MONTHLY MAGAZINE AND LITERARY JOURNAL

Published in the isolated small town of Winchester, Virginia, in 1812 and 1813, this monthly held itself strangely aloof from the War of 1812 and other political concerns of that troubled period. For a small-town periodical, the sixty-four page *Monthly Magazine* was a decidedly ambitious publishing venture. Winchester was hardly a major seat of literary endeavor, and Editor/Proprietor John Heiskell used selected material, that is, articles and verse that had appeared earlier in other periodicals or books, to an extent that by today's standards would seem almost inconceivable. This policy was made quite plain in his address to patrons in number 1.

In the same address Heiskell portrays his new monthly as the best magazine bargain in the nation. While the *Port Folio* had more pages, wrote Heiskell, the *Monthly Magazine* would sell for $4 yearly, as opposed to *Port Folio*'s $6. At the same time that the new editor compared his own product favorably with the celebrated *Port Folio*, it was this magazine that he most often tapped for material. Other periodicals from which articles and poems were lifted were the *American Review*, the *Mirror of Taste*, the *Analectic Magazine*, the *Monthly Review*, the *Literary Panorama*, the *Universal Magazine*, the *Freemason's Magazine*, the *Quarterly Review*, and the *Edinburgh Review*.

Heiskell promised that the *Monthly Magazine* would be "regularly embellished with Engravings, executed by the ablest artists, and embracing subjects best calculated to amuse and instruct" (1, 1: 4). No more than two or three engravings appeared during the magazine's one-year life, however, due in part to cost, in part to difficulty in obtaining suitable plates. In the final number of the first semi-annual volume, the editor apologizes for the absence of illustrations, citing an unnamed Philadelphia artist as the culprit (1, 6: unnumbered page facing p. 317). On the same page, the editor, now fully aware of the troubles by which editor-publishers of his era were beset, begs his subscribers to make payment, saying politely and optimistically, "The Editor confidently relies on their embracing the earliest opportunity of discharging their accounts."

Issue number one, typical of those to follow, began with an article on Valley Forge, taken from the *Freemason's Magazine*. Other contents of number 1 were "Comparative Traits of English and American Character" and "Particulars on the Death of Capt. Lewis,"[1] both from the *Port Folio*, as were "A Retrospect on the Year 1811" and "Biographical Sketches of Major General Henry Knox." From the *Mirror of Taste* came "Life of George Frederick Cooke, the Justly Celebrated Actor." Some items are unattributed, such as "Gossipping," a dialog; "Letter from a Young Lady on Her Death Bed to Her Sister"; and commentary on physical beauty, which included a poem by Gray that concludes, "In beauty, faults conspicuous grow/The smallest speck is seen on snow."

A small amount of the prose in number 1 was original. In "A Prudent Hint to Young Ladies," the editor warns the fair against premature loss of virtue; and an unsigned travel piece, "A Short Account of the Azores or Western Islands," was written especially for the *Monthly Magazine*. A collection of amusing snippets appears near the back of the first number. In one a sailor is asked why a ship is always called *she*. "O, faith," said the sailor, "because the rigging costs more than the hull." In another example, a country gentleman asks his college-student son what is meant by a *Bachelor of Arts*. "One (said the student) who woos the arts, but never weds them!"

A four-page poetry department completed the issue, as it did future issues. Like the prose copy, most of the verse in the *Monthly Magazine* had first appeared elsewhere. Much of it was palatable, and Editor Heiskell had a liking for the light and witty, as in the epigram,

> Let the loud thunder roll along the skies,
>   'Clad in my virtue, I the storm despise.'
> 'Indeed,' cries Peter, 'how your lot I bless,
>   To be so *sheltered* in so *thin* a dress.' [1, 1: 64]

or in these lines,

> By our parson perplext,
>   How shall we determine?
> 'Watch and pray,' says the text,
>   'Go to sleep,' says the sermon. [1, 3: 192]

or this epitaph:

> Here lies Tom Paine, who wrote in
>   Liberty's defense,
> But in his 'Age of Reason' lost his
>   'Common Sense.' [1, 4: 252]

Returning to the magazine's article content, much space was taken up with looking back at Europe and England, as in "Female Heroism, As Evinced during the Reign of Terror of the French Revolution" (2, 5: 298–308), "Life of Soult, the Present Duke of Dalmatia" (2, 2: 329–31), "Character of Hume, by the Earl of Charlemont" (2, 6: 333–37), and "The Story of Don Estevan de Xeres" (2, 3: 176–81).

The editor also showed a marked penchant for the battle of the sexes. Scores of inconsequential articles appeared under such titles as "A Good Husband," "A Good Wife," "The Old Bachelor," "The Old Maid," "Advice to Husbands by a Lady,'' "Picture of Connubial Felicity,'' and the like. An unusual offering was "On the Absurd Compliments Which People Pay to Parents on the Likenesses of Children" (1, 4: 243–44).

Heiskell continued to suffer delinquent accounts and declined to publish further after the final number of his second volume (April 1813). After informing readers that such was the case, he suggested, probably with an optimism born of desperation, that subscribers who had not yet paid could send $5 that they might satisfy their obligation and receive the *Winchester Gazette* for the next year, as well.

The last item to appear in the *Monthly Magazine* was its first obituary—three pages with heavy black borders on twenty-year-old William Ball, a popular Winchester man who was murdered at Fort Nelson in the Norfolk area (2, 6: 367–69).

Note

1. The piece on Capt. Lewis was in the form of a letter from Alexander Wilson, author of *American Ornithology*, and was more nearly about birds and Chickasaw customs than about the unfortunate captain.

Information Sources

INDEX SOURCES: Indexed at end of each volume.
LOCATION SOURCES: American Periodical Series microfilm, Library of Congress.

Publication History

MAGAZINE TITLE AND TITLE CHANGES: *The Monthly Magazine and Literary Journal*.
VOLUME AND ISSUE DATA: Vols. 1–2 (May 1812-April 1813), monthly.
PUBLISHER AND PLACE OF PUBLICATION: John Heiskell. Winchester, Virginia.
EDITOR: John Heiskell.
CIRCULATION: Unknown.

MONTHLY MISCELLANY. *See* THE MEDLEY

THE MONTHLY REVIEW AND LITERARY MISCELLANY OF THE UNITED STATES. *See* THE MONTHLY REGISTER, MAGAZINE, AND REVIEW OF THE UNITED STATES

THE MONTHLY REGISTER, MAGAZINE, AND REVIEW OF THE UNITED STATES

Charleston's eighth magazine,[1] the *Monthly Register and Review of the United States*, was founded in January of 1805 by expatriate Englishman Stephen C.

Carpenter, who had served the Crown in India and had done journalistic writing in England before settling in Charleston as editor of the *Courier*. The first volume of his new magazine was most unusual in that it included a separate, independently paginated section with its own title page, which read, the *Monthly Review and Literary Miscellany of the United States*. This odd two-magazines-in-one approach was dropped after volume 1, and the title *The Monthly Register, Magazine, and Review of the United States* was employed. Volume 1, containing twelve numbers, was printed by Gabriel Manigault Bounetheau at the Apollo Press, No. 3 Broad-Street, near the Exchange.

In each number of volume 1 the *Monthly Register* was divided into two departments: "Retrospective History," devoted to assembling a record of the American Revolution, and "History of the Passing Times," given over to literary and miscellaneous matter. Carpenter modeled the *Monthly Register* section of his double-barreled magazine after the *English Annual Register*; his ambition was to edit a "journal of record," or as he stated in his prospectus, to provide "a permanent record of all the public transactions of the time; which would enlighten the minds, and improve the morals and the manners of the existing generation, and deliver down to posterity, for the use of the future historian, all the political facts and public transactions of the day, untinged with false colouring and unsullied by political prejudice."

His *Monthly Review and Literary Miscellany* contained a series of essays entitled "The Wanderer" and another serialized feature called "Men and Women," which Carpenter termed "a moral Tale, portraying the human character, as it really exists in the world, and developing the springs and movements of the human heart." The *Monthly Register* also contained literary reviews and poetry.

One of the most interesting items in volume 1 appeared in the first number in the "Retrospective History" section. Here Carpenter comments on the difficulties of writing history, compares the work of ancient and modern historians, and reflects on the nature and use of history in general. The historian's dilemma, he says, is to convey factual truth without becoming dry and dull. He speaks of

> those graces of composition, which relieve subjects of a dry nature from wearisome dullness, which attract attention, where interest flags, and give annimation, and spirit, to the most cold and lifeless materials. Upon the reading of a dry, jejune narrative of events, utterly destitute of ornament, few will bestow time or trouble. To render history generally useful, therefore, it must be made attractive, and, to that end, decorated with the finest, but most simple drapery.

One must, he continued, "steer a middle course between dry narrative and frothy relation . . . to give to history its measure of reflections, without . . . falling short of propriety; for, while mere narrative, without those, is to be regarded as little better than a file of newspapers, a redundance of reflections without a proportionate share of facts, differs but little from a novel or romance.'' The true historian, he concluded, was neither a plodding compiler nor a "vain pedant" who tries to dazzle the reader with a "gaudy display of bloated sentiments, and pompous, turgid phraseology.''

Carpenter's own writing might be regarded as somewhat "precious" or over-ripe, yet somehow he usually managed to produce a pleasing result with it. Consider his apologia offered in the preface to volume 1:

> Conscious of the very humble rank in letters, to which he can venture to aspire, and at the same time aware of the difficulties that beset him, he considers it to be his duty not to shrink from the task he has undertaken, and, while he feels the disproportion of his capacity to the magnitude of such a work, to strain that capacity to the utmost, and to draw upon industry for deficiencies of genius.

The *Monthly Register* appeared irregularly during its first year and was sus-pended from September 1805 until March 1806 and again from September through November 1806. In December 1806 Carpenter recommenced publication, this time from New York City, where, as he put it, he could "stand at the confluence of the greatest number of streams of knowledge, flowing from the most distant sources, that meet at any one point of this great continent" ("Introductory Essay," 2, December 1806: 2).

Carpenter chose as his associate editor the well-connected John Bristed, who married a daughter of John Jacob Astor;[2] publication became regular, with the magazine appearing monthly. Upon completion of volume 2, Carpenter turned over the editorial reins to Bristed.[3] In his preface to the annual collection of volume 2, Bristed boasted that the *Monthly Register* was the only magazine in America offering impartial and independent reviews of American authors. Other U.S. reviewers, he said, "suppose that they could encourage the efforts of American *genius*, by *praising* every American publication. . . . It were much to be desired that all, who take upon themselves the office of Reviewers, would attend to the words of Publius Syrus; —Judex damnatur, cum nocens obsolvitur. —The *Judge* is *condemned*, when the *guilty* is *absolved*.'' The magazine failed to prosper under Bristed and ceased publication after the December 1807 number.

Especially during Carpenter's tenure as editor, the magazine not only provided a wealth of historical information on the Revolutionary era but showed flashes of wit amid the "fine" prose of the editor and the serious historical content. In the seemingly endless (424-page) supplement to volume 1 suddenly appeared a delightful poem, "On Being Left Alone after Dinner" (pp. 65–66),[4] accom-panied by "An Epigram on An Epigram":

> The qualities all in a bee that we meet,
>   In an epigram never should fail;

> The body should always be little and sweet,
> And a sting should be felt in its tail.

Perhaps the most endearing single feature of this magazine, however, is the brash idea of an editor setting out single-handedly to provide the public with a "journal of record," a task to which even the most lavishly staffed and best-financed modern periodical is barely equal.

Notes

1. Earlier Charleston magazines were the *Traiteur** (1795–96), the *South Carolina Weekly Museum** (1797–98), the *Vigil* (1798), *L'Echo Du Sud: Moniteur Francais* (1801), the *Toilet** (1801), *Charleston Medical Register* (1803), and the *Sociable Magazine and Quarterly Intelligencer* (1803–4).

2. Frank Luther Mott identifies Bristed as "the 'Oxonian Bristed' whom Halleck satirized in *Fanny* and Neal lambasted in *Blackwood's*" (November 1824). See Mott's *A History of American Magazines, 1741–1850* (New York, 1930), I: 261.

3. Carpenter also edited the *People's Friend*, a New York City daily, and later the *Mirror of Taste*, a theatrical periodical, in Phiadelphia.

4. The anonymous poem's first two verses read:

> How shall I here employ my time
> Alone, without or prose or rhyme,
>   Or pencil to amuse me?
> Nor pen, nor paper, to be found,
> No friend to push the bottle round,
>   Or for its stay abuse me.

> The servants come and find me here,
> And stare upon me like the deer
>   On Selkirk, in Fernandez;
> And quite as tame, they wipe the chairs,
> And scrub; and hum their fav'rite airs,
>   And ask what my command is.

Information Sources

BIBLIOGRAPHY:
Mott, Frank Luther. *A History of American Magazines, 1741–1850*. New York, 1930. I: 260–61.
INDEX SOURCES: None.
LOCATION SOURCES: American Periodical Series microfilm, Atlanta Public Library, Boston Athenaeum, Miami University Library (Oxford, Ohio), State Historical Society of Wisconsin (Madison).

Publication History

MAGAZINE TITLE AND TITLE CHANGES: *The Monthly Review and Literary Miscellany of the United States* (a separate section in volume 1 bore its own title page: *The Monthly Register, and Review of the United States*, January 1805-

December 1806); the separate sections were discontinued as of vol. 2, which was published as *The Monthly Register, Magazine, and Review of the United States* (January-December 1807).

VOLUME AND ISSUE DATA: Vols. 1–4 (January 1805-December 1807); irregular until November 1806, then monthly.

PUBLISHER AND PLACE OF PUBLICATION: Stephen C. Carpenter (Charleston, South Carolina, January 1805-November 1806); E. Sargeant, (New York City), S. F. Bradford (Philadelphia), and Marchant, Willington & Co. (Charleston, South Carolina, December 1806-December 1807).

EDITORS: S. C. Carpenter (January 1805-May 1807); John Bristed (June-December, 1807).

CIRCULATION: Unknown.

MOONSHINE

One of the South's earliest attempts at a humor magazine[1] was *Moonshine*, a sixteen-page weekly that shone but briefly in June and July 1807. Published by Samuel Jefferis at No. 212 Market-street in Baltimore, this little sheet was edited by a group of friends who called themselves the Lunarian Society. It sold for 12.5¢ a copy or $1 in advance for eight issues.

Page 1 of the maiden number, headlined "By the Man in the Moon," introduced the new periodical to its readers via a convoluted, bogus tale about a role of papyrus "found in the small pyramid of Gizeh" and provided voluminous explanation and description of its appearance and contents. At considerable length the reader is led to the translation of the papyrus' message: that the pyramid was built to preserve the ancient Egyptian recipe for moonshine. This singular introductory essay concludes by detailing what the editors planned for their new vehicle:

> Our chief employment shall be to present . . . sundry pieces of Moonshine[2] of our own weaving, according to the newest fashions. . . . For those who are fond of comparing their own excellencies with the deficiencies of other poor devils around them, we have in store a budget of satire. . . . For those of merrier frame, we shall work hard to manufacture a few easy jokes; for dull dogs we shall sometimes even condescend to be dull . . . for the young ladies we shall cull from among the inditings of our younger days many a tender ode and dying ditty.

All readers who might wish to contact the society were advised to address their letters "To the Man in the Moon" and deposit them in the box in Mr. Jefferis' window.

A romantic sonnet is offered on page 16 of number 1 for the use of ladies whose gentlemen admirers are incapable of writing romantic verse of their own. "To every fair forlorn," the editors write, "whose admirers may not have the skull to perceive that 'rhyme' and 'time,' and 'love' and 'dove' jingle together, we offer the following. Let her make them transcribe this upon gilt paper, and then, as a great secret, she may show it to all her acquaintances as a copy of verses addressed to herself'':

'Twas not the liquid lustre of thine eye,
   Nor thy fine form, to which might ill compare
   The bending statue, nor thy glossy hair,
Nor thy cheek ting'd with health and beauty high,
Not yet thy honied lip, nor those bright rows
Of pearl, thro' which thy breath more fragrant flows,
   Than balmy Zephyr when he wooes the May,
That won my heart: for beauties I have known
   That *almost* equal'd thine, and have not lov'd!
   It was thy gentleness my bosom mov'd,
Thy heart to feel for others' miseries prone,
   Thy converse sweet, and (unaffected) gay.
These shall endure when other charms are past,
And while these shall endure, so long my love shall last.

The "Lunarians," who signed their contributions "Vincent Lunardi," "Timothy Varnish," "Copernicus Ptolemy," etc., seem to take special relish at poking fun at themselves:

The gentle reader of our pages, if he has ever had the good luck to increase his knowledge of natural history by stumbling over a hornet's nest, may form some notion of the situation of authors on their first appearance before the public. The buzz and general commotion of the venemous insects that sally forth on the first attack of their hive, are a perfect type of the din and persecution that surround the wight who has dared to tread within the purlieus of a printing office. Assailed on all sides by their stings and their hummings, you know not whether to advance or retreat, amid the shower of hail shot that whizzes by you.

And again:

On Saturday morning, then, I arose with the sun, shaved myself with such expedition as to slice off the point of my chin . . . and sallied out to hear what the world said of us. I had scarce got into Market-street when I saw several of the *literati* of the city hurrying along as if in eager pursuit of something. 'Now,' said I to myself, 'shall I witness the triumph of our society; with what anxiety do these gentlemen haste to the bookseller's to peruse our pages!' I stopped the first I met and asked him why he went so fast. 'I am afraid, answered he, that I shall find nothing fit to eat if I do not make haste to the market,' and left me. The next gave me a similar answer, and so did the third. 'Strange!' thought I, 'that intellectual food and even Moonshine, should be neglected, for the sake of the vulgar gratification of a good dinner!' Home I went again, muttering to myself all the way, and lamenting the degeneracy of these latter times.

On being asked whether *Moonshine* would succeed, "Tim Varnish" replied with accuracy of foresight:

> Indeed, my dear friend, I could wish that it might;
>   But I fear it will go to the d . . . l:
> For most men love darkness far better than light;
>   Because all their doings are evil. [No. 2: 29–30]

Moonshine's publisher, anticipating that a general miscellany would be more widely and warmly received, soon announced plans to commence a second periodical, the *Baltimore Magazine*, a weekly that managed to publish only one issue (in July 1807) before being absorbed by the Philadelphia *Port Folio*. The two Baltimore magazines were offered as a package deal, costing $3 for six months, in advance.

Notes

1. Others were the *Vigil* (Charleston, S.C., 1798), *Spectacles* (Baltimore, Md., 1807), the *Red Book** (Baltimore, 1819–21), and the *Microscope and General Advertiser* (Louisville, Ky., 1824–25).

2. The term "moonshine" is used two ways: one to denote the liquid variety, the other in the sense of "foolishness" or "whimsy."

Information Sources

INDEX SOURCES: None.
LOCATION SOURCES: American Periodical Series microfilm, Library of Congress.

Publication History

MAGAZINE TITLE AND TITLE CHANGES: *Moonshine*.
VOLUME AND ISSUE DATA: Nos. 1–5, weekly (irregular; June 20-July 23, 1807).
PUBLISHER AND PLACE OF PUBLICATION: Samuel Jefferis. No. 212, Market-
    street, Baltimore, Maryland.
EDITORS: "The Lunarian Society."
CIRCULATION: Unknown.

THE MOTHER EARTH NEWS®

In Madison, Ohio, in January 1970 began a magazine distinguished by a really different appeal. It was directed at a young, activist audience—people who had picketed and held vigils, worked as fundraisers, appeared before planning boards, demonstrated, participated in happenings. People who probably prefaced many of their statements with the word ''man,'' or with ''like, man,'' but who nevertheless had something of value to say. People who had come to want more action and less talk.

It was for them, America's blue-jean men and blue-jean women, that the *Mother Earth News*® was created. Its creators directed their efforts at those who dreamed of a simpler, more natural lifestyle, but not at those who dreamed faintly. The message was direct: drop out of the unreality of city life and the corporate life structure, and tune into nature and self-sufficiency in a rural setting.

Volume 1, number 1, began with the announcement that the issue had been put together ''in one solid month of 14-hour days'' by two people, John and Jane Shuttleworth. ''If you like us,'' added the Shuttleworths, ''we're *The Mother Earth News*®. If you don't like us . . . we're *The Saturday Evening Post*!'' (p. 5). A notice on the title page identified the new magazine as ''a bi-monthly publication edited by, and expressly for, today's influential 'hip' young adults. The creative people. The doers. The ones who make it all happen.'' Emphasis would be placed, the notice continued, on alternative lifestyles, ecology, working with nature, and doing more with less. Single copies were priced at $3, high for a slim all-newsprint periodical of sixty-four pages in which the only color work was the one-color cover. A yearly subscription was $15. Today, page length approximates 200 pages, and a substantial amount of full-color work appears. The magazine has remained a bimonthly. The single copy price also remains the same; a yearly subscription is now $18.

One of the first articles in the initial issue was ''How to Make It Your Way'' (pp. 6–7), reprinted from an earlier appearance in *Cavalier*. The drop-out-and-tune-in advice it contained was couched in the hip language of the day (''If you don't have the bread, don't sweat it''; ''That's a drag''; ''Make the scene''; etc.) The article's author cited Gladys Laubin's book, *The Indian Tipi*, and Euell Gibbons' *Stalking the Wild Asparagus*, *Stalking the Blue-Eyed Scallop*, and *Stalking the Heathful Herbs*.

Other articles in the first issue were also reprinted by permission. ''Living High on $6,500 a Year'' (pp. 8–11) had appeared in the *Saturday Evening Post*, and a series of articles on freelance cartooning, gag writing, and humor writing were reprinted from *Information Guide* (pp. 12–28).[1] Still other articles in this issue were a detailed how-to piece on building and living in an Indian tipi (pp. 29–40), and a profile of Twin Oaks, a Virginia commune known for the excellent rope hammocks and hammock chairs made there (pp. 56–59).

Articles chosen for a subsequent issue (number 39) were ''How to Eat Better for Less: The Secrets of Organ Meat Cookery,'' offering recipes for kidneys, tongue, heart, sweetbreads (thymus and/or pancreas, pp. 66–70); ''Smoke Your Way to Independence,'' not about marijuana—Mother stays well away from this topic—but on smoking fish (pp. 79–83); and ''We Built a Spinning Wheel for $2.50'' (p. 106). Another issue (number 60) offered articles on how to build a firewood splitter (pp. 80–82); dog sledding (pp. 88–89); wild foods, with a detailed chart listing the nutritional components of chicory, fennel, day lily, knotweed, etc. (pp. 110–113); and "Four Arguments for the Elimination of Television" (pp. 122–124, 126).

A regular feature that pokes fun at *Playboy* is the "Plowboy Interview." A recent example is an interview with Dr. Andrew Saul, a naturopath, or practitioner of natural healing (no. 85: 17–20, 22–23). Rather than prescribing drugs or surgery, the naturopath is more inclined to prescribe vitamins or vegetarian diets. Dr. Saul's book, *Doctor Yourself*, is described as a "health homesteader's handbook," certainly appropriate for Mother's readers. The same issue also contains articles on how to deliver a calf (pp. 74–76), folk music instruments (pp. 90–92), how to build Mother's waterless compost commode—a modern outhouse (104–6), chimney sweeping as a career field (pp. 108–11), dowsing (pp. 124–26), foraging for wild foods in the dead of winter (130–31), and home schooling (pp. 139–41).

A regular department called "$uccessful $waps" began with number 39, inspired by an article on bartering that had appeared in number 37. The magazine itself will swap a year's subscription for acceptable selections sent in by readers.

The magazine's personals department, "Lifemates and Companions," began as "Positions and Situations," intended as a means of helping those who wanted to escape The System get in touch with those who had dropped out earlier. In this space appear the messages of creative, caring, nonviolent, nature-loving, mellow Aquarians, Geminis, etc. in search of a like-minded someone, usually of the opposite sex, with whom to enjoy organic farming, solar energy, geodesic dome living, vegetarian diets, communicative relationships, and total commitment. A similar department, "Lost Souls," was instituted to help readers locate long-lost friends and relations—people who had *really* dropped out.

A department called "Mother's Calendar" lists folk festivals, crafts fairs, poetry competitions, awareness workshops, meditation seminars, and the like. Under the heading "Mother's Lifers" are printed the names of readers, now numbering more than 6,000, who have paid $600 each to become lifetime subscribers. The funds generated from this source are used to help support Mother's 622-acre research center, Eco-Village, located between Hendersonville and Brevard in the North Carolina mountains. Eco-Village is a research and teaching center with programs in ecology, organic gardening, and alternative energy generation.

The magazine's management has also branched out into The Mother Earth News® Tours, featuring exotic tours to such places as Ladakh in the Himalayas, Inner Mongolia, or Rwanda's Mountains of the Moon. Other adjuncts are Mother's newspaper column—mailed free in both manuscript and camera-ready format and carried by 1,150 papers—and three-minute radio segments, now carried by some 900 stations, including some as far away as Saipan, Agana (Guam), and Pago Pago.

Mother has created her own Environmental Hall of Fame. Among the environmentalists, activists, explorers, and scientists inducted have been Jacques-Yves Cousteau, Davis Ross Brower, Jerome Irving Rodale, Aldo Leopold, Barbara Ward, Sir Albert Howard, Rene Jules Dubos, and Anwar Fazal (no. 84: 96–97).

The magazine's ad/editorial ratio is weighted in favor of the editorial, 60:40. Roughly 80 percent of income is generated by subscriptions and newsstand sales, unusually high in today's market.

Noneditorial space is occupied by ads for sensible shoes, garden tillers, vitamins, food processors, seeds, backpacks for dogs, windmills, tents and tipis, woodstoves, well-drilling equipment, all-natural toothpaste, mauls for splitting firewood, and the How-To Book Club. The magazine enjoys a good number of full-page ads on various ways to make money independent of the corporate world by such means as worm farming or becoming a chimney sweep. Mother lets herself in for some criticism by occasionally accepting ads for vague get-rich-quick schemes, which might tend to lessen the magazine's otherwise excellent credibility, and has in the past accepted ads of an alarmist nature—what to do in the coming depression, for example.

From its first home in Madison, Ohio, the magazine moved in 1973 to Hendersonville, North Carolina, where it remains. Today its subscribers are still relatively young, median age thirty-eight; modestly prosperous, with median household income $27,684; and moderately well educated—40 percent attended or were graduated from college and 14 percent did postgraduate work. The magazine's substantial readership—912,000 paid plus 25,000 nonpaid—is scattered throughout the nation, with their biggest region for subscribers being the East North Central states, followed by the South Atlantic, Mid-Atlantic, and West South Central regions. A little more than half Mother's subscribers (54.5 percent) are males. A telephone conversation with staffer Joanne Dufilho (June 4, 1984) confirmed that the *Mother Earth News®* has no direct competitor, that is, no other magazine devoted to the same range of interests.

In January 1980 the Shuttleworths sold the magazine to three of the company's employees: David Adams, formerly treasurer and now president; Robert M. Lieb, formerly media director, now publisher; and Bruce Woods, ex-managing editor, now editor. The magnitude of the purchase price has not been revealed, but presumably the Shuttleworths no longer have to concern themselves with "doing more with less."

Note

1. This magazine was later retitled *Cartoon World*.

Information Sources

BIBLIOGRAPHY:
Hirsley, Michael. "Getting Down to Mother Earth at a Modern Walden." *Chicago Tribune*, December 19, 1983, 1: 13.

Meals, Cynthia. "The Mother Earth News." *Business: North Carolina*, 3, 5 (May 1983): 35–36.

Salmans, Sandra. "Beyond Mother Earth News." *New York Times*, August 9, 1983, p. D7.

Smart, William. "Wheels: Keep on Stokin'." *Washington Post*, September 23, 1982, p. D5.

INDEX SOURCES: Access: The Supplementary Index to Periodicals, New Periodicals Index, Reader's Guide to Periodical Literature.

LOCATION SOURCES: Boston Public Library, Columbia University Library, Duke University Library, Library of Congress, University of Arkansas Library, University of Kentucky Library, University of Oregon Library, Yale University Library.

Publication History

MAGAZINE TITLE AND TITLE CHANGES: *The Mother Earth News®*.

VOLUME AND ISSUE DATA: Not grouped in volumes; Nos. 1–86 (January 1970-March/April 1984), bimonthy.

PUBLISHER AND PLACE OF PUBLICATION: John Shuttleworth (1970- 1980); Robert M. Lieb (1980-present). Madison, Ohio (January 1970–1973); Hendersonville, North Carolina (1973-present).

EDITORS: John Shuttleworth (1970–1980); Bruce Woods (1980-present).

CIRCULATION: 912,000 paid, 25,000 nonpaid.

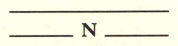

NATIONAL MAGAZINE (1799)

This thoroughly political periodical, Virginia's first magazine, was issued twice quarterly in Richmond during 1799 and 1800. Edited, published, and printed by James Lyon, this short-lived magazine was a forceful spokesman for the Anti-Federalist, or Republican, cause.[1]

With the full title of the *National Magazine; or, A Political, Historical, Biographical, and Literary Repository*, the contents page of volume 1, number 1, reads like a course in U.S. history, including the texts of the Declaration of Independence, the U.S. Constitution, the Alien and Sedition Acts, the Virginia and Kentucky Resolutions, the Constitution of Virginia, and other documents central to the early history of our nation. An extract from the trial of Mathew Lyon ("the Roaring Lyon of Vermont")[2] appears here, as does the monarchical constitution proposed by Alexander Hamilton, as well as Hamilton's biographical memoirs and a history of the National Mint.

Also in the 103-page first number appears a "Triune Dedication," 10 pages in length: to the Republicans throughout the United States; to John Adams, Esq., President; and to the aristocrats generally. The first part begins:

> To your patronage I submit this publication; for the dissemination of your principles it is instituted; and by your support, or your neglects, it must flourish, or must fade. In your cause I have embarked; —with you I must rise or fall.

This portion of the dedication then launches into an eloquent but seldom quoted defense of press freedom:

> A press properly conducted, is justly numbered among the most powerful weapons of liberty against slavery, virtue against vice, and patriotism

against ambition. But its qualities are perverted, its influence becomes pernicious, when it falls into the hands of sychophants, and hirelings, who are always ready to varnish over, with fulsome adulation, the follies and vices, treacheries and enormities of their patrons, and drown their crimes in praise. . . .

When offices and vice, honor and corruption, influence and treachery, flow from the same fountain, accountability is but a name; —then the freedom, the terror, and censorious power of the press, is the only check to the injustice and avarice, the rapine and cruelty, of the subordinate tyrant.

The purpose of the *National Magazine*, Lyon tells his Anti-Federalist readers, would be to lay bare "the plans and villanies of an aspiring faction, who are trampling on your liberties, abusing your confidence, despising republican virtues, and usurping power necessary for the execution of their conspiracies."

In the second and third portions of the dedication, and throughout his magazine's short life, Lyon berates the Alien and Sedition Acts[3] and President John Adams' part in their passage and attacks the Northeastern establishment aristocrats. True to his promise, Lyon never smooths over "with soft words and silken sentences" the excesses of the Adams administration.

In volume 1, number 3, Lyon prints the text of Adams' speech to the Sixth Congress, then adds his own commentary, the nature of which is made clear in this excerpt:

At the opening of each session of Congress, it has been customary for the president to make a speech to the two houses. This practice issues in a mere waste of time. The president can tell them nothing but what they have heard already by other channels. The harrangue has often been employed as a convenient organ for the voice of faction and defamation.

Lyon's favorite personal target, however, was Alexander Hamilton, whom he describes as a man "whose transcendent capacity for mischief entitles him to the epithet of *the most dangerous man in the Union*." Had he not been disappointed in seeing his strong central government fully established, Lyon said, "he would be a *Caesar* without his *virtues*, and a *Cataline* with all his *vices*." (1, 1: 91).

The pages of the *National Magazine* were open to other vehement Jeffersonian spokesmen. An example is the valedictory address of Thomas Cooper upon his relinquishing the editorship of a Pennsylvania newspaper, the *Sunbury and Northumberland Gazette*. In it, says Lyon in his introduction, Cooper "developes step by step the destructive measures of the faction which has been running these states to ruin for several years."[4]

Space is given essays on press freedom, such as "Essay on Liberty of the Press" (1, 4: 352–71) by "Hortensuis," actually George Hay of Petersburgh,

Virginia, and "Remarks on the Liberty of the Press" (2, 5: 19–20) by David Hume, Esq. Much attention is paid to economics in such articles as "Political Arithmetic" (2, 5: 7–8; 2, 6: 111–20), a reprint of the nation's first bankruptcy law, and several treatments of the national debt. Also given prominent play were essays on libel (2, 5: 172–78) and slander ("Slander the worst of poison, ever finds/An easy entrance in ignoble minds"; 2, 8: 392–93). In later numbers poetry, miscellaneous material, and filler supplant some of the political content, though general political material—as in "On the Rights of Woman" (2, 7: 204–5)— and direct, partisan political material—such as "Serious Considerations Why John Adams Should Not Be Re-elected President" (2, 7: 232–37)—still predominate.

A note at the conclusion of volume 2, number 8, informs readers that the magazine, which had been moved to the District of Columbia before the appearance of number 7, would be "blended" with the *Cabinet* and published in a weekly quarto pamphlet of twelve pages, to be stitched together in a cover, except in the District, where four pages of the combined periodical would be delivered every second day. Number 8 appears to be the last issue available to researchers.

Though historians have paid little attention to this magazine, its importance lies in having been a bold regional spokesman for Jeffersonian principles at this crucial, formative time in our new nation's development.

Notes

1. These "Republicans," it should be noted, were the political faction that later became today's Democratic Party.

2. See Adoleph O. Goldsmith, "The Roaring Lyon of Vermont," *Journalism Quarterly*, Spring 1962, pp. 179–86.

3. In the magazine's prospectus, Lyon refers to the Sedition Act as "the scalping knife of government, and tomb-stone of American Liberty" and to the Alien Act as "its sister in iniquity, and hand-maid in oppression."

4. From the prospectus that precedes the front page of vol. 1, no. 2.

Information Sources

BIBLIOGRAPHY:
Mott, Frank Luther. *A History of American Magazines, 1741–1850*. New York, 1930. I: 204–5.
INDEX SOURCES: None.
LOCATION SOURCES: American Antiquarian Society (Worcester, Massachusetts), American Periodical Series microfilm, Library of Congress.

Publication History

MAGAZINE TITLE AND TITLE CHANGES: *National Magazine; or, A Political, Historical, Biographical, and Literary Repository* (June 1, 1799-December 22, 1800); united with the *Cabinet* in 1801 to form the *National Magazine; or, Cabinet of the United States* (October 1801-January 1802).

VOLUME AND ISSUE DATA: Vols. 1–3 (June 1, 1799-January 1802), twice quarterly.
PUBLISHER AND PLACE OF PUBLICATION: James Lyon. Richmond, Virginia (June
      1, 1799-December 22, 1800); District of Columbia (October 1801-January 1802).
EDITOR: James Lyon (1799–1802).
CIRCULATION: Unknown.

THE NATIONAL MAGAZINE (1830)

Clearly the best of the early Southern women's magazines was the *National Magazine; or, Lady's Emporium*, edited and published in 1830–1831 in Baltimore by Mrs. Mary Chase Barney, daughter of Justice Samuel Chase, a signer of the Declaration of Independence, and daughter-in-law of Commodore Joshua Barney. It was the first of these magazines[1] to be directed by a strong woman editor, whereas earlier magazines of the genre had been edited by men who had a well-meant but somewhat clumsy desire to "improve the female mind and morals."

Mrs. Barney entered the journalistic lists at a time when women were expected to be seen, not heard. Though she introduced herself to her readers as one who entered upon the publication of a magazine out of financial necessity and as one who felt "as the doe chased from its covert of years" ("To Patrons," 1, 1: 1–3), Mrs. Barney soon showed herself a forceful spokesperson for her sex. Objections had been raised to the portion of her prospectus that promised some political content. Her wish was not to engage in party warfare, she promised her readers, yet "because we have no voice in the government, have we no voice in the nation?" She recognized the delicacy of her position from the start and for the most part kept her magazine from party strife as promised, save in the case of President Andrew Jackson, who had earlier relieved her husband from his naval post in Baltimore. For Jackson she had never a kind word, describing him as violent, ambitious, and ruthless:

> His conduct . . . must have convinced every intelligent and impartial man that he is completely destitute of intellectual ability, and even of those Pagan virtues, which might excuse if they could not justify the infatuation of a gallant and spirited people. Putting *goodness* out of the question, he does not seem to possess a single *great* quality. His mind, in every respect appears to be of the lowest order—utterly incapable either of generating or comprehending an elevated and liberal idea. . . .
>
> If General Jackson did not 'fill the measure of his country's glory,' he has at least filled that of its dishonor. We do not think that it is in his power to add to the disgrace which he has brought upon it. [2, 3: 210–11]

Mrs. Barney's editorial judgment was such that she did not shrink from presenting her readers such "manly" copy as "The Baltimore and Ohio Rail Road," "The

Late Revolution in France,'' ''The American System,'' and ''The State of the Union.'' Certainly she was criticized for doing so.

Lighter fare also appeared, of course. Representative titles are ''The Flower Market of Paris''; ''The Logierian System,'' on a new method of teaching pianoforte; ''Italian Opera''; and ''Fashionable Scandal,'' a humorous piece on the progress of rumor. A serialized feature in fiction entitled ''The Circulating Library'' related the adventures of Clara Jones and Mr. Barnacle. A letter to the editor from a woman reader began, ''Madam, I have looked with great eagerness through the pages of your Emporium, in the expectation of finding an enigma, a rebus, or a connundrum, which from 'time immemorial' have been considered as appropriate 'trifles' for a Lady's Magazine; but I am sorry to say I looked in vain'' (1, 3: 210). Mrs. Barney not only obliged by printing an enigma sent in by the reader but in a later number included another, as appears below:

> The noblest object in the works of Art;
> The brightest Gem which nature can impart;
> The point essential in a Lawyer's lease;
> The well known signal in the time of peace;
> The ploughman when he drives his plough;
> The soldier's duty, and the lover's vow;
> The planet seen between the Earth and Sun;
> The prize which merit never yet has won;
> The miser's treasure and the badge of Jews;
> The wife's ambition and the parson's dues.
> Now if your noble spirit can divine,
> A corresponding word for every line,
> By all these lessons clearly will be shown,
> An ancient City of no small renown. [1, 5: 398][2]

Also providing entertainment for the magazine's readers were curiosities, such as the copy from a watch-maker's sesquipedalian signboard that read:

> Here are fabricated and renovated, trochiliac horologies, portable and permanent, linguacious, or taciturnal; whose circumgyrations are performed, by internal spiral elastic, or extensive pendulous plumbages; diminuatives, simple, or compound, invested with aurent or argent integuments. [1, 2: 109]

Other examples of the curious were an announcement of a Mr. McGlue's separation from his wife (''We should suppose a husband, so *tenacious* of his rights as this *adhesive* name would indicate, would *stick* closer to his partner'') and a brief item on a gigantic flower found in Sumatra.

Poetry, predominantly original, made up an important part of the eighty-page *Emporium*'s content. It varied from the highly sentimental ''The Widowed

Mother'' (1, 3: 209) to verse of considerable dignity, such as "Are There No Wreaths" (2, 2: 151). Most of the poetry was anonymous, usually signed "A," "F," etc., and most was doubtless the product of women contributors. In complimenting the contributor of "Tribute to the Memory of a Young Lady," Mrs. Barney wrote: 'Few things are more gratifying to the Editor than to maintain this literary intercourse with the learned and distinguished females of her Country'' (2, 1: 78).

Much of the prose, too, was anonymous, identified only as "selected" or "for the *National Magazine*." An occasional item might better have been anonymous, as in the case of Georgian C. R. Floyd's burbling description of the South as a latter-day Eden:

> As free, as exuberant as the branching vine is the Southern generosity; as soft as the air is its country; but as stern and unyielding as the native Oak when threats or injustice assail. —Man is rich in noble traits and personal graces—and Woman, the loveliest work of creation, is bewitchingly attractive in our soul-healing climate. [2, 1: 119]

Though Mrs. Barney had agents as far north as New Hampshire and Vermont, as far west as Indiana, and throughout the South, the female world did not beat a path to her door to pay the $5 subscription rate, causing her to begin her second volume "under a weight of despondency, enough to sink the stoutest heart" ("Prolegomena," 2, 1: 2). Readers who complained of the lack of love stories in the magazine were told to make love for themselves, for the editor was too old to help them.[3] At the end of volume 2, in July 1831, the magazine was discontinued, stilling the voice of a pioneer American feminist who had given her public a most respectable editorial product.

Notes

1. Earlier entries were the *Toilet** (Charleston, 1801); the *Charleston Spectator, and Ladies Literary Portfolio* (1806); the *Emerald** (Baltimore, 1810–11); the *Masonic Miscellany and Ladies Literary Magazine* (Lexington, Ky., 1821–23); the *Ladies' Literary Boquet* (Baltimore, 1823–24); and the *Ladies' Garland* (Harper's Ferry, Va., 1824–28).

2. A solution to this enigma was submitted by a New York woman and appeared in vol. 2, no. 1, pp. 73–74:

"The noblest object in the works of art,"
Apollo di Belvidere.
"The brightest gem which nature can impart,"
Diamond.
"The point essential in a lawyer's lease,"
Rent.
"The well known signal in the time of peace,"
Illumination.
The ploughman when he drives his plough,"
Aration, (act of ploughing.)

"The soldier's duty and the lover's vow,"
Naught, or Nonsense.
"The planet seen between the earth and sun,"
Orb.
"The prize which merit never yet has won,"
Paradise.
"The miser's treasure and the badge of Jews,"
Lucre.
"The wife's ambition and the parson's dues."
Expenses.

Using the first letter of each word, then, the answer to this enigma was Adrianople.

3. Reported in Bertha-Monica Stearns, "Southern Magazines for Ladies," *South Atlantic Quarterly*, 31 (January 1932): 76.

Information Sources

BIBLIOGRAPHY:
Stearns, Bertha-Monica. "Southern Magazines for Ladies, 1819–1860." *South Atlantic Quarterly*, 31 (January 1932): 70–87.
INDEX SOURCES: None.
LOCATION SOURCES: American Antiquarian Society (Worcester, Massachusetts), American Periodical Series microfilm, Peabody Institute Library (Baltimore).

Publication History

MAGAZINE TITLE AND TITLE CHANGES: *The National Magazine; or, Lady's Emporium*.
VOLUME AND ISSUE DATA: Vols. 1–2 (November 1830-July 1831), monthly.
PUBLISHER AND PLACE OF PUBLICATION: Mary Barney. Baltimore, Maryland.
EDITOR: Mrs. Mary Barney.
CIRCULATION: Unknown.

THE NEW EAST. *See* CAROLINA LIFESTYLE

NEW ORLEANS MAGAZINE

One of the South's most readable city magazines is *New Orleans*, an 88 to 120-page monthly published since 1966 and currently one of the properties of ARC Publishing Company, which also publishes *Sun Belt Executive Magazine*.[1] Like many other city books in metropolitan areas of modest size, *New Orleans'* editorial content is illustrated in black and white. The only color is on the slick, full-color cover and in some advertisements.

The magazine's circulation of 40,500 consists of roughly 18,000 copies that are distributed as an in-room periodical in local hotels, 15,000 sold by subscription, and 4,500 to 6,000 sold on newsstands. The rest are placed free of charge in doctors' offices and other high-visibility outlets. Subscribers have a median income of $54,000 and a mean age of 40.4. Sixty-five percent of subscribers are female, 35 percent male, and according to publisher Paul Richardson,[2] more than 90 percent of the city's professional men and women receive the magazine.

Again, like most other city magazines in middle-sized markets, most ad matter is local. About 18 percent of yearly ad revenues come from national advertisers, with the pre-Christmas months of October through December accounting for much of this total. The two largest ad categories are dining/entertainment and fashion/jewelry. New Orleans, of course, is a city noted for fine dining, and the magazine gets good ad support from the city's legion of "apostrophe restaurants": Antoine's, Brennan's, Begue's, Moran's, Menefee's, Christian's, Monte's, Ralph & Kacoo's, and Nuvolari's, the last of which was singled out in a February 1984 restaurant article as offering "creative upscale pastas" (19, 5: 85).

Jewelry advertising occupies considerable space in this city book, with national ads by De Beers and local advertisements by Adler's, Godchaux's, Boudreaux's, and Hausmann's ("apostrophe jewelers"), plus antique and estate jewelry from Nancy Kittay and J. Herman. Shoes, liquors, hotels, automobiles, banks, and condos are also well represented.

What makes *New Orleans* worth selecting over others of its kind, however, is its editorial content, which does a good job of reflecting the unique character of the city. In company with Charleston, South Carolina; Savannah, Georgia; and a few other Southern cities, New Orleans has successfully resisted taking on the bland, franchised appearance of "Anywhere, U.S.A.," and still has a clear, distinctive personality. In covering its home city, the magazine's management divides editorial content into three parts: departments, feature articles (45 percent freelanced and uninterrupted by advertising matter), and a third section that has not been given a name on the contents page. Asked how he would characterize this no-name third of editorial content, Richardson replied that it might be thought of as the "Looking Good" section, as much of it is built around dining, entertainment, home improvement, fashion, and other "good life" copy. It also contains items on New Orleans' business scene and miscellaneous news notes about life in the city.

Among the magazine's regular departments are "Griffiti" (formerly "Up Front"), a brief column on society and other city matters by Tommy Griffin; "Dossier," a sprightly miscellany of snippets of local interest; "Backstage," on the city's theater scene; and the standard calendar of dance, music, theater, museums, and other sources of public entertainment. This magazine's calendar is unique for at least part of the year, when parades (Momus, Endymion, Venus, Bacchus, Zulu, Rex, etc.) rate their own category in the listings. One of the best departments is "Local Color," the magazine's last page, a short monthly write-up of the likes of ex-prizefighter Willie Pastrano, Mardi Gras "Indian tribes," and Smile's Pool Room.

Best of all are *New Orleans'* feature articles, which show greater breadth and imagination than do those found in many other similar magazines. One 1984 issue contained a piece on increased teenage alcoholism in the city, a likely side-effect of the "Mardi Gras mentality" (19, 5: 48–53); an article on how the state's law schools are cranking out virtual armies of young lawyers and how New Orleans law firms are soaking them up (19, 5: 55–59); and a food piece titled "Hello Deli" on the welcome emergence in the city of delicatessens, an institution sorely lacking in most parts of the South (19, 5: 78–80).

Another 1984 issue contained features on city churches that invoke the spirit of Black Hawk, an early nineteenth-century Indian chief who led the Sacs and Fox tribes against white settlers (18, 6: 24–27, 71, 94–95); the mysterious disappearance of Spanish moss from New Orleans; the meaning of the term "creole"; and the city's traditional Monday repast of red beans and rice, which the Spanish originally called *Moros y Cristianos* (Moors and Christians). In a later issue, "Raiders of the Lost Art" profiled the city's dealer in primitive art Charlie Davis, New Orleans' own version of Indiana Jones (19, 4: 60–64).

Notes

1. Other ARC efforts of recent years were *A. C. Flyer* (1968–1977) and *Louisiana Industry Review* (1982 only).

2. Telephone conversation with the author, July 12, 1984.

Information Sources

INDEX SOURCES: Access: The Supplementary Index to Periodicals.
LOCATION SOURCES: Library of Congress, Louisiana State University Library, Loyola University Library.

Publication History

MAGAZINE TITLE AND TITLE CHANGES: *New Orleans Magazine.*
VOLUME AND ISSUE DATA: Vols. 1–19 (September 1966-present), monthly.
PUBLISHER AND PLACE OF PUBLICATION: Joe David, Jr. (1966–1975); Ben Turner (1975-June 1984); Paul Richardson (July 1984-present). New Orleans, Louisiana.
EDITORS: James L. Townsend (1966-April 1970); editors for May 1970-November 1974 could not be located; Thomas Fitzmorris (December 1974-December 1976); C. P. Rumph (January-March 1977); Joe Manguno (April-September 1977); Bonnie Crone (October 1977-September 1978); Ron Faucheaux (October 1978-February 1979); Don Lee Keith (March-July 1979); Clarence Doucet (August-December 1979); Jean Stewart (January 1980-September 1982); Linda Matys (October 1982-September 1984); Don Washington (October 1984-February 1985); Sandra Shilstone (March 1985-present).
CIRCULATION: 45,000 (June 1985).

NILES' NATIONAL REGISTER. *See* NILES' WEEKLY
REGISTER

NILES' WEEKLY REGISTER

If any title deserves the distinction of being called the most outstanding non-literary Southern magazine of the 1800s, it is *Niles' Weekly Register* of Baltimore (1811–1849). Its founder was Hezekiah Niles, earlier a printer and bookseller, publisher of a literary magazine,[1] and editor and publisher of the Baltimore *Evening Post*. The thirty-four-year-old Niles first published his new property as the *Weekly Register* but in March 1814 changed the title to *Niles' Weekly Register*. Years later the magazine's title was changed again to *Niles National Register*, the version that remained in its masthead for the twelve years leading up to the magazine's demise.

In his prospectus, which appeared in volume 1, number 1, Niles explained the rationale of his new periodical, writing with the force and flair that marked his tenure as editor:

> The newspapers of the day, devoted to *party* and *partizans*, seldom dare to '*tell the truth, the whole truth, and nothing but the truth.*' Every city, town and village has its *little-great* men, whose interests and views must be subserved, and the dignity of the press is prostrated to the will of aspiring individuals. . . . The editor does not intend to interfere in the *petty* disputes betwen the *ins* and *outs*; as he hopes the Register will receive a general support. . . . Its politics shall be *American*—not passive, not luke-warm, but active and vigilant—not to support individuals, but to subserve the *interests of the people*.

The *Register*, Niles promised, would be published every Saturday at noon, printed on a fine sheet of super royal paper with a nonpareil or brevier type and would contain sixteen pages octavo at $5 a year,[2] payable at the expiration of six months and annually thereafter. A year's numbers would constitute two volumes. Niles further indicated that content would be divided into the following departments: politics; history; biography; geography; notices of the arts, sciences, manufacturing, and agriculture; miscellany; and a "neat summary of the news." His prediction that "we think it promises something interesting at the present moment, and as a Book of Reference" (1, 1: 2) was certainly borne out, as the *Register*'s impartiality, objectivity, and accuracy made it the unrivaled journal of record of its time—one of the best examples ever of a mass medium serving as an ongoing recorder of history in the making. Niles' *Register* became an essential reference work, kept by most libraries and known not only throughout America but in Europe as well. The status this magazine attained is attested to by the fact that while in Baltimore in 1825, the Marquis de Lafayette called to pay his respects to Niles and said that he intended to take a complete set of the *Register* back to France.[3] In a preface to volume 58 of the *Register* (1839–40), the editor proudly quoted his counterpart at the *United States Gazette* of Philadelphia, who had called the *Register* "a textbook for those that dealt in facts" (p. iv).

The *Register*'s original motto was a quotation from Shakespeare's *Henry VIII*:

> I wish no other herald,
> No other speaker of my living actions,
> To keep mine honor from corruption
> But such an honest chronicler.

A later motto was shorter—*Hoec olim meminisse juvabit*, a line from Virgil, which Norval Neil Luxon translates as "to remember these things hereafter will be a pleasure."[4]

The one group that could have found little pleasure in the *Register*'s pages were America's Anglophiles. Niles was bitterly anti-British, and his copy from the era of the War of 1812 teems with this sentiment. Some of the most forceful, and probably persuasive, copy Niles ran concerned atrocities committed by English soldiers and their Indian allies. A news story headlined "His Majesty's Allies" (4, 8: 135) told a story of savage brutality on the banks of the Ohio, where a band of Indians tricked and murdered two families of settlers. "The situation of Mrs. Kennedy," read an extract from this copy, "was shocking beyond description. She having been pregnant, her body was found entirely naked, cut open and the child taken out and hung up on a peg in the chimney. Her entrails were scattered all about the door and the hogs were eating them."

Another selection from later in 1813, "The Monsters at Hampton" (4, 21: 332–37), gave an account of not only pilferage ("spoon stealing," Niles called it) by the British army but of brutal "ravishment," or rape, and an episode in which British troops stripped a number of local women naked and marched them at bayonet point through the streets of the city.

In chronicling the American political scene, the *Register* provided unbiased coverage of ten presidential elections, fought for a protective tariff on behalf of U.S. industry, and opposed the congressional caucus method of selecting presidential candidates. Niles argued unsuccessfully for a single presidential term of six or eight years (32: 339) and provided his readers a concise history of U.S. political party activities in a two-part piece, "The Old Landmarks" (24, 18: 274–80; 24, 19: 291–93).

Niles gave his readers a wealth of facts and statistics on the economic scene and showed a strong interest in Latin America and the American West, at the same time encouraging Westward expansion and the rights of Indians. An especially interesting part of Norval Luxon's extensive writing on the *Register* concerns Hezekiah Niles' coverage of improvements in transportation—steamboats, canals, the railroads—that influenced the opening of the West.

Like today's James J. Kilpatrick or Scotty Reston, Niles was what might be designated a *likable* writer whose work was filled with solid facts and whose presentation of these facts was accomplished with wit and grace. The reader who might be tempted to regard Niles as a gray compiler of facts and figures should also read his reflections on "the editorial we," which Niles called a "foolish, pompous and regal fashion" in periodicals having but one editor. "The use of 'we,' " he continued, "when a writer has to speak of himself, is often ridiculous in the extreme. I well remember a hearty laugh I had at a certain editor, giving an account of a personal affray that he had with another person, somewhat in these terms—'As *we* were passing through —— street, *we* were assaulted by ——, notwithstanding he saw *our* wife looking out of the window; and *we* being of much less bodily strength than ——, he beat *us* and struck *us* in the most barbarous manner, until *we* were rescued by some of *our* neighbors who rushed to *our* relief' " (24, 19: 289).

In a similar vein, Niles had from the start promised to sign, or at least initial, whatever he wrote in the *Register*, "confident that what I have to say will not be one jot or tittle the better for being signed *Cincinnatus*, or *Thales*, or *Washington*, or *Franklin*. It is the fashion, to be sure, to attach great names to little pieces. . . . The ass was chiefly despised for pretending to be a lion" (1, 1: 8).

On September 3, 1836, Niles announced his retirement after having been paralyzed on his right side by a stroke, which he attributed to the constant stress of the editorship. His old post was turned over to his eldest son, William Ogden Niles, who moved to Baltimore from Frederick to assume his new responsibilities. The younger Niles said that he accepted the position fully aware that he was rendering himself "liable to all the imputations which may arise from the contrast" between himself and his illustrious father and promised to keep the *Register* free of party taint and to preserve its national character (51, 1: 1).

The younger Niles moved the magazine from Baltimore to Washington, D.C., altering its title a year later to *Niles' National Register*. His performance could not equal his father's, and when Hezekiah Niles died in 1839, his administratrix, Sally Ann Niles, sold the *Register* to Jeremiah Hughes, who returned the magazine to Baltimore, where he edited and published it until 1848. In a brief farewell to his readers, William Niles expressed regret that the *Register* could not remain in the family of its founder but warmly commended the new owner, who had been an old friend of the elder Niles.

Hughes' age made it difficult to keep up the exertions necessary to a magazine like the *Register*, and at age sixty-five he sold it to a young man named George Beatty, who moved it to Philadelphia. In his nine years as editor, said Hughes in his valedictory, the obligations of his office had been "fulfilled amidst such a series of embarrassments, difficulties and disheartening circumstances as few publishers have been subjected to" (74, whole no. 1901: 1).

Under Beatty, the battered old *Register* was published for an additional year with much difficulty and considerable irregularity. After the end of the seventy-fifth volume came a suspension of two and a half months, followed by three final numbers in September 1849. These three issues contained the only advertisements ever to appear in the *Register*. These few pathetic columns of advertising space were sold in a last effort to keep the venerable old magazine afloat. Most of the ads were for other magazines, including the *Southern Literary Messenger*,* then in its fifteenth year. Also advertised was a 24″ × 32″ engraving entitled "The First Prayer in Congress."

The *Register* deserves an important place in any history of American magazines, as it was the new nation's first news magazine, or at least the first to achieve quality and recognition. As a repository for the public documents, important speeches, and national news of its day, it is unsurpassed.

Notes

1. *Apollo or Delaware Weekly Magazine* (February 12-August 24, 1805).
2. The $5 subscription cost remained in effect for thirty-seven years until on January 3, 1849, it was reduced to $4 annually.
3. Lucretia Ramsey Bishko, "Lafayette and the Maryland Agricultural Society: 1824–1832," *Maryland Historical Magazine*, 70 (Spring 1975): 54. Also, John Adams, Thomas Jefferson, James Madison, and Andrew Jackson were among Niles' subscribers.
4. Norval Neil Luxon, "Niles' Weekly Register—Nineteenth Century News-magazine," *Journalism Quarterly*, 18 (September 1941): 273.

Information Sources

BIBLIOGRAPHY:
Luxon, Norval Neil. "Niles' Weekly Register—Nineteenth Century News-magazine." *Journalism Quarterly*, 18 (September 1941): 273–90.
———. *Niles' Weekly Register: News Magazine of the Nineteenth Century*. Baton Rouge, 1947.
Mott, Frank Luther. *A History of American Magazines, 1741–1850*. New York, 1930. I: 268–70.
INDEX SOURCES: Poole's Index to Periodical Literature. *Niles' Weekly Register: General Index to the First Twelve Volumes, or First Series of Niles' Weekly Register. Being a Period of Six Years: from September 1811 to September 1817*. (Baltimore: Franklin Press, 1818).
LOCATION SOURCES: American Antiquarian Society (Worcester, Massachusetts), Boston Public Library, Duke University Library, Library of Congress, New York Public Library.

Publication History

MAGAZINE TITLE AND TITLE CHANGES: *The Weekly Register*, vols. 1–5 (September 1811-February 1814); *Niles' Weekly Register*, vols. 6–52 (March 1814-August 1837); *Niles' National Register*, Vols. 53–76 (September 1837-September 1849).
VOLUME AND ISSUE DATA: Vols. 1–76 (September 1811-September 1849), weekly.
PUBLISHER AND PLACE OF PUBLICATION: Hezekiah Niles (Baltimore, 1811-August 1836); William Ogden Niles (Washington, D.C., September 1836-October 1839); Jeremiah Hughes (Baltimore, October 1839-February 1848); George Beatty (Philadelphia, July 1848–1849).

EDITORS: Hezekiah Niles (1811-August 1836); William Ogden Niles (September 1836-
    October 1839); Jeremiah Hughes (October 1839-February 1848); George Beatty
    (July 1848–1849).
CIRCULATION: Unknown.

THE NORTH CAROLINA MAGAZINE

Historians differ as to whether the *North Carolina Magazine; or, Universal
Intelligencer*, published in 1764 and early 1765, should be more properly regarded as a magazine or a newspaper.[1] On one hand, a substantial portion of
its contents appears to have been lifted from English newspapers, and significant
space in each extant issue is given over to news items. Its overall physical
appearance is more nearly that of a colonial newspaper. On the other hand,
Editor-Publisher James Davis surely must have understood the import of the
word "magazine" and must have used it in his masthead for a purpose. There
was magazine material aplenty in each number. Perhaps Mr. Davis, who is
thought to have come to Newbern from Virginia in 1749, possibly after having
served an apprenticeship under William Parks in Williamsburg,[2] had plans to
make this periodical somewhat different from the usual colonial newspaper but
in practice found obtaining newspaper-type copy easier in his relatively isolated
setting than obtaining magazine-type material. His intentions were very likely
explained to his readers in his first number, but numbers 1 through 4 of volume
1 are unavailable to researchers.

Page 1 of the first extant issue (volume 1, number 5) begins with a quotation
from Dryden:

> Hard steel succeeded then,
> And stubborn as the Metal were the Men
> Truth, Modesty and Shame the World forsook;
> Fraud, Avarice and Force their Places took.

Then follows a long essay reflecting on how the world had changed since the
time of Ovid—certainly more nearly magazine than newspaper copy. Next ensues
the continuation from the previous number of another magazine-like discourse
on Roman history. Most of the following three pages contain an extended essay
on Moses. The remainder of this number is filled with newspaper-style material:
notices of runaway slaves, a public meeting in Craven County, and a livestock
sale, plus two advertisements for books.

Number 6 is similar in content, but number 7 has more nearly the contents
of a newspaper, including a curious little item about the death at her Piccadilly
lodgings of one Elizabeth Taylor, age 131. Number 8 begins in magazine style
with an attractive colophon and quotation ("O sacred Hunger of pernicious Gold/
What Bands of Faith can impious Lucre hold!"), followed by a two-and-a-half-

page essay overloaded with classical allusions, itself followed by the next installment on Roman history, then three pages of news items.

As might be expected for 1764, a considerable portion of the magazine's
content was devoted to developments in the mother country. In volume 1, number
11, Davis' North Carolina readers are given a strong dose of the kind of language
necessary in a monarchy in a long report entitled "To the King's Most Excellent
Majesty. The humble Address of the People of Great Britain," which begins:

> We, Your Majesty's most dutiful and loyal Subjects, the People of Great
> Britain, humbly beg Leave to approach your Royal Throne, not as Flattering
> Sycophants, or Party Tools, but as Honest Men, with our real and undis-
> guised Sentiments; which, from the high Opinion, we truely entertain of
> the Goodness of Your Majesty's Heart, we doubt not, will be more ac-
> ceptable to Your Majesty than the highest Strains of Adulation.

Presumably it was necessary to perform this sort of verbal two-step when com-
plaining about something His Majesty's government was doing, which in this
case centered on trade and relations with France.

Other copy hits closer to home, as in a two-page essay on whether the seat
of government for North Carolina should be fixed at Newbern or Wilmington.
"And now my Countrymen," Davis asks, "what would some of you give to
have the Seat of Government again at Newbern? . . . Methinks I hear some of
you break out, 'O Newbern! Newbern! When shall I again tread thy Grassy
Plains, and shake the Wilmingtonian Dust from my Feet!' " (1, 12: 95).

The lead story to volume 1, number 14, contains a quaint description of an
elephant that had been presented to the king by a Captain Sampson of Bengal:
"The bodies of these creatures are heavy and gross, and far from being beautiful;
their eyes are like those of a hog; their legs and feet resemble columns." Also
in this number is a poem by G. Hayden of Epsom, "The Choice of a Husband,"
at which today's feminist might take some small offense. An excerpt from it
reads:

> And females must exert their care
> When patching cheeks, or curling hair
> Dress, pleasantry, and show,
> Is all they're taught, and all they know:
> On pride and fashion so intent,
> On folly so entirely bent;
> 'Tis question whether one in ten
> Knows how to spell her name—what then!
> She's been three years, or more, at school,
> And learn'd how to compliment by rule:
> Learn'd how to dress, and how to dance;
> Can tell what mode came last from France

Can cut a fowl the modish way,
And knows the art of drinking tea.
On these acquirements, when compounded,
Is female education grounded.

It would appear that James Davis began this venture with the intention of publishing a sheet that dealt in longer, more substantial articles than did the typical newspapers of his day. The *North Carolina Magazine* was, in fact, part magazine, part newspaper, and is presented here as such.

Notes

1. Lyon Richardson lists it as the thirteenth magazine in the colonies and the first in the South; Frank Luther Mott considers it a newspaper. The editors of the American Periodical Series refer to it as "a newspaper which somewhat resembled a magazine" (*American Periodicals 1741–1900, An Index to the Microfilm Collections*. Ann Arbor, 1979, p. 168.) Lossing calls it North Carolina's "first periodical paper," Lawrence Wroth refers to it as a "journal," and Isaiah Thomas doesn't mention it at all. (*See* "Bibliography.")

2. Davis' first journalistic effort in Newbern, and North Carolina's first newspaper, was a weekly called the *North Carolina Gazette*. This paper began in August of 1751, continued for six to eight years, and was revived by Davis on May 27, 1768.

Information Sources

BIBLIOGRAPHY:
Lossing, Benson. *Field Book of the Revolution*. Ed. of 1860. II: 360.
Richardson, Lyon N. *A History of Early American Magazines, 1741–1789*. New York, 1931. Pp. 140, 148.
Thomas, Isaiah. *The History of Printing in America*. 2d ed., vol. 2. New York, 1967. (Original edition published in 1874, pp. 166–68.)
Wroth, Lawrence C. *The Colonial Printer*. Charlottesville, Va., 1931. P. 48.
INDEX SOURCES: None.
LOCATION SOURCES: American Periodical Series microfilm, Library of Congress.

Publication History

MAGAZINE TITLE AND TITLE CHANGES: *The North Carolina Magazine; or, Universal Intelligencer* (June 1, 1764-January 11, 1765).
VOLUME AND ISSUE DATA: Vols. 1–2 (June 1, 1764-January 11, 1765), weekly.
PUBLISHER AND PLACE OF PUBLICATION: James Davis. Newbern, North Carolina.
EDITOR: James Davis.
CIRCULATION: Unknown.

O

THE OBSERVER

An early Baltimore weekly miscellany devoted to light literature was the *Observer, and Repertory of Original and Selected Essays, in Verse & Prose, on Topics of Polite Literature, &c.* (1806–1807). The magazine's prospectus, which occupied the first five pages of volume 1, number 1, set forth the anonymous editor's belief that "variety is the essence of amusement." To succeed, the editor continued, "a publication of this kind must display a spirited versatility: It must treat by turns of morals, politics, and fashions; 'Must move from grave to gay with ready art, now play the sage's, now the trifler's part.'" Johnson and Addison would be emulated, the editor said, in essays on men and manners designed to "amuse the grave, and detain the idle." Biographies were promised, as were literary criticism, reports on important judicial decisions, and travel narratives. The metaphysician would be accorded space to "spin his cob-webs, and the philosopher have a corner for his theories. Poetry may wing her daring flight" (1, 1: 2). Partisan politics, the editor promised, would be avoided.

The original poetry that appeared in the *Observer* seems at least a bit superior to most other early Southern magazines. Much of its serious poetry was less cloying than the usual run of poetic effusions of the period, as exemplified in "To Laura" (1, 1: 16), "The Tear" (1, 1: 32), and "To a Lady, Who Requested a Description of Love" (1, 6: 96). The verse which was designed to amuse probably did so, as in this brief reflection:

> Which would thee, if the wish were thine,
> Be out of wind, or out of wine?
> Let merchants rule the wind, say I;
> Give me good wine, or let me die!
> Physicians, who are always kind,

> If paid, will try to give you wind—
> But good madeira, while you live,
> If you love me, always give. [1, 20: 320]

Selected verse was also printed, as in the amusing "Copy of verses on Mr. Day, who from his landlord ran-a-way," which began:

> Here Day and night conspir'd a sudden flight,
> For Day, they say is run-a-way by night,
> Day's past and gone, why landlord, where's your rent?
> Did not you see that Day was almost spent?
> Day pawn'd and sold, and put off what he might;
> Tho' it be ne'er so dark, Day will be light . . .
> Day is departed in a mist, I fear;
> For Day is broke, and yet does not appear [1, 3: 48]

The persons who provided most of the *Observer*'s original copy delighted in teasing readers with vague hints as to their identities. The second appearance of a feature called "The Cameleon," by "Thomas Fickle, Esq.," informed the reader that this contributor was a lawyer, not long in practice and "not over-burdened with business," who had the leisure to mingle in the amusements of the town and write anonymously of its citizens' frivolities "without exposing myself to their invective" (1, 7: 97).

The cover page of number 8 presents "Beatrice Ironside" as a woman of thirty who "is neither ugly enough to frighten a fiery courser from his repast, nor handsome enough for the Parson of the Parish to turn aside from his discourse whilst he admires her beauty. In point of years she is old enough to have set aside some of the levities of youth, and young enough to remember that she has had her share of them." She will, it is promised, always laugh at the affected and ridicule the vain and if attacked, will defend herself. "Porcupine like, she will always have a quill ready to dart at those who may assail her."

In "Beatrice Ironside's Budget," on the cover page of number 9, her co-writers are introduced as "Hypathia," of a more grave and pious persuasion than Beatrice; "the Rev. Mr.Supple," a carefree cleric inclined to tipple; and a third contributor identified only as H——, possessing "an extensive acquaintance with elegant literature." "We shall henceforth leave it to the sagacity of our readers," adds the editor, "to discover which of us supplies the literary repast of the day."

Though a considerable variety of serious material appeared in the *Observer*—intelligence from other countries, historical anecdotes, essays on the fine arts, and the like—the magazine's main thrust was entertainment, not information, though this emphasis was not quite as marked as in the earlier Baltimore weekly continued by the *Observer*, which was the *Companion and Weekly Miscellany*, printed by Cole and Hewes and edited in 1804–1805[1] by "Edward Easy, Esquire" ("A Safe Companion and an Easy Friend").

After little more than a year's life, the grim inevitable became apparent, and the editor announced her intention to close the *Observer* and go on to other pursuits. To other tasks I go, she said in the concluding paragraph of the final number, "and therefore bid you the eternal adieu of Beatrice Ironside."

Note

1. November 3, 1804-October 16, 1805. This periodical is also available on American Periodical Series microfilm.

Information Sources

BIBLIOGRAPHY:
McLean, Frank. "Periodicals Published in the South before 1880." Ph.D. dissertation, University of Virginia, 1928. Pp. 15–16.
Mott, Frank Luther. *A History of American Magazines, 1741–1850*. New York, 1930. I: 204.
INDEX SOURCES: None.
LOCATION SOURCES: American Periodicals Series microfilm, Library of Congress.

Publication History

MAGAZINE TITLE AND TITLE CHANGES: *The Observer, and Repertory of Original and Selected Essays, in Verse & Prose, on Topics of Polite Literature, &c.*
VOLUME AND ISSUE DATA: Vols. 1–2 (November 29, 1806-December 26, 1807), weekly.
PUBLISHER AND PLACE OF PUBLICATION: Joseph Robinson, printer and publisher. 4 North Charles-Street, Baltimore, Maryland.
EDITOR: "Beatrice Ironside."
CIRCULATION: Unknown.

OMNIUM BOTHERUM

When a magazine is founded, it is common enough to find another new entry springing up to compete with it for a share of the market. It is rare, however, to find a competitor whose sole purpose is to ridicule the earlier magazine and put it out of business. Such an unusual competitor was *Omnium Botherum; or, Strictures on the Omnium Gatherum*, a Charleston, South Carolina, magazine of 1821.

Omnium Botherum's ridicule was directed at Thomas Bee's weekly, the *Omnium Gatherum*,* also of 1821 Charleston.

Bee's critics fired their initial round in the *Charleston Courier* of July 27, 1821, after having read *Gatherum*'s first two issues. This article was later reproduced in *Omnium Botherum*. Its slashing lead appears below:

We remember to have once heard of an industrious Porter, who, after a protracted life of fruitless and ill-directed labor, died as he had lived, indigent and obscure. He had one consolation, however, with which he was wont to sooth the reflections of his declining years; although it did not effectively minister to the relief of his condition, yet as it derived its elasticity from his vanity and self-love, it mingled no small portion of pride with his poverty. He left the world, it is true, without leaving a ducat behind him; but as he was born for nothing more than to be *a carrier of other men's wares*, and had, in his vocation, sweated under many a goodly pack, he died with the glorious certainty, that had all the lumber which had loaded him in life been set down to his own account, he might have shaken hands with the richest nabob in the land. Such is emphatically the character, and such will for ever be the destiny of all those who float into momentary distinction upon the reputation of others—all compilers of other men's thoughts—collectors of other men's opinions—propagators of other men's sentiments—and retailers of other men's wit—They are literally the hewers of wood and drawers of water, that stand by the well-springs and upon the eminences of literature, wearing the chaplets and adorned with the wreaths that belong to other brows. Unblessed with the possession of genius themselves, they live and breathe in the sunshine of superior minds, and as they pass on through life, gather in a kind of false reputation, in which they strut to their graves, tricked out, like jackdaws, in the golden plumage of more splendid birds. [Reprinted in *Omnium Botherum*, no. 1: 5–6]

The first indictment of *Gatherum*'s editor, then, was for lack of original material, which rendered him, said *Botherum*, "a solemn pretender to honors to which he has no legitimate claim" (no. 1: 7).

Botherum's second criticism was that although Thomas Bee had read and transcribed much, he had transcribed injudiciously, making *Omnium Gatherum*'s first two issues "a manifest incoherent piece of patchwork" (p. 7). Furthermore, he had committed a:

literary hocus-pocus, in which subjects, as remote in character, as they are discordant in connexion, are thrown together like the ingredients with which the gizzled hags in MacBeth compose the 'thick gruel' of their 'charmed pot.' We have a little of everything:

Eye of newt, and toe of frog,
Wool of bat, and tongue of dog,
Adder's fork, and blind worm's sting,
Lizzard's leg, and owlet's wing.

> We have no objection to variety, provided there is consistency in it. . . .
> No man admires the patchwork of a Harlequin's coat, although it has all
> the colors of a rainbow. [*Omnium Botherum*, no. 1: 10]

Bee's detractors also assailed him for pedantic trifling, fondness for the com-
monplace, and "the leaden gravity of sermonizing dullness" (no. 1: 11). Their
final complaint was concerned with violations of the common decencies that
might offend the delicate sensibilities of Charleston womanhood. Scarcely a
page, they wrote, "is not stained with some gross indecency, or rendered loath-
some by some disgusting allusion" (p. 12).

After the third *Gatherum* had been published, and after having leveled its
initial criticisms against the *Gatherum* in the *CharlestonCourier*, the *Omnium
Botherum* made its appearance in magazine form, printed by T. B. Stephens of
Charleston to look as identical to *Omnium Gatherum* as possible. On its cover,
where *Gatherum* ran its three mottos, appeared the following, culled from the
Edinburgh Review of April 1810:

> He who has seen a barn-door fowl flying—and only he—can form some
> conception of this Tutor's eloquence—with his neck and hinder parts brought
> into a line—with loud screams, and all the agony of feathered fatness—
> the ponderous little glutton flaps himself up into the air, and, soaring four
> feet above the level of our earth, falls dull and breathless on his native
> dunghill.

Next in the forty-two page issue was a sort of preface in with the editor and his
supporters claimed that their only purpose was to show *Gatherum*'s editor the
"necessity of a complete revolution in the character of his compendium" and
admitting that in bringing *Botherum* before the public, they, too, like Bee, were
heir to the vanity of seeing one's work "garnished out in a spruce dress of new
type and wire-wove paper," employing the delightful quotation:

> 'Tis pleasant, sure, to see one's name in print,
> A book's a book, altho' there's nothing in't. [*Omnium Botherum*,
>   no. 1: iii-iv]

The *Courier* article, already quoted here at some length, appeared next, followed by two responses to it that had been run in Charleston's *Southern Patriot*
in late July. The first of these was signed by the editor of *Omnium Gatherum*,
the second by "A Plain Man," who argued that the material in *Gatherum* suited
his needs, as he was a plain man of commerce, not a scholar or philosopher,
and that "Little things are great to little men" (p. 21).

Next, the editor of *Botherum*, whom Hoole identifies as Edwin C. Holland,
accuses Bee of having written the "Plain Man" letter himself, which appears
quite likely true. The third number of *Gatherum*, Holland continues, was "ten

times more replete with imperfection'' than the first two, and presents the image of a mind ''thrown into undistinguishable chaos by the worst possible system of education,'' which probably included having been ''stuffed with Latin and Greek at Eton College, or bloated afterwards to a plethora at the literary commons of Oxford University'' (pp. 31–32).

Poor Bee is berated for his ''habitual contempt'' for native literature and his ''slavish admiration'' for the imported article. As to Bee's selection of material, ''Nature seems to have intended him for nothing more than a very plodding, dull and diligent Compiler—a hunter merely in the lower grounds of Literature— and a kind of packing machine to compress and spoil the thoughts of others. . . . The editor of 'The Omnium Gatherum' is as preposterously blind as he is insufferably ignorant'' (pp. 35–36).

Such rough treatment of Bee would seem to indicate that something more than literary cricitism was at work here—something far more personal, but at least the harsh invective was cut by occasional doses of wit, as when *Gatherum* was characterized in verse as:

> ————That motley Magazine
> Of stale severities, and pilfer'd spleen;
> Where *insect* puns their feeble wings expand,
> To speed, in little flights, their lord's command—
> Where, in the paper *chrysalis*, we see
> *Specks* of *bon-mots* and *eggs* of repartee—
> Where Boswell's *chitchat* lives without his sense,
> And *just enough* of Johnson for *offence*. [*Omnium Botherum*, no. 1:
>   37]

The biting comments of Holland, Henry Farmer, William Crafts, and probably other Charlestonians accomplished the desired end; *Omnium Gatherum* was put to rest after only nine numbers. Best available evidence indicates that only one number of *Omnium Botherum* appeared in magazine form, though other *Botherum* copy had been printed earlier in the Charleston *Courier* of July 27, 1821.

Information Sources

BIBLIOGRAPHY:
Hoole, William Stanley. A Check-List and Finding-List of Charleston Periodicals, 1732–
       1864. Durham, N.C., 1936. P. 23.
INDEX SOURCES: None.
LOCATION SOURCES: South Carolina Historical Society (Charleston).

Publication History

MAGAZINE TITLE AND TITLE CHANGES: *Omnium Botherum; or, Strictures on the
       Omnium Gatherum.*

VOLUME AND ISSUE DATA: No. 1 (August 13, 1821) irregular.
PUBLISHER AND PLACE OF PUBLICATION: T. B. Stephens, printer; published by
    Edwin C. Holland, Henry T. Farmer, William Crafts, and probably others;
    Charleston, South Carolina.
EDITOR: Edwin C. Holland.
CIRCULATION: Unknown.

OMNIUM GATHERUM

In June of 1821 Thomas Bee, under the *nom de plume* Papirius Cursor, gave
Charleston, South Carolina, a new miscellany bearing the grand, all-encom-
passing title *Omnium Gatherum*.[1] His hope was that it would be viewed as similar
to the English essay papers so popular in the previous century. A preface to the
first number admitted that virtually all the magazine's contents would be selected
rather than original—the product of the editor's habit of reading and extracting
that which he felt deserved further consideration. "These extracts increased at
length, to an inconvenient bulk," wrote Bee, "and it became a question whether
they should be committed to the flames, or whether a part of them might not,
with some advantage to others, be committed to the press." Noting that he had
first considered the title *Farrago*[2] for his magazine, Bee offered his hope that
his efforts might at least prove useful in increasing the city's stock of "harmless
gaiety."

Charlestonians Edwin Holland, Henry Farmer, William Crafts, and others of
their set were not amused, however, and attacked Bee's efforts in a short-lived
periodical of their own, which they called *Omnium Botherum; or, Strictures on
the Omnium Gatherum*.* According to William Stanley Hoole,[3] *Botherum* put
Gatherum out of business after only nine numbers of the latter had been published.[4]

This most unusual episode of magazine trench warfare long remained obscure;
neither *Gatherum* nor *Botherum* is mentioned in most previously published works
on Southern magazine history. Neither magazine appeared, for example, in Frank
McLean's "Periodicals Published in the South before 1880"[5] or in Gertrude
Gilmer's *Checklist of Southern Periodicals to 1861*.[6]

Reading Hoole's brief comments on these periodicals, one might have assumed
that *Botherum* would be nothing more than fun-filled satire. Such was not the
case. The criticism in *Botherum* was usually deadly serious, even vehement in
places. The motives behind *Botherum* could only be guessed at today, but at
this remove, the object of their vehemence appears innocent enough, if
unexceptional.

Printed and published by Duke & Browne of No. 4 Broad-street in what has
been called in more recent times "digest-size" format (7 1/4″ × 4 1/2″), the
thirty-six page *Gatherum* sold for 25¢ and exhibited three mottos on its cover:

Nihil legebat quod non excerperet[7] — Pliny

Il ne lit rien qui'il ne trouve a en extraire quelque chose.[8]
—Guillaume le frank Parleu

From grave to gay; from lively to severe. —Pope

The first issue made it abundantly clear that Papirius Cursor's taste ran almost exclusively to classical and European literature, and much of his magazine's content was devoted to reflections on marriage and the battle of the sexes, with selections from *Boswell's Life of Johnson*, *Torrent des Passions*, Rousseau, Lord Erskine, Dr. Johnson, Swift, and *Exprit du Mercure*. From the last named of these (volume 1, p. 460) was lifted an eight-line epigram for which the following English translation was provided:

> Bless'd is the man above his kind,
> Whose wife is charming, chaste, refined;
> Possess'd of temper and discretion,
> Humble in thought, mild in expression;
> Whose rhetoric is from the heart,
> Untainted by the sophist's art:
> Happy who such a wife has got!
> As happy he who has her not!! [*Omnium Gatherum*, no. 1: 12]

As the foregoing is indicative, the copy in *Omnium Gatherum* was mainly meant to amuse. Other bits and pieces appearing under such heads as "Grimmiana," "Mile. Guimard and the Curate," "Fontenelle," and "Dialogue between John Wilkes and a Roman Catholic" were similarly lighthearted. Sixteen maxims by Dr. Johnson were included, as were three short pieces of "pop etymology" on the terms "jury-mast," "pic-nic," and "blunderbus."

Bee, struggling against such criticism as few editors have had to endure, began his fourth number with four favorable notices about *Omnium Gatherum* from local newspapers. Bee took care in this issue to print nothing that might offend female sensibilities. The most interesting of its articles for today's reader is an eleven-page piece on the character of William Cobbett, lifted from an unspecified English publication of 1821, in which the writer refers to Cobbett as "a kind of *fourth estate*" in the politics of England (*Omnium Gatherum*, no. 4: 10–20). Toward the end of the issue Bee informs his readers that he had been tempted to change his magazine's title to "The Echo" to thwart his critics, who had written as "Sudorifecum, Catharticum, Emeticum, and last not least Botherum" (*Omnium Gatherum*, no. 4: 32). Addressing *Botherum*'s editor as "Sir Fretful Plagiary," Bee tweaks his critic's nose about the latter's earlier works that had apparently been rejected by the *Analectic Magazine*.

In number 5 Bee attempts to put his detractors behind him by ignoring them. All of number 6 and most of number 7 were devoted to coverage of the literary tiff between Lord Byron and the Rev. W. L. Bowles over the character and talent of Pope. After two further issues, the contents of which were once again miscellaneous, the strictures of economics caught up with *Omnium Gatherum*, and Bee's magazine was no more.

Notes

1. At least two magazines bearing this title had appeared earlier, the first in Boston (November 1809-October 1810), the second in Bath, England, in 1814. A fourth *Omnium Gatherum* was published in New York City from December 1864 until October/November 1866.

2. A medley or mixture.

3. *A Check-List and Finding-List of Charleston Periodicals, 1732–1864* (Durham, N.C., 1936), p. 23.

4. All nine issues of *Gatherum* but only one number of *Botherum* have been secured. What Hoole listed as a *Botherum* dated July 27, 1821, was actually a newspaper article in the *Charleston Courier*. It is possible, then, that the August *Botherum* was the only one in magazine form, and that the September *Botherum* listed by Hoole also appeared in a newspaper.

5. Ph.D. diss., University of Virginia, 1928.

6. Boston, F. W. Faxon Co., 1934.

7. "He read nothing except for the purpose of excerpting it."

8. "In everything he reads, he finds something to extract."

Information Sources

BIBLIOGRAPHY:
Hoole, William Stanley. A Check-List and Finding List of Charleston Periodicals, 1732–1864. Durham, N.C., 1936. P. 23.
INDEX SOURCES: None.
LOCATION SOURCES: South Carolina Historical Society (Charleston).

Publication History

MAGAZINE TITLE AND TITLE CHANGES: *Omnium Gatherum*.
VOLUME AND ISSUE DATA: Nos. 1–9 (June 24-November 1, 1821), irregular.
PUBLISHER AND PLACE OF PUBLICATION: Duke & Brown. No. 4 Broad-street, Charleston, South Carolina.
EDITOR: Thomas Bee ("Papirius Cursor").
CIRCULATION: Unknown.

THE ORION

The *Orion: A Monthly Magazine of Literature, Science and Art* was a Southern magazine of the 1840s that was edited and published in a small Georgia town by a transplanted Englishman, William Carey Richards (1818–1892). Richards and his younger brother, Thomas Addison Richards (1820–1900), were born in London, sons of a Baptist minister who moved his family to America when his boys were adolescents. The Richards brothers' first appearance in Southern periodicals was in William Tappan Thompson's *Augusta Mirror: A Semi-monthly Journal Devoted to Polite Literature, Music, and Useful Intelligence*, published in Augusta, Georgia, 1838–1841. Both brothers contributed poetry and prose, and Thomas, who later became a well-known landscape painter of the Hudson River School, also contributed artwork in the form of a series of scenes entitled "Georgia Illustated."[1] Thompson encouraged William Richards' plans to found his own magazine and even suggested its unusual name, after Orion, the brightest constellation in the Southern hemisphere. It was an optimistic name, an original name, but a name that caused public uncertainty as to its pronounciation. To clear up this matter, the editor ran a happy little poem in his third number:

> Three syllables distinct and clear
> In this euphonious word appear,
> The *first* a single vowel O—
> In full and lengthened tone should flow;
> The *second* is an accented Ri—
> Go ask the ancient classics why;—
> The *third* the lips their skill may try on,
> And thus pronounce the whole ORION! [June 1842, p. 180]

Orion was, according to mythology, the son of Neptune and Queen Euryale, a huntress of the Amazon. He became the greatest hunter in the world before being killed by a scorpion's bite. A well-executed likeness of the hunter holding club and shield adorns the magazine's cover page. "We shall be ambitious to deserve the bright name we have assumed," said Richards in his first "Editor's Department" column, "and with this assurance, gentle reader, we commend us to thy favor" (March 1842, p. 55).

To commemorate the month of the *Orion's* founding, Richards penned two "March Sonnets," a tradition he continued in subsequent monthly issues. "Let us hope," he wrote, "that the rising of our constellation, in a month so gemmed with names of glory, is but a true augury of its waxing and long-continuing-brightness" (March 1842, p. 55). In this same "Editor's Department," Richards notes that though the *Orion's* illustrations, or embellishments,as they were more commonly called in the mid–1800s, were not as numerous as those of some other magazines of the period, "they are at least vastly superior, and indeed in this department . . . we may challenge competition with any American or European work whatever." The drawings for these embellishments were done exclusively by the editor's brother, and their engraving was the work of James Smillie, Esq., "without question the best landscape engraver in the United States." Each plate the magazine used, Richards told his readers, would cost $300.

In the first number, the editor also gives a fraternal nod to three Southern contemporaries, the *Mirror*, the *Magnolia*,* and the *Family Companion*, saying:

We know how hard it is to establish a popular and permanent magazine
. . . we have urged upon our friends the duty of supporting them, and aiding
their projectors in the accomplishment of their common noble aim—the
advancement of literature in the South—we will not say southern literature,
for we have a decided distaste for such local expressions, as if literature
were of different characters in the South and the North. It is the same
everywhere except in degree and tone, and its advancements, its elevation
in the South, is the proper object of our desires and efforts [March 1842,
p. 63]

The literary quality of the *Orion*, said its editor, "will be as elevated as the
best writers of the South with much talent from various parts of the world, can
make it." Its articles, he said, would be strictly original and would measure up
to a high standard. "This practice," he wrote, "will benefit even young writers,
who, since we shall not *stoop* to their standard, will strive to *rise* to ours"
(October 1863, outside back cover). For $3 yearly, in advance, the reader was
promised a monthly magazine of forty-eight to fifty-six pages on history, biography, narrative, philology, ethics, metaphysics, physical science, fiction,
poetry, and the fine arts. "Our aim is not to make a Magazine of Love Tales
and Ghost Stories—the mere froth of Literature—but to contribute to the real
mental wealth of our readers." Further, Richards claimed that his was "the only
magazine in America which publishes original pictures of American Scenery,"
done in Lithotint.

Creditable nature poetry was presented in the *Orion*, and the editor contributed
some fine social commentary in the form of short essays on topics ranging from
dueling to plagiarism to copyright law to country singing. Another of William
Richards' best contributions to his own pages was a series, "Smithville Sketches,"
on Georgia village life of the period. A long sentimental poem that was one of
T. Addison Richards' best contributions in verse was "The Trysting Rock: A
Tale of Tallulah," which was serialized in several early numbers.

The editor avoided political controversy but did not shrink from offering harsh
literary criticism. On one occasion Richards commented, "We have reexamined
the multifarious contents of our 'Drawer for Rejected Beams.' Most of the articles
are more like leaden bars than glittering rays, and must be consigned to the
fire—*en masse*" (September 1842, p. 399). On an earlier occasion he had been
even more blunt in offering "editorial guidance" to young would-be poets:

to the thousand half-fledged bardlings who . . . bring ridicule and contempt
upon the name of poetry by their vile attempts to manufacture rhymes and
stanzas, and who, not content with spoiling whole reams of virgin paper,
and shedding floods of ink in the production of their miserable, senseless
rhymes—must, in the exceeding generosity of their souls, inflict these
rhymes upon some unfortunate editor, obliging him . . . to read the enclosed

verses, distinguished only by long and short lines placed alternately, and each beginning with a capital letter. . . . What a privilege! [May 1842, p. 124]

Not content to leave off at this, the editor, who must have been having a truly excruciating day, proceeded to offer his readers a sample of such poetical effusions ("we should call them *con*fusions," said Richards) in the form of verses sent as the unfortunate poet's admitted "first attempt to the muses" ("we hope he will never make a second effort!") The example was entitled, incredibly, "Lines to the Beautiful Black Eyes of My Cousin Sally"; just as Richards says, the stanzas are quite pathetic. This was not the only occasion on which Richards used his "Editor's Department" to discuss the reasons for rejecting copy, sometimes even identifying the contributor.

Harsh as he could be, and moralizing as he often was, Richards' sense of humor shined through and gave his magazine a pleasant, witty tone more often than not. Keeping to the theme of his hard criticism, apt examples might be this "Epitaph for a Deceased Poetaster":

> Here lies a bard, whose wretched verses ran
> To dark oblivion faster than the man;
> But Death took pity on his hapless lot,
> And now both rhymes and author are forgot. [March 1842, p. 28]

or "Pat and the Author, An Original Irish Bull":

> 'Ye'er writen's so bad,' quoth Patrick the printer
> 'It looks like ye' scratch'd off the lines with a splinter;
> And faith, but I'm shure, I niver shall rade it,
> Till in illegeant type, Sir, I've set and displayed it! [March 1842,
>   p. 23]

It should be mentioned in the *Orion*'s favor that the magazine evidenced interest in all the arts, not just literature. Unlike most magazines of its time, it commented little on the slavery issue. In spite of quality copy on serious subjects, leavened by enough good humor to keep the magazine's contents from becoming impossibly heavy, subscriptions were disappointing. The magazine was abruptly moved to Charleston, South Carolina, in March of 1844, probably in hopes of attracting support from a larger, more affluent, and presumably more cultured public. Advertisements were accepted for the first time, and the subscription price was reduced from $5 to $3 a year. These efforts were of no avail, however, and the magazine was discontinued in August of the same year.

The versatile William Richards went on to edit the *Southern Literary Gazette* at Athens, Georgia, and later Charleston, South Carolina, from 1848 to 1852; became a Baptist minister in 1855; taught chemistry in a medical college; and was awarded a Ph.D. by Colgate University in 1869. T. Addison Richards moved to New York and contributed to *Harper's Magazine* and *Knickerbocker*, wrote several books on art and travel, established himself as a painter, and was a professor of art in New York City.

Notes

1. See Gertrude Gilmer, "A Critique of Certain Georgia Ante Bellum Literary Magazines Arranged Chronologically, and a Checklist," *Georgia Historical Quarterly*, 18 (December 1934): 300.

Information Sources

BIBLIOGRAPHY:
Abney, Beth. "The Orion As a Literary Publication." *Georgia Historical Quarterly*, 48 (December 1964): 411–24.
Gilmer, Gertrude. "A Critique of Certain Georgia Ante Bellum Literary Magazines Arranged Chronologically, and a Checklist." *Georgia Historical Quarterly*, 18 (December 1934): 293–334.
Tucker, Edward L. "Two Young Brothers and Their Orion." *Southern Literary Journal*, 11 (Fall 1978): 64–80.
INDEX SOURCES: None.
LOCATION SOURCES: American Periodical Series microfilm, Library of Congress, Mercer University Library, University of Georgia Library, University of Minnesota Library, University of Texas Library (Austin).

Publication History

MAGAZINE TITLE AND TITLE CHANGES: *The Orion: A Monthly Magazine of Literature, Science, and Art* (vols. 1–2); *The Orion: A Monthly Magazine of Literature and Art* (vol. 3); *The Orion; or, Southern Monthly: A Magazine of Original Literature and Art* (vol. 4).
VOLUME AND ISSUE DATA: Vols. 1–4, no. 6 (March 1842-August 1844), monthly.
PUBLISHER AND PLACE OF PUBLICATION: William Carey Richards. Penfield, Georgia (March 1842-February 1844); Charleston, South Carolina (March-August 1844).
EDITOR: William Carey Richards.
CIRCULATION: Unknown.

OUR LIVING AND OUR DEAD

There are some moments when a nation's heart
    Is wrung with anguish to its inner core
When joy on pinions wild is seen to start
    And its flight to some far distant shore;
    When wailing dirges rise where oft before

The midnight revel rose with noisy glee;
   When million bitter tears are known to pour
   On earth which covers for eternity,
   One of her gallant sons who died to make her free.[1] [July 9, 1873]

These lines aptly describe the feelings in the defeated South that led to the establishment of a number of postbellum literary/historical magazines. One of these reflective periodicals, and probably the one with the most unusual title, was *Our Living and Our Dead*, introduced in Newbern, North Carolina, on July 2, 1873, as a weekly. Its complete title was *Our Living and Our Dead; or, Testimony from the Battle-Fields*, and though it was printed in the four-page folio style of a newspaper and, in fact, referred to itself as a newspaper, its contents were markedly more magazine-like than the typical newspaper of the day due to the predominance of historical material that appeared in it.

Its editor and publisher, Stephen D. Pool, had been a North Carolina artillery colonel and had gone into newspaper journalism after the war, editing and publishing the *Weekly Journal of Commerce* and the *Newbern Journal of Commerce*, a daily.[2] In introducing *Our Living and Our Dead*, Pool explained to his readers that his *Weekly Journal of Commerce* was a political paper "conservative in tone, firm and reliable, but neither denunciatory nor abusive" (July 2, 1873). His new paper, he declared, would be "chiefly devoted to the War Record of North Carolina, but will contain several columns of local, state and general news. Nothing like political discussions will find a place in its columns." He went on to claim that his new periodical was "rapidly securing a circulation *second to none* in the State" and listed its price as $2.00 yearly, in advance, or $3.50 for both weeklies. *Our Living and Our Dead* appeared on Wednesday, the *Weekly Journal of Commerce* on Saturday.

In his first issue Pool offered a 10 percent discount to anyone who would obtain subscriptions from not less than five additional persons, a sales scheme that proved unsuccessful. He claimed an initial subscription list of 1,500 and said that he had subscribers in every North Carolina county, adding:

Our new barque to be freighted with the glorious deeds of *our* living and *our* dead, is fairly launched upon the sea of public opinion, and is seeking its cargo from every county, city, town, hamlet and neighborhood of the Old North State, or of any other State where a native North Carolinian resides. [July 2, 1873]

Under the standing headline "From the Roll of Honor" appeared registers of North Carolina regiments, of historical value, no doubt, but awfully dull reading. Camp and battlefield reminiscences occupied considerable space, as did selections from the wartime journals of Southern ladies. Letters to the editor were given space, as were news items having North Carolina connections. Another content category of this cross between a newspaper and a magazine was poetry, which from the first issue was run in the left-hand column of page 1. The first poem to occupy this space was a tribute by "Luola" to Stonewall Jackson, who had died after a successful battle. One verse read:

With throbbing heart and downcast eye
    Each would in silence turn away
To weep the price for victory paid,
    The cost of this triumphant day.

The poetry that would be run in *Our Living and Our Dead*, said the editor, would be "commemorative of events which occurred during the war, or of the sentiments and feelings of those who participated in it, and memorial sketches in verse of gallant officers and men who fell in battle, or significantly distinguished themselves." Many of these poems had appeared previously in earlier Southern magazines.

Finally, a variety of fairly brief miscellaneous items appeared, many of them borrowed from other U.S. periodicals. In today's terms, this copy might be regarded as feature material, and it included such stories as an accidental boat ride down a wild Colorado river in which two young boys traveled 140 miles in two hours, an article on the nicknames of cities (New Orleans—The Crescent City; Louisville—The Falls City; Nashville—The City of Rocks; Newbern—Elm City; Raleigh—The City of Oaks; etc.), and a paean of praise headlined "Mrs. Robert E. Lee: Her Pedigree and Her Interests at Arlington."

After only three months, *Our Living and Our Dead* was converted into a 128-page monthly which sold for $3 a year and became the official publication of the North Carolina branch of the Southern Historical Society. It was published in Raleigh beginning in September 1874.[3] As associate editors Pool chose writer-editor-author-minister Theodore Bryant Kingsbury and James H. Pool, Editor Pool's brother. Of the two, Kingsbury appears to have been far and away the more talented. The monthly's four departments were the historical and biographical, the descriptive and statistical, the literary, and the editorial. Kingsbury designed a new cover for the monthly, which pictured a Confederate war memorial copied from one in downtown Wilmington, North Carolina. Due to costs, very few other illustrations appeared.

"A Summer Idyl," a story set in the mountains of western North Carolina, was one of the best works serialized in the magazine; its author was Miss Frances C. Fisher ("Christian Reid"). Professor Ray Atchison ranks as the magazine's most outstanding piece of short fiction Theophilus F. Kluttz's "Buried Alive," a tale reminiscent of Poe.[4] Atchison also points out that of this postwar genre of literary/historical magazines, *Our Living and Our Dead* was the most provincial, restricting most of its attention to North Carolina and North Carolinians.

As had been the lot of so many Southern magazines before it, this periodical's subscription list never advanced to a profitable level, and the end came with the March 1876 number. Likely, the sentiments of the editors were similar to those of Fanny Downing, whose poem "Confederate Grey" appeared in the magazine's early Newbern days:

> You're like your master, worn and old,
>   And scarred with wounds, my suit of grey;
> I'll smooth you free of crease and fold,
>   And lay you tenderly away.
>
> But ere I hide you from my sight—
>   Forgetting all that's lost and gone—
> Let me recall the visions bright,
>   I saw when first I drew you on. [July 9, 1873]

Notes

1. The commemorative poem from which this verse was extracted was "General S. D. Ramseur" by "Pelloy."

2. Pool also edited the *Southern Historical Monthly* (Raleigh, 1876–77?) and the *North Carolina Journal of Education* (Raleigh, 1874–75?).

3. The magazine's full title was altered to read *Our Living and Our Dead: Devoted to North Carolina—Her Past, Her Present, and Her Future.*

4. "Our Living and Our Dead: A Post-Bellum North Carolina Magazine of Literature and History," *North Carolina Historical Review*, 40 (1963): 431.

Information Sources

BIBLIOGRAPHY:
Atchison, Ray M. "Our Living and Our Dead: A Post-Bellum North Carolina Magazine of Literature and History," *North Carolina Historical Review*, 40 (1963): 423–33.

INDEX SOURCES: None.

LOCATION SOURCES: Library of Congress, Newberry Library (Chicago), New York Public Library, University of North Carolina Library (Chapel Hill), University of Texas Library (Austin), Yale University Library.

Publication History

MAGAZINE TITLE AND TITLE CHANGES: *Our Living and Our Dead; or, Testimony from the Battle-Fields* (July 2, 1873-August 5, 1874); *Our Living and Our Dead: Devoted to North Carolina—Her Past, Her Present, and Her Future* (September 1874-March 1876).

VOLUME AND ISSUE DATA: Vols. 1–2, no. 5 (July 2, 1873-August 5, 1874), weekly; Vols. 1–4, no. 1 (September 1874-March 1876), monthly.

PUBLISHER AND PLACE OF PUBLICATION: Stephen D. Pool (Newbern, North Carolina, July 2, 1873-August 5, 1874); North Carolina Branch, Southern Historical Society (Raleigh, North Carolina, September 1874-March 1876).

EDITOR: Stephen D. Pool.

CIRCULATION: About 2,000.

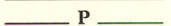

P

PALM BEACH LIFE

Of all the magazines published on the east coast of the United States, Florida's *Palm Beach Life* probably appeals to the most exclusive audience—23,000 subscribers whose mean annual income is an impressive $145,260. Following the lead of St. Augustine's *Tatler of Society in Florida** (1892–1908), *Palm Beach Life* was founded in December 1906 for the entertainment of the wealthy. Like the *Tatler*, the later magazine was originally published only during the "season"—from January until April. Its founder was Englishman Richard Overend Davies, who had the backing of South Florida's legendary developer, Henry Morrison Flagler. Until 1945 the magazine was published as a weekly, then as a semimonthly. Later, frequency edged up to ten issues yearly, then eleven, and in 1980 it went monthly.

Flagler (1830–1913) was co-founder of the Standard Oil Company and before zeroing in on Palm Beach, had built St. Augustine in northern Florida into a posh resort. In the early 1890s he decided to build a railroad along the Indian River to Miami, and in 1894 his 540-room Royal Poinciana Hotel opened to house the likes of John Jacob Astor, Admiral George Dewey, Harold Vanderbilt, and Henry P. Whitney. Two additions later, the Royal Poinciana had 1,150 rooms and was the world's largest wood building. Flagler then built an oceanfront hotel, the Palm Beach Inn, which burned in 1903 but was rebuilt as The Breakers. The boom was on, and *Palm Beach Life* has chronicled most of it.

In the magazine's pages one can read about the institutions of this gilded town—Bradley's Beach Club, Florida's answer to Monte Carlo, where America's fiscal elite and imported continental croupiers came together for mutual enjoyment; the Beaux Arts Theater, scene of innumerable movie premiers in the 1920s; the Paramount Theater, which opened in 1927 with *Beau Geste*; The Everglades Club; The Society of the Four Arts; the Round Table speaker series; The Norton

Gallery of Art; the Henry Morrison Flagler Museum; the Palm Beach Playhouse; the Seminole Golf Club; and later the Palm Beach Opera and Palm Beach Festival. Society watchers and those given to what might be more accurately termed "wealth watching" should find the seventy-seven years of *Palm Beach Life* a font of endless fascination. Other readers might find the accounts of galas, yachts, nine-course dinners, golf tournaments and polo matches, thirty-carat diamonds, and grande dames cloyingly opulent, all to be wealth overwhelming reason. One might be tempted to view as wretched excess any man's need for a forty-car garage, a feature of Edward Stotesbury's Palm Beach home, El Mirasol.

Even so, the fabulous characters who have peopled the pages of this magazine make for undeniably tempting reading: financier Otto Kahn; Barbara Hutton; Joseph Widener, founder of Hialeah racetrack; the Duke and Duchess of Windsor; Marjorie Merriweather Post; Consuelo Vanderbilt; radio pioneer Atwater Kent; Gurnee Munn of the Wannamaker department store family; polo star Winston Guest; Evalyn Walsh McLean; Henry Carnegie Phipps; auto maker Walter Chrysler; Dr. Aldo Gucci; Joseph Kennedy; William Randolph Hearst—the merest sample from a glittering universe.

In 1910 Ruby Edna Pierce became editor. "Miss Ruby," who believed in packing the magazine with as much society news as possible, remained in this post until 1954, directing coverage of activities in the major hotels, clubs, restaurants, shops, and yacht basins, and reporting on the owners of the island's "cottages," a dysphemism for the opulent private homes of Palm Beach. Edward Stotesbury's "cottage" had 147 rooms, for example; Marjorie Post's Mar-a-Lago had 115. Miss Ruby guided the magazine through the Roaring Twenties, the more subdued era of the Great Depression, and World War II, when Palm Beach suffered through a golf-ball shortage and some hotels and clubs were given over to the war effort. During the forties the magazine ran a column entitled "Resorters in the Armed Forces."

In April 1948 Oscar G. Davies, son of the founder, sold *Palm Beach Life* to John H. Perry, Sr., of Perry Publication Inc., whose firm managed the magazine until 1960, when Donald S. Greenlief took over for a one-year term as publisher. Greenlief was followed by Cecil B. Kelly, who directed the magazine until the mid–1970s.

In the 1960s color photography began to be used, and the magazine broadened its coverage to Miami, New York, and other cities frequented by its highly affluent, mobile readership. In July 1969 the magazine was bought by Cox Enterprises, which is still owner, though the company's name appears nowhere in the magazine. Under Cox ownership, more travel stories were used, as were more celebrity interviews and articles on gourmet foods. In 1970 the magazine added a horoscope column, "The Stars and You." The column still appears and is of droll interest because it is written especially for the well-to-do. Sample entries appearing in one issue begin:

Libra: You are not a social climber by nature, but associating with the right people is going to play an important part in your life.

Taurus: Delaying your move to your winter home has made you irritable. [75, 11: 150–51]

Other regular departments in today's *Palm Beach Life* are a crossword puzzle by William Lutwiniak; "First Editions," a book-review column conducted by Alden Whitman; a health column called "In Good Shape"; Charles Calhoun's column, "The Wine Mystique"; "Days and Nights," a listing of theater, music, dance, and other area entertainments; "Distinctive Dining," a listing and gentle review of local restaurants ranging all the way from Hamburger Heaven to the Cafe L'Europe; and Shannon Donnelly's "Cottage Colony" on society activities, illustrated with small black-and-white photos and peppered with Biddles, Newhouses, Sarnoffs, McLeans, Kellogs, Guests, Shrivers, etc.

From time to time the world's great hotels are profiled, and travel or travel/ history features appear. An example of the latter is a well-written piece on "Monsieur Eiffel's Extraordinary Tower" (69, 6: 44–45, 52–53) built in 1889 by A. G. Eiffel, who also built the first wind tunnel.

A noteworthy historical article closer to home was "Worth Avenue: The Start of a New Era" (77, 1: 4, 6, 10, 12, 14, 18, 20, 22–24, 26, 28, 30, 32, 34–36, 38W) on the contributions to Palm Beach of Paris Singer, son of the sewing machine tycoon, and Addison Mizner. The article is illustrated with photos of celebrity visitors: Andy Warhol, Ann Margaret, Warren Burger, Zsa Zsa Gabor, Jackie Onassis, Ted Kennedy, King Hussein, Cary Grant, plus regulars of the Old Guard: Jean Flagler Matthews (Henry Flagler's granddaughter), Pete Widener, and others.

Personality profiles, such as one of tenor Placido Domino (77, 3: 86–87, 120, 122, 124, 126, 128), appear, as do house-and-garden features and trendy art pieces with titles like "Post-Modern Art Goes Public" (75, 11: 58–63). Food articles are used, such as one suggesting roast duckling marinated in lemon juice and honey for Thanksgiving dinner (75, 11: 79, 138), and articles on the area's flora and fauna appear, as in a special foldout feature on Florida's turtles (77, 2: 113–16).

Upscale sports news articles address the Gucci Cup Internationale, the Piaget World Cup and other polo competitions, the Palm Beach Classic Horse Show, and the National Club Team Croquet Tournament. Feature articles on steeplechase racing and croquet (originally called *paille-maille*) are used. Most issues include fashion features, the models for which are posed with that carefully modulated ennui that bespeaks wealth, or at least the way fashion photographers imagine the wealthy might look if they looked that good.

Opportunities for grand gestures in acquisition merit space, as with ex-managing editor Ava Van de Vater's article on a forthcoming auction at Christie's of the splendid jewelry collection of Florence Gould (77, 2: 81–85). Part of the collection was displayed by having the choicest pieces modeled by prominent ladies of Palm Beach society, some of whom were a decided improvement over the lank professional models that usually fill this role.

With its ultra-affluent readership, the magazine has always enjoyed good advertising support. Innumerable bank ads picture silver-haired bankers with dependable Rock of Gibraltar features. Gucci and Van Cleef & Arpels jewelry; fashion from Saks Fifth Avenue, Richilene, Bonwit Teller, Givenchy, and Harold Grant; watches by Piaget; Razook's furs; Boehm porcelain; Mussallem Oriental rugs; Ferrari automobiles—all are advertised here, as are condominium developments, such as Sailfish Point, where the units start at $400,000, and such developments as The Sanctuary, where homes sell from $600,000 to $3 million. Luxury hotels, yacht builders and yacht dry dock service, art dealers, fine restaurants, antique dealers, interior designers, and other businesses that appeal to the affluent also advertise.

The magazine, now as much as 180 pages per issue, is beautifully printed and is well laid out with one exception—the irritating number of "jumps" that hopscotch the reader of its feature articles. The apparent causes of these frequent jumps are economy in placing color ads and the management's desire to create an "editorial well" for feature articles. About 90 percent of articles are freelanced as opposed to staff written, according to the new editor, Anne Wholf, whose correct title is "editorial and design director."[1]

For $2.50 a copy or $20.00 for a year's subscription, readers of *Palm Beach Life* get a quality product reflecting a six-square-mile world that is luxurious to a fault. The usual magazine term "upscale" pales.

Note

1. Telephone conversation with the author, May 23, 1984.

Information Sources

BIBLIOGRAPHY:
Furstinger, Nancy. "Turning Back the Pages." *Palm Beach Life*, December 1981.
Rout, Lawrence. "The Special Business of 'Elite' Magazines Is to Flatter the Rich." *Wall Street Journal*, July 22, 1980.
INDEX SOURCES: None.
LOCATION SOURCES: None.

Publication History

MAGAZINE TITLE AND TITLE CHANGES: *Palm Beach Life*.
VOLUME AND ISSUE DATA: Vols. 1–77 (December 1906-present), weekly for the Palm Beach Season: January-March (1906–1944); semimonthly January-March (1945–1954); eight times a year: semimonthly January-March, monthly July and August (1955–1961); ten times a year: monthly November-August (1962–1967); eleven times a year: monthly with September and October combined (1968–1979); monthly (1980-present).

PUBLISHER AND PLACE OF PUBLICATION: Richard O. Davies (1906–1925); Oscar G. Davies (1925–1948); John H. Perry (1948–1960); Donald S. Greenlief (1960–1961); Cecil B. Kelly (1962–1975); Daniel J. Mahoney (1975–1976); Agnes Ash (1976-present). Palm Beach, Florida.
EDITORS: Richard O. Davies (1906–1910); Ruby Edna Pierce (1910–1954); Thomas E. Penick (1955–1961); Toni Veverka (1962–1969); Martha Parrish (1969–1972); Martha Musgrove (1972–1975); Kathryn Robinette (1975–1978); Christopher Salisbury (1978–1979); Ava Van de Water (1979–1984); Anne Wholf (1984-present).
CIRCULATION: 23,000.

THE PLANTATION

The *Plantation: A Southern Quarterly Journal* is not included in this selection of Southern periodicals as much for the periodical itself as for the man who founded and edited it. Having been published in 1860, it was not one of Georgia's early magazines,[1] nor is it demonstrably one of the state's best; yet its editor, Joseph Addison Turner, was a rare individual who was in some ways symbolic of the ante bellum South and of an era in which magazine publishing was still an intensely personal business.

The versatile Turner—teacher, lawyer, legislator, farmer—was also a man with literary aspirations. Two of his books were collections of verse;[2] between the two he published a modest literary magazine entitled *Turner's Monthly*[3] (1848) and another periodical called *Red Lion* (1849).[4] In 1850 Turner married a wealthy Eatonton woman and bought a nearby plantation, which he christened Merry Dale. When his younger brother took over the Turner family plantation and began calling it "Turnwold," Turner, whose new property adjoined it, discontinued Merry Dale; henceforth both properties were known as Turnwold.

In 1853 a long satirical poem of Turner's, "The Times," was published in book form by Charles B. Norton of New York City, who then refused to market it for fear of a libel suit. That same year saw the birth and hasty demise of another Turner magazine, the *Tomahawk*. As in the case of the *Red Lion*, no known copies remain. The only evidence of their existence is Turner's *Journal*, a microfilmed copy of which is in the Emory University Library in Atlanta.

Finally, in 1860, came Turner's best periodical effort to date, the *Plantation*, a quarterly patterned after the prestigious *North American Review*. In his second number (June 1860), Turner explains his unusual arrangement with Messrs. Pudney and Russell of New York City to publish his oh-so-Southern magazine:

In the first place, it takes the labor of publication off our hands, and leaves us more time to devote to the editorial department of this journal. No one man is adequate to the task of editing and publishing a quarterly—happy he is if adequate to the task of either editing or publishing. In the next place, the *Plantation* is published by a house which has all the appliances, and all the machinery, for pushing out this journal into a circulation in a section where it is most needed to combat abolitionism. [Pp. 500–501]

He would have otherwise preferred, he said, to have it printed in Georgia but had been unable to come to a satisfactory agreement with the two in-state newspapers he had earlier approached. Better equipment and cheaper labor and materials in the North, Turner said, caused him to arrange for printing there "in order to prevent our journal from sharing the death which has heretofore generally been allotted to Southern magazines."

Uncertainties over printing arrangements had caused the March number to be delayed until May and the June number to appear in July. The contract with Pudney and Russell regularized his schedule until the onset of hostilities in 1861, which gave the magazine its premature death.

Turner's approach to his own magazine's content can be seen in comments run in the June 1860 number regarding the "changing of the guard" taking place at the *Southern Literary Messenger** in Richmond. John R. Thompson was retiring as editor and Dr. George W. Bagby was replacing him and had announced his intention to illustrate the *Messenger* more profusely. ("As the devil must be fought with fire, so must the Northern papers and periodicals be fought with pictures, and we intend to do it.") Of this move to popularize the distinguished *Messenger*, Turner writes:

> The Doctor is wise. Of what avail is the strength of the eagle's wing if he has not the element upon which to poise his noble pinion? What availeth the lofty thought of princes in the dominions of intellect, if there is no medium through which to communicate with the people? What does a magazine amount to without a long list of subscribers and readers? [P. 500]

Some of the *Plantation*'s contents addressed interesting individuals: "William H. Seward As a Schoolmaster in Georgia," "Edgar A. Poe," "Barnum and Burnham; or, Swindlers' Self-made Heroes." Some were heavily Southern in one way or another: "Two or Three of Mr. Spratt's Slave-Trade Arguments," "What Is Slavery?" and "Walter Early's Love for His Cousin, Cleopatra Clare."

Perhaps the most bizarre and unexpected item Turner himself wrote for the magazine was a five-act farce called "Julius Sneezer." Much of the *Plantation*'s content, in fact, was penned by Turner, incuding a good many poems and a number of so-so short stories, but the most enduring work he did for this magazine was a series called "The Old Farm-House of My Uncle Simon; or, Sketches of Southern Life," which appeared in the March, June, and September issues. The sketches are peopled with Southern archetypes: Aunt Parmela, the thrifty, resourceful plantation mistress; Emily, the Southern belle; Dorothy, the old maid; Aristides, the professional bachelor; and several others. These sketches, thirty-seven in all, are done from the point of view of young Abraham Goosequill.

Their importance lies in the insights they offer into plantation life. As Lawrence Huff [5] points out, Turner was inspired to do these sketches by Washington Irving's *Bracebridge Hall*; both works romanticize country life—Irving's the English manor and Turner's the Southern plantation.

Though Turner's *Plantation* ended with the Civil War, he returned to magazine editing again in 1862 with his *Countryman*.*

Notes

1. At least seventy-seven nonnewspaper periodicals preceded it, the first in Georgia being the *Georgia Analytical Repository* of Savannah (1802–3).

2. *Kemble's Poems* (1847) was the first; no copies are extant. The second was *The Discovery of Sir John Franklin, and Other Poems* (Athens, Ga., 1858).

3. Three numbers were published. A partial file of *Turner's Monthly* is available at the Atlanta Historical Society.

4. Only the first number was published; none has survived.

5. Lawrence Huff, "The Literary Publications of Joseph Addison Turner," *Georgia Historical Quarterly*, 46 (1962): 229.

Information Sources

BIBLIOGRAPHY:
Huff, Lawrence. "The Literary Publications of Joseph Addison Turner." *Georgia Historical Quarterly*, 46 (1962): 223–36.
INDEX SOURCES: None.
LOCATION SOURCES: Boston Public Library, Duke University Library, Emory University Library, Library of Congress, University of Georgia Library.

Publication History

MAGAZINE TITLE AND TITLE CHANGES: *The Plantation: A Southern Quarterly Journal*.
VOLUME AND ISSUE DATA: Vols. 1–2 (March-December 1860), quarterly.
PUBLISHER AND PLACE OF PUBLICATION: Joseph Addison Turner, (Eatonton, Georgia) and Pudney & Russell (79 John Street, New York City).
EDITOR: Joseph Addison Turner.
CIRCULATION: Unknown.

A POLITICAL, HISTORICAL, BIOGRAPHICAL, AND LITERARY REPOSITORY. *See* NATIONAL MAGAZINE (1799)

THE PORTICO

A true heavyweight among early Baltimore magazines was the *Portico: A Repository of Science & Literature*, an eighty-page monthly of considerable dignity, worth, and reputation.[1] Founded in January 1816 by Dr. Tobias Watkins[2] and brother-in-law Stephen Simpson, who referred to themselves in their masthead as "Two Men of Padua," the magazine derived its name from the columned porticos of Classical Athens where poets, philosophers, statesmen, and orators met and exchanged ideas. What the editors of the *Portico* longed for was a blossoming of a distinctly American literature with "Taste once more pure, Wit aiming her shafts at folly, Wisdom denouncing turpitude, and Genius crowned with perfection" (1, 1: iii).

These grand aims had emerged in a Baltimore that at this time expected to become America's premier city, culturally as well as financially. The years immediately following the War of 1812 were marked by patriotism and chauvinism, and the literati of Baltimore saw themselves as occupying an excellent position for furthering a fresh, new American literature divorced from the nation's earlier dependence on European letters. "Dependence," said Watkins and Simpson, "whether literary or political, is a state of degradation, fraught with disgrace; and to be dependent on a foreign mind, for what we can ourselves produce, is to add to the crime of indolence, the weakness of stupidity" (1, 1: iii-iv).

Toward this end, and doubtless for pure enjoyment as well, Baltimore gentlemen who shared these literary aspirations formed The Delphian Club, whose members contributed to the *Portico* and later Baltimore magazines. The club's membership included novelist John Neal, Francis Scott Key, Edward Pinkney, John P. Kennedy, William Wirt, John Pierpont, William Gwynn, Paul Allen, Jared Sparks, and Rembrant Peale.

In their prospectus the editors accurately assess the difficulties that faced their new venture, saying, "When every variety of literary enterprise has long ceased to be a novelty to American readers; when every thing has been attempted, and almost every thing has miscarried; it will naturally be inquired, whether the authors of a new Literary project come better prepared to command success, whether they possess more exhaustless materials." The key to success, they felt, was variety, and they promised that "the entertaining narrative, and the profound dissertation, will be equally regarded" (1, 1: 1-4).

Their contents were distributed into four main departments: "The Review," which presented original and selected literary criticism; "The Chronicle," a record of national facts, presented without party favor; "The Repository," almost exclusively original poetry; and "The Miscellany," which contained letters and essays on biography, travel, religion,and science.

As did many other early magazines, the *Portico* helped set its tone by means of a motto, which appeared in its masthead. Until volume 4 the motto used lines from Akenside:

> Different minds
> Incline to different objects; one pursues
> The vast alone, the wonderful, the wild;

> Another sighs for harmony and grace
> And gentlest beauty.
> Such and so various are the tastes of men.

With the first issue of volume 4 the motto was changed to four excellent lines borrowed from Pope:

> With mean complacence ne'er betray your trust,
> Nor be so civil as to prove unjust.
> Fear not the anger of the wise to raise;
> Those best can bear reproof who merit praise.

That the editors took seriously Pope's injunction not to "be so civil as to prove unjust" is often reflected in the severity of the magazine's literary criticism, as in these comments on *Narrative of a Journey in Egypt, and the Country Beyond the Cataracts*, by Thomas Legh (Philadelphia, 1817):

> The volume has, at least, one thing to recommend it—its brevity. If we gain but little information from its perusal, we cannot complain that it imposes a very severe tax upon our time. Authors, in general, are too apt to consider their readers as a species of intellectual dray-horses, upon whom they may lay the heaviest burdens. [5, February/March 1818: 1]

The *Portico* was typical of early Southern magazines in that it lags well behind its Northeastern competitors in the use of illustrations. Aside from two handsome engravings by George Fairman of Philadelphia that adorned volume 1, illustrations appeared with great rarity.

Heaviest of all the magazine's contributors were Editor Simpson and the prolific John Neal.[3] With their fellow Delphians, they filled the *Portico*'s pages with copy of solid quality until its demise in 1818 and made the magazine, as Marshall Fishwick once aptly put it, "a busy nurse to the infant that was American literature."[4]

Notes

1. Writing in the *William and Mary Quarterly* in 1951, Marshall Fishwick cites an article in the *Edinburgh Magazine* of August 1815, p. 91, that named the *The Portico*, the *Port Folio* (Philadelphia), the *Analectic Magazine* (Philadelphia), and the *North American Review* (Boston) as the best magazines in the United States.

2. Dr. Watkins had already edited the *Baltimore Medical and Physical Recorder* (1809–10), which is available on American Periodical Series microfilm. After the *The Portico* was discontinued, Watkins became assistant surgeon general of the United States.

3. See Neal's autobiography, *Wandering Recollections of a Somewhat Busy Life* (1869), as well as his novels, which included *Logan*(1822), *Errata* (1823), *Seventy-Six* (1823), *Randolph* (1823), *Brother Jonathan* (1825), and *The Down-Easters* (1833).

4. Fishwick, "The Portico and Literary Nationalism," p. 244.

Information Sources

BIBLIOGRAPHY:

Edgar, Neal L. *A History and Bibliography of American Magazines, 1810–1820*. Metuchen, N.J., 1975. P. 220.

Fishwick, Marshall W. "*The Portico* and Literary Nationalism after the War of 1812." *William and Mary Quarterly*, 1951, pp. 238–45.

McCloskey, J. C. "A Note on the Portico." *American Literature*, 8 (1936): 300–304.

————. "The Campaign of Periodicals after the War of 1812 for National American Literature." *Publications of the Modern Language Association*, March 1935, pp. 262–73.

Mott, Frank Luther. *A History of American Magazines, 1741–1850*. New York, 1930. I: 204, 293–96.

INDEX SOURCES: None.

LOCATION SOURCES: American Antiquarian Society (Worcester, Massachusetts), Duke University Library, Georgetown University Library, Harvard University Library, Library of Congress, New York Public Library, University of North Carolina Library (Chapel Hill).

Publication History

MAGAZINE TITLE AND TITLE CHANGES: *The Portico: A Repository of Science & Literature*.

VOLUME AND ISSUE DATA: Vols. 1–4, no. 4/6 (January 1816-April/June 1818), monthly. (July-December 1817 in three double issues, January-June 1818 in two quarterly issues.)

PUBLISHER AND PLACE OF PUBLICATION: Neale Wills & Cole (1816); E. J. Coale and Cushing and Jewett (1817–1818). Baltimore, Maryland.

EDITORS: Dr. Tobias Watkins and Stephen Simpson (January 1816-June 1817); Tobias Watkins (July 1817-June 1818).

CIRCULATION: Unknown.

THE PROGRESSIVE FARMER

By the early 1960s the *Progressive Farmer* of Birmingham, Alabama, founded in 1886, could claim the largest circulation[1] of any farm magazine in the South and first place in advertising lineage among all U.S. farm magazines. Though down from those heights, the venerable *Farmer* is still a powerful force in agricultural publishing, its influence extending well outside the South.

The magazine's founder was Leonidas LaFayette Polk, who had been reared on a farm in Anson County, North Carolina, served in that state's legislature in 1860 and 1861, and saw active duty in the Civil War.[2] During Reconstruction he converted his farm into a town, Polkton, and in April 1874 began publishing his own newspaper, the *Ansonian*, which he used as a vehicle to argue for the establishment of a state department of agriculture. In this he was successful and was named the state's first commissioner of agriculture in 1877. He resigned in

1880, and after trying his hand at a number of jobs, including selling a patent medicine called Polk's Diptheria Cure in Boston and New York, began the *Progressive Farmer* in Winston, North Carolina, on February 10, 1886. The four-page, statewide weekly, done in newspaper format, was devoted to "the industrial and educational interests of our people paramount to all other considerations of state policy." Its editor/publisher promised that his farm journal would "speak with no uncertain voice, but will fearlessly the right defend, and impartially the wrong condemn."

The *Progressive Farmer*'s pages contained articles on farming, export figures, voluminous correspondence from readers, recipes, brief news items of interest to rural North Carolinians, and even poetry. Advertising support was adequate from the start. Editorial space was used to speak for two primary concerns: reorganization of the state's department of agriculture and establishment of an agricultural and mechanical college, as well as campaigning for better rural roads, crop diversification, and the other usual concerns of farm publishers. Polk's efforts were an important factor in the chartering in 1887 of the North Carolina College of Agriculture and Mechanic Arts, now North Carolina State University.

In April 1887 the periodical was moved to Raleigh, and soon thereafter it became the official organ of the 42,000-member North Carolina Farmer's Alliance. In July 1888 it was also made the organ of Virginia's Farmers' Alliance. The regular subscription price of $2 was reduced to $1 for alliance members, and circulation grew rapidly, from 1,200 in July 1887 to 11,760 in January 1890, with subscribers in roughly two-thirds of the states of the union.[3] Polk was thrust into national prominence in late 1889 when he was elected president of the National Farmers' Alliance and Industrial Union; he moved to Washington, D.C., and edited the *Progressive Farmer* from there during 1890–1892 with the editorial help of J. L. Ramsey and Baylus Cade in Raleigh. In 1892 there was talk of running Polk as the People's Party candidate for the U.S. presidency, and in June of that year Polk resigned from his editorship to keep the journal nonpartisan and for health reasons. His sudden death was announced on page 2 of the June 14 issue of the *Progressive Farmer*.

The farm paper was continued in much the same format under the ownership of Polk's widow, with J. L. Ramsey as editor and J. W. Denmark as business manager. An interesting new feature during this period was "Zeke Billings, M.A.," political commentary written in crackerbarrel style in the form of telephone conversations between farmer Billings and editor Ramsey. Circulation declined somewhat, but in 1896 the paper became the national organ of the Farmers' Alliance and Industrial Union.

In May of 1897 a sixteen-year-old farm boy named Clarence Poe was employed as assistant editor, and on July 4, 1899, the talented youth became editor. In the interim the paper placed considerable emphasis on politics, devoting much space to coverage of the Spanish-American War. Despite his tender age, Poe editorialized effectively against trusts and lynchings and pioneered the sale of books as a means of improving the *Progressive Farmer*'s profit picture. Due to

Poe's fondness for poetry, the verse content of the paper also increased during this period; Poe's personal favorite was Edwin Markham's "The Man with the Hoe," which appeared in the *Farmer* in 1899. This period also saw the reorganization of the "Home Department" under L. L. Polk's daughter, Mrs. Juanita Polk Denmark, who wrote about rural family life under the pen name "Aunt Jennie."

After becoming editor, Poe steered the paper away from partisan politics and restressed its role as an agricultural periodical. The new editor argued for better education in rural areas, more funding for rural school libraries, improved facilities for Raleigh's Agricultural and Mechanical College, and rural free mail delivery.

Mrs. L. L. Polk, sole owner of the *Progressive Farmer*, died in June 1901, and in August of the same year, Business Manager J. W. Denmark bought the periodical from her estate, expanding the *Farmer*'s size from eight to sixteen pages. In December 1903 Denmark sold out to Clarence H. Poe and four backers[4] for $6,000 plus the journal's liabilities. Together the buyers constituted the shareholders of the Agricultural Publishing Company, with Poe as its president.

In 1908 Bailey, Burkett, and Parker sold their shares in the company to Dr. Tait Butler and John S. Pearson. Butler had edited and published the *Southern Farm Gazette* in Starkville, Mississippi, and after he joined Poe's company, the Starkville periodical was purchased, which boosted circulation to 38,000 and gave the *Progressive Farmer* an Eastern edition (for the Carolinas and Virginia) and a Western edition (for Mississippi, Arkansas, and Louisiana), apparently a first in farm periodical publishing. In 1911 the headquarters of the firm was moved from Raleigh to Birmingham, Alabama, and the company's name was changed to The Progressive Farmer Company soon thereafter. A third edition was added upon the purchase of the *Texas Farmer*. Also absorbed before 1920 were the *Carolina Farmer*, *Southern Fancier*, *Tennessee Farmer*, and *Southern Farming*; by 1920 circulation stood at 227,000. Two more regional editions appeared, and by 1930 circulation had reached 618,000. This impressive period of growth was capped in 1930 by a merger with the *Southern Ruralist*, which boosted circulation to more than one million. The periodical went bimonthly in 1931 and was published monthly in magazine format beginning in 1932. Eugene Butler succeeded Poe as editor in 1958 and was in turn succeeded in 1982 by C. G. Scruggs.

Company management shrewdly foresaw that as the years passed, fewer Americans would be farming, and in 1966 a new magazine was spun off from the *Progressive Farmer*. The profitable newcomer, *Southern Living*,* provided a cultural link between the tremendous number of Southerners who had left farm or rural settings for more urban or suburban lifestyles, and its circulation soared in ten years from 200,000 to 1,300,000. The same trend has caused a decline in the *Progressive Farmer*'s circulation, around 573,000 in 1984. The magazine sells mainly in a sixteen-state area and currently has regional editors for the Southwest, Midsouth, Southeast, Upper South, Central, and Midwest states.

Another addition to the firm's magazine stable was *Decorating & Craft Ideas*, purchased in 1974 from the Tandy Corporation, owners of Radio Shack. In 1969 the parent firm expanded into book publishing through its Oxmoor House division, which started with cookbooks and volumes on travel and gardening. Big-selling coffee-table books from Oxmoor have been *Jericho, the South Beheld* (1974), *A Southern Album* (1975), and *The World of Bob Timberlake* (1979).

Other activities under the aegis of Chairman and President Emory Cunningham is Akra Data, the firm's data-processing operation; a travel division; and an insurance division. In 1981 the company name was changed to the Southern Progress Corporation.

Today's *Progressive Farmer*,[5] averaging about 130 pages per issue, is filled with the kinds of articles one would expect in any farm magazine—"Soil Insecticides Perk Up Yields," "What Cotton Regions Want in the Next Farm Bill," "How Much Is a Good Bull Worth?" and the like, but at the same time its contents look current: "What Kind of Neighbors Are Foreign Landowners?" or "Computer Records Keep Him Organized." Ads for fancy Nocona Boots vie for space with those for Digital or Radio Shack's Agri Star On-Farm computers that come with special agribusiness software. Farmers in once remote areas now read *Progressive Farmer* articles from its "Country Living" section on backyard satellite dish antennas. Most of the illustrations that accompany the editorial copy are in black and white; only a few per number are in four-color. All in all, the *Progressive Farmer* is an intensely practical magazine, but it is an attractive brand of practicality.

Notes

1. Around 1,400,000 in 1962.

2. After being wounded at Gettysburg, Polk was again elected to the North Carolina legislature in 1865.

3. See William D. Poe, Jr., "*The Progressive Farmer*, 1886–1903" (Master's thesis, University of South Carolina, 1971), p. 48.

4. The four were Dr. B. W. Kilgore, director of North Carolina's State Experiment Station; Dr. Charles W. Burkett, head of the agriculture program at A & M College; T. B. Parker of the North Carolina Farmer's Alliance; and J. W. Bailey, editor of the *Biblical Recorder*.

5. The word *The* was dropped from the magazine's nameplate in 1973.

Information Sources

BIBLIOGRAPHY:

Cunningham, Emory. "The Progressive Farmer Co. Found the '70s a Decade of Soaring Growth in Many Ways." *Birmingham News*, January 6, 1980.

"Emory Cunningham Is National 'Magazine Publisher of Year.'" *Vestavia Sun*, 1976.

"Grown Up at Seven." *Birmingham News*, April 7, 1972.

Lazarus, Geroge. "*Progressive Farmer* Deep in Pay Dirt." *Chicago Tribune*, November 26, 1975.

Parham, Linda. "Alabama Firm Finds Success in Southern Lifestyles." *Alabama Journal*, August 21, 1977.

Poe, William D., Jr. "*The Progressive Farmer*, 1886–1903." Master of Arts thesis, University of South Carolina, 1971.

Reed, Roy. "Birmingham Publisher Propelled by Regionalism." *New York Times*, September 7, 1976.

"South's Top Farm Magazine: *The Progressive Farmer*." *Birmingham Magazine*, March 1962.

Tharpe, Gene. "Two Magazines of Real Use." *Atlanta Constitution*, April 27, 1978.

INDEX SOURCES: None.

LOCATION SOURCES: Library of Congress, North Carolina State Library (Raleigh), University of Virginia Library.

Publication History

MAGAZINE TITLE AND TITLE CHANGES: *The Progressive Farmer* (1886–1973); *Progressive Farmer* (1973-present).

VOLUME AND ISSUE DATA: Vols. 1–99 (February 10, 1886-present); weekly (1886–1930), bimonthly (1931), monthy (1932-present).

PUBLISHER AND PLACE OF PUBLICATION: Leonidas LaFayette Polk (February 10, 1886-June 1892); Mrs. L. L. Polk (June 1892-June 1901); Estate of Mrs. L. L. Polk (June 1901-August 1, 1901); J. W. Denmark (August 1, 1901-December 1903); Agricultural Publishing Company (December 1903–1905); The Progressive Farmer Company (1906–1981); Southern Progress Corporation (1981-present). Winston, North Carolina (February 10, 1886-March 30, 1887); Raleigh, North Carolina (April 14, 1887–1911); Birmingham, Alabama (1911-present).

EDITORS: Leonidas L. Polk (February 10, 1886-June 11, 1892) with Baylus Cade (December 9, 1890-June 23, 1891) and J. L. Ramsey (June 21, 1892-June 27, 1899); Clarence Poe (July 4, 1899–1958); Eugene Butler (1958–1982); C. G. Scruggs (1982-present).

CIRCULATION: 564,000 paid, 9,000 nonpaid.

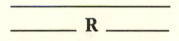

R

THE RED BOOK

Pulitzer-Prize winning historian Frank Luther Mott devotes but half of one
sentence to the *Red Book*, calling it a "pleasantly amateurish periodical" of
Baltimore.[1] One might add that by their very nature, virtually all early humor
magazines might be termed amateurish. At the far end of the seriousness spectrum, the same might be said of a great many early religious periodicals.

The *Red Book* was published erratically during 1819–1821; it was the joint
editorial effort of Peter H. Cruse and John Pendelton ("Horseshoe") Kennedy,
though their names never appear in the periodical. Instead they style themselves
Pentagruel and Sidrophel. In an advertisement following the title page of the
bound volume of their less than digest-size magazine appears the following:

> This little book comes before the public eye, the careless offspring of
> chance, unsupported by patronage and unadorned by the tinsel of name or
> fashion. It is vain to seek into its origin, for no man shall tell whence it
> comes.

A worthy feature of the *Red Book* is that its humor is aimed at its own city
and most especially at the pretentions of the early nineteenth-century urbanite.
An introductory passage in number 1 reads:

> Our city—Baltimore, it is said abroad, is celebrated for three things—its
> *music*,—its *churches* and its *military*. In each of these, are strange an-
> omalies. *Music* is patronized by those who have least *ear* and most *money*
> (which is only another name for discord.) The best *churches* are built by

the worst christians; and in the *military* department, it is observed, that all logick is set at defiance in making *majors* of *minors*.

If today's reader can forgive Cruse and Kennedy for their constant use of classical allusions and comparisons, their humor remains remarkably intact. Much of their most effective humor is in verse form, as in the feature ''Sidrophel's Letters to Mr. Drytext,'' which began:

> A Book-Worm, rear'd in rural shades,
> Emerging lately from his glens and glades,
>   Came hither to complete his education,
>   To learn a modish air,
>   And study with some care
> What we town-folks acquire without a set probation.
>
> Our hero was not void of common sense,
>   Although he had, we own, some small book-knowledge;
> Could parse a Greek verb through each mood and tense,
>   And was an honour-man at Princeton college.
>
>   Our well bred gentlemen may smile to hear
>   That he, with all this learning, was no bear;
>   Had master'd logic with no wish to prose,
>   And bowing, seldom trod on ladies' toes. [2, 10: 156–158].

The further verses of this item are devoted to puncturing the inflated pride of city folk who look down their noses at their country cousins. By like token the city woman of place and fashion is lampooned in ''Smilinda,'' the first verse of which appears below:

> Smilinda has a sportive eye,
> A polish'd cheek of rosy die,
> A rounded neck, a taper waist,
> And lips—exactly to my taste.
> Her skin is perfect, —and her air
> Just what a shepherdess might wear,
> So little is it shap'd by rule;
> I'm only sorry she's a fool. [2, 10: 151–153].

The brightest star in this magazine's heavens, however, is a series of witty verses printed under the running head ''Horace in Baltimore,'' one of which began:

> There are some criticks, as I hear,
> Who think the Red Book too severe;
> On modern sins as great a libel

> As Pope, Swift, Horace, or the Bible;
> And likely less to mend than vex,
> By its stern strictures on the *sex*.
> Others, (for doughtiest doctors differ,)
> Exclaim, "Was never satire stiffer!"
> The style is loose, the morals worse,
> Pointless the prose, and tame the verse;
> And dolts and knaves may flourish long,
> Attack'd by prosing and sing-song [2, 10: 146–151].

The *Red Book*'s final issue, March 16, 1821, was mainly given over to good-byes—said, of course, in their usual satirical style. Toward the end, "Horace" said of his magazine:

> But go! you idle, insect thing;
> You brought some honey with your sting,
>   More merriment than trouble:
> Like other things that aim at *style*,
> 'Twas yours to soar and shine awhile,
>   A breath-inflated bubble [P. 155].

Note

1. *A History of American Magazines, 1741–1850* (New York, 1930), I: 204.

Information Sources

BIBLIOGRAPHY:
Edgar, Neal L. *A History and Bibliography of American Magazines, 1810–1820*. Metuchen, N.J., 1975. Pp. 223–24.
Mott, Frank Luther. *A History of American Magazines, 1741–1850*. New York, 1930. I: 204.
INDEX SOURCES: None.
LOCATION SOURCES: Library of Congress, Yale University Library.

Publication History

MAGAZINE TITLE AND TITLE CHANGES: *The Red Book*.
VOLUME AND ISSUE DATA: Vols. 1–2, no. 10 (October 23, 1819-March 16, 1821), irregular.
PUBLISHER AND PLACE OF PUBLICATION: Printed by J. Robinson. Baltimore, Maryland.
EDITORS: Peter H. Cruse and John P. Kennedy.
CIRCULATION: Unknown.

REED'S ISONOMY

A feisty, irreverent Texas monthly that carried on the tradition of William Cowper Brann[1] was *Reed's Isonomy: A Journal of Justice*, published from 1902 until 1905 in San Antonio. Its editor, J. Guy Reed, had published from December 1895 to December 1901 a weekly newspaper called *La Salle's Isonomy* at Cotulla, in La Salle County, Texas, of which *Reed's Isonomy* was a continuation. Known at that time as J. Guy Smith, the editor had petitioned the La Salle district court for a judicial order changing his name from Smith to Reed. The apparent reason for the change of surname stemmed from a provision in connection with property interests bequeathed to him (7, 2: 10).

Three years before his move to San Antonio, Reed (then Smith) was shot in the back while arresting two Mexicans in his capacity as deputy sheriff. Though the shot pierced one of his lungs, the editor/deputy turned and shot his assailant dead. Smith's wound took three months to heal and left him with health problems.

Volume 7, number 2, of the *Isonomy*, in its magazine form—the earliest available—includes a page of comments from Texas newspapers welcoming the appearance in San Antonio of the peppery Reed and his associate editor, James Armstrong, Jr., who for a time had edited and published a Texas paper called *Armstrong's Autonomist*. The *San Antonio Daily Express* noted that *Reed's Isonomy* was similar to Brann's *Iconoclast* in typographical style as well as in content. San Antonio's *Record* said the *Isonomy* dealt with questions of sociology "with a vigor and bluntness which readers of the *Iconoclast*, when under the editorial control of the late W. C. Brann, will recall with supreme satisfaction" (7, 2: 7).

The editor of the Grimes County *Record* of Anderson, Texas, helpfully explained that the arcane title "Isonomy" means "equal law" or "common rights and privileges," calling Reed honest and courageous and predicting that "until the enemies of justice—whom he deals unmerciful drubbings without fear or favor—do get him (if this shall be his fate), he will continue to hand 'em hot ones properly mixed with tabasco sauce. His style is decidedly Brannic" (7, 2: 7). In a later issue the editor explained his methods:

> The *Isonomy* is sometimes taken to task for its frank and candid speech. It says "bellyache" instead of "a disturbance in the abdominal region." This is a horrible shock to the sensibilities of the superaesthetic, and they have a sorrowful time recovering. . . . It is not our province to serve up dishes of altruistic gush for the delectation of intellectual milksops, but to show things up as they are; to give cynical, concise and close-reasoned arguments, and to clothe them in language at once forceful and picturesque. . . . We must act on the hypothesis that a "desperate disease requires a radical remedy." [8, 4: 85]

In fact, the *Isonomy* was a crazy-quilt of opinion. With one breath Reed defends womanhood, the sanctity of the family, or religion; with the next he issues something as wildly blasphemous as an article entitled "The Virgin Mary" (8, 4: 80–81), which he lifted from the *Truthseeker* of Bradford, England. Elsewhere in this issue, with reasoned arguments he protests capital punishment, but the same page includes the violently bigoted article "Is the Negro a Beast?" (8, 4: 73–75).

The lead article to volume 8, number 5, presents Reed's outraged response to reports that for the first time a black man had been listed in the New York "Four Hundred." His tirade spills over to address the excesses and deficiencies of the rich. "This particular class," writes Reed, "possesses the manly physique of a toothpick. . . . It has to put on an overcoat in order to make a shadow." By like token, the news of Booker T. Washington's celebrated White House dinner is likened to "a jackass eating with a mule" (7, 2: 5).

Local items Reed spoke out against included overhead wires, unsightly telephone poles, the patrol wagon ("a jail on wheels"), and assignation houses in the very shadow of city hall. The outspoken editor could not abide what he considered Americans' tendency to slobber over European royalty, and he frequently took a swipe at prohibitionists.

A target of some of Reed's most vehement attacks was James Stephen Hogg, governor of Texas. "If bluster were brains," Reed wrote, "Mr. Hogg would be the profoundest thinker that ever lived." Hogg, he went on, "is a natural born demagogue. He is an instinctive pettifogger. He is the Sir John Falstaff of American politics. . . . Mr. Hogg has struck oil in Beaumont, but he might bore forever into the depths of his fathomless nescience without striking a flow of original thought. . . . Possessed of boundless ignorance, he has peddled small chunks of it at fabulous prices." Nature occasionally almost exhausts herself, Reed tells his readers, as when she poured genius into William Shakespeare. "Upon Mr. Hogg she showered mountains of gall. She loaded him with irrepressible audacity like a Mexican peon loads a jackass with wood" (7, 3: 8).

As detestible as the blustering politician in Reed's eyes was the medical charlatan. The *Isonomy* was instrumental in ridding San Antonio of one Dr. Frederick J. Fielding, a heavy advertiser in the city's dailies. In "Fielding the Great; or, Consumption Cured While you Wait," Reed wrote:

> San Antonio appears to be pre-eminently the American Mecca for the mind reader or the charlatan. The smooth individual whose graft is getting something for nothing seems to find this city a Paradise. If he has a reservoir of gall and advertises like a fire sale, he will fall in the swim immediately, and the suckers will push him along. He may be as ignorant as a mud turtle and as homely as the butt end of a bat, but he'll get there. [8, 5: 101]

In "An Inspired Jackass: Otherwise, The Rev. Sam Jones," Reed denounces another favorite target: the cash-hungry evangelist. "Jones poses as a reformed sot and soul-saver," says Reed, "but in fact he is a vulgar-mouthed ass." He characterizes Jones as "fat as a seed-tick and as lusty as a willie-goat" and calls him a jackass, a cur, a mountebank, and an unmitigated liar. "Instead of being greeted with a brass band ovation by a lot of namby-pamby fanatics, who mistake an atribilarious liver for the gospel of Christian religion, he should be tickled and touched with a horse-whip. . . . The secret of Sam Jones' attractiveness is the same that impels the morbid in curiosity to visit the cadavers in a morgue" (7, 3: 3). Similar treatment was later accorded John Alexander Dowie, who, wrote Reed, "claims to be a divine healer, whatever that means, and thinks God has made him his special deputy. . . . Like the rest of the wind-jammers, he is strictly out for the cash" (7, 8: 180).

Reed remained outspoken even in the face of a threatened libel suit. In volume 8, number 5, appears just such a letter to the editor written by one C. F. King, president of King-Crowther Corporation, a Texas developer. In a reply headlined "The Isonomy Stands Pat," the editor wrote:

> Rash, reckless *Isonomy*! . . . Is annihilation to be our destiny for daring to impugn the motives of a spread-eagle corporation which advertises oil fields that do not exist, a pipe line that was never constructed and a railroad that was never built? [8, 5: 129]

It is impossible to discover what brought this twenty-four-page monthly to a close in 1905, as few copies are extant. The little magazine sold for $1 a year or 10¢ a copy, and ten of its twenty-four pages usually contained advertisements for Caney Creek Whisky, Marlin cartridges, Winchester shotgun shells, business colleges, jewelers, insurance agents, and professional men. Certainly *Reed's Isonomy* was a colorful part of a gunslinging brand of magazine journalism not practiced in the more reticent parts of the South.

Note

1. See William L. Rivers, "William Cowper Brann and His 'Iconoclast'," *Journalism Quarterly*, Fall 1958, pp. 433–38.

Information Sources

INDEX SOURCES: None.
LOCATION SOURCES: Library of Congress, New York Public Library.

Publication History

MAGAZINE TITLE AND TITLE CHANGES: *La Salle's Isonomy* (1895–1901); *Reed's Isonomy: A Journal of Justice* (1902–1905).
VOLUME AND ISSUE DATA: Vol. 1–10 (1895–1905); weekly (1895–1901), monthly (1902–1905).
PUBLISHER AND PLACE OF PUBLICATION: J. Guy Smith (Cotulla, Texas, 1895–1901); J. Guy Reed (San Antonio, Texas, 1902–1905).
EDITOR: J. Guy Reed (formerly J. Guy Smith).
CIRCULATION: Unknown.

A REPOSITORY OF SCIENCE & LITERATURE. *See* THE
PORTICO

THE ROLLING STONE

An important influence in transforming William Sidney Porter, bank clerk,
into O. Henry, celebrated shorty-story writer, was a slender humor magazine
entitled the *Rolling Stone*, which Porter edited and published during 1894 and
1895 in Austin, Texas. The first two issues, no longer extant, were published
as the *Iconoclast*, continuing William Cowper Brann's apt title after the latter
had moved to San Antonio to become editor of the *Express*, selling the press
he had used for his *Iconoclast* to Porter for $250. Shortly therefter, Brann left
the *Express*, moved to Waco, and decided to revive his crusading magazine.[1]
Porter agreed to discontinue using the title *Iconoclast* and rechristened his periodical the *Rolling Stone*, adding into its nameplate the combination motto-
subtitle "Out for the Moss."

A few words of explanation are in order regarding how a man born in Greensboro, North Carolina, came to edit a Texas magazine. Porter's mother died of
tuberculosis when he was a toddler; fearing he, too, might have the disease,
relatives took him to live on a Texas ranch where it was hoped the drier air
would be beneficial to his health. Here Porter learned the skills of a cowboy,
read voraciously, and became an amateur caricature artist. His first job was as
a clerk for Morley Brothers Drug Store in Austin (1884). Later he clerked and
kept books for an Austin cigar store, was bookkeeper for a big Texas real estate
firm (1885), and was a draftsman in Austin's General Land Office (1887). Also
in 1887, Porter eloped with Miss Athol Estes, age seventeen, whose mother had
also died of tuberculosis. The couple had a daughter, Margaret, in 1890, and in
January 1891 Porter left the land office to become a clerk at the First National
Bank of Austin.

Having done a little freelance writing, Porter decided to edit a periodical of
his own and in March 1894 concluded his deal with W. C. Brann. Porter's first
number appeared on April 14, 1894; the first number as the *Rolling Stone*
appeared on April 28 of the same year, an eight-page weekly printed in five-
column format on low-quality newsprint. With number 14, the format was changed
to three-column quarto-size pages, done on slick paper. Number 36 saw the
magazine back to newspaper size but retaining the better paper stock and three-
column layout. Volume 2 retained the same format, but sinking ad lineage
dictated a return to printing on cheap paper.

The *Rolling Stone* was basically a humor magazine, though it occasionally
made serious comments on local or state political issues, related news events,
and made sporadic attempts at *belles lettres*. Most of its space was given to
cartoon drawings—done in chalk by Porter himself—short humor poems, par-

odies, short stories, and satirical editorial comments. Most of this copy was written by the editor.

In October 1894 appeared the "Plunkville Patriot," Porter's parody of Southwestern country weekly newspapers. Frank Luther Mott called this feature "a work of grotesque art. . . . It was a typographer's nightmare, with more wrong fonts, 'typos,' and general compositor's cussedness than any printer has ever condensed into such a limited space before or since."[2] The "Patriot's" imaginary editor, Col. Aristotle Jordon, was forever crusading to clean up local pigpens, which in Porter's mind seems to have represented the banality of the issues with which the crossroads newspaper editor had to deal. A typical treatment made use of an awkward jumble of multideck headlines which, with the misspellings and upside-down letters removed, reads: "VICTORY!! Perkins Hog-Pen Squashed by a Habeas Corpus & an Axe. Perkins Makes a Bold Resistance. The Hog Takes a Hand in the Proceeding." Extracts of the copy read:

> Judge Perkins sat on the edge of the pen barefooted, with a long, single barreled shot gun in his hand. He was breathing hard, and his big toes were working viciously. . . . "Judge Perkins," we said in a loud voice, "by the authority invested in us by the Commonwealth of Plunkville and the power of the Press, we command you to remove, take away, . . . and disperse yourself and aforesaid hog contrary to the peace and dignity of the State of Texas until death you do part, so help you God!" "Go to h— l!" says the Judge. [2, 12: 9]

On the same page of this "Patriot" was Porter's parody of disreputable newspaper ads. "Widows!" it begins, "Send your name, height, weight, reach, inches around bicepts and forearm and $4.75, and receive by return mail a picture of your late husband, free!" Also on this page was a separate item just three words long—a comment elegant in its comic simplicity on the paucity of local copy available to the editor of a country paper: "Spring has come." "The Plunkville Patriot" was a regular feature until the magazine's demise with the April 27, 1895, issue.

Another example of Porter's style of humor was an article headlined "Austin by Gaslight," in which he writes:

> Chicago may be a gay and wicked city, New York undoubtedly is, but after the lights are lit, the student of the dark side of city life would have much to learn, if, sufficiently furnished with police protection, he should penetrate the depths of wild abandon and dissipation of Congress Avenue, Austin, Texas. . . .

> How strange it is to note the difference between the great city of Austin by daylight and by gaslight. We seem to be transferred to another, and a gayer, wickeder world. All the dark passions of humanity seem to be loosed.

We stand beneath the windows of the Austin Club.

Ah! the Austin Club. What scenes of reckless dissipation, of sensuous abandonment to pleasure, of all the giddy, butterfly whims that flutter in the brains of society.

On the long gallery above us two blase members of the club—the wickedest and most aristocratic of its members—are eating tamales, and conversing in low, ribald tones about the price of socks. . . .

The mad revelry of a night in Austin under the gaslight is nearly over. In a few minutes it will be ten o'clock. [1, 3: 1]

In another item on the same page, Porter delivered a neat one-liner: "A woman generally likes her husband's mother-in-law the best of all his relatives." Later in the same issue he writes of a woman in Paris, Texas, who had recently given birth to her third pair of twins, commenting that "this is indeed a living illustration of the fact that three of a kind beat two pair" (p. 4).

One of Porter's neater parodies was a spoof of Rudyard Kipling, entitled "On the Punjab," which includes a bit of verse that reads like a combination of Kipling and Pogo:

The Blooming Goat kicked over the cliff,
    And Truth spake from the Rhyme,
And Craft and Sin and the bow-legged Wolf
    Came smilingly up to Time.
And thus the Story was made to Run
    By the Thing which rules the Roost;
And the Son-of-a-gun that raised the Wind
By the Unsaid Words was loosed. [1, 36: 1]

This poetic effort Porter entitled "The Ballad of the Mixed Drink."

To poke fun at the pretensions of a rival city's supporters of culture, Porter ran a chalk engraving of a landscape that looked as though it had been done by a five-year-old and captioned it: "View of San Antonio from Alamo Heights (copied from a picture by the San Antonio Art League.)"

The work of the more established humorist Bill Nye also appeared in the *Rolling Stone*. Typical of his contributions was this excerpt from "Nye in the St. Croix":

Here, where the shriek of the locomotive on half of a dozen Chicago lines entering St. Paul and Minneapolis echoes up and down the beautiful lake, and where the godless barbarian rose from his couch unblest and uncivilized, there now stands a penitentiary with a seating capacity of 1,800 and turning away business every day. [1, 36: 5]

Porter put together the earlier copies of his magazine after banking hours. Then in December 1894 he resigned from the bank and had the *Rolling Stone* as his sole means of support. Hoping to broaden his advertising base, Porter in January 1895 took as co-editor Henry Ryder-Taylor, an Englishman who contributed a one-page "San Antonio Department"; the magazine began publishing simultaneously in both cities. His plan backfired, however, when the co-editors opposed the popular Callaghan administration in San Antonio and offended the sizable German population of that city. As circulation dwindled, Porter suffered an attack of measles. During his convalescence Porter took as co-publisher Mr. Hec A. McEachin of Austin, but after his serious attack of measles, only four numbers were published before Porter threw in the towel.

Thereafter Porter wrote for the Houston *Post* (October 1895-July 1896), doing a humor column called "Some Postscripts and Pencillings." After a trip to Central America, the death of his wife, and a short prison term caused by his bookkeeping while in his old post at the bank, Porter moved to New York City and achieved lasting fame as O. Henry, a *nom de plume* he had adopted while passing through New Orleans. Surely the *Rolling Stone*'s importance lies in the part it played in developing the skills of America's best-known short-story writer.

Notes

1. See William L. Rivers, "William Cowper Brann and His 'Iconoclast'," *Journalism Quarterly*, Fall 1958, pp. 433–38.
2. *A History of American Magazines, 1885–1905* (New York, 1957), IV: 668.

Information Sources

BIBLIOGRAPHY:
Davis, Robert H., and Arthur B. Maurice. *The Caliph of Bagdad*. New York, 1931.
Mott, Frank Luther. *A History of American Magazines, 1885–1905*. Cambridge, 1957. IV: 665–70
Rollins, Hyder E. "O. Henry's Texas Days." *The Bookman*, 40 (September 1914-February 1915): 154–65.
Smith, C. Alphonso. *O. Henry Biography*. New York, 1931.
Tracey, Paul Aubrey. "A Closer Look at O. Henry's Rolling Stone." Master of Arts thesis, University of Texas, 1949.
INDEX SOURCES: None.
LOCATION SOURCES: University of Texas Library (Austin).

Publication History

MAGAZINE TITLE AND TITLE CHANGES: *Iconoclast* (April 14–21, 1894); *The Rolling Stone* (April 28, 1894-April 27, 1895).

VOLUME AND ISSUE DATA: Vols. 1–2 (April 14, 1894-April 27, 1895), weekly.
PUBLISHER AND PLACE OF PUBLICATION: William Sidney Porter (April 1894-
    March 1895); W. S. Porter and Hec A. McEachin (March-April 1895). Austin,
    Texas.
EDITORS: William Sidney Porter (April 1894-January 1895); W. S. Porter and Henry
    Rider-Taylor (January-March 1895).
CIRCULATION: Approximately 1,500.

THE ROSE BUD

> John had a par-rot. It was a pret-ty par-rot. It could whis-tle and laugh,
> and say "bad-boy."[1, 2: 6]

This Dick and Jane-like copy, carefully presented in syllables of pablum
simplicity, are from a department called "For My Youngest Readers" in the
Rose Bud; or, Youth's Gazette, a Charleston, South Carolina, weekly of the
1830s that claimed to be the nation's first children's magazine.[1] Printed by J. S.
Burgess of 44 Queen Street, the four-page, three-column *Rose Bud* was edited
by Caroline Howard Gilman, the talented wife of Unitarian minister Samuel
Gilman, who had been educated at Harvard and who came to Charleston from
Gloucester, Massachusetts.

The periodical first appeared on August 11, 1832; to underscore its title, its
flag included a wood engraving of a rosebud. The periodical's original motto,
or caption, was a line from Scott, "The Rose is Fairest When 'Tis Budding
New," and its price was $1 a year, in advance. In her maiden issue Mrs. Gilman
tells her young readers that she will "always encourage your holy feelings, and
assist you in being pious and humble. I have chosen the Rose Bud for my
emblem, partly because it is one of God's gifts to us" and partly to encourage
the reader to reflect on the rose and think, "I will try to be like you, so perfect,
so desirable. God has folded up my heart in pure freshness. I will let it open
for him" (p. 1). She encourages contributions from her youthful readers but
warns that they must never mention political parties or religious controversy.

Some readers obliged. Other letters to the editor were obviously the work of
Mrs. Gilman herself, as in this entry:

> Mrs. Editur, i wish you wud rite a peese to My muther about macking me
> go to skool she maks me go to skool wether I want to or wether i don't
> want to—you seem so kind tu lettle people i think you will tak my part.
> I am with Respec, Sally Hatebook. [1, 1: 3]

The early issues of the *Rose Bud* also carried children's stories, enigmas,[2]
news of children's organizations, a book column concerned with juvenile literature, and a considerable portion of verse, most of it from the pen of the

prolific Mrs. Gilman. Much of the material the editor used had a decided Low
Country flavor, as in "Sullivan's Island" and "The Planter's Son," two stories,
and "On the Spire of St. Michael's Church" by the editor, extracts of which
read:

> Symmetric Spire! Our city's boast,
>   In scientific grandeur pil'd
> The guardian beacon of our coast,
>   The seaman's hope, when waves are wild!
>
> All sleep but thee—Thy tuneful bells,
>   Hymn to the night-wind in its roar,
> Or float upon the Atlantic swells,
>   That soften summer on our shore. [1, 4: 16]

Six years later, one of the few illustrations used by Mrs. Gilman was of the
graceful spire of St. Michael's (7, 1), which today remains one of Charleston's
outstanding attractions.

In a brief prospectus for volume 2, Mrs. Gilman notifies her readers that the
magazine's title was being changed to the *Southern Rose Bud*, since periodicals
"of a similar character have increased so rapidly at the North" since the *Rose
Bud*'s founding. Under this prospectus appeared the testimonials of a number
of influential Charlestonians, including Thomas Lee, C. E. Gadsden, C. J. Col-
cock, and the *Rose Bud*'s main financial backer, Thomas S. Grimke (3, 5: 37).
In volume 2 the editor began to provide more copy for mature readers alongside
the juvenile material.

With volume 3 the magazine's motto was changed to "Devoted to the Culture
of the Imagination, the Understanding, and the Heart," and its page length and
frequency of publication changed to an eight-page biweekly in order to save
postage and accommodate articles of greater length. New departments were
added: "The Leaf-and-Stem-Basket—or Items of News"; a miscellaneous collection called "The Flower Vase"; and for extracts and selected material, "The
Pruning Knife."

Volume 4 saw another title change, to the *Southern Rose*, accompanied by
the new caption "Flowers of All Hue, and without Thorn the Rose," a line
borrowed from Milton. By this time the magazine had been adapted to older
subscribers, with a department called "The Bud" serving juvenile readers. Translations appeared under the standing head "Exotic," and Doctor Gilman, writing
as "Apollos," provided essays on religious and moral topics. Mrs. Gilman's
own reflections appeared in "Editor's Boudoir," and page 8 was filled with
original poetry, some of it occasionally in French.

Outstanding among the editor's prose contributions were two series entitled
"Recollections of a Southern Matron" and "Notes of a Northern Excursion."
Well-known Southern writers contributed: William Gilmore Simms, William

Henry Timrod, Elizabeth Ellett, and others. The editor called her Southern readers' attention to an up-and-coming New England writer, Ralph Waldo Emerson, and Nathaniel Hawthorne made a three-page contribution to the *Southern Rose* : "The Lilly's Quest, An Apologue" (7, 11: 161–64).

With volume 6, page size was reduced and pages per issue increased to sixteen. One can see Mrs. Gilman beginning to tire of her editorial exertions in volume 7, and with the August 17, 1839, number she laid her *Rose* to rest, saying she "would prefer some mode of publication less exacting than the rigorous punctuality of a periodical work' (7, 26: 416). She subsequently published several books, among them *The Rosebud Wreath* (Charleston, 1841), *Oracles from the Poets* (Philadelphia, 1845), *Sibyl, or New Oracles from the Poets* (New York, 1849), *Verses of a Life Time* (Boston, 1849), and *Inscriptions in the Unitarian Cemetery of Charleston* (Charleston, 1860).

In the quaint, chirpy sentimentality of the *Rose*'s pages, one can get an unusual perspective on the mind-set of the genteel lifestyle of uppercrust ante bellum Charleston, and one can follow the progress of a magazine that literally matured with its readers. A fitting way to end this selection is to quote a verse from one of Caroline Gilman's poems:

> How frequently in life's long way,
>   A Bud, a Leaf, when well bestow'd,
> Will give the kind affections play,
>   And cheer and bless the thorny road. [1, 2: 8][3]

Notes

1. See William Stanley Hoole, "The Gilmans and the Southern Rose," *North Carolina Historical Review*, 11 (April 1934): 120.

2. An example, from vol. 1, no. 23, p. 92, is:

> There is a word of plural number,
> A foe to peace and human slumber,
> Now any word you chance to take,
> By adding S you plural make;
> But if an S you add to this,
> How strange the Metamorphosis!
> Plural is plural then no more,
> And sweet what bitter was before.

The enigma's solution is cares (caress).

3. The poem is entitled "To a Flower Sent Me by Mrs. ——" (in return for the first number of the *Rose Bud*).

Information Sources

BIBLIOGRAPHY:
Hoole, William Stanley. "The Gilmans and the Southern Rose." *North Carolina Historical Review*, 11, (April 1934): 116–28.

Kennedy, Fronde. "The Southern Rose-Bud and the Southern Rose," *South Atlantic Quarterly*, 23 (1924): 10–19.
INDEX SOURCES: None.
LOCATION SOURCES: American Periodical Series microfilm, Columbia University Library, Duke University Library, Harvard University Library, Library of Congress, Yale University Library.

Publication History

MAGAZINE TITLE AND TITLE CHANGES: *The Rose Bud; or, Youth's Gazette* (August 11, 1832-August 24, 1833); *Southern Rose Bud* (August 31, 1833-August 1835); *The Southern Rose* (September 1835-August 1839).
VOLUME AND ISSUE DATA: Vols. 1–7; weekly (August 11, 1832-August 1834), biweekly (September 1834-August 1839).
PUBLISHER AND PLACE OF PUBLICATION: W. Estill (August 1832-February 1833); J. S. Burges (March 1833-August 1838); B. B. Hussey (September 1838-August 1839). Charleston, South Carolina.
EDITOR: Caroline H. Gilman.
CIRCULATION: Unknown.

RUSSELL'S MAGAZINE

Another idealistic ante bellum Southern literary monthly was *Russell's Magazine*, published in Charleston from April 1857 to March 1860. It was unusual in that it was spawned not by an individual, but by committee—the congenial group of Charleston literati who often met at William Gilmore Simms' townhouse "The Wigwam" and in somewhat greater numbers at John Russell's Charleston bookstore. The group was not the kind of middle-class, homogenized coterie today's reader might expect to find in the Old South but included businessmen, a rabbi, a Roman Catholic bishop, an Anglican rector, professors, jurists, planters, physicians, and journalists. Among its members were lawyers James Petigru, Samuel Lord, Jr., Middleton Michel, Mitchell King, and Benjamin Whaley; physicians Samuel Dickson, John Dickson Burns, and F. Peyre Porcher; clergymen James Miles and Father Patrick Lynch; and professors Basil Gildersleeve and Alfred Huger. Primary literary figure of the group was the prolific Simms, and chosen to edit the new "depository for Southern genius" was the well-to-do Charlestonian poet Paul Hamilton Hayne.[1] William B. Carlisle of the Charleston *Mercury* was to be assistant editor, and the collegial John Russell agreed to serve as publisher. "Lord John," as Russell was called by his friends, agreed to meet all expenses not satisfied by subscription revenues. As in most committee work, the chairman—in this case the editor—did most of the work, for which he received no pay.

The new ninety-six-page magazine, selling for $3 a year, in advance, or 25¢ a number, was anything but unusual in that its *raison d'être* was to provide an outlet for serious Southern letters which the North could not so readily belittle.

In Hayne's first editorial address to his readers, he said: "A few years ago, Sydney Smith sneered at American literature. The North was indignant. They have never ceased to allude to it. . . . But now the North has turned sneerer and sneers at Southern literature. Our turn may come next, who knows?" (1, 1: 83). In any case, he solicited the public's support for his new periodical exponent of Southern thought and feeling, talent and culture.

Usual, too, were delays in initial publication and overly optimistic plans to pay contributors.[2] Simms became miffed at not being consulted often enough; one of the magazine's backers, William Tabor, editor of the Charleston *Mercury*, died in a duel; two more members of the group, Gildersleeve and Dickson, moved away; and the assistant editor apparently was not inclined to put much time into the project.

Of the original "committee," only Hayne, Simms, and their discovery, Henry Timrod, remained regular contributors, and July 1858 found Hayne saying in his department entitled "Editor's Table":

> The professional author writes for his profit—perchance his bread—and this is, of course, a sufficient inducement for him to write freely. But professional writers in our regions are indeed *rarae avis*, and in the infancy of our literary achievements, or rather efforts, we have to depend on amateur authors. [3, 4: 370]

In December of the same year George C. Hurlbut, who later became secretary of the New York Geographical Society, was named associate editor and provided much of his own work to fill the magazine's pages.

Probably the finest accomplishment of *Russell's Magazine* was launching the literary career of poet Henry Timrod, a boyhood friend of Hayne. Writing in the *Southern Literary Journal* in 1970, Richard Calhoun rates as Timrod's best contributions to the magazine's poetry "The Arctic Voyager" (1, 1: 46), "Praeceptor Amat" (2, 5: 404–5), and "Lines" (5, 5: 409) and as his best essays "The Character and Scope of the Sonnet" (1, 2: 156–59), "Literature in the South" (5, 5: 385–95), and "What Is Poetry?" (2, 1: 52–58).

The last named of the essays above was written by Timrod in answer to an earlier essay bearing the same title, this one by lawyer William J. Grayson (1, 4: 327–37). Timrod favored the newer techniques of the Romantic poets; Grayson had taken the traditionalist view. It was Grayson who had done the lead article for *Russell's* maiden issue, "The Edinburgh Review Reviewed," in which he presented proslavery arguments and in doing so set the tone for the one constant theme that runs through the magazine's six volumes—the ardent defense of slavery. Though Hayne's editorial policy was to eschew partisan politics in favor of the rarefied realms of literature, the slavery issue was so vital in the South of the late 1850s that it could not possibly have been avoided. Aside from the slavery question, Hayne held to his policy of avoiding the party shackles and petty combat of politics. Even in literary criticism he espoused the genial approach, saying, "The fabric of no man's reputation can be strengthened by the wanton destruction of another's fame," and holding himself above those editor/critics whose work, he said, usually alternated "between detraction and deification" (1, 4: 376).

Another of William Grayson's strongly held convictions was that dueling, still in use in the Southern states at that time, should be outlawed (1, 5: 439–54). Here his opponent in *Russell's* pages was the eminent physician and professor of medicine Dr. Samuel H. Dickson, who defended the code duello as a more elegant, and therefore more desirable, solution of men's differences than "the gouging and biting scuffles of our rude pioneers, or the . . . legal manslaughter of the ready Bowie knife" (1, 2: 133).

Other contributions worth mentioning are Simms' essay on Francis Marion (4, 1: 1–16; 4, 2: 113–28) and another, "Literary Prospects of the South" (3, 3: 196–206); Hayne's "The Poets and Poetry of the South" (2, 2: 152–60); and James Wood Davidson's defense of Poe (2, 2: 161–73).

Filling considerable space, but adding little to the lasting glory of *Russell's*, were the frothy effusions of Essie Cheseborough and the stories and reviews of Mrs. H. C. King, a Charleston socialite. Numerous translations appear, including quite a few from the then-faddish works of Persian writers. Oddly enough, these were sometimes used to lighten the preponderantly serious tone of the magazine's pages.[3]

The editors of the American Periodical Series, who borrowed heavily from Frank Luther Mott, characterize *Russell's Magazine* as aspiring to be a literary work but failing in the attempt. Others regard it more highly. William Trent calls it "one of the best periodicals ever published in the South,"[4] Richard Calhoun "the most significant periodical published in South Carolina and one of the two or three most important of all ante-bellum Southern magazines,"[5] pointing out also that it was the last significant attempt at a literary magazine in the region before the Civil War. Fronde Kennedy felt the magazine had "embalmed the very spirit of the Old South."[6] It was most certainly a literary periodical and an important one, but not all can go so far as Trent and Calhoun in its praise. Its brief life span alone prevented it from even approximating the importance of *Niles' Weekly Register*,* the *Southern Literary Messenger*,* or *DeBow's Review.** It was, nevertheless, a magazine of real importance but, alas, not the brand of importance that builds long lists of paying subscribers.

Notes

1. Hayne had had previous editorial positions with the *Southern Literary Gazette** and Washington *Spectator*.

2. See Richard J. Calhoun, "The Ante-Bellum Literary Twilight: Russell's Magazine," *Southern Literary Journal*, 3 (Fall 1970): 92–93.

3. On p. 81 of vol. 1, no. 1, appears "A Jar of Wine," from the Persian:

Day and night my thoughts incline,
To the blandishments of wine;

Jars were made to drain, I think,
Lips, I know, were made to drink!
When I die (the day be far!)
Should the potters make a jar
Out of this poor clay of mine,
Let the jar be filled with wine!

4. William Peterfield Trent, *Southern Writers* (London, 1905), p. 178.
5. Calhoun, "Literary Twilight," p. 99.
6. "Russell's Magazine," *South Atlantic Quarterly*, 18 (April 1919): 144.

Information Sources

BIBLIOGRAPHY:

Calhoun, Richard J. "The Ante-Bellum Literary Twilight: Russell's Magazine." *Southern Literary Journal*, 3 (Fall 1970): 89–110.

Kennedy, Fronde. "Russell's Magazine." *South Atlantic Quarterly*, 18 (April 1919): 125–44.

Moore, Rayburn S. "The Old South and the New: Paul Hamilton Hayne and Maurice Thompson." *Southern Literary Journal*, 5 (Fall 1972): 108–22.

———. "Paul Hamilton Hayne as Editor, 1852–1860." *South Carolina Journals and Journalists*, edited by James B. Meriwether., Spartanburg, S.C., 1975. Pp. 91–108.

INDEX SOURCES: None.

LOCATION SOURCES: American Periodical Series microfilm, Duke University Library, New York Public Library.

Publication History

MAGAZINE TITLE AND TITLE CHANGES: *Russell's Magazine*.
VOLUME AND ISSUE DATA: Vols. 1–6 (April 1857-March 1860), monthly.
PUBLISHER AND PLACE OF PUBLICATION: John Russell. Charleston, South Carolina.
EDITOR: Paul Hamilton Hayne.
CIRCULATION: Unknown.

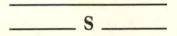

S

SANDLAPPER: THE MAGAZINE OF SOUTH CAROLINA. *See* CAROLINA LIFESTYLE

SCOTT'S MONTHLY MAGAZINE

It would be difficult to imagine less favorable circumstances for introducing a new magazine than existed in Atlanta, Georgia, just after the Civil War; yet in December of 1865 the Rev. William J. Scott (1826–1899) founded *Scott's Monthly Magazine*. With the war to reflect upon, what in prewar years would likely have been simply a literary magazine was published with a combined literary and historical focus. Though this monthly lasted for only four years, it published the work of some of the South's finest writers of that era.

Scott's Monthly had moral overtones, but it was one of those rare instances of a minister publishing a magazine that was clearly secular rather than religious. Perhaps this can be explained by noting that Scott had been a lawyer prior to entering the Methodist ministry and hence had more experience of worldly affairs than did many of the other minister-editors of the 1800s South.[1]

Publisher, or as he termed it, proprietor, of the magazine was J. J. Toon, an enterprising printer, who also owned the *Christian Index* and the *South Western Baptist*.[2] The magazine began with a length of seventy-two pages, offered at $5 annually. As one might imagine, subscriptions were not easy to attract, and both special rates and package deals with Toon's other magazines were offered. Three or four pages of advertisements were carried in most issues, and in its final year, the subscription price was lowered in a vain attempt to boost subscriptions. Few illustrations could be afforded, and the only engravings that appeared were ten portraits of well-known men: Lee, Davis, Jackson, and others, all executed by New York engraver George Perine. Circulation probably never far exceeded

5,000 (October 1867, p. 844), and as *Scott's Monthly* was one of the South's leading magazines of its era,[3] the difficulties of magazines in war-torn Dixie stand out in stark contrast to the 100,000+ circulations of the leading city-based Northern magazines of the day.

Scott must surely have had difficulty securing sufficient original copy, for his issues contained substantial amounts of material selected from other magazines, both domestic and foreign, much of it from British periodicals. Serialized novelettes and short stories appeared regularly. Much of the fiction in the magazine's pages came from the pens of Southern amateur women writers who employed heroes and heroines too saccharine and too stereotyped to be of much enduring interest. Ray Atchison singles out the Rev. R. Wilson's "The Symbie of Moore's Fountain" as worthy of special recognition for its use of Negro dialect, a style popularized in later years by Joel Chandler Harris, George Cable, and others.

Where the magazine shined was in literary criticism and poetry. Probably the best of the criticism was contributed by the distinguished Paul Hamilton Hayne, who had edited *Russell's Magazine** in Charleston from 1857 to 1860. Edgar Allan Poe received much favorable attention; less favorable criticism was usually the fate of Northern writers, such as Hawthorne, Emerson, Thoreau, and Longfellow. Somewhere between in the literary opinions of the magazine's reviewers were British literati: Tennyson, Shelley, Keats, Byron, and Hartley Coleridge (the eldest child of Samuel Taylor Coleridge).

It is likely that the monthly's finest hour was in its original poetry, most of it by Southern poets whose stars were rising. Much of this poetry—by Hayne, Sidney Lanier, Henry Timrod, Maurice Thompson, James Russell Barrick, and others—addressed mournful themes connected with war and dying. Representative poems that have been singled out by literary scholars are Timrod's "Our Willie," Hayne's "Rhoecus and the Dryad," and Lanier's "The Raven Days."

A poetic tribute to Stonewall Jackson taken from the *Petersburg Express*, whose editor had in turn borrowed it from, to one's surprise, the *New York Citizen*, began:

> He sleeps all quietly and cold
>   Beneath the soil that gave him birth—
>
> Then break his battle-brand in twain,
>   An lay it with him in the earth!

and ended:

> And oft, when white-haired grandsires tell
>   of bloody struggles past and gone,
>
> The children at their knees shall hear
>   How Jackson led his columns on! [1,5:409]

Typical of the home-grown war-reminiscence verse published in the magazine was "The Camp Scene" by A. R. Watson. Its first verse read:

Midnight lay along the dunes
    That walled the town of Richmond in;

The weariest of weary moons
    Had climbed where Pleiades had been,
And threw its light in silvery flames
Along the waters of the James [1,2:112]

Editor Scott took a hopeful attitude toward Southern poetry, saying in his first number:

It is a noteworthy fact that Poetry has not flourished to any great extent in the Southern States of the Union. It cannot be attributed to our climate, for that is not unlike the climate of Greece and Italy, which produced a Homer and a Virgil. . . . We have been justly proud of Poe, and Simms, and Meek, and Wilde, and others who belong to the past generation; but yet candor constrains us acknowledge our comparative inferiority. Our settled conviction is, that in the new era now dawning on the South, this state of things will not exist. . . . We venture to predict that the next quarter of a century will be the Augustan age of Southern literature. It will be emphatically the era of Southern song. The stern discipline of adversity will, we verily believe, elevate our poetry in the same ratio in which we have suffered from the "slings and arrows of outrageous fortune" (p. 63).

Some other departments of the magazine were "Our Tripod" and "Editorial Brevities," the editor's remarks on a multitude of subjects; "Monthly Gleanings," short items clipped from other periodicals; "Salmagundi," humorous material; and "The Pantry," a pioneer magazine effort to provide recipes and other ideas for the housewife.

"Crumbs from the Countryman's Table" by J. A. Turner, editor of the *Countryman*,* appeared, subheaded "Course No. 1," "Course No. 2," etc., and Major B. W. Frobel contributed a series of field and camp reminiscences of a sort given greater circulation some years later in such magazines as the *Land We Love*,* *Southern Bivouac*,* and *Our Living and Our Dead*.* There were also essays on farming, travel, education, and other assorted topics.

Over the magazine's life, Scott had two associate editors: James Russell Barrick (1866–1867) and H. T. Phillips (1869). Unable to make a financial success of his venture, Scott gave up his editorship to Col. William H. Wylly, who edited *Scott's Monthly* for but one issue, then changed its title to the *Cosmopolitan Monthly*, only one or two issues of which were ever published (January and perhaps February 1870).[4]

Like so many of its Southern predecessors, *Scott's Monthly* died an early death, and like the multitudes of men killed in the Civil War, these magazines have long lain at rest, evoking the sentiments of a W. H. Thompson poem once published in Scott's pages, the first verse of which read:

> The shout of the charging lines has ceased
>   By the shores of the rushing river,
>   And the waves that break
>   Shall never awake
>   The sleepers that sleep forever.[4,6:891]

Notes

1. While editing *Scott's Monthly*, the Rev. Scott was also active in the ministry in Atlanta and Acworth. His books show his interest in both spiritual and temporal affairs: *South Side Views* (Atlanta, 1883); *From Lincoln to Cleveland and Other Short Studies in History and General Literature* (Atlanta, 1886); *Biographic Etchings of Ministers and Laymen of the Georgia Conferences* (Atlanta, 1895).

2. See Ray M. Atchison, "Scott's Monthly Magazine: A Georgia Post-Bellum Periodical of Literature and Military History," *Georgia Historical Quarterly*, 49 (1965):303.

3. See Frank Luther Mott, *A History of American Magazines, 1865–1885*, (Cambridge, 1938), III:45–46.

4. The University of Georgia Library has the January 1870 issue.

Information Sources

BIBLIOGRAPHY:
Atchison, Ray M. "Scott's Monthly Magazine: A Georgia Post-Bellum Periodical of Literature and Military History." *Georgia Historical Quarterly*, 49 (1965):294–305.
Mott, Frank Luther. *A History of American Magazines, 1865–1885*. Cambridge, 1938. III:45–46.
INDEX SOURCES: None.
LOCATION SOURCES: Library of Congress, University of Georgia Library.

Publication History

MAGAZINE TITLE AND TITLE CHANGES: *Scott's Monthly Magazine* (December 1865-December 1869); *Cosmopolitan Monthly* (January-February? 1870).
VOLUME AND ISSUE DATA: Vols. 1–8 (December 1865-January/February 1870), monthly.
PUBLISHER AND PLACE OF PUBLICATION: J. J. Toon (Atlanta, Georgia, 1865-August 1867); J. W. Burke & Co. (Atlanta and Macon, Georgia, September 1867-December 1869); William H. Wylly (Atlanta, Georgia, January-February?, 1870).
EDITORS: William J. Scott (December 1865-December 1869); William H. Wylly (January-February?, 1870).
CIRCULATION: About 5,000.

THE SEWANEE REVIEW

Oldest of the nation's literary quarterlies is the *Sewanee Review*, published since 1892 at the University of the South, Sewanee, Tennessee.[1] Standing, as one observer put it, "in the front ranks of the battle for a mature literature,"[2] this university-based review was joined in the South by the *South Atlantic Quarterly* (1902, at Trinity College, now Duke University), the *Texas Review* (1915, at the University of Texas, but moved to Southern Methodist University in 1924 and rechristened the *Southwest Review*), the *Virginia Quarterly Review* (1925, at the University of Virginia), and the *Southern Review* (1935–1942, at Louisiana State University).

As one of the journal's early editors, John Bell Henneman, expressed it in his retrospect of the *Sewanee Review*'s first ten years, the *Review* "has stood for the culture of the literary spirit first, and all else was of second importance" (10,4:490). Years later in succeeding Monroe Spears as editor, Andrew Lytle commented on the *Review*'s "allegiance to the humane tradition in learning and letters" and promised that "the perversion of language will of necessity be the chief concern of this magazine, for the word is creative, even in its diluted form, and hence can destroy as well as make" (69,4:711–712).[3] Still later, editor William Ralston, in a seventy-fifth anniversary essay entitled "An Earthen Vessel," stated the magazine's purpose in these words: "We are doing everything we can to provide a place where the unity and the continuity of writing in English can be celebrated—in verse, in fiction, and in criticism" (75,3:12).

Most recently one reads present editor George Core's remarks about the place of a literary journal in 1984. "In a postliterate culture that wearily derives from a society in which reading is little valued," he writes, the defense of *belles lettres* should be "greeted enthusiastically by the few surviving members of the reading public." We live in an age, Core tells us with some bitterness, "whose citizens view writing anything more demanding and sustained than a check as an epic feat," an age in which "computer literacy is thought more significant than the ability to read well" (92,1:iii), a technological age in which reading is viewed only as a practical means to an end—improving one's own writing.

Surely editing a literary magazine is something of a lonely vigil—manning the ramparts of civilization backed by thinning ranks while encircled by the ravening Hun. But this has always been true, as the strewn bones of so many Southern literary journals attest. Given these difficulties, one must admire a journal that has manned the ramparts for so many years, thanks in the early years to the financial commitment of various faculty members at Sewanee and since 1927 to the generosity of the University of the South itself.

Presiding at the *Review*'s birth were young Sewanee professor of English and history William Peterfield Trent, who felt the lack of U.S. magazine reading of the sort supplied British readers by that country's quarterlies; B. Lawton Wiggins, Sewanee's chief administrative official, who provided guidance; and Telfair

Hodson, Sewanee's dean of theology, who assumed the journal's financial risks for its first year and under the misleading title managing editor saw to its book-keeping and advertising.

The 128-page first number opened with Trent's review of *Tess of the D'Ubervilles* (New York, 1892) by Thomas Hardy. Following were a piece on Theodore of Canterbury and his part in founding the Church of England and an essay on modern Spanish fiction, both by B. W. Wells; S. C. Hughson's "Early Piracy and Colonial Commerce"; F. A. Shoup's "The Education of Memory"; an article on U.S. missions in China by someone using the pen name "Partridge"; and another Trent review, this one on Thomas Nelson Page's *The Old South; Essays Social and Political* (New York, 1892). At the end of the journal appeared a section of eight shorter book reviews and seven pages of "Minor Notices"—Trent's comments on still other new books or new editions of older books. Articles and reviews in the first number were run unsigned in imitation of the British quarterlies, but thereafter articles were signed.

In January 1897 Trent's brother-in-law, professor of modern languages Benjamin W. Wells, became associate editor but after two years moved to New York City to accept a similar post on the *Churchman*. After another year Trent also moved to New York to teach English at Columbia University, whereupon John Bell Henneman came to Sewanee to replace Trent both as editor and as chair of English.

When Henneman looked back at the *Review*'s first ten years, he found that literature—general, Greek, Latin, Sanskrit, Semitic, British, U.S., French, Italian, German, Scandinavian, Russian—greatly predominated,[4] followed in descending order by history/biography, current questions, education, philosophy, theology, art, music, and science. The journal received manuscripts from all over the nation and hence did not become overly sectional. Articles were contributed, for example, from Harvard, Yale, Columbia, and the universities of Chicago, Minnesota, Indiana, and Pennsylvania. Like virtually all university-based journals, the *Review* from the start has been what Henneman called an "organ of academic opinion" (10,4:486), and as that editor also pointed out, a number of its articles have been developed into book-length works. Early examples are Trent's *John Milton: A Study of His Life and Works* (New York, 1899) and *War and Civilization* (New York, 1901), Wells' *Modern German Literature* (New York, 1895 and 1901), Theodore Roosevelt's *Essays* (New York, 1897), and G. B. Rose's *Renaissance Masters* (New York, 1898).

The *Review* originally sold for 75¢ an issue or $3 a year and had a circulation of around 500. Current rates are $4 a number or $12 yearly, and circulation in 1984 was 3,350. The journal nearly expired during World War I when promised alumni support failed to materialize, but the old *Review* was saved by the efforts of faculty who organized The Sewanee Review Incorporated, the magazine's publisher from 1913 to 1926. One of these faculty members was professor of English John McLaren McBryde, Jr., who became editor after Henneman's death and held the post for nearly a decade until leaving Sewanee for Tulane University.

His successor, George Herbert Clarke, a poet, was the first editor to use original poetry in the *Review*.

The magazine remained at a circulation of about 500 until 1945, when editor Allen Tate, realizing that his only subscribers were libraries and writers, decided to promote the magazine, which brought its circulation to over 2,000. During its long tenure, the *Review* has published the work of many fine writers—John Crowe Ransom, T. S. Eliot, W. H. Auden, Wyndham Lewis, E. E. Cummings, Cleanth Brooks, Katharine Ann Porter, Eudora Welty, and Robert Penn Warren, to name a few.

In discussing the *Sewanee Review*, Frank Luther Mott made an observation that was at once a criticism and a compliment, that "here were poets writing for poets; story writers providing entertainment for their kind; and poets, story writers, and critics writing for critics. If the circle was small, it was at least select."[5]

Writing in Elliott Anderson and Mary Kinzie's *The Little Magazine in America* (Yonkers, 1978), the late Charles Robinson contended that university-based literary magazines have fallen into a sterile academism relative to short-lived independent "little magazines," such as the *Double Dealer** in New Orleans, the *Fugitive** in Nashville, and the *Reviewer* in Richmond. Whether this charge is accurate or exaggerated, the university literary journal doubtlessly operates under expectations and constraints that make it somewhat more conservative, less avant garde. Writing for a journal like the *Sewanee Review*, moreover, has much in common with doing papers at scholarly conferences: one is writing for a small audience consisting, in the main, of one's contemporary academicians and their more advanced students. Southerners in particular, as Reed Whittemore remarked in his book *Little Magazines*, have taken a stern line against the revolutionary historical processes of industrialism around them and made a point of not being 'progressive' but 'reactionary,' not 'in the vanguard' but 'in the great tradition' . . . retiring gracefully into 'the tradition of aestheticism.' "[6]

This last contention seems borne out in *Sewanee Review* Editor William Ralston's essay "An Earthen Vessel" that discussed the *Review*'s role after seventy-five years of publication. The *Review*, he wrote, seeks the classic literary spirit, steeped in tradition. "It does not consider tradition as immutable or set rigid bounds on invention. But it desires that each new presentation of truth and beauty shall show us the old truth and the old beauty, seen only from a different angle and colored by a different medium. It wishes to add link by link to the chain of tradition, but it does not wish to break the chain." Ralston quoted an English critic as saying the *Sewanee Review* was continuing discretely its somewhat Sibylline course, then adds, "But the Sibyl's discrete murmur may continue to be heard long after the louder voices have shouted themselves hoarse" (75,3:551–52).[7]

Notes

1. An earlier magazine effort at this institution was the *University of the South Magazine* (April-December 1890).

2. Frederick J. Hoffman, *The Little Magazine: A History and a Bibliography* (Princeton, N.J., 1946), p. 1.

3. Lytle added on p. 12: "The University of the South is a Liberal Arts institution in its true sense, as opposed to the liberalism everywhere about us, and nowhere more strongly entrenched than in the Colleges of Education, those abstractions of spiritual and intellectual illiteracy."

4. By Alice L. Turner's count in *A Study of the Content of The Sewanee Review* (Nashville, Tenn., 1931), p. 273, roughly 60 percent of the articles in the *Review*'s first thirty-seven years dealt with literary topics.

5. Frank Luther Mott, *A History of American Magazines, 1885–1905* (Cambridge, 1957), IV:740.

6. Minneapolis, 1963, p. 24.

7. Certainly this is a fit sentiment for the journal of a university affiliated with the Church of England.

Information Sources

BIBLIOGRAPHY:

Anderson, Elliott, and Mary Kinzie, eds. *The Little Magazine in America: A Modern Documentary History.* Yonkers, N.Y., 1978. P. 733.

Henneman, John Bell. "Ten Years of the Sewanee Review: A Retrospect." *Sewanee Review*, 10:477–92.

Mott, Frank Luther. *A History of American Magazines, 1885–1905.* Cambridge, 1957. IV:733–40.

Ralston, William. "The State of Letters." *Sewanee Review*, 75,3:550–55.

Turner, Alice Lucille. *A Study of the Content of The Sewanee Review, with Historical Introduction.* Nashville, Tenn., 1931.

INDEX SOURCES: Abstracts of English Studies, Bibliography of English Language and Literature, Current Contents, Humanities Index, Literary Criticism Register.

LOCATION SOURCES: Duke University Library, Library of Congress, New York Public Library, Tennessee State Library (Nashville), University of North Carolina Library (Chapel Hill), University of Tennessee Library.

Publication History

MAGAZINE TITLE AND TITLE CHANGES: *The Sewanee Review.*

VOLUME AND ISSUE DATA: Vols. 1–92 (November 1892-present), quarterly.

PUBLISHER AND PLACE OF PUBLICATION: Telfair Hodgson (1892–1893); B. Lawton Wiggins (1893–1902); other Sewanee faculty (1902–1912); Sewanee Review Incorporated (1913–1926); University of the South (1927-present). Sewanee, Tennessee.

EDITORS: William P. Trent (1892-July 1900, with Benjamin W. Wells, January 1897–1899); John Bell Henneman (October 1900-January 1909, with Burr James Ramage, 1900–1903); John McBryde (January 1910-October 1919); George Herbert Clarke (1920-October 1925); Seymour Long (1926); William S. Knickerbocker (1926-July/September 1942); Tudor Seymour Long (October/December 1942-July/September 1944); Allen Tate (October/December 1944-July/September 1946); John James Ellis Palmer (October/December 1946-July/September 1952); Monroe K. Spears (October/December 1952-July/September 1961); Andrew Lytle (Oc-

tober/December 1961-October/December 1973); George Core (January/March 1974-present).
CIRCULATION: 3,350 in 1984.

SHENANDOAH VALLEY MAGAZINE. *See* THE VIRGINIAN

SHENANDOAH/VIRGINIA TOWN & COUNTRY. *See* THE VIRGINIAN

SOUTH CAROLINA WEEKLY MUSEUM

In his epic work, *A History of American Magazines*,[1] Frank Luther Mott incorrectly names the *South Carolina Weekly Museum and Complete Magazine of Entertainment and Intelligence* of Charleston as the first real magazine published south of Baltimore; it was in fact preceded by two years by the *Traiteur*,* a Charleston monthly that maintained life from October 1, 1795, to June 15, 1796.

The *Museum*, a thirty-two page weekly issued on Saturdays from January 1797 to July 1798, was a miscellany of essays, poetry, and "foreign and domestic intelligence" intended to entertain, inspire, and inform. Its tone was nicely captured on the title page of its bound volume in two sprightly lines from Pope: "Eye Nature's Walks, Shoot Folly As It Flies, And Catch The Living Manners As They Rise," lines adopted as a slogan by other magazine publishers, as well.[2] Under this slogan appears a dubiously executed likeness of George Washington, recognizable only because it is labeled as such.

The *Museum*'s contents are either unsigned or signed in the "genteel" manner as "A Friend to the Museum," "A Subscriber," "An Egotist," and the like. Though some of its contents are material one might more reasonably expect in a newspaper than a magazine—lists of cargo in recently arrived ships, marriage and death notices, etc.—the vast majority of its offerings are clearly magazine copy.

An essay entitled "Taste" (January 1, 1797, p. 9) begins with the couplet, "True taste to me is by this touchstone known, that's always best that's nearest to my own." The first number also contains advice for women readers: "Some rules to the ladies for choosing husbands of agreeable tempers, by the cut of the nose" (p. 16). In the second number appears a whimsical reply from another contributor:

As a subscriber and well-wisher to your Magazine, I cannot avoid taking notice of a paragraph in your last, respecting Noses. Your correspondent has neither signed himself Long Nose, nor Short Nose; I will therefore conclude that he has got a *marvellous proper Nose, at the ladies' service* (January 14, 1797, p. 53).

signing himself "Roman Nose."

Another contributor congratulates the editor on having started a weekly magazine and advises, "To cook a dish to suit all palates will be a vain attempt; yet from a well chosen variety, each guest may find something agreeable." Further advice from the same contributor is given in verse:

> To your young writers, lend a friendly ear,
>   Nor check their progress by reproof severe;
>
> Tho' wit and fancy, injudicious roam,
>   A mild rebuke will bring the wand'rers home;
>
> Prepared, secure, again they'll mount on high,
>   And shine like stars, to guild Columbia's sky. [January 14, 1797,
>   p. 53]

Typical of the *Museum*'s more playful content is a treatise headlined "On Sluttishness in Married Ladies," written by a man who had married a young lady of "the utmost elegance of person" who later metamorphosed into an unkempt slob: "that fine head of hair . . . which I used to contemplate with so sensible a satisfaction . . . was continually bloused, like the tuft on the back of a camel; or clumsily matted, like the tail of a dray horse." The article is poignantly signed "Benedict, the married man" (March 4, 1797, pp. 279–81).

Much space was occupied by moralistic essays: "On Morals," "On Imagination," "Of Dueling," "On Literary Pride," "Thoughts on Drunkennes," "The Swearer Corrected," "On Bigotry," "On the Sentiments of the Soul," "Essay on Fortitude." Tales likewise appeared frequently, some of the moralistic variety, as in "The Unfortunate Daughter," others of the voguish Eastern school, for example, "Oriental Apologue" or "Beneficence, A Persian Tale."

A department on foreign affairs usually appeared, as did a poetry department. A considerable portion of the two or three pages usually devoted to verse was selected, as opposed to original. There were the usual odes and epitaphs, effusions in honor of the ladies, and translations from the classics. Most of the original poetry was of inferior quality; only occasionally does a contribution stand out, as in "Monsieur Kaniferstane, A Tale" (April 1, 1797, pp. 405–7).

Though the *South Carolina Museum* cannot be remembered as a profound or influential periodical, it does its share in giving the lie to the many historians and other critics who have parroted the false charge that Southern magazines were above all else the stuff of dullness.

Notes

1. *A History of American Magazines, 1741–1850* (New York, 1930), I:32, 205.
2. These lines, or portions of them, were also employed by the *Vigil* (Charleston, S.C., 1798) and the *Microscope and General Advertiser* (Louisville, Ky., 1824–25).

Information Sources

BIBLIOGRAPHY:
Mott, Frank Luther. *A History of American Magazines, 1741–1850.* New York, 1930. I:32, 205.
INDEX SOURCES: None.
LOCATION SOURCES: American Periodical Series microfilm, Library of Congress.

Publication History

MAGAZINE TITLE AND TITLE CHANGES: *South Carolina Weekly Museum and Complete Magazine of Entertainment and Intelligence.*
VOLUME AND ISSUE DATA: Vols. 1–3 (January 1, 1797-July 1, 1798), weekly.
PUBLISHER AND PLACE OF PUBLICATION: Printed by William Primrose Harrison and Company. No. 32, Church-Street, Charleston, South Carolina.
EDITOR: Unknown.
CIRCULATION: Unknown.

SOUTHERN ACCENTS

Picture, if you will, a world of flame-stitch sofas, Flemish bond or herringbone brickwork, Aubusson carpets, decks cantilevered into treetops, warm earth tones, color schemes of pale aqua and apricot, livable spaces, natural areas, parquet floors with lively sheens, Killim pillows, Kravet moiré, Brunschwig and Fils taffeta, inlaid medallions, rich patinas, hidden demarcations seen only by the gifted, translucent Sèvres porcelain, artful tablescapes, infusions of color, muted wall coverings set aglow by diffused natural light, ambience, provenance, and museum-quality everything, and you have a reasonably good picture of the South's superslick house-and-garden magazine, *Southern Accents*, which began publication in November 1977.

This extremely well-laid-out periodical, which has thickened to as much as 180 pages per issue and strives for a comfortable 50:50 ad/editorial mix, aims at an audience of high affluence. Its subscribers' mean annual income is more than $112,000; the mean value of subscribers' principal residences is $213,000.

Publisher Walter Mitchell, Jr., was asked[1] what percentage of readers were bona fide participants in the lifestyle *Southern Accents* pictures, a standard to which not even successful medical specialists might aspire unless they have truly gifted brokers, and what proportion were merely onlookers or "wish book readers." Mitchell's reply was that he didn't know, but at least his advertisers appeared satisfied that they were reaching the right people, as they tended to stay with the magazine.

Though perhaps 80 percent of the magazine's circulation is in the South, the magazine is distributed nationally through Warner Communications. This circulation pattern is reflected in *Southern Accents'* advertising. Though many of its regular advertisers are companies that sell nationally—Beefeater Gin, Baker Furniture of Michigan, Henredon and Heritage furniture, Frederick Cooper lamps and chandeliers, Brunschwig and Fils fabrics, Brown Jordan outdoor furniture, Kirk sterling silverware, Waterford crystal, Aynsley bone china, Tiffany jewelry—a great many of its ads are for Southern products and services.

Most of the oriental rug ads are for firms located in the South—Yamin's, House of Persia, and Sharian of Atlanta; Behgooy of Dallas; Stephen Croft of New Orleans; Shaia of Williamsburg. Art-sellers Clements Northgate Gallery of Chattanooga, Robert Rice of Houston, and W. Graham Arader III of Atlanta and Houston advertise here, as do many antique dealers: Boone's of Wilson, North Carolina; Heinsmith of Lexington; Otto Zenke of Greensboro; Emily Zum Brunnen of Shreveport; Bradford's of Nashville; Brannon of Griffin, Georgia; Trosby and The Gables of Atlanta. Georgia's Sea Island, South Carolina's Hilton Head Island and Kiawah Island, and Florida's Boca West are resorts that find *Southern Accents* readers an appropriate market, as does the Boar's Head Inn of Charlottesville, Virginia. Southern portrait artists often advertise here: Frances Lynch Bennett of Charleston; Dale Kennington of Dothan, Alabama; and Arthur Stewart of Mountain Brook, Alabama; to name a few. Realtors accustomed to dealing in houses that sell for, say, $250,000 to $2 million also advertise: Myriad Properties and Harry Norman of Atlanta; Frank Hardy of Charlottesville. The Southern bias also shows up in the ads of interior designers, jewelers, and others who mainly serve the well-to-do. It is probably true that most of *Southern Accents'* subscribers can afford to purchase many of the items advertised in these pages but will never be able to take them home to residences that equal in sumptuousness the houses featured in this magazine.

Southern Accents' main magazine competitor and its original inspiration is *Architectural Digest*. The chief differences between the two are that *Architectural Digest* pictures the homes of celebrities wherever they might live, and *Southern Accents* restricts its features to the homes of very wealthy, though usually nonfamous, Southerners.

Another non-Southern competitor, says Walter Mitchell, is *Home and Garden* in its new format. In Texas three even more recent Southern magazines compete—*Texas Homes*,* *Dallas-Fort Worth Home/Garden*,and *Houston Home/Garden*—each of which has grown rapidly, though not so rapidly as *Southern Accents*.

The Atlanta magazine, which has attracted national attention by its growth, almost fizzled before its first issue. The management of W.R.C. Smith of Atlanta, a longtime publisher of trade periodicals, tested subscribers by direct mail in 1976 but was disappointed by the results. Some months later a prominent Atlanta saw the promotional brochure and called to subscribe. Told about the poor public response, she constructed her own list of potential subscribers, drawn from time-honored repositories of Southern society: the Junior League, garden clubs, historical societies, and the like. This time the response was excellent, and 11,000 copies of the maiden issue were mailed free to good prospects, roughly half of whom subscribed.[2] The 1,500 copies placed on newsstands were sold out in three weeks, and a major magazine venture was well launched. The young Atlanta woman who saw such promise in the magazine is Lisa Newsom, who immediately joined the staff and took over as editor in 1980 when the first editor, James Hooten, resigned for health reasons.

Between 1978 and 1979 the magazine enjoyed a circulation growth of 103 percent; from 1979 to 1980 the rate was 68 percent, which qualified it as second in circulation growth in the nation, behind *Geo*, another beautifully produced new magazine.[3] The circulation climb has slowed since then, of course. Publisher Mitchell estimates his maximum potential circulation at 250,000; the present figure is 174,000, 77 percent of which is sold by subscription and 23 percent at newsstands. Growth for 1984 could not be safely estimated, as the magazine converted from quarterly to bimonthly in January 1984 and the subscription price was increased from $13 to $18 to compensate for the two additional issues.[4] This rate hike is not likely to have adverse consequences, as the magazine enjoys a loyal readership which is 82 percent female. About 80 percent of readers report keeping their copies indefinitely, and nearly half report having given someone else a gift subscription. A readership that is both happy and affluent enables *Southern Accents* to command substantial ad rates—$6,195 for a full-color page.

Editor-in-Chief Lisa Newsom is aided in running the magazine by an associate editor, Helen Candler Griffith of the Coca-Cola family, Managing Editor Diane Burrell, and Assistant Editors Susan Hewitt and Susannah Wilson. The magazine's staff also includes a copy editor, special projects editor, four feature editors, and eight contributing editors. Articles are for the most part freelanced. This is a magazine of a genre that depends heavily on pictorial content, presided over by Art Director Oscar Almeida; originality of approach and writing has limits when one is usually limited to describing houses and gardens.

In launching *Southern Accents* Mitchell and the W.R.C. Smith Company stuck their financial neck out by sparing no expense in publishing a top-quality product. From the graphic standpoint the magazine could scarcely be prettier. All photo work is in full color; choice of feature material is splendid, and presentation is always tasteful. For the South's upper crust and for those who like to dream, the six annual issues represent $18 well spent. From the publisher's viewpoint, any new magazine that breaks even in a year and a half and keeps gaining is a success indeed.

Notes

1. In telephone conversation with the author, May 17, 1984.

2. Sharron Hannon, ''Magazine Publishers Here Gambling with Slim Chance of Profit,'' *Atlanta Business Chronicle*, November 28, 1983.

3. Andria Krewson, "Southern Accents Ranks 2nd in Growth," *Atlanta Journal*, July 31, 1981.

4. Newsstand price per issue is now a hefty $3.95.

Information Sources

BIBLIOGRAPHY:
Hannon, Sharron. "Magazine Publishers Here Gambling with Slim Chance of Profit." *Atlanta Business Chronicle*, 6, 27 (November 28, 1983).
Krewson, Andria. "Southern Accents Ranks 2nd in Growth." *Atlanta Journal*, July 31, 1981.
Melton, Martha Faye. "Buckhead Boy of the Year." *Georgia Alumni News*, 61, 3:13–14, 50.
————. "Starting a New Magazine." Master's Thesis, University of Georgia, 1982.
INDEX SOURCES: None.
LOCATION SOURCES: Library of Congress, University of Texas Library (Austin).

Publication History

MAGAZINE TITLE AND TITLE CHANGES: *Southern Accents*.
VOLUME AND ISSUE DATA: Vols. 1–7; quarterly (November 1977–1983), bimonthly (January 1984-present).
PUBLISHER AND PLACE OF PUBLICATION: W.R.C. Smith Publishing Company; Walter Mitchell, Jr., publisher. Atlanta Georgia.
EDITORS: James A. Hooten (November 1977–1980); Lisa Newsom (1980-present).
CIRCULATION: 174,000.

THE SOUTHERN AND WESTERN LITERARY MESSENGER AND REVIEW: DEVOTED TO EVERY DEPARTMENT OF LITERATURE AND THE FINE ARTS. *See* THE SOUTHERN LITERARY MESSENGER

SOUTHERN APALACHIAN. *See* THE MAGNOLIA

THE SOUTHERN BIVOUAC

In September 1882 the Southern Historical Association of Louisville, Kentucky, began publishing the *Bivouac*, a monthly periodical devoted to preserving accounts of the Civil War and the Confederacy that might otherwise die with the passing generations. In August 1883 W. M. Marriner and W. N. McDonald began editing the magazine, altering its title to the *Southern Bivouac: A Monthly Literary and Historical Magazine* and broadening its content to include papers read before the sponsoring association, battle accounts and other war-connected stories, poetry, and a section of miscellany. They wished to preserve, the editors said:

> the life and body of Confederate times. It is believed that the soldiers of neither side desire the remembrance of that period to perish. Its very bitterness has its lessons, while the good and brave deeds that adorned it are the precious heritage of our common country.
>
> But the survivors of the lost cause can least of all afford to be silent. The fairest history a victor may write never does justice to the cause of the conquered. [August 1883]

Definitely not a Southern spokesman of the ''Fergit, hell!'' school, the *Bivouac* maintained a gentlemanly and conciliatory tone, probably more so than its distinguished predecessors *Scott's Monthly Magazine** (Atlanta, Georgia, 1865–1870), *The Land We Love** (Charlotte, North Carolina, 1866–1869), *Our Living and Our Dead** (Newbern, North Carolina, 1873–1876), or the *Southern Historical Society Papers* (Richmond, Virginia, 1876–1959). The editors solicited manuscripts from Northern as well as Southern writers and in cooperation with Boston's monthly *Bivouac* offered both magazines for $2.50 a year. The *Southern Bivouac*'s terms singly were $1.50, in advance, or 15¢ a number.

It might fairly be observed that by 1882, battle accounts and other such copy from the war had come to be quite familiar to Southern readers. Perhaps it had, in fact, been ''done to death'' in the manner of present-day television, which seizes on a major news development and ''talks it to death,'' wringing every conceivable drop of saleability from it before passing on to something new. At least it may be said that the *Bivouac*'s war accounts were often done in sprightly, appealing style, as in this extract from ''Vicksburg in 1862'':

> On the 19th day of June, 1862, our division (Breckinridge's) was detached from Bragg's army at Tupelo, Mississippi, and we moved westward. The first day's march was to Pontotoc; the next to Lafayette Springs, then in disuse as a place of summer resort, however, and that night our bivouac fires lighted up the groves which had, no doubt, been the scene of many a ''Meet-me-by-moonlight alone'' campaign in former times. [September 1884]

In September 1883, Editor Marriner resigned and E. H. McDonald took his place; the McDonald brothers edited volume 3 together. They claimed in this month and year to have the largest circulation of any magazine published south of the Ohio River—3,000. They predicted a circulation of 5,000 by 1885 (actually it reached 7,500) but added that ''reconstruction has taught us to advance cautiously, and at every halt to fortify.''

The growing magazine was purchased by B. F. Avery and Sons, publisher of Louisville's *Home and Farm*, the South's most successful nonnewspaper periodical of its day, and a new editorial duo took over beginning with the June 1885 issue. They were Basil W. Duke, a former Confederate general, and Richard W. Knott, editor of the biweekly *Home and Farm*. Their wish, they told their readers, was to present the South "not as something separate from the national but as an inseparable and integral part of it."

As indicated by Professor Rayburn Moore,[1] the *Bivouac*'s most enduring contribution was in its nonfiction essays. Outstanding among these was the three-part (September-November 1885) "Ante-Bellum Charleston" by Paul Hamilton Hayne. In part 1 Hayne describes the city's early years, painting a picture of its tranquil, aristocratic culture in the prewar era, and describing Hugh Swinton Legare (1797–1843) and Robert Young Hayne (1791–1839), his uncle. Part 2 was a very personal essay on his friend William Gilmore Simms; and part 3 treated John Russell, the Charleston literati who gathered at Russell's book store, and *Russell's Magazine*.*[2]

Another of Paul Hayne's excellent nonfiction contributions was a three-part essay (June-August 1886) on Charles Gayarre of New Orleans, his politics, and his literary contributions. Gayarre himself had contributed an interview with Secretary of State Seward on reconstruction (February 1886). Other interesting nonfiction works included Alexander Stephen's "My Impressions of General Robert E. Lee," George Devereux's "Southern Ghost Stories," Kate Rowland's "The Virginia Cavaliers," Polk Johnson's "Jefferson Davis at Home," and Lafcadio Hearn's "New Orleans Fencing Masters." After Paul Hayne's death in July 1886, a long essay on his life and literature was done for the *Bivouac* by his old friend Margaret J. Preston (September 1886). Three memorial poems also appeared in the August, September, and December numbers, the best of which was also by Mrs. Preston.

Less important, but of interest, were Felix Oswald's "Southern Summer Resorts," D. L. Wilson's controversial "The Beginnings of the Ku-Klux Klan," and Alpheus Baker's "The Pocahontas of the South," about the Creek girl Malee, who saved a white man named McCrimmon from execution.

A section of respectable poetry followed the essays in this forty-eight-page monthly. Rayburn Moore rates as its best poem "Robert Lee" by Paul Hayne, who characterized Lee as "calmly benignant, and superbly bold, all incorruptible—unbought, unsold—a steadfast splendor in a stormy sky" (February 1886).

Comment and criticism was a department of the magazine that dealt with battles and the war, as well as such diverse topics as Southern dialect, Persian wit, and "Hadrian's Address to His Soul." In the "Editor's Table" section appeared remarks on Christmas as celebrated in the North and South, education in the South, and George Eliot's life and letters. In general, the *Bivouac* was strong in literary criticism, not so strong in original fiction.

Never able to attain its circulation goal of 25,000, the magazine's owners sold out to the *Century* in 1887. By this purchase the *Century* eliminated its Southern competitor, and the New York monthly began publishing the work of several *Bivouac* regulars.

Notes

1. " 'A Distinctively Southern Magazine': The Southern Bivouac," *Southern Literary Journal*, 2 (Spring 1970):60.

2. For a full account of this series, see Daniel Morley McKeithan, "Paul Hamilton Hayne and The Southern Bivouac," *University of Texas Studies in English*, 17 (1937):114–18.

Information Sources

BIBLIOGRAPHY:

McKeithan, Daniel Morley. "Paul Hamilton Hayne and The Southern Bivouac." *University of Texas Studies in English*, 17 (1937):112–23.

Moore, Rayburn S. " 'A Distinctively Southern Magazine': The Southern Bivouac." *Southern Literary Journal*, 2 (Spring 1970):51–63.

Mott, Frank Luther. *A History of American Magazines, 1865–1885*. Cambridge, 1938. III:47.

INDEX SOURCES: None.

LOCATION SOURCES: Library of Congress, Newberry Library (Chicago), New York Public Library, University of Chicago Library, University of Georgia Library, University of North Carolina Library (Chapel Hill), University of Texas Library (Austin).

Publication History

MAGAZINE TITLE AND TITLE CHANGES: *The Bivouac* (September-October 1882); *The Southern Bivouac: A Monthly Literary and Historical Magazine* (November 1882-May 1887).

VOLUME AND ISSUE DATA: Vols. 1–2, New Series Vols. 1–2 (September 1882-May 1887), monthly.

PUBLISHER AND PLACE OF PUBLICATION: Southern Historical Association of Louisville, Kentucky (September 1882-July 1883); W. N. McDonald and E. H. McDonald (August 1883-May 1885); B. F. Avery and Sons (June 1885-May 1887). Louisville, Kentucky.

EDITORS: Members of the Southern Historical Association of Louisville (September 1882-July 1883); W. M. Marriner and W. N. McDonald (August-September 1883); W. N. McDonald and E. H. McDonald (October 1883-May 1885); Basil W. Duke and Richard W. Knott (June 1885-May 1887).

CIRCULATION: About 15,000.

THE SOUTHERN CULTIVATOR

One of the most successful of Southern farm journals was the *Southern Cultivator*, which appeared in Augusta, Georgia, in 1843, moved to Athens in 1865, and was relocated to Atlanta in 1880. Among the South's ante bellum farm magazines, the *Cultivator*'s 93-year span was exceeded only by its Richmond contemporary the *Southern Planter*'s* 130 years (1841–1969). It is worth noting that of all the region's various periodicals, farm journals and religious magazines enjoyed by far the greatest longevity. One might deduce that these were the two subject fields that "hit Southerners where they lived." A caveat must be added, however, in that the religious magazines' longevity was partly due to their sponsorship by organized church groups that could provide financial underpinning. The best of the agricultural magazines, one assumes, lasted well because of their practicality and everyday usefulness to the working farmer in an era before government and universities provided much agricultural advice.

The magazine was founded by J. W. and W. S. Jones of Augusta. Its original subtitle read: *A Semi-Monthly Journal, Devoted to Southern Agriculture, Designed to Improve the Mind, and Elevate the Character of the Tillers of the Soil, and to Introduce a More Enlightened System of Culture*. In later years this subtitle was simplified in variations and in the late 1890s was changed to *The Representative of Southern Agriculture*.

Page one of the first number of the sixteen-page magazine featured a long letter on farming methods written in 1793 by George Washington. Editor J. W. Jones remarked that the document was "valuable not only because it affords many excellent lessons from an able and practical farmer. . . . We see here the exercise in private life of that attention to detail, that inflexible devotion to order and discipline, which so eminently mark the public character of Washington."

That the new magazine was sold by what was then called the cash system provides evidence of Jones' own practicality. Subscribers were to hand their $1 for twelve yearly issues to their postmasters, who would place the order for them. Jones candidly advised his readers that "we cannot afford to send a collector over the country to collect bills of one dollar each, and shall not attempt such a piece of folly" (1,24:206), a policy that saved him from the sorry fate of so many more trusting editors.

Like other farm journals of the era, the *Cultivator* offered brief articles in the how-to-do-it vein and gave farmers a platform for offering the benefit of their experience to their fellows. After two years, Jones retired as editor, citing the necessity of spending more time with his other more profitable interests, and the editor's chair was then occupied for another two years by James Camak of Athens, who converted the *Cultivator* to monthly publication in 1845. Upon Camak's death in 1846, Daniel Lee, M.D., formerly with New York's *Genesee Farmer*, became editor. Lee was joined as co-editor in 1852 by D. Redmond, whose editorial association with the magazine lasted until 1867. In 1861 Redmond adopted as the *Cultivator*'s motto or slogan: "AGRICULTURE is the most general pursuit of man. It is the BASIS of all things; and, therefore, the most USEFUL and HONORABLE."

Issues of the Civil War era may be of special interest to the historian. Noteworthy articles on the South's "peculiar institution" are "The African Slave Trade" (17,3:68–71) by Garnett Andrews of Washington, Georgia; "Serfs, Not Slaves; or, the Relation between the Races at the South" (19,4:105–11) by a South Carolinian who signed himself "H"; and "The African Mystery" (21,3/4:42–43). In a letter in the May/June 1862 number, the writer concludes that the Negro should be kept enslaved "because the African is an inferior being, differently organized from the white man, with wool instead of hair on his head" (20,5 and 6:110). Despite the appearance of such bigoted rhetoric in their journal, and despite their own reference to blacks as "Sambo and Cuffee," the editors took no strong stand on the slavery question but kept mainly to questions of farming. In the same issue a department called "Recipes &c" contained tips on how to make cottonseed soap and homemade starch, how to treat sprains and repair broken china, and a dubious cure for chills involving a turpentine rubdown.

During the difficult days of 1864 Redmond tried operating the magazine as a weekly, but shortages of paper and labor caused this arrangement to sour. The *Cultivator* reappeared as a monthly in January 1865, this time in Athens, Georgia. William and W. L. Jones again became owners in late 1867 and were the magazine's editors and publishers until 1872, when W. L. Jones took over as sole editor and publisher.

After the Civil War, about all that was left to Southerners was the land. The central importance of agriculture in the impoverished region resulted in the birth of a good many new farm periodicals in the years immediately following the war.[1]

In 1880 the *Cultivator* was moved to Atlanta, with W. L. Jones remaining as editor and the Constitution Publishing Company taking over as publisher. The *Georgia Grange* of Atlanta; the *Rural Sun* of Nashville, Tennessee; and the *Plantation* of Montgomery, Alabama, were absorbed by the *Cultivator*, and in November 1886 its title was enlarged to the *Southern Cultivator and Dixie Farmer*. In the years immediately following, a fashion department was added, and folksy humor appeared in the crackerbarrel prose of Bill Arp (as in "Bill Arp Writes of the Beauties of Nature," 43,1:21) and the homely effusions of Bill Simmons, "The Cracker Poet."[2] By 1887 the magazine, which now contained enough advertising to make it profitable, had also absorbed the *Southern Farmer's Monthly* of Savannah, the *Phoenix Agriculturist* of Marietta, and the *Southern World* of Atlanta and had considerably increased both the quality and quantity of its engravings. By 1895 a few photographs appeared, interspersed among the engravings. In 1899 the *Southern Farm* was absorbed.

Gains in the scientific study of agriculture were reflected in 1901 in a new motto for the *Cultivator*: "The Text-Book of the Tiller of the Soil." By 1905 the magazine advertised a "sworn average circulation" of 50,000, of which about 19,000 subscribers were in Georgia. Issues at this time were thirty-six pages long. Content was divided into the following departments: editorials, timely suggestions, letters from the field, the farm home, horticulture, gardening, poultry, dairy, live stock, and publisher's notes.

After absorbing *Farming* of Knoxville in 1926, the magazine again altered its title, this time to *Southern Cultivator and Farming*. A file of these more recent copies of the *Cultivator* has not been located, but according to the best information available, it was merged into the *Southern Farmer* after July 1935.

Notes

1. Farm magazines that began between the end of hostilities and 1870 were *Farmer: Devoted to Agriculture, Horticulture, the Mechanic Arts and Household Economy* (Richmond, 1866–67); *Southern Ruralist* (Tangipahoa, La., 1866–67); *Farmer's Home Journal* (Lexington, Louisville, Ky., 1867–1932); *Phillips' Southern Farmer* (Memphis, Tenn., 1867–74); *Banner of the South and Planters' Journal* (Augusta, Ga., 1868–72); *Dixie Farmer* (Knoxville, Tenn.; Atlanta, Ga., 1868–82); *Farm and Family* (Louisville, Ky., 1868–1918); *Farm and Garden* (Clinton, S.C., 1868); *Rural Southerner* (Atlanta, Ga., 1868–76); *Dixie Farmer* (Nashville, Tenn., 1869); *Farmers' Gazette and Industrial Index* (Richmond, Va., 1869–71); *Model Farmer* (Corinth, Miss.; Nashville, Tenn., 1869-?); *Reconstructed Farmer* (Tarboro, N.C., 1869–72); *Rural Carolinian, an Illustrated Magazine of Agriculture, Horticulture and the Arts* (Charleston, S.C., 1869–76); *Southern Agriculturist* (Corinth, Miss.; Nashville, Tenn., 1869–1949); *Southern Farm and Home* (Macon, Ga.; Memphis, Tenn., 1869–73); *Southern Horticulturist* (Canton, Miss., 1869–70).

2. See "The Yearlins," vol. 43, no. 1, p. 45. The poem began:

> Hits forty years ago sence me
>   An' Hitty Ann was hitch't.

> No prearter nor a hansomer
>   Than her, the boys bewitch.

With his wife came a dowery of two fine yearling calves. One night this farmer was returning home from a trip when he saw a fiery glow:

> I knowed at once the Injun sign,
>   An' hid till airly dawn—

> Lord bless me, boy, my wife was dead,
>   My house an' fixin's gone,

> But what I hated wust of all—
> I low hit made my spirits fall—
>   The Injuns tuk them yearlins!

Information Sources

BIBLIOGRAPHY:
McLean, Frank. "Periodicals Published in the South before 1880." Ph.D. dissertation, University of Virginia, 1928. Pp. 94–104.
McMillen, James A. "Mr. McMillen's Address." *Bulletin of the American Library Association*, 28 (December 15, 1933):626–28.
INDEX SOURCES: None.
LOCATION SOURCES: American Periodical Series microfilm (vols. 1–64), Atlanta Public Library, Carnegie Library of Pittsburgh, Duke University Library, New York Public Library, Princeton University Library, University of Massachusetts Library (Amherst), University of Texas Library (Austin), U.S. Department of Agriculture Library.

Publication History

MAGAZINE TITLE AND TITLE CHANGES: *The Southern Cultivator* (1843–1886);
The Southern Cultivator and Dixie Farmer (1886–1926); *Southern Cultivator and
Farming* (1927–1935).

VOLUME AND ISSUE DATA: Vols. 1–93 (March 1843-July 1935); semimonthly (1843–
1845), monthly (1845–1864), weekly (1864), monthly (1865-?).

PUBLISHER AND PLACE OF PUBLICATION: J. W. Jones and W. S. Jones (1843–
1851); William S. Jones (1852–1860); D. Redmond (1861–1864); D. Redmond
and William M. White (1865–1867); D. Redmond and J. Camak (1867); William
Jones and W. L. Jones (1868–1872); W. L. Jones (1872–1878); Constitution
Publishing Company (1880–1881); James P. Harrison & Co. (1882–1885); The
Cultivator Publishing Company (1885-?). Augusta, Georgia (1853–1865); Athens,
Georgia (1865–1880); Atlanta, Georgia (1880–1935).

EDITORS: J. W. Jones (1843–1845); James Camak (1845–1847); Daniel Lee (1847–
1851); Daniel Lee and D. Redmond (1852–1858); D. Lee, D. Redmond, and
C. W. Howard (1859); D. Redmond and C. W. Howard (1859–1861); D. Redmond (1862–1863); D. Redmond and William N. White (1863–1867); D. Redmond and J. Camak (1867); William Jones and W. L. Jones (1868–1872); W. L.
Jones (1872–1878, 1880–1898); James B. Hunnicutt (1899–1902); G. F. Hunnicutt (1906–1919); unknown (1919–1935).

CIRCULATION: 50,000 in 1906.

SOUTHERN EXPOSURE

Among Southern magazines *Southern Exposure* is unique. Where most recent
magazines with a regional slant have appealed to the affluent in order to attract
advertisers, this periodical, which began publication in May 1973, totally dis-
regards its readers' prosperity and has hardly any advertisers at all. While most
of the South's magazines stay away from politics or adopt a conservative stance,
Southern Exposure is very, very liberal. Whereas most of the region's magazines
speak for the comfortable, self-satisfied South, *Southern Exposure* is the voice
of the South's righteous indignation.

This bimonthly is published by The Institute for Southern Studies in Durham,
North Carolina, a nonprofit corporation dedicated to progressive change in the
region. In answer to frequent inquiries about both institute and magazine, the
magazine's inside front cover now lists the organization's three goals: (1) building
grass-roots organizations with effective strategies and leadership, (2) providing
current information and historical understanding of Southern social struggles
necessary for long-term change, and (3) aiding communication and understanding
among the South's diverse cultural groups.

The concept of a research institute for what was then termed The Movement
originated in 1965 with black Georgia politician Julian Bond and Sue Thrasher,
a white Southern activist, now a staffer with the Highland Center in New Market,
Tennessee. A brief account of this period penned by Thrasher appeared in *South-*

ern Exposure's tenth anniversary issue (May/June 1983) and told of the Southern liberal's need in the mid–1960s to know more about "the System"—"how it worked. Who it helped, and who it hurt. And who, besides us, wanted to change it" (11,3:3).

By 1969 plans for the institute had crystallized, and with the help of Howard Romaine, who had also helped found Atlanta's underground newspaper *Great Speckled Bird*,[1] Bond and Thrasher set up shop at 88 Walton Street in Atlanta. The institute's first public seminar featured Gunnar Myrdal, author of *The American Dilemma*. Another prominent speaker was Daniel Ellsberg, who had come into the public eye in the Pentagon Papers affair.

The institute's initial efforts centered on the antiwar movement. Later Bob Hall, now *Southern Exposure*'s publisher, joined the institute and began a corporate research project. Hall's wife Jacquelyn, Sue Thrasher, and another new staffer, Leah Wise, became interested in oral history as a means of evolving a fuller picture of Southern history by including the voices of the working class, the poor, and the black. A later arrival, Jim Trammel, spoke of this as "uncovering our own true history, and not buying the history of 'lies agreed upon' " (11,3:9).

The push to have the institute publish its own magazine came from Bob Hall, the only founder still with *Southern Exposure* today. He saw it as a means of reaching new people and developing a larger constituency for the institute and a way to involve liberal Southern scholars with the organization's work. A magazine, he said, would help staffers discipline their work by providing deadlines, would contribute toward a broader analysis of the South, and might provide a limited amount of subscription revenue.[2] The first issue, "The Military and the South," appeared in May 1973 and included an exposé of Lockheed's $2 billion overrun on the C–5A aircraft and a 40-page, state-by-state analysis of defense spending in the South. The second issue was built around an energy theme; the third and fourth numbers of volume 1, entitled "No More Moanin'," offered a 225-page picture of the Great Depression-era South, depending heavily on the oral history method. Theme issues have been more the rule than the exception. The magazine's name was suggested by Sue Thrasher, who took it from a 1946 book by that title written by Stetson Kennedy. The magazine began as a quarterly and in 1982 was converted to bimonthly publication. Single issue price is either $3 or $4, depending upon length of issue; annual subscription rates are $16 for individuals, $20 for libraries. Issues typically run from 72 to 120 pages in length.

In 1973 the magazine moved with the Halls to Chapel Hill, where it remained until the autumn of 1979. In November 1979 it moved to new quarters at 604 West Chapel Hill Street in nearby Durham, North Carolina. Some persons who have seen issues of *Southern Exposure* assume that because of its locations in Chapel Hill and Durham the institute must be affiliated with the University of North Carolina or Duke University. Actually it is an independent organization supported by small donations, small grants, and subscription revenues. Of its

8,000 subscribers, 90 percent are individuals, 10 percent are libraries. Subscribers are scattered throughout the South, with subscriptions heaviest in North Carolina, Georgia, and Tennessee.

The magazine's contents are a curious study in contrasts. Those who write and edit its copy are at the same time Southern radicals and Southern chauvinists. It must be admitted that this approach results in a fuller picture of the South than most other magazines have provided, though the middle-class, heterosexual, mortgage-paying Southern male with a steady job could get a complex from reading some of *Southern Exposure*'s articles. More than anyone else, Bob Hall is responsible for the magazine's tone. Former staffer Steve Cummings describes Hall as combining "the innocent guilelessness of a Jesuit with the easy-going laziness of John Calvin. As talkative as a Trappist monk, as tolerant as Torquemada," and reflects that the magazine's work atmosphere "captured the best aspects of the sweat shop and the Spanish Inquisition" (11,3:7). Certainly no one has worked for *Southern Exposure* for the money. Working there has been more a matter of mission. Jacquelyne Hall characterizes the magazine as a way station that has allowed a stream of individuals a chance to do something tangible and lasting with their political convictions and a place to develop their writing skills.

In theme issues, guest editors who were not regular staff members have made large contributions: Tobi Lippin and Candace Waid on Southern women, Peter Wood and Tema Okum on Southern sports, Stephen March and Bob Brinkmeyer on Southern literature, Tony Dunbar on Southern prisons, Jim Sessions and Bill Troy on religion in the region, Allen Tullos on Southern folklife.

The magazine's physical appearance, which has remained fairly constant over its first decade, was largely the work of Stephanie Coffin, who had earlier worked on graphics for the *Great Speckled Bird*. The most striking feature of the photographs in *Southern Exposure* is that they are of working people in their natural settings, which the magazine views as something of an antidote to the posed shots of beautiful models and upper-middle-class Southerners doing upper-middle-class things that one expects to find in most other magazines. Photos are strictly black and white; only the covers are in color. The magazine also differs from most others in that it feels an obligation to use the work of Southern photographers and artists, even if better-quality illustrations might be available elsewhere. Artwork varies from excellent to the occasionally amateurish, and of the photography, the best work consists of shots that show the dignity of blue-collar labor and humble dwellings and portraits of the Southern poor. An example of the former is the work of Kenneth Murray in the July/August 1982 number (in "People Pieces," 10,4:17–21), and of the latter, the close-up of Miss Susie Walker by Reesa Tansey in January/February 1983 (11,1:64).

Of the multitude of ills addressed by this magazine—agent orange, the boll weevil, brown lung, convict labor and peonage, corporate dominance, the death penalty, Hilton Head Island ("a Disneyland for wealthy WASPS"), hookworm, the Klan, the McDonaldization of bookshops, the mosquito, nuclear energy, strip mining, urban renewal that equates with Negro removal, vigilante violence—the region's race problems predominate. Another of the magazine's continuing missions is to show the poor and lower-middle-class Southerner that he or she has more in common with the area's blacks than with the kind of whites pictured in *Southern Living** or *Texas Monthly.** The magazine's protest copy is often right on target, but some of its gripe pieces put one in mind of Al Capp's mythical protest organization SWINE, or, Students Wildly Indignant about Nearly Everything. Disney World, instead of being enjoyed for what it is, is seen by one *Southern Exposure* writer as evidence that Americans are so "profoundly alienated from creativity, community and realization that they must be told when to have a good time" (1,2:23–28). Black writer Alice Walker complains that Joel Chandler Harris stole part of her heritage when he popularized the Uncle Remus tales by somehow making her feel ashamed (9,2:29–31).

Some of *Southern Exposure*'s best contributions come when it burrows beneath the accustomed veneer of New South prosperity to tell us many things about our region. In "A Mighty Fortress," Jim Sessions informs us that there are 245 Baptist churches in Houston, Texas, and 152 in Dallas, compared to but 65 for the entire state of West Virginia (4,3:88–91). Allen Tullos introduces us to Arthur "Peg Leg Sam" Jackson, hobo, a man so poor that "if I was to die, they'd make me walk to the cemetery" (3,4:40–45). Chris Walters-Bugbee writes about black midwife Gussie Jackson (5,1:4–12); Sue Thrasher tells us how Minnie Pearl made her start in show business in Aiken, South Carolina (2,4:32–40); and Peter Guralnick profiles Sleepy Labeef, a Shreveport rockabilly singer (9,3:68–72). Nick Lindsay interviewed Edisto Islanders Sam Gadsden and Bubberson Brown for their first-hand accounts of the great earthquake of 1886 and the storm of 1893 (10,3:27–32). Those of us who lead ordinary, "average" lives might be surprised, and even shocked, upon reading "Lesbian Writing in the South" (9,2:53–62).

Regular features in *Southern Exposure* are "Facing South: Voices of Tradition in a Changing Region," which also goes out as a weekly syndicated column to more than eighty newspapers, newsletters, and other magazines; a book review section; an additional listing of books about the South; and "Voices from the Past," a one-page feature that tries to recapture "the indomitable spirit of those who have spoken for human dignity for egalitarianism and for collective social action."

Southern Exposure has a lot to recommend it. For those of us who are fairly well-off whites, it can cut through our traditional complacence and make us look at the South's vulnerable underside. It can also leave us with a vague feeling of uneasiness. In a review of *The Redneck Way of Knowledge: Down-Home Tales*, author Blanche McCrary Boyd is quoted by the reviewer as saying, "Being a white Southerner is a bit like being Eichmann's daughter: people don't assume you're guilty, but they wonder how you've been affected" (11,1:68).

Notes

1. Romaine is now a Baton Rouge attorney.
2. Hall's memo arguing for establishing the magazine is reprinted on p. 176 of the tenth anniversary issue, vol. 11, no. 3.

Information Sources

BIBLIOGRAPHY:
Boyd, Richard. "Southern Magazine Delighted to Turn 10." *Times-Picayune/States-Item*, July 21, 1983.
Hartman, Leda. "10 Years of Southern Exposure." *Ruralamerica*, July/August, 1983.
Jones, Gregg. "Southern Exposure Opens a Window for Liberals in Region." *Atlanta Journal and Constitution*, June 26, 1983.
Pressley, Sue Anne. "Magazine Marks Decade as a Voice of Southern Liberalism." *Charlotte Observer*, August 15, 1983.
Turner, Paul. "Liberal Magazine Defies Odds, Lives." *Commercial Appeal* (Memphis), June 19, 1983.
INDEX SOURCES: Alternative Press Index, Historical Abstracts, Humanities Index, Sociological Abstracts.
LOCATION SOURCES: Duke University Library, Library of Congress, New York Public Library, University of Georgia Library, University of South Carolina Library, University of Tennessee Library.

Publication History

MAGAZINE TITLE AND TITLE CHANGES: *Southern Exposure*.
VOLUME AND ISSUE DATA: Vols. 1–12; quarterly (May 1973-December 1981), bimonthly (January 1982-present).
PUBLISHER AND PLACE OF PUBLICATION: Institute for Southern Studies. Chapel Hill, North Carolina (May 1973-October 1979); Durham, North Carolina (November 1979-present).
EDITORS: Bob Hall, managing editor and publisher (May 1973-December 1983); Michael Yellin, managing editor (January 1984-present).
CIRCULATION: 8,000 paid.

THE SOUTHERN LADIES' BOOK: A MAGAZINE OF LITERATURE, SCIENCE AND ARTS. *See* THE MAGNOLIA

THE SOUTHERN LITERARY GAZETTE

The best of William Gilmore Simms' early magazine efforts[1] was the *Southern Literary Gazette*, published in Charleston, South Carolina, in 1828 and 1829. Simms and his co-editor, Harvard-educated James Wright Simmons, had originally proposed to call their magazine the *Tablet* and were to publish it as an eight-page weekly.[2] Within three weeks they had reevaluated their prospects and opted for the more manageable pace of a monthly[3] and somewhat later selected a more descriptive title: the *Southern Literary Gazette*. The magazine appeared in September 1828 as a sixty-four-page literary miscellany printed in one-column format, published by P.M.S. Neufville of Charleston.

Despite a favorable reception by the local newspaper press, subscriptions at $4 per annum were slow and contributors few. In March 1829 Simmons withdrew from the venture and left his younger partner to sole conduct of the *Gazette*. Simms began a new series in May, issuing the magazine as a twenty-four-page semimonthly done in two-column format and published by A. F. Cunningham. Using the *Critic* of New York as a model, Simms divided content into three departments: critical notices of new publications, original poetry, and general miscellany. Criticism would follow the example of the *London Literary Gazette* by using liberal extracts of the works reviewed. John C. Guilds contends that the critical notices department was the most valuable part of Simms' work and that "the heavy hand of morality and sentimentality rules the poetry and the fiction."[4]

Today's magazine editor might well be staggered at the amount of the *Gazette*'s content actually written by the editor. According to John Guild's count, twenty-eight of the forty-one poems in volume 1 were written by Simms, and six of the remaining thirteen were written by Co-editor Simmons. The situation was probably similar for the magazine's prose content, though the case cannot be proved because so many contributions were run unsigned.

Even the most ardent defender of Southern letters would have to admit that Simms' poetic efforts were marked more by quantity than quality. Most of his prodigious outpouring of verse was mired to the axles in a quagmire of sentimentality that makes it distasteful to today's reader. Still, one cannot help liking Simms better after reading "Sketch of a Gobbler, By Ourself," a sentimental last look at the family turkey, which ended:

> He was not singular, nor differed he
> In instinct or in appetite, or look
> From any of his *race*, except in this—
> He was our own, the only one we had,
> And therefore was he *singular* to us.
> But Christmas came apace—a merry time,
> And gobbler died at last, and meekly dress'd,
> Was brought upon the table, where he lay—
> Forgetting he is dead, we long for him—
> "Life was in him so passing beautiful!" [N.S.1,4:78]

One wonders if a little poem entitled "Ladies' Bonnets" was also Simms' work. It was signed EBO, which is suspiciously close to the E with which he signed nine poems in the *Gazette* and Nemo, another of his many known pen names,[5] and reads:

> Good Fates, if it be crime to be a man
> The crime's in you—I'll leave it if I can.
> For danger and much evil's to be found,
> For all our sex not underneath the ground.
> The Fair, I (think) they're call'd, not satisfied,
> To blind our eyes and win our hearts beside,
> Fleece our strong coffers, revel in our spoils,
> The sole reward of many heavy toils;
> Not now content as once of old they were,
> To leave their wicked faces to our stare,
> As some small compensation for the great
> And heavy evils sent with them by fate,
> Now take this last enjoyment from our sight,
> And wear umbrella hats to keep out light—
> The lovely, to enhance, by Fancy's skill
> The sweets beneath and make them sweeter still—
> The ugly—(God forbid that there should be
> An ugly woman,) that we should not see
> The shrivelled face and floured check below—
> Made, unlike "Pindar's razors"—not for show. [1,3:192]

Taken on the whole, the *Gazette*'s prose was superior to its poetry. An early example of an interesting prose piece was "Duelling," which began, "The efforts of the Legislature, and the denunciations of the Pulpit, having equally failed to put an end to this pernicious and unchristian practice," only education could "counteract those principles of false honor." The article points out that "the Greeks, Spartans and Romans, though certainly sufficiently high minded and warlike, fought no duels—an apparent anomaly which has sadly puzzled our modern men of the sword," which the writer ascribes to the result of education (1,2:65–73).

An unusual review in the same issue was done of *The Art of Tying the Cravat* by Eugene Victoire. Giving a history of the cravat, the writer delivers up a droll review of upper-crust interest (pp. 92–98).

One of Simms' best contributions to his general miscellany department was a series of six pieces that ran from August 1, 1829, entitled "Chronicles of Ashley River." Chronicle No. 1 was written in a curious, churchly style, beginning "Now it comes to pass in those times that the village being grown into size and appearance" and concluding "Here endeth the first Chronicle." The "Chronicles" tell the story of conflict between the Yemassee Indians and white settlers in the Charleston area, and this early work prefigures his later historical novels *The Yemassee* and *The Cassique of Kiawah*.

The *Gazette*'s last number was published on November 1, 1829. This number is unavailable on film but was located in 1968 among uncataloged materials in the South Caroliniana collection at the University of South Carolina in Columbia. It is thought possible that Simms joined forces with publisher-printer James S. Burgess of Charleston and that one number of the *Pleiades* and *Southern Literary Gazette* may have been published.[6] No copies have been found.

For a second time Simms' ambition to further the cause of Southern periodical letters had died an early death. In considering this, one is put in mind of the last verse of "The Lost Pleiad," which Guilds rates as far and away the best of Simms' poems to appear in this magazine:

A strain—a mellow strain
Of parting music fell'd the earth and sky;—
The stars lamenting in unborrowed pain,
That one of the selectest ones must die,
The brightest of their train!
Alas! it is the destiny—
The shortest lived are loveliest,
And like yon full orb shooting down the sky
Are always brightest when about to fly
From the lone spot they blest! [1,2:74]

Notes

1. His first experience as a magazine editor was with the *Album*, Charleston, 1825. See John C. Guilds, "Simm's First Magazine: The *Album*,"*Studies in Bibliography*, 8, (1956):169–83. Simms' third such effort was with the *Cosmopolitan: An Occasional*, Charleston, 1833. See John C. Guilds, "William Gilmore Simms and the *Cosmopolitan*," *Georgia Historical Quarterly*, 41 (1957):31–41.

2. See their prospectus in the *Charleston Courier* of June 7, 1828.

3. See their revised prospectus in the *City Gazette and Commercial Daily Advertiser* of June 27, 1828.

4. "William Gilmore Simms and the *Southern Literary Gazette*," *Studies in Bibliography*, 21 (1968):65.

5. See James E. Kibler, Jr., *Pseudonymous Publications of William Gilmore Simms* (Athens, Ga., 1976), p. 3.

6. See prospectus for the *Pleiades: A Weekly Literary Gazette*, in the *Charleston Courier*, August 29, 1829. See also John C. Guilds, "The 'Lost' Number of the *Southern Literary Gazette*," *Studies in Bibliography*, 22 (1969):266–73.

Information Sources

BIBLIOGRAPHY:
Guilds, John C. "The 'Lost' Number of the *Southern Literary Gazette*." *Studies in Bibliography*, 22 (1969):266–73.
———. "William Gilmore Simms and the *Southern Literary Gazette*." *Studies in Bibliography*, 21 (1968):59–92.

Mott, Frank Luther. *A History of American Magazines, 1741–1850*. New York, 1930.
    P. 382.
INDEX SOURCES: None.
LOCATION SOURCES: American Periodical Series microfilm, Library of Congress.

Publication History

MAGAZINE TITLE AND TITLE CHANGES: *The Southern Literary Gazette.*
VOLUME AND ISSUE DATA: Vol. 1 (September 1828-March 1829), monthly; New
    Series vol. 1 (May 15-November 1, 1829), semimonthly.
PUBLISHER AND PLACE OF PUBLICATION: P.M.S. Neufville (September 1828-
    March 1829); A. F. Cunningham (May 15-November 1, 1829). Charleston, South
    Carolina.
EDITORS: William Gilmore Simms and James Wright Simmons (September 1828-March
    1829); W. G. Simms (May-November 1829).
CIRCULATION: Unknown.

THE SOUTHERN LITERARY JOURNAL

> The influence of a popular national literature upon the social and political
> condition of those among whom it exists, is correctly regarded as of the
> highest importance. In a country like our own, where the sovereign power,
> in practice no less than in theory, resides in the people, it is necessary that
> the people should be intelligent. On this foundation only can the fabric of
> our institutions firmly rest. On this account, our country requires for its
> highest prosperity, a popular literature of a peculiar kind; a literature
> deserving the name of American, alike in its range of subjects, and its
> tone of feeling. [1,1:1]

With these idealistic words began the *Southern Literary Journal, and Monthly
Magazine*, a regional literary miscellany located in Charleston and founded in
1835 by Daniel K. Whitaker. The *Journal*'s life was brief—two years under
Whitaker's ownership and one additional year under Bartholomew R. Carroll—
yet it added a respectable chapter to the literary history of Charleston. Printed
in one-column format by James S. Burges of 18 Broad-Street, the *Journal* began
as a sixty-four-page monthly, later increased to eighty pages.

Editor Whitaker's own comments were issued in a department called "From
Our Arm-Chair." His first such editorial column drew an analogy between his
new magazine and a chair:

> it is not a rocking-chair—but is planted firmly on the floor upon its four
> legs, as if to indicate that the position of an editor should be a steady
> one—that he should not be always bobbing up and down like a man rocking
> himself to sleep after a hearty dinner. Neither is it a trundle-chair, which

> may be made to change places at the pleasure of every whimsical and capricious person who may wish to see it put in motion. Neither is it a high-backed, well-stuffed, old-fashioned easy-chair, fit only for an invalid who has a headache.... Neither is it a professor's chair from which he reads lectures, nor a chairman's chair in which he presides at literary, political, commercial, or agricultural meetings; but simply an editor's chair constructed after the most approved fashion. [1,1:55]

The *Journal*'s motto, Whitaker told his readers, would be "Post Nubila Pheobus," or "After the Clouds the Sun," which on hindsight might have been more appropriate to a Southern magazine founded *after* the Civil War. The aim of the magazine, he added, would be "to rouse a spirit of inquiry and improvement among our citizens—to diffuse information and intelligence on interesting and important subjects among all classes of readers . . . , stimulate literary ambition, and elevate the standard of taste and feeling" (1,1:56). Pledges of assistance had been obtained from members of the Literary and Philosophical Society of South Carolina, under the auspices of which the *Journal* was published, and from members of the state's bar, clergy, medical profession, authors, and poets. The *Journal* would "at all times breathe a Southern spirit and sustain a strictly Southern character," despite the fact that Editor Whitaker was a Harvard-educated New Englander. Contributors were asked to select topics "bearing directly upon the customs, opinions, peculiarities, and general tone of thinking" of the South. "Come," wrote Whitaker with a flourish, "and bring your beautiful offerings to the consecrated ground and costly altar dedicated to the Muses. . . . Come! . . . stretch every nerve, spread every sail, and catch every breeze that can waft us to the future" (1,1:60).

Subsequent installments of "From Our Armchair" greeted the reader with essays: "The Seminoles" (2,2:153–55); "Natural History of the Negro Race," in which Whitaker defends the institution of slavery;[1] "Southern Literature" (3,1:72–76); and "Modern Novels" (2,3:235–37). Sometimes Whitaker's column began with reviews, a good example of which comments on *The Life of Wm. Cobbett, Dedicated to His Sons*:

> Cobbett, we should judge from the work before us, had the organ of self-esteem very strongly developed upon his cranium, or at any rate, ought to have had. Few individuals ever entertained a higher opinion of their own talents and achievements than he did. . . . He loved to set the tongues and the pens of other men in motion, and he did not grieve much when he himself was the principal subject of their remarks and criticisms— Whether good or ill were said of him he cared little: if good, he accepted the praise only as his due; if evil, he was both ready and able to avenge himself. [2,2:155–59]

Essays, sketches, and poetry were interspersed throughout each issue rather than being segregated into departments. Perhaps the essays are the magazine's most memorable content. Some were preachy (''On Sacred Poetry and Literature'' [2,1:1–10]; ''On the Pleasure of Sorrow'' [3,2:91–97]), others pedantic (''On Medical Jurisprudence'' [1,6:369–80]; ''Etruscan Remains'' [2,2:81–89]; and ''Thea Orientalis'' [1,6:383–92]). Longer selections were serialized, such as ''Sketches of Indian Culture'' or ''Italian Poets of the Eighteenth Century.''

An interesting poetic feature was ''Southern Passages and Pictures,'' a series of four unsigned poems in volume 2, number 2 (pages 90–93). A frequent contributor was William Gilmore Simms, the South's leading literary light.

Three years into the venture, including a one-year suspension, editor Whitaker announced that for personal reasons he was ending his association with the *Journal*, saying ''I have not abandoned my offspring, but have only sent it from home'' (''Valedictory,'' 3,1:75–76), selling his interest to B. R. Carroll, who also succeeded him as editor. The conduct of the *Journal* was much the same under its new editor. An outstanding serialized feature under Carroll was ''Medical Sketch of South Carolina'' by W. G. Ramsay, M.D.; perhaps the most interesting of these selections is the second, on ''country fever'' (alias bilious fever, congestive fever, or miasmatic fever), a serious problem in extremely hot, humid areas of the un-air-conditioned South (n.s. 3,1:32–39; also n.s. 1,6:493–99; n.s. 3,5:385–91). The new series of the *Journal* also contained, according to Carroll's own summation, poetry, essays, tales, sketches—historical and fanciful—reviews and critical notices, general literary intelligence, pieces on philosophy and science, and articles on drama and the fine arts.

Carroll's valedictory in December 1838 began, ''The short span of the *Southern Literary Journal* is now brought to an untimely close. The last attempt at reviving the dying energies of Southern Literature has utterly failed,'' and ended, ''It is a fearful thing, this passing out of existence—becoming absolutely annihilated, void and of none effect. . . . We die like many flowers of brightest hue, with the year. Farewell, then, long suffering reader, 'vale, iterum atque iterum vale,' and as the old Roman comedian was wont to bid the audience on his departure from the stage, so say we, with all humility, 'Plaudite' '' (n.s. 4,6:474–75).

Note

1. ''It is very questionable whether the abolutionists in their efforts for the emancipation of the Negro race, are not attempting a thing, physically and morally impossible—if by emancipation be meant, enabling them to be republicans. . . . Of this republican liberty in government we believe the black race absolutely incapable'' (3,2:151).

Information Sources

BIBLIOGRAPHY:
Mott, Frank Luther. *A History of American Magazines, 1741–1850.* New York, 1930. Pp. 664–65.

INDEX SOURCES: None.
LOCATION SOURCES: American Periodical Series microfilm, Library of Congress,
    University of North Carolina Library (Chapel Hill).

Publication History

MAGAZINE TITLE AND TITLE CHANGES: *The Southern Literary Journal, and Monthly
    Magazine* (September 1835-August 1836); *The Southern Literary Journal, and
    Monthly Review* (September 1836-August 1837); *The Southern Literary Journal,
    and Magazine of Arts* (January-December 1838).
VOLUME AND ISSUE DATA: Vols. 1–3, new series vols. 1, 3–4 (September 1835-
    December 1838), monthly.
PUBLISHER AND PLACE OF PUBLICATION: Daniel K. Whitaker (September 1835-
    August 1837); Bartholomew R. Carroll (January-December 1838). Charleston,
    South Carolina.
EDITORS: Daniel K. Whitaker (September 1835-August 1837); Bartholomew R. Carroll
    (January-December 1838).
CIRCULATION: Unknown.

THE SOUTHERN LITERARY MAGAZINE

Yet another vain hope that the people of the South would support a literary
magazine prompted Henry E. Harman of Atlanta to found the *Southern Literary
Magazine* in July 1923. Published by the Harman Publishing Company, the
monthly was edited by Harman with help from Archibald Henderson of the
University of North Carolina; George A. Wauchope, University of South Carolina; Harry Stillwell Edwards of Macon, Georgia; Mary Brent Whiteside of
Atlanta; and Henry Bellamann of Chicora College. The magazine is included in
this selection of titles because it represents an attempt to be "literary" but to
reach a larger popular audience than had been the case with most of the region's
earlier literary periodicals, or with the so-called little magazines of the present
era.[1]

As had been the case with so many of his predecessors, the editor's first task
in volume 1 was an acknowledgment of the difficulties before him. The usual
causes of failure, he said, were lack of sufficient financial backing, lack of
literary ability, and lack of practical experience in the publishing business. During
his thirty years of managing technical publications in Atlanta, wrote Harman, a
dream had haunted him—a desire "to do something better than make money."
His pages in the *Southern Literary Magazine*, he went on, would be open to
aspiring writers presently unable to get a hearing in the Northern magazines;
like so many before him, Harman wanted to be instrumental in building a
Southern literature.

He would appeal to Northern book publishers for advertising patronage, rea-
soning that the encouragement of letters in the South would work to their advantage. Publishers advertising in the first issue were Lippincott; Boni & Liveright;

Heath & Co.; The W. G. Burke Company; The State Company; Martin, Hoyt & Co.; The Dial; Current History; The Lyric; McMillan; and Doubleday, Page & Co.

Represented in the new magazine were essays, poetry, history, biography, editorials, news items, and criticism, supported by a reasonably liberal supply of illustrations, among the most interesting of which was a series of forty-three drawings depicting Indian life in Georgia and Florida (1,1:7). The artist was Jacques Le Moyne de Morgues of Dieppe, France, a member of the Laudonniere expedition who escaped the Spanish massacre at Fort Carolina and lived for four years among the Indians before being rescued and returned to France.

Much of the magazine's prose content revolved around Southern literary figures, such as an article on how Tom Moore wrote "The Firefly" at Williamsburg, Virginia, or another concerning the letters of Edgar Allan Poe and Thomas Holley Chivers and the controversy over who originated the style in which "The Raven" was written. Other articles dealt with nonliterary historical topics: the route of De Soto through Florida, Georgia, Alabama, and Mississippi; the mysterious disappearance of Theodosia Allston, daughter of Aaron Burr; the early history of St. Simons Island. Poems published in the magazine were usually short, regionally oriented, and aimed at a fairly wide audience.[2]

In the second number, Harman suggested an ambitious plan to encourage Southern letters: the forming of a Southern Authors' Association. Harman's scheme called for a parent organization in Atlanta, with which local poetry societies, writers' clubs, and book clubs around the South could affiliate. He felt that the region had "reached a point in industrial and commercial development which puts us on the safe road to an era of great prosperity" and that like himself, the South might now afford to devote more of its attention to its literature.

Even the severest critics of Southern literature had by this time noticed something of a rebirth of the region's writing. Baltimore's H. L. Mencken, whose description of the cultural South as the "Sahara of the Bozart" had caused widespread consternation in Dixie, had by 1921 seen new hope for Southern literature in such periodicals as the *Double Dealer*,* the *Southerner*, and the *Reviewer*.[3] Contributing Editor Archibald Henderson asked Mencken to write a piece on Southern literature and art for the *Southern Literary Magazine*, and Mencken obliged. The October 1923 number's cover carried a portrait photo of the young Mencken. On page 3, headlined "Oases in the Desert," were Henderson's comments on Mencken and his "Sahara of the Bozart" charge. "The emotions aroused in Southern breasts by this cubist sketch," wrote Henderson, "which nevertheless bore many revealing lines of truth, ranged all the way from pained astonishment to blind rage. . . . Let us not mistake caricature for portraiture. H.L.M. is the G.B.S. of America." Henderson called Mencken a "desperado in depreciation, an *enfant terrible* of caricature. . . . No one enjoys shooting up the town more than Mencken, and he has no pity for the innocent bystander," yet, he wrote, Mencken spoke forcefully for Southern writers he favored "as loudly as ever he clamoured for the wholesale extinction of Southern Sweet Songsters, piffling poetasters, and feeble fictionists.''

Henderson's remarks were followed by ''Is the South a Desert?'' by Mencken. ''The South today is by no means illiterate; on the contrary, it is producing a great deal of writing,'' wrote the Sage of Baltimore. ''But the trouble is that most of that writing is conventional, sentimental and feeble, and that sectional sensitiveness protects it against the attack that ought to dispose of it. . . . How can dignified and serious poets flourish on a soil where neighborhood jinglers are hailed as geniuses, and ninth-rate doggerel is solemnly compared to the work of the great masters?'' Mencken praised the constructive literary criticism of two North Carolina journalists, Gerald Johnson of the Greensboro *Daily News* and Nell Battle Lewis of the Raleigh *News & Observer*, but excoriated ''the senseless praise of cross-roads bards, gurgling old maids, literary schoolmasters and other such dull frauds.''

Racial antipathy, Mencken predicted, would continue to cast a pall not only over the South's personal relationships, but its literature as well, saying:

> No great work of art was ever produced in a town in which half of the citizens turned out in night shirts and side-arms to terrorize the other half. And no great work of art was ever produced in a town which yielded itself at intervals to debauches of religious frenzy, with some preposterous moun-tebank of an evangelist roaring objurgations from his platform at every idea and ideal upon which the civilization of the modern world is based. Try to imagine a Shakespeare beset by fundamentalism, or a Goethe trying to work with the Ku Klux Klan roaring under his door!

In the autumn of 1923, founder Harman stepped aside as an editor in favor of Mary Brent Whiteside of Atlanta. In November the picture cover was replaced with a more somber journal-style cover with no illustration.

The March 1924 number was published in Nashville, Tennessee, under new management and under an altered title, the *Southern Magazine*, with Joseph H. Lackey as publisher and Walter F. Coxe as managing editor. Harman and Mary Whiteside remained as members of the editorial advisory board, as did Archibald Henderson, George Wauchope, Harry Stillwell Edwards, and Wrightman Fletcher Melton. The picture cover was revived, and quite a lot of interesting prose copy appeared in the five numbers before the magazine's discontinuance.

Harry Edwards, author of the very successful *Eneas Africanus*, contributed ''The Female of the Species''; H. A. Smith wrote a piece on Daniel D. Emmett, the author of ''Dixie.''[4] ''The Morgue of Lost Hopes'' by Dixon Merritt discussed the U.S. Patent Office, and Sterling Tracy wrote on J. P. Alley of the Memphis *Commercial Appeal* and his now forgotten cartoon feature ''Hambone's Meditations,'' then distributed by The Bell Syndicate. Despite interesting content, the magazine was not a financial success, and the July 1924 issue was its last.

Notes

1. By "little magazines" is meant such literary periodicals as the *Black Mountain Review* (1954–57), *Carolina Quarterly* (1948-present), *The Outsider* (1961–63), the *Sewanee Review** (1892-present), and the *Southern Review* (1965-present).

2. Vol. 1, no. 1, p. 14, provides an interesting example. A second example is "Sunset Over Pisgah" by George Armstrong Wauchope, on p. 15 of the same issue.

3. For a detailed discussion, see chapter 3 of Fred C. Hobson, Jr., *Serpent in Eden: H. L. Mencken and the South* (Chapel Hill: University of North Carolina Press, 1974), pp. 33–55.

4. It is a curious quirk of history that this song, which so inspired the South, was written in New York City by a native of Ohio and that its first use was by a minstrel troupe wearing blackface.

Information Sources

BIBLIOGRAPHY:
Hobson, Fred C., Jr. *Serpent in Eden: H. L. Mencken and the South.* Chapel Hill, N.C., 1974. Pp. 33–55.
INDEX SOURCE: None.
LOCATION SOURCES: Duke University Library, Houston Public Library, Library of Congress, University of Georgia Library, University of North Carolina Library (Chapel Hill), University of Tennessee Library, University of Virginia Library, Yale University Library.

Publication History

MAGAZINE TITLE AND TITLE CHANGES: *The Southern Literary Magazine* (July 1923-February 1924); *The Southern Magazine* (March-July 1924).
VOLUME AND ISSUE DATA: Vol. 1, nos. 1–13 (July 1923-July 1924), monthly.
PUBLISHER AND PLACE OF PUBLICATION: The Harman Publishing Company (Atlanta, Georgia, July 1923-February 1924); Joseph H. Lackey (Nashville, Tennessee, March-July 1924).
EDITORS: Henry E. Harman (July-October 1923); Mary Brent Whiteside (November 1923-February 1924); Walter F. Coxe (March-July 1924).
CIRCULATION: Unknown.

THE SOUTHERN LITERARY MESSENGER

The most acclaimed of all nineteenth-century Southern magazines is the *Southern Literary Messenger: Devoted to Every Department of Literature and the Fine Arts*, published in Richmond, Virginia, from 1834 to 1864. This attempt to provide the South with a "cultural spokesman" of its own was the rash gamble of Thomas Willis White, the son of a Williamsburg tailor who by his thirties had established himself as a printer in Richmond. White realized the risk he was taking, which he acknowledged in his May 1834 prospectus, pointing out that not one of the South's earlier literary magazines had long survived. As Robert Jacobs has put it, "the South, slumbering by its unsharpened pens," needed to "be rallied to defend its intellectual honor against the barbed comments of the complacent North."[1]

White's first number was issued in August 1834, edited by Virginia novelist James Ewell Heath,[2] who served without pay and shared White's hope of making the South less dependent on the North for its literary pleasures. "The first number of the 'Messenger,' " White wrote in an introductory essay, "will be sent forth by its Publisher, as a kind of pioneer, to spy out the land of literary promise, and to report whether the same be fruitful or barren, before he resolves upon future action" (1,1:1).

Also on page one of the maiden issue were the good wishes of a number of well-known writers, including these comments from James Fenimore Cooper:

The South is full of talent, and the leisure of its gentlemen ought to enable them to bring it freely into action. I made many acquaintances in early youth, among your gentlemen, whom I have always esteemed for their manliness, frankness, and intelligence. If sons, whom I could name, were to arouse from their lethargy, you would not be driven to apply to any one on this side the Potomac for assistance.

It was, however, not the South's landed gentlemen of leisure who would write for the *Messenger*, but the middle class—the lawyers, doctors, teachers, and clergy. Cooper's hopes for the literary awakening of the Southern upper crust would seem to have pertained more to the ladies of the region.

By October the publisher felt secure enough to begin regular monthly publication,[3] each issue containing essays, poetry, book reviews, a short story, and an installment of a novel. The texts of public lectures also appeared frequently and certainly represented one of the magazine's dullest features. Under Heath, the *Messenger*'s contents tended to the moralistic. Like other literary periodicals of the day, it was besmeared with cloying sentimentality, especially in its verse selections. At least the saccharin brand of poetry epitomized by the contributions of the popular Northern writer Lydia Huntley Sigourney and the effusions of a flock of Southern amateur poets, most of whom sensibly remained anonymous, were occasionally interrupted by the more likable verse of Edgar Allan Poe and Giles McQuiggin.

After editing eight numbers of the *Messenger*, Heath concluded that his magazine duties were demanding more time than he had bargained for, and White sought to replace him with lawyer Lucian Minor, one of his better contributors. Minor declined; Edward Vernon Sparhawk, a young New England-born poet and newspaperman was engaged but remained as editor for only three months. In July 1835 Edgar A. Poe came to Richmond from Baltimore to assume the post but offended the straightlaced White with his drinking and returned to Baltimore in September. Shortly thereafter White relented and rehired Poe, but with a warning about his drinking habits.

Poe had been a frequent contributor to the *Messenger* before becoming its

editor, beginning in March 1835 with "Berenice—A Tale."[4] Now his editorial
duties were restricted to writing book reviews and proofreading, with White
retaining control over acceptance and rejection of manuscripts. Yet much of the
Messenger's influence is owed to Poe's outspoken reviews. Until this time,
reviewers for Southern periodicals had been overly kind to American writers,
especially those from their own region. Poe, on the other hand, could be dev-
astating, even to so well-known a Southern author as Charleston's William
Gilmore Simms. In commenting on Simms' *The Partisan*, Poe details its "manifest and manifold blunders and impertinences," though he does allow that it
contains interesting historical details and that some of Simms' passages describing swamp scenery are exquisite. "Mr. Simms has evidently the eye of a painter,"
said Poe. "Perhaps, in sober truth, he would succeed better in sketching a
landscape than he has done in writing a novel" (2,2:121). In his review of Joseph
Robinson's *The Swiss Heiress; or The Bride of Destiny—A Tale*, Poe's lead goes
straight for the jugular: "The Swiss Heiress should be read by all who have
nothing better to do" (2,11:715–16).

Poe had little sympathy for the unsuccessful amateur author, as one can see
in his comments on *The Old World and the New* by the Reverend Orville Dewey.
In the book's preface, says Poe, Dewey tells his readers that his remarks on a
recent tour of Europe should not be considered an itinerary. Poe scoffs that "it
is difficult to say in what other light they should be regarded. They are indeed
an itinerary . . . a journal in which unconnected remarks follow upon one another
. . . with a scrupulous accuracy in regard to dates. . . . We cannot understand Mr.
Dewey in declaring his book not to be what it most certainly is, if it is any thing
at all" (2,9:582).

In a favorable review of an address on public education that Lucian Minor
delivered at Virginia's Hampden Sidney College, Poe's outspokenness doubtlessly ruffled many Virginian feathers:

> The most lukewarm friend of the State must perceive—if he perceives
> anything—that the glory of the Ancient Dominion is in a dying condition.
> Her once great name is becoming, in the North, a bye-word for imbecility—
> all over the South, a type for 'the things that *have been*.' " [2,1:66–67]

Aside from his reviews, Poe's own contributions to the *Messenger* in this
period vary from "The Duc De L'Omelett" (2,3:150–51), in which a satirical
Poe has a little fun at the expense of the French, to a dismal, mystical poem
entitled "The City of Sin" (2,9:552),[5] typical of the brooding Poe to whom
most of us are accustomed.

After one year as editor, Poe was let go, either for his drinking or his acid
pen[6] or a combination of the two factors. White began listing himself as editor
and publisher in February 1837. After Poe's departure the review section, for
one year the magazine's true claim to fame, fell into the sear and yellow leaf.
White began publishing a considerable amount of Simms' less than memorable

poetry, translations of foreign works, and a variety of contributions from Northern writers, including Henry Wadsworth Longfellow, Park Benjamin, both Seba Smith and Mrs. Smith, and H. T. Tuckerman, which he needed to keep up his circulation in the Northeast. Though controversy was removed, the *Messenger* maintained its position as a major literary periodical for White's six years as editor, during the last three of which he was assisted by Matthew F. Maury. Maury, who sometimes used the pen name "Harry Bluff," was a Navy lieutenant whose first appearance in the *Messenger* was in a laudatory review by Poe of Maury's book *Navigation*. Maury's own contributions began appearing in January 1839; the most important of these pressed for various naval reforms: the need for officer grades above captain, the need to experiment with steam warships, added protection for American merchant ships in the Pacific, and the need for a naval academy comparable to West Point.[7] Most of the reforms that Maury argued for in the *Messenger*'s pages were realized, which added considerably to the magazine's prestige.

In January 1843 Thomas White died from the effects of a stroke, and the influential but impecunious magazine passed to the ownership of Benjamin Blake Minor, a young Virginia lawyer of scholarly leanings, who also became editor in August of that year. In December 1845 the *Messenger* merged with William Gilmore Simms' *Southern and Western Monthly Magazine and Review* and for a year was published as the *Southern and Western Literary Messenger and Review* before reverting to its original title. Under Minor the magazine lost ground as a voice for *belles lettres* but shone as a recorder of Southern history. Minor published Captain John Smith's *True Relation* and a long series on Virginia history by Charles Campbell. The *Messenger*'s book review section also regained some of its prominence under Minor, thanks in large part to reviewer Henry C. Lea, though the criticism was of the gentle variety. Poe began contributing again, sending the *Messenger* "The Literary Life of Thingum Bob" and a revised version of "The Raven."

In the autumn of 1847 Minor became principal of the Virginia Female Institute at Staunton, Virginia,[8] and the *Messenger* was sold to John Reuben Thompson, another young Virginia lawyer. History gave way to the literary, and for the early portion of Thompson's thirteen years as editor—the longest editorship in the magazine's entire history—the *Messenger* could hold its head high in the company of other literary journals. Criticism became more demanding, thanks in part to Poe's return to these pages; some of White's Northern contributors returned; and the gifted young Charleston poets Paul Hamilton Hayne and Henry Timrod were featured, as was Philip Pendleton Cooke, who wrote on the Virginia frontier.

As had ever been the case with Southern literary periodicals, the *Messenger* was on the brink of financial ruin. Appeals to the South's regional pride did little good, and in January 1853 Thompson sold out to his printer, Macfarlane & Fergusson, but remained as editor through May 1860. The subscription price was reduced from $5 to $3, yet many subscribers remained in arrears. John

Esten Cooke became a prominent contributor, and Joseph Glover Baldwin's *Flush Times of Alabama and Mississippi* made its first appearance in the *Messenger*. The place of history again increased in the magazine, proslavery pieces became more frequent, and eventually its literary distinction faltered.

In May 1860 Thompson resigned to become editor of *Southern Field and Fireside* and was replaced by Virginia physician and writer of dialect George W. Bagby, who earlier had his "Letters of Mozis Addums to Billy Ivvins" published in the *Messenger*. Now on the very brink of civil war, the *Messenger*, formerly moderate in its political stance, became an ardent secessionist organ. Bagby wanted to develop a truly Southern literature, with Southern protagonists portrayed in Southern settings, which quickly alienated the magazine's last Northern subscribers. He tried to rid the *Messenger* of sentimentalism and was the first editor to use fairly frequent woodcuts and engravings in its pages. Bagby joined the Confederate Army, and the magazine was sold to two well-to-do young men named Wedderburn and Alfriend. The latter owner, Frank H. Alfriend, edited the last few numbers. Good paper stock was unobtainable by this time; wartime inflation had pushed the magazine's subscription price to $15; and as a final blow, the *Messenger*'s printers were pressed into the defense of Richmond, which closed the *Messenger* after its June 1864 issue.

After seventy-five years, a new incarnation of the *Southern Literary Messenger* appeared in Richmond in January 1939, edited by F. Meredith Dietz, who invited the contributions of Southern writers and in each number printed under the standing head "Résumé Original 'Messenger' " contents from the nineteenth-century *Messenger*. The first four volumes of the new *Messenger* were done in roughly the same size, page length, and format as the original, and publication was monthly. Volume 5 (1943) appeared as a bimonthly in digest size on cheaper paper ("designed for war-time") and with a one-color picture cover. By 1944 the *Messenger* had become far more popular than literary, featuring pictures of movie stars and articles with such titles as "The Truth About Halitosis" (April 1945, pp. 25–27). The September/October 1944 issue was published under the title *Southern Literary and Radio Messenger*. Thus deflated, the magazine was sold to Richard Eaton in 1945, and publication resumed in Washington, D.C. Eaton claimed, inaccurately, that the *Messenger* had been "published for many years by Edgar Allen [*sic*] Poe. In 1946 the title changed to *Best, Combined with Southern Literary Messenger* after a merger with *Best: The Popular Digest*. In 1947 this sad relation of the once eminent *Messenger* finally disappeared into a Chicago magazine called *American Family*.

Notes

1. Robert D. Jacobs, "Campaign for a Southern Literature: The Southern Literary Messenger," *Southern Literary Journal*, 2 (Fall 1966):68.

2. Heath's best-known literary work was the romantic plantation novel *Edge-Hill, or the Family of Fitzroyals*. He earned his living as Virginia's state auditor, a post he held for thirty-two years.

3. A second, shorter break occurred the following year when the October and November 1835 numbers were not published.

4. Other prose contributions by Poe in volume 1 were "Bon-Bon, a Tale," "Hans Phaal, a Tale," "Lionizing, a Tale," "Loss of Breath, a Tale, *à la* Blackwood," and "The Visionary, a Tale."

5. The poem began:

> Lo! Death hath rear'd himself a throne
> In a strange city, all alone,
> Far down within the dim west—
> Where the good, and the bad, and the worst, and the best,
> Have gone to their eternal rest.
> There shrines, and palaces, and towers
> Are—not like any thing of ours—
> O no!—O no!—*ours* never loom
> To heaven with that ungodly gloom!

6. Actually, only a few of Poe's many reviews were caustic. For details, see Frank Luther Mott, *A History of American Magazines, 1741–1850* (New York, 1930), I:637.

7. See Charles Lee Lewis, "Maury and the 'Messenger,'" *Southern Literary Messenger*, 1 (March 1939):165–71.

8. Minor later became president of the University of Missouri and late in life published *The Southern Literary Messenger, 1834–1864* (New York, 1905), a history of the magazine.

Information Sources

BIBLIOGRAPHY:

Jackson, David K. "An Estimate of the Influence of 'The Southern Literary Messenger,' 1834–1864." *Southern Literary Messenger*, August 1939, pp. 508–14.

———. "Poe and The 'Messenger.'" *Southern Literary Messenger*, January 1939, pp. 5–11.

———. *The Contributors and Contributions to The Southern Literary Messenger.* Charlottesville, Va., 1936.

Jacobs, Robert D. "Campaign for a Southern Literature: The Southern Literary Messenger." *Southern Literary Journal*, 2 (Fall 1966):66–98.

Lewis, Charles Lee. "Maury and The 'Messenger.'" *Southern Literary Messenger*, March 1939, pp. 165–71.

Minor, Benjamin Blake. *The Southern Literary Messenger, 1834–1864.* New York, 1905.

Mott, Frank Luther. *A History of American Magazines, 1741–1850.* New York, 1930.

Rogers, Edwin Reinhold. *Four Southern Magazines.* University of Virginia, Studies in Southern Literature, 1902.

Tucker, Edward L. "The Southern Literary Messenger and the Men Who Made It." *Virginia Cavalcade*, 21 (Summer 1971):14–20.

Watts, Charles H. "Poe, Irving, and The Southern Literary Messenger." *American Literature: A Journal of Literary History, Criticism, and Bibliography*, 27 (1955–56):249–51.

INDEX SOURCES: Poole's Index to Periodical Literature.

LOCATION SOURCES: American Periodical Series microfilm, Library of Congress, University of Michigan Library.

Publication History

MAGAZINE TITLE AND TITLE CHANGES: *The Southern Literary Messenger: Devoted to Every Department of Literature and the Fine Arts* (1834–1845, 1848–1864); *The Southern and Western Literary Messenger and Review: Devoted to Every Department of Literature and the Fine Arts* (1846–1847).

VOLUME AND ISSUE DATA: Vols. 1–36 (August 1834-June 1864), monthly. No numbers issued September 1834, October and November 1835, December 1836.

PUBLISHER AND PLACE OF PUBLICATION: T. W. White (1834–1843); B. B. Minor (1843–1847); John R. Thompson (1847–1852); Macfarlane & Fergusson (1847, 1853–1863); Wedderburn and Alfriend (1864). Richmond, Virginia.

EDITORS: James E. Heath (August 1843-April 1835); Edward V. Sparhawk (May-July 1835); Thomas W. White (August-September 1835, February 1837-December 1839); Edgar Allan Poe (December 1835-January 1837); Thomas White (February 1837-December 1839); Thomas W. White and Matthew F. Maury (January 1840-September 1842); Matthew F. Maury (October 1842-July 1843); Benjamin B. Minor (August 1843-October 1847); John R. Thompson (November 1847-May 1860); George W. Bagby (June 1860-January 1864); Frank H. Alfriend (February-June 1864).

CIRCULATION: Unknown.

SOUTHERN LIVING

The unquestioned leader among regional magazines in both the South and the nation is *Southern Living*, spawned in February 1966 by the venerable Progressive Farmer Company of Birmingham, Alabama. The company's first periodical, the *Progressive Farmer*,* dates from 1886 and is still going strong, though its circulation has dropped to about 573,000 in 1984 from a peak of 1,400,000 in 1962.

The planning of *Southern Living* is an example of near-perfect timing. Just as the *Progressive Farmer* was enjoying record circulation, company planners realized the magnitude of the change occurring in the region as people moved out of farming and into city jobs. In its quiet way, the South was becoming urbanized and suburbanized, and the Progressive Farmer Company understood that the demand for their farm magazine was sure to decline. What was needed to maintain their strong position, they reasoned, was a new magazine to serve the reader who lived in the South's modest-sized cities or their suburbs but who was not fully divorced from his or her rural roots. The company's first efforts in this direction appeared in what had been called "The Progressive Home" section of the *Progressive Farmer* but was retitled "Southern Living"in October 1963. After the new magazine was launched in 1966, the home section of the older periodical was rechristened "Southern Farm Living."[1]

Introducing the new magazine in volume 1, number 1, company president Eugene Butler spoke of the South as a region of "changing habits and customs, blooming economy, and favorable climate . . . where emphasis is given to social, cultural, and recreational life.'' The new magazine, he continued, would be a special-interest family magazine for both men and women who want to improve their homes, enjoy good food, take part in community affairs, and learn more about their region's people and progress. Life in Northern cities, Butler wrote, had become frustrated by "dirty air, filthy water, growing crime, traffic jams, noise, and tension." Long-range planning for most Southern cities, he went on, had sidestepped "the obvious mistakes that have blighted so many Northern urban areas."

Many of the readers of these introductory remarks had responded to a direct mail campaign that went to urban readers of the *Progressive Farmer*. Lists of other relatively affluent Southerners were also used for the initial direct mail appeal. Response was strong, and the magazine began with a paid circulation of more than 250,000.[2] The several magazine consultants who had advised against publishing *Southern Living*[3] were confounded, and not even the most optimistic of its advocates would have believed that eleven years later *Forbes* would declare the Southern newcomer the most profitable magazine in the United States,[4] calling it a "Dixiefied version of *Better Homes & Gardens*" and pointing out that in 1976 it "posted twice the profits of *Playboy* and double the bottom line of *The New Yorker* and *New York* magazine combined." Certainly no one would have imagined that by 1984 *Southern Living*'s paid circulation would reach 2,225,000, largest of any regional magazine and rivaled only by *Sunset*,[5] a much older California regional which provided a model for *Southern Living*'s early editorial management. Both magazines have concentrated on "hitting readers where they live": travel, food and entertaining, homes and decorating, and landscaping/gardening. Both have chosen to leave controversy and unpleasantness to the newspapers and to accentuate the positive in covering their region.

The latter decision has proved to be a sound business move but has, of course, resulted in slighting remarks aimed at the magazine by serious-minded social critics. As once remarked, "The Big Picture in *Southern Living* is of a relaxed, unhurried South, a South that never runs short of money near the end of the month, a South that keeps touch with the great outdoors—if only via one's multilevel deck or herringbone patterned old-brick patio—and close to the soil, if only in one's herb garden. It is a South without memory of pellagra or racial unrest, a South where none of the parents are divorced, where burglary and street crime are unknown, where few have Hatteras yachts but one and all play golf and tennis at the club—and in the right outfits."[6] The magazine, in other words, pictures only part of the South, the comfortable part. Perhaps its critics would be mollified if *Southern Living* subscribers also had to read *Southern Exposure*,* a periodical that concentrates on the uncomfortable elements of life in the South.

It bears mentioning that *Southern Living* is not directed at the rich, merely at the reasonably affluent. The mean annual household income of its subscribers was $43,148 in 1983, enough to qualify it for the magic magazine term "upscale" but modest compared to *Ultra Magazine*'s* $212,500, *Texas Homes*'* $146,400, or *Palm Beach Life*'s* $145,200. The median age of *Southern Living*'s readers is 45.4, 84 percent are married, and 93 percent own their own home, the median value of which is $80,174.

While *Southern Living*'s subscribers are undoubtedly out for the good life, they are doers, not just spenders, which is reflected in the magazine's pages. A great deal of how-to copy appears, including endless recipes; gardening tips; and detailed schema for building garden benches, gazebos, decks, green-houses, and other additions or improvements in which the editors clearly expect their readers to take a personal hand. In contrast to "way upscale" magazines whose readers might be expected to hire an architect or a decorator to do such things for them, *Southern Living* readers are more in sync with the traditional middle-class, Southern Protestant values of being able to "do for yourself."

At the same time, the people who appear in the magazine look decidedly preppy—nothing flashy, but the way one might expect an off-duty cardiologist to dress when he goes to the club on Wednesday. The women are not sleek or leggy like New York fashion models, but have the appearance of Junior League officers who have taken good care of themselves.

A curious thing about *Southern Living* is that its articles are not people oriented; it concentrates instead on places and things. The people who appear in its photos are often incidental, there only to demonstrate the enjoyment of a *Southern Living* recipe or to make a more interesting shot or establish scale in depicting a redecorated room or a new landscaping plan, in just the way that drawn figures of people are included in architects' renderings. This paucity of people copy is scarcely noticeable to the casual reader since the magazine's tremendous volume of ads are filled with people smoking, drinking, eating, sunning, playing, strolling, hugging, mugging, posing.

In attracting advertisements, *Southern Living* has been a phenomenal success. During its initial decade, annual ad pages rose from 268 to 1,265 and revenues grew from $555,890 to $13,845,000.[7] In 1983 ad pages totaled 1,511 and revenues were $46,894,640. The magazine began turning a profit within eighteen months of its founding, unusually fast for the industry, and by 1984 was the twenty-fourth largest magazine in America and still growing.

Despite high ad rates—a full-page, full-color ad is $36,300 for a single insertion—national advertisers believe that *Southern Living* delivers the South and have made the magazine a veritable gold mine for its owners.[8] The magazine's coverage area is also growing and now contains more than a third of America's population, which has been an important factor in the periodical's success story. More than 80 percent of the magazine's advertising is national,[9] and ad copy exceeds editorial matter by 52.5 to 47.5 percent. The two biggest ad categories are travel and food. Automobile, appliance, cigarette, and yard care ads are also prominent.

As the magazine became ever more thick and slick, the original cover price of 25¢ increased to the present $2.25. A year's subscription, $2.00 in 1966, is now $17.95 in seventeen ''Southern'' states and the District of Columbia, $22.00 elsewhere. Circulation is heaviest in Texas, Florida, Virginia/Delaware/D.C., North Carolina, and Georgia, in that order, with only about 100,000 subscriptions outside the South.[10] About 99 percent of circulation is by subscription, with the remainder coming from newsstand sales. Subscriptions to *Southern Living* have been a big gift item in the South, and the magazine has never had to resort to premiums or other such promotional devices to build circulation.

The person most responsible for this success story is Emory Cunningham, a small-town boy from Alabama who studied agriculture and played football at Auburn University, was a World War II pilot, and rose through the magazine ranks to become the *Progressive Farmer*'s advertising manager in 1960. In 1966 he became publisher of both *Southern Living* and the *Progressive Farmer* and a year later was made president of the parent company. In 1983 the publisher's duties were turned over to James De Vira; Cunningham now is chairman and president of the company, which was renamed The Southern Progress Corporation in 1981. In this age of relatively impersonal, corporate magazine publishing, Cunningham has been a real public presence, acting as his magazine's spokesman. Credit is also due Cunningham for keeping the company's management structure simple and cost-effective.[11]

Southern Living is unusual for a magazine its age in that it has had but two editors—Otis Copeland (1966–1969) and Oklahoman Gary McCalla, who has held this post since 1969 and who has helped personalize the magazine's editorial workings by his short monthly column ''Life at Southern Living,'' which includes a photo of *Southern Living* writers, editors, or photographers and discusses their work on some part of the issue's feature articles.

The magazine's features have been criticized for their brevity and for bland writing, which a Knight Ridder reporter once characterized as ''small-bore snippets and unpolished prose.''[12] A noteworthy exception might be the Charles Kuralt-like prose of a former travel editor, Caleb Pirtle III.[13] Aware of these criticisms, management hired a writing coach in 1982 and in March of the same year increased the length of some of its features. The first such piece was ''On the Face of the Sea: Reflections of the Fisherman,'' twelve pages on the South's commercial fishing industry. Two further examples of these beefed up feature pieces are ''Louisiana's River Plantations'' (19,3:110–19) by Assistant Travel Editor Pat Zajac, with the fine photography of Frederica Georgia, and Features Editor Mark Childress' admirable ''Places of the Man'' (19,4:162–73) on the homes of Robert E. Lee.

Layout and photography are of high quality, and editorial copy is virtually free of the irritating jumps (''continued on p. —'') found in so many other regional magazines. *Southern Living*'s optimistic, soothing approach and its tersely written, useful copy have made it into a bona fide Southern institution. It is in many ways the touchstone of magazine publishing in its region.

Notes

1. Ernest Hynds, "The Recent Rise of Southern Magazines," an unpublished paper presented to the Association for Education in Journalism in Athens, Ohio, July 1982, pp. 6–10.

2. Ibid., p. 7.

3. Emory Cunningham, quoted in a UPI story in the *Rockdale Citizen* (Conyers, Georgia), November 18, 1981.

4. "The Most Profitable Magazine in the U.S.," June 15, 1977, pp. 30–31.

5. Paid circulation in 1984 was 1,422,600.

6. Sam G. Riley, "The New Money and the New Magazines," *Journal of Regional Cultures*, Fall/Winter 1982, p. 114.

7. Hynds, "Recent Rise," p. 9.

8. *Southern Living* was until 1985 the property of a privately held company, for the most part in the hands of descendants of the families that controlled the *Progressive Farmer*. In 1985 both magazines were bought by Time Inc. for $480 million.

9. Mary McCabe English, "Good Climate for Regionals," *AdvertisingAge*, April 5, 1982.

10. The magazine's coverage in 1966 was eleven states: Alabama, Arkansas, Florida, Georgia, Kentucky, Louisiana, Mississippi, North Carolina, South Carolina, Tennessee, and Virginia. Since then the *Southern Living* definition of the South has broadened by five: Delaware, Maryland, Missouri, Oklahoma, and West Virginia, plus the District of Columbia. Mexico and the islands of the Caribbean also receive some editorial coverage.

11. Cunningham was named Magazine Publisher of the Year in 1975 by the Magazine Publisher's Association in New York.

12. Louise Hickman Lione, "Southern Living Formula Success with Sun Belt Readers," *The State* (Columbia, South Carolina), April 11, 1982.

13. Pirtle left the magazine for Texas, where he freelances Hollywood screenplays and writes for airline magazines and for *Southern Outdoors*. This information, as well as the 1983 figures cited in this entry, were provided by *Southern Living* spokesmen in July 17, 1984, telephone conversations with the author.

Information Sources

BIBLIOGRAPHY:

Bennett, Elizabeth. "Southern Living: Publisher Cunningham Credits a Simple Concept for Making His Magazine a Success." *Washington Post*, July 7, 1978.

Dougherty, Philip H. "Southern Admanship Comes to New York City." *New York Times*, August 3, 1978.

English, Mary McCabe. "Good Climate for Regionals." *Advertising Age*, April 5, 1982.

Goolrick, Chester. "One Way to Succeed in Sun Belt Is Simply to Sing Its Praises." *Wall Street Journal*, November 23, 1981.

Hynds, Ernest C. "The Recent Rise of Southern Magazines." Unpublished paper delivered to the Magazine Division of the Association for Education in Journalism, Athens, Ohio, July 1982. Pp. 6–10.

Lione, Louise Hickman. "Southern Living Formula Success with Sun Belt Readers." *The State* (Columbia, South Carolina), April 11, 1982.

"Magazine Makes Its Debut; Editorial Office Located Here." *Birmingham News*, January 19, 1966.

"The Most Profitable Magazine in the U.S." *Forbes*, June 15, 1977, pp. 30–31.

Reed, Roy. "Birmingham Publisher Propelled by Regionalism." *New York Times*, September 7, 1976.

Riley, Sam G. "The New Money and the New Magazines." *Journal of Regional Cultures*, Fall/Winter 1982, pp. 107–15.

White, Beville Comer. "Eleven Years of Southern Living: 1966 to 1976." Unpublished honors thesis, University of Georgia, 1977.

Yahn, Steve. "Ecology, Profitability Pace Southern Living Journalism." *Advertising Age*, September 26, 1977.

INDEX SOURCES: Access: The Supplementary Index to Periodicals.

LOCATION SOURCES: Library of Congress, many other libraries.

Publication History

MAGAZINE TITLE AND TITLE CHANGES: *Southern Living*.

VOLUME AND ISSUE DATA: Vols. 1–19 (February 1966-present). Monthly.

PUBLISHER AND PLACE OF PUBLICATION: Southern Living, Inc. (part of the Southern Progress Corporation): Emory Cunningham (1966–1983); James E. De Vira (1983-present). Birmingham, Alabama.

EDITORS: Otis B. Copeland (1966–1969); Gary E. McCalla (1969-present).

CIRCULATION: 2,225,000 paid, 20,000 nonpaid.

THE SOUTHERN MAGAZINE (1893). *See* FETTER'S SOUTHERN MAGAZINE

THE SOUTHERN MAGAZINE (1924). *See* THE SOUTHERN LITERARY MAGAZINE

THE SOUTHERN MAGAZINE (1934)

Southern womanhood has always wanted to do its share of preserving the region's history and furthering regional pride. A manifestation of this desire was the *Southern Magazine*, published for four years in Wytheville, Virginia. The rather plain cover of its early numbers featured a cotton ball superimposed on a five-pointed star. On the visible tips of the star appeared the words Love, Live, Pray, Think, Dare. The title page notified readers that the new monthly was published by the News Publishing Company of Wytheville in the interests of the United Daughters of the Confederacy (UDC) and the Southern States and that it would be "devoted to the truth of Southern history, literature, art, music and poetry—past and present."

Editor of the UDC's magazine was Miss Claudia M. Hagy, who was assisted by a bevy of subeditors scattered about the South and even beyond. The April 1935 issue (volume 2, number 1) identified the following department editors: Historical—Mrs. Walter D. Lamar (Historian General of the UDC), Macon, Georgia; Educational—Mrs. John C. Abernathy of Chicago; Children of the Confederacy—Mrs. Frank Dennis, Eatonton, Georgia; Jefferson Davis Historical Foundation—Mrs. John F. Weinmann of Little Rock; Jefferson Davis Highway— Mrs. John L. Woodbury, Louisville, Kentucky; Lee-Stratford Memorial—Mrs. Frank P. Canby, Smithburg, Maryland; Sidney Lanier for Hall of Fame—Mrs. Walter D. Lamar of Macon; Poetry Page—Mrs. Grace Dupree Ridings, Sherman, Texas. (Department editors were no longer listed after the issue of December 1935.) Added to this elaborate editorial structure were four associate editors: Mrs. John Huske Anderson, Mrs. John L. Woodbury, Miss Anne V. Mann, and Miss Decca Lamar West.

The magazine soon adopted a geographical theme format. Volume 2, number 1, was a mountain number; the volume's succeeding issues were devoted to individual states in this order: Texas, Virginia, Arkansas, North Carolina, Kentucky, California,[1] Missouri, West Virginia, South Carolina, and Mississippi. With the theme issues came much improved covers and full-page frontispiece photos of old Southern homes or public buildings.

The contents of one poetry page (2,1:31) should serve as an adequate example of the kind of verse the magazine welcomed. Titles such as "Slave's Shawl," "Grey Roofs," "Gray Battalions," and "Old Sweethearts" are indicative of the sentimental, historical orientation that is hardly surprising for an organization called the United Daughters of the Confederacy. "Fire Hazards" appeared in Negro dialect.

In the same issue appear notices about various prizes to be given by the UDC for chapters that best promote the arts in Dixie and to individuals for essays on a variety of topics: best essay on Jefferson Davis, on Confederate newspapers, on the military genius of Stonewall Jackson, on plantation life in the Old South.

A tiny amount of advertising appeared on the inside front cover. The George Washington Hotel in New York City; Homewood, a summer resort near Wytheville for artists and writers; and flagmaker J. A. Joel & Co. were frequent advertisers. Also appearing were house ads for the UDC's own 466-page book *Women of the South in War Times* and for Emma A. Fox's *Parliamentary Usage*. The ad for the latter book began ominously: "YOU may be chosen as an officer in your organization." On the outside back cover often appeared an advertisement for Wedgewood dinner plates on which was displayed a scene of Robert E. Lee's home, Stratford Hall.[2]

Two of the magazine's continuing campaigns were in support of poet Sidney Lanier's candidacy for New York University's Hall of Fame and the Jefferson Davis Highway, a route proposed by the UDC and laid out so as to pass through most of the South's state capitals.[3]

Some of the monthly's best articles were written by Associate Editor Decca West, whose contributions included "Reagan the Commoner," on John H.

Reagan of Tennessee and Texas, a judge/general/senator often referred to as "The Grand Old Roman," and another historical piece on Mirabeau B. Lamar, hero of San Jacinto and father of public education in Texas (both articles in volume 2, number 2).

Presented here as an example of the contents of the magazine's theme issues, the North Carolina number (2,5) contained messages from U.S. Ambassador to Mexico Josephus Daniels and Governor John Ehringhaus and articles on the restoration of Fort Raleigh; the Great Smokey Mountains National Park; the "Appalachian Parkway" (now called the Blue Ridge Parkway); the Wright Memorial; Governor Zebulon Vance; the state's coastal defenses during the Civil War; Confederate Brigadier General Collet Leventhorpe; and Orren Randolph Smith, designer of the Confederate flag.

Articles in the South Carolina issue (2,10) chronicled the restoration of Fort Hill, the home of John C. Calhoun; the state's signers of the U.S. Constitution; the beginnings of Southern slavery; judge/scientist/educator/authorThomas Cooper; Beaufort County, where the first ship built in America was constructed; the Citidel at Charleston; and the Ladies' Benevolent Society of that city.

The *Southern Magazine*'s content was respectable, yet even with the support of a sizable organization, it, too, became part of Southern history after the May 1938 issue.

Notes

1. The California issue (2,7) explored connections between the South and the West Coast's largest state, with articles on trees in the sequoia forest named for Robert E. Lee, Southerners who were among the early settlers of the state, Southerners then active in the California-based film industry, and Southerners and their descendants who figured prominently in the civic and social life of California.

2. In 1935 these plates sold for $1.50 each, or $16.50 for twelve.

3. The road missed only three Southern capitals.

Information Sources

INDEX SOURCES: None.

LOCATION SOURCES: Indiana University Library, Los Angeles Public Library, New York Public Library, University of Georgia Library, University of North Carolina Library (Chapel Hill), University of Texas Library (Austin), University of Virginia Library, Virginia State Library (Richmond).

Publication History

MAGAZINE TITLE AND TITLE CHANGES: *The Southern Magazine*.

VOLUME AND ISSUE DATA: Vols. 1–4 (March 1934-May 1938), monthly.

PUBLISHER AND PLACE OF PUBLICATION: News Publishing Company, under the auspices of the United Daughters of the Confederacy. Wytheville, Virginia.

EDITOR: Claudia M. Hagy

CIRCULATION: Unknown.

SOUTHERN MONTHLY: A MAGAZINE OF ORIGINAL LITERATURE AND ART. *See* THE ORION

THE SOUTHERN MONTHLY

On first glance it would seem surprising that during the Civil War, when already-established Southern magazines were finding survival difficult, anyone in the Confederacy would be rash enough to launch a new magazine. One of these wartime newcomers that has heretofore received scant attention from historians and literary scholars was the *Southern Monthly* of Memphis, Tennessee, which appeared from September 1861 to May 1862. Others also profiled in this volume are the *Countryman** (1862–1865) in Georgia and Richmond's *Southern Punch** (1863–1865). Magazines in this wartime category not described in this work were Richmond's *Southern Illustrated News* (1862–1865), *Magnolia* (1862–1865),[1] *Bohemian* (1863), and *Age: A Southern Eclectic Monthly* (1864), plus Raleigh's *Illustrated Mercury* (1863–1864).

Time and again the introductory editorial or salutatory in the literary magazines of this region have sounded the same melancholy chord: that the South needed a literature of its own. This deeply felt need appears not to have been pushed to the back burner after the war began but was given new urgency. In "Southern Literature," the essay that introduced this eighty-page monthly, the anonymous editor speaks of the "magnificent disdain of mental labor" shown by Southerners as bitter medicine, and indeed a sin. "We have sinned, and that deeply," he writes, "for we have betrayed the holiest trust man receives from God—*the proper fashioning of immortal minds*. The sages of the South have repeatedly warned us that if we continued to depend on the North for clothing, the day might come when ingenuity would be tasked to avert nakedness . . . 'Sans le Nord, le Sud ne saurait lire'—without the North, the South couldn't learn to read—said a shrewd French observer" (1,1:1), a prophecy the editor found humiliating. The texts from which Southern children are taught, the editor complains, were written in the North and contain subtle, insidious propaganda. "Pass we now from the schoolroom to the parlor," he continues, "and lo! on yonder table lies not one Southern book, but the *Atlantic Monthly*, with Harriet Beecher Stowe's last novel *continued*; Holmes' ingenious diatribes against our country, polished as a Damascene blade" (1,1:2).

The magazine's plain green cover bears the title *Hutton & Freligh's Southern Monthly*; the nameplate on the title page reads *The Southern Monthly*. Publishers Hutton and Freligh had from 1858 to 1861 published the *Aurora: A Southern Literary Magazine*. They would include in their new venture, they wrote in a publishers' notice on the inside back cover of volume 1, "good articles—warm, glowing, true, high toned; articles on all subjects—Politics in an enlarged sense, not mere partisanship; Science, Morals, Arts, General Literature, Tales, Essays, Poetry, Sketches, Biographies." The publishers' aim was to combine the "weightier essays of the solid Quarterly with the lighter literature of the popular magazine" (back cover of final issue, 2,1). The hope was to emulate *Harper's* in Dixie. Few illustrations appeared due to wartime costs. The first number contained an engraving of Jefferson Davis, the second a fine portrait of General Beauregard.

Beginning to end, the *Southern Monthly*'s price was $3 per annum. Circulation is unknown, but the magazine had subscription agents in Tennessee, Arkansas, Mississippi, Louisiana, North and South Carolina, Georgia, Kentucky, Virginia, and Texas.

Most articles were run unsigned; most poems bore the names of their authors. Nowhere does the editor identify himself by name, but in "Our Sanctum," first run in volume 1, number 2, he describes himself thus:

> Conceive a florid-complexioned, good-natured looking man of half-a-century's experience in worldly matters, but who has not yet dropped all the blossoms that are supposed to dissappear with youth, or harvested a new crop of more doubtful character, and the editor is before you [1,2:145]

Another department whose conductor remained anonymous was a likable miscellany called "The Rambler." Its writer called himself "a rambler in literature as in life, a skimmer of surfaces, abhorring labor but loving art, though artless as a lady 'widowed for the third time' " (1,1:73). A final department began in the first number as "Monthly Summary of Foreign News," containing brief items on the Legitimists and Mazzinites in Italy, a new sultan in Turkey, and the like. By the second number domestic news had replaced this exotic fare, and the department's title had been changed to the more general "Compendium of News."

The magazine's copy, as one might expect, was much taken up with the war and its causes. In January 1862 appeared a scholarly essay on chivalry (1,5:345–51), a topic much on the Southern mind in that era. Biographical articles treated Jefferson Davis (1,2:143–44) and the popular General Beauregard (1,3:168–71); lead article in the final number was "The Negro Not a White Man" (2,1:1–4), a purportedly scientific explanation of white supremacy.

In no other literary magazine of its time can one find more war-related poetry, typical of which is "The Invocation," the first verse of which reads:

> God bless the land of flowers,
> And turn its winter hours
> > To brightest summer time!
> Be the brave soldier's friend,
> And from dangers defend
> When Northern balls descend
> > On the Southern line! [1,4:306]

In the same issue appeared the popular poem "The Sword of Harry Lee" (pp. 344–45), and other representative efforts are "A Voice from Virginia," selected from the *Richmond Whig*, and William Gilmore Simms' "O, The Sweet South" (both in 1,1:10–11).

"To Fred" was written by Lena Lyle of Germantown, Tennessee, for her son. An excerpt follows:

> You ask me for a story now,
>   My dearest little boy,
> So I will try to tell you one
>   To thrill your heart with joy;
> 'Tis of Manassas' battle-field,
>   Where the Southrons won the day,
> And the Northerners' 'grand army'
>   So bravely *ran away*. [1,2:127]

Not all the poetic contributors to the *Southern Monthly* expressed proud, war-like sentiments, however. A contributor who used the pseudonym Tin Pan wrote in "To the Man in the Moon":

> Hold! hold! great monarch of yon changing orb,
>   Whose influence felt, makes lunatics of all,
> But most of statesmen, for they most absorb,
>   And feel the influence of thy rolling ball.
> No doubt you see what mighty things we're doing,
>   But can you think how strongly we are bent on
> Urging mad war, and widely scattering ruin
>   O'er all the land, that your mild beams are sent on?
>
> O Great Lunatic! thy power has been too great,
>   Profusely pour'd upon each ruler's head;
> Reckless, they urge along the car of State,
>   And all their brains seem only turn'd to lead.
> We've mighty men! yes, plenty of that class!
>   Plenty enough to damn a generation,
> With leaden brains and faces made of brass,
>   To bring on wars and with them ruination! [1,3:226]

In the April 1862 number came an announcement that due to the fall of Fort Donalson and the strategy of Buell, Halleck, and McClellan, the Union occupation of Memphis had become a possibility; consequently the magazine had removed to Grenada, Mississippi. "Our prudence may seem to many to savor of a timidity too anticipative of evil," wrote the editor," and we hope that the success of Beauregard will make it a standing jest at our expense." Still, he wrote, the magazine wanted to "keep beyond the stretch of Lincoln's arm" (1,8:626). Only the May 1862 number was published in Grenada before the monthly succumbed to wartime pressures. It seems a fair supposition that the feelings of those who conduced the magazine through its last days were in accord with the anti-Union sentiments expressed in A. J. Requier's "Our Faith in '61":

Oh, sordid age! oh, ruthless rage!
    Oh, sacrilegious wrong!
A deed to blast the record page,
    And snap the strings of song;
In that great character's name, a band
    By groveling greed enticed,
Whose warrant is the grasping hand
    Of creeds without a Christ! [1,1:9–10]

Note

1. First published as *Magnolia: A Southern Home Journal*, then in 1863 as *Magnolia Weekly: A Home Journal of Literature and General News*.

Information Sources

BIBLIOGRAPHY:
McLean, Frank. "Periodicals Published in the South before 1880." Ph.D. dissertation, University of Virginia, 1928. P. 47.
Mott, Frank Luther. *A History of American Magazines, 1850–1865*. Cambridge, 1938. II:111.
INDEX SOURCES: None.
LOCATION SOURCES: Duke University Library, Library of Congress, New York Public Library, Virginia State Library (Richmond), Yale University Library.

Publication History

MAGAZINE TITLE AND TITLE CHANGES: *The Southern Monthly (Hutton & Freligh's Southern Monthly)*.
VOLUME AND ISSUE DATA: Vols. 1–2 (September 1861-May 1862), monthly.
PUBLISHER AND PLACE OF PUBLICATION: Southern Publishing House. Memphis, Tennessee (September 1861-April 1862); Grenada, Mississippi (May 1862).
EDITOR: Unknown.
CIRCULATION: Unknown.

THE SOUTHERN PLANTER

The longest lived and one of the most important agricultural magazines born in the ante bellum South was the *Southern Planter* of Richmond, Virginia. Its 130-year life span, in fact, qualifies it as one of the region's most durable magazines of whatever category, exceeding by a considerable margin the 93-year life of its Georgia contemporary, the *Southern Cultivator**(1843–1935), and the 74 years of the earlier *American Farmer** of Baltimore (1819–1897), with a period of suspension during the Civil War.[1]

The Southern Planter: Devoted to Agriculture, Horticulture, and the Household Arts first appeared in January 1841, edited and published at No. 3 Governor Street by Charles Tyler Botts. The masthead of this modest sixteen-page monthly bore dual mottoes: "Agriculture is the nursing mother of the Arts," Xenophon, and "Tillage and Pasturage are the two breasts of the State," Sully. Both mottoes were retained into the early 1900s and occasionally recalled thereafter; the magazine's subtitle was changed several times, then eliminated.

In his prospectus and introductory address to his readers, Botts explained that his intention would be to reject long essays and print instead, in condensed form, "the observations and deductions of practical men" (1,1:1–2). In so doing, he wrote, he would follow the lead of Northern agricultural magazinists whose technique was "to publish an agricultural paper at so small a price, as to bring it within the reach of all." Botts' hope was to reach "plain, economical men, who are frequently deterred from subscribing to a more expensive work." The *Southern Planter*, Botts continued, was to be a medium for the exchange of opinions and observations among Southern farmers. To these, his potential readers and contributors, he directed a plea to give one another the benefit of their experience, recognizing "the difficulty of eliciting communications from men unaccustomed to writing for the public eye."

On page 3 of the maiden issue appeared an anecdote on "book farming," ostensibly a letter to the editor but doubtlessly penned by Botts himself. It was the account of a "strong-minded but conceited and uneducated" old farmer who frequently sneered at "working by book rules." His younger neighbor, to whom the older man often gave advice, asked his mentor to write out his plan for the cultivation of sweet potatoes, a crop with which the older farmer had been especially successful. This resulting copy was sent secretly to a farm magazine, which published it in the next number. The younger farmer then sent a copy of this issue to his "advisor," appending a note saying "the directions, although valuable in themselves, had become worthless because having been printed" they now properly came under the head of *book farming*. After mulling this over, the older farmer concluded that putting advice in print does not hurt it at all and thus became a converted "book farmer," though he still insisted "(drawing himself up with considerable importance) that nobody but an individual rather advanced in life, skillful and experienced, should be permitted to write for agricultural papers."

From the appearance of America's first farm periodicals in the early 1800s until the last decades of the nineteenth century, there were no agricultural colleges, no state experiment stations, and no county agents. The farm periodical, therefore, was primarily a how-to-do-it medium—a source of practical information. Resistance to so-called book farming was the great hurdle these magazines had to get over before they could prosper. Botts realized that this problem would be especially pronounced in the more conservative, less educated South.

Editor Botts gave his readers a magazine filled with short articles, mostly of a how-to nature: the use of bone dust in turnip culture, the preparation of tobacco beds, how to train cows not to kick during milking, "ripening" manure, protecting peaches against worms, how to render leather waterproof, a "Heimlich's maneuver" to relieve a choking cow, how to build a better rat trap, how to cure mange. Only occasionally did tips for farm wives appear: a recipe for laundry soap, an earache remedy, cures for warts, how to preserve butter; copy aimed at women readers was given far greater prominence in the magazine's later years.

Early volumes were illustrated regularly, if not profusely, with small engravings of farm implements and machines: corn planters, straw cutters, potato steamers, mollebarts (scoops), harrows, hay presses, shingle makers, threshers, drag rakes, churns, rasps, stump extractors, homminy mortars, and the like. At the conclusion of his first year, Botts apologized for not having run more illustrations, saying that in all Richmond there was "not a single individual who makes a profession of engraving" (1,11/12:260).

In the midst of all this practicality, Botts occasionally allowed himself a touch of whimsy. The fat of human beings, he wrote, is said to make the finest candles. "What a use for some old ladies and gentlemen we have seen!"

After publishing seven volumes, Botts surrendered the editorship to John M. Daniel, whose two years in the post was typical of the brief tenure many of the magazine's subsequent nineteenth-century editors enjoyed. One of the more durable of these editors was Frank G. Ruffin of Albermarle, editor from 1851 to 1858, who pointed out that of Virginia's roughly 80,000 farmers, only 4,600 subscribed to the *Planter* and that he himself had brought that number up from 1,800 (15,1:17).[2] Ruffin's successor, Dr. James E. Williams of Henrico County, introduced poetry to the *Planter*'s last page, space occupied in many earlier issues by commodity prices, exchange information, and freight rates. A major article that appeared during Williams' years as editor (1858–1860, plus parts of 1861–1867 as co-editor with William Gilham) was "Slavery and Free Labor Defined and Compared," contributed by Edmund Ruffin (19,12:723–41; 20,1:1–10).[3]

Though it began without advertising, by 1860, before the five-year suspension (1862–1866) caused by the Civil War, the *Southern Planter*'s ad pages had burgeoned handily. Advertising sections were fat with the entreaties of commission agents, nurserymen, hotels, and railroads. The farmer and his wife were wooed by sellers of fertilizers, plows, wagons, sewing machines, dry goods, and many other such practical items.

The magazine's last owner was the Southern Planter Publishing Company, which took over in 1889. In January of the following year J. F. Jackson became editor and held that position until the magazine's May 1912 number. A subsequent editor who held his post for more than a decade was Dr. Meade Ferguson, under whose leadership the *Planter* went to the larger "life-size" format and became a semimonthly in July 1919. Ferguson also introduced picture covers beginning with the January 1, 1921, number. By this time the words "The Oldest

Agricultural Journal in America'' appeared on the cover of each issue. The *Planter* reverted to monthly publication in June 1932 under Editor T. K. Wolfe, and Paul D. Sanders, a former U.S. Department of Agriculture extension agent who was to edit the magazine for thirty-five years, took over in 1934.

Two issues of special note are the January 1, 1930, number, which commemorated the magazine's ninetieth anniversary, and the January 1940 number, which celebrated the start of the *Planter*'s second century. Both contained appraisals of the magazine's history.

The *Planter*'s circulation had seen many ups and downs. Its peak before the Civil War was probably about 5,000. This number dwindled to about 2,000 after war's end, and on the night of April 3, 1865, the magazine's records were destroyed in the fire following the evacuation of Richmond. By 1893 circulation had climbed to 20,000, by 1929 to 220,000, and in 1949 the *Planter* claimed 350,000 subscribers.

The venerable old journal's last editor was George W. Ijams of Maryland, formerly with the *Cooperative Farmer* and the *Del Mar Va Farmer*. The magazine's demise came after the November/December 1969 number.

For its 130 years the *Planter* published original observations and opinions on farming and gardening, selections from other agricultural periodicals and news of them, reports of farmers' clubs and organizations, reports of agricultural tours, discussion of various theories of tillage, price information, and other items of practical value to the farmer. Its later issues reflect the increasing importance of government to U.S. farmers, but start to finish, the magazine's many editors and proprietors kept it geared to the strictly practical. Botts would likely have been pleased.

Notes

1. Other ante bellum Southern agricultural magazines of various kinds are: the *Carolina Journal of Medicine, Science and Agriculture* (Charleston, S.C., 1825–26); *Southern Agriculturist, Horticulturist, and Register of Rural Affairs* (Charleston, 1828–46); *Virginia Farmer* (Scottsville, Va., 1829–33); *Farmer's Register* (Shellbanks, Petersburg, Va., 1833–42); the *Farmer and Gardener and Live Stock Breeder and Manager* (Baltimore, Md., 1834–39); *Magazine of Gardening and Botany* (Baltimore, 1834); *Tennessee Farmer* (Jonesborough, 1834–40); *Southern Botanic Journal* (Charleston, S.C., 1837–41); *Franklin Farmer* (Frankfort, Lexington, Ky., 1838-?); *Journal of American Silk Society and Rural Economist* (Baltimore, 1839–40); *Mountpleasant Silk Culturist and Farmer's Journal* (Brandonville, Va., 1839); *Dollar Farmer* (Louisville, Ky., 1842–46); the *Southern Planter: A Monthly Magazine of Husbandry* (Natchez, Washington, Miss., 1842-?); *South-Western Farmer* (Raymond, Miss., 1842–44); *Carolina Planter* (Columbia, S.C., 1844–45); *Farmers' Gazette* (Cheraw, S.C., 1844); *Valley Farmer* (Winchester, Va., 1844–46); *Journal of Agriculture* (Baltimore, 1845–48); *North Carolina Farmer* (Raleigh, N.C., 1845–50); *Alabama Planter* (Mobile, 1846-?); *DeBow's Review** (New Orleans, La., 1846–80); *Tennessee Farmer and Horticulturist* (Nashville, 1846); *Georgia Botanic Journal and College Sentinel* (Macon, 1847–48); *Colman's Rural World* (St. Louis, Mo.; Louisville, Ky., 1848–1916); *Southern Botanico-Medical Reformer* (Macon, 1849–51);

Naturalist (Franklin College, Tenn., 1850); *Soil of the South* (Columbus, Ga., 1851–57); *Cultivator* (Covington, Ky., 1852-?); *Farmer's Journal* (Bath, N.C., 1852); *American Cotton Planter* (Montgomery, Ala., 1853–61); *Cotton Plant* (Baltimore, 1853); *Kentucky Farmer* (Frankfort, Ky., 1853–60); *Southern Agriculturist* (Laurensville, S.C., 1853–54); *Agricultural and Commercial Journal* (Nashville, Tenn., 1855-?); *Carolina Cultivator* (Raleigh, N.C., 1855–57); *Farmers' Banner* (Nashville, 1855–60); *South Carolina Agriculturist* (Columbia, 1856); *Tennessee Farmer and Mechanic* (Nashville, 1856–57); *Virginia Farmer* (Harrisonburg, 1856); *Western Farm Journal* (Louisville, 1856–57); *North Carolina Planter* (Raleigh, 1858–61); *Valley Farmer* (Louisville, Ky., 1858–62); *Southern Field and Fireside* (Augusta, Ga., 1859–64); *Southern Rural Magazine* (Montgomery, Ala., 1860-?); *Virginia Farm Journal* (Richmond, 1860).

2. Ruffin again served as editor, co-editing the *Planter* in 1870 with Charles B. Williams while Williams was ill, and in 1875 served as an interim editor.

3. Ruffin had been the South's foremost agriculturist when the *Planter* was founded, and he was a frequent contributor. His own agricultural journal, the *Farmer's Register*, was published from 1833 to 1842. Ruffin fired the first shot at Fort Sumter on April 12, 1861, beginning the Civil War, and committed suicide in 1865 when the South was defeated.

Information Sources

BIBLIOGRAPHY:
Manchester, Harland. "The Farm Magazines." *Scribner's Magazine*, October 1938, pp. 25–29, 58–59.
Mott, Frank Luther. *A History of American Magazines, 1741–1850*. New York, 1930. I:154.
INDEX SOURCES: None.
LOCATION SOURCES: American Periodical Series microfilm, Duke University Library, Henry E. Huntington Library (San Jose, California), Library of Congress, Princeton University Library, University of Illinois Library, University of Massachusetts Library, University of Michigan Library, University of Texas Library (Austin), University of Richmond Library (Virginia), West Virginia University Library.

Publication History

MAGAZINE TITLE AND TITLE CHANGES: *The Southern Planter: Devoted to Agriculture, Horticulture, and the Household Arts* (January 1841–1862); *The Southern Planter and Farmer: Devoted to Agriculture, Horticulture, and the Mining, Mechanic and Household Arts* (January 1867-December 1881); *Southern Planter: Agriculture, Horticulture, Live Stock and the Household* (January 15, 1882-May 1889); *The Southern Planter: Devoted to Practical and Progressive Agriculture, Horticulture, Live Stock and the Home Fireside* (June 1889-December 1906); *The Southern Planter: Devoted to Practical and Progressive Agriculture, Horticulture, Trucking, Livestock and Fireside* (January 1907–1969).
VOLUME AND ISSUE DATA: Vols. 1–27 (January 1841-December 1861), new series, vols. 1–9 (February 1867-December 1877), vols. 39–130 (January 1878-December 1969); monthly except for January-June 1882 and July 1919-May 1932, when it was semimonthly.
PUBLISHER AND PLACE OF PUBLICATION: C. T. Botts (1841); C. T. Botts and

L. M. Burfoot (1842–1843); C. T. Botts (1843–1846); P. D. Bernard (1847–1854); Frank G. Ruffin (1855); F. G. Ruffin and N. August (1856–1858); August and Williams (1858–1861); Charles B. Williams (1867–1870); Ferguson and Rody (1870–1871); John W. Rison (1871–1872); Rison and Dickinson (1872–1873); L. R. Dickinson (1873–1881); Rolfe S. Saunders (1882); Aubrey H. Jones (1882); T. W. Ormond (1882–1885); O'Ferrall and Co. (1885–1889); Southern Planter Publishing Company (1889–1969). Richmond, Virginia.

EDITORS: C. T. Botts (1841); C. T. Botts and L. M. Burfoot (1842–1843); C. T. Botts (1843–1847); John M. Daniel (1847–1849); Richard B. Gooch (1849–1851); Frank G. Ruffin (1851–1858); James E. Williams (1858–1860); J. E. Williams and William Gilham (1861); Charles B. Williams (1867–1869); Charles B. Williams and Frank G. Ruffin (1870); Charles B. Williams (1870); James T. Johnson and John M. Allan (1870–1871); John W. Rison (1871–1872); Rison and Dickinson (1872–1873); L. R. Dickinson (1873–1874); Frank G. Ruffin (1875); L. R. Dickinson (1875–1880); Rolfe S. Saunders (1880–1882); Aubrey H. Jones (1882); W. C. Knight (1882–1889); J. F. Jackson (1890–1912); J. S. Cates (1912–1914); Meade Ferguson (1914–1929); T. K. Wolfe (1929–1933); Westmoreland Davis (1934); Paul D. Sanders (1934–1968); Doris B. Barksdale-Justice (1969); George W. Ijams (1969).

CIRCULATION: 350,000 in 1949.

THE SOUTHERN PLANTER AND FARMER. *See* THE SOUTHERN PLANTER

SOUTHERN PUNCH

It is decidedly difficult to imagine anyone starting a humor magazine in Richmond, Virginia, after Lee's defeat at Gettysburg. Yet in August of 1863 former New Orleans journalist John W. Overall introduced *Southern Punch*, an eight-page weekly modeled on the famous English original. Overall's salutatory in his first number read, in part:

This hearty, laughing disciple of Momus, is a legitimate son of that world-renowned 'London Punch,' whose sides have been made to ache when tickled by such men as Jerrold, Thackeray, and their wit-loving compeers of the 'Fast-anchored Isle.'

Our 'Punch' is a genuine Confederate. He prefers the Virginia mint julep and the mixed drinks of the Cotton States, to the Brown Stout and Cheshire cheese. In a word, the young Punch is a Southron.

He can be serious, as will be seen, when indulging his passion for polite literature; satirical, as the humbugs of the age will discover; and woe to him at whom he shakes his big-bellied fun, for his ridicule is more powerful than a thousand logicians.

There will be no resisting 'Punch.' Independent, fearless, he will go on
his way conquering and to conquer. Public abuses will fall before his satire
and plethoric humor. Charlitanism, in all its protean shapes will quail when
he speaks. [August 15, 1863, p. 2]

A notice to advertisers in the same issue claimed that *Southern Punch* would
have "the largest circulation of any paper in the South. Even before the first
number was issued, orders had accumulated to over fifteen thousand" (p. 8).

Overall's *Punch* was copiously illustrated with cartoon drawings of admirable
quality, most of which were done by engraver W. B. Campbell of Richmond.
The cover, like the London original, featured a jester, this time portrayed against
a Southern background.

A regular feature on page 2 was devoted to *belles lettres*, the magazine's
concession to the serious. Page 8 contained advertisements and usually one
cartoon illustration. On this page in volume 1, number 1, also appeared a single
column of information concerning the city's public amusements, notably those
at the New Richmond Theater and Metropolitan Hall. These establishments also
placed ads on this page, the New Richmond Theater advertising "Miss Mary
Partington, Danseuse, with an efficient corps de ballet," assisted by "Professor
Loebman, leader of the best Orchestra in the Confederacy." Other advertisers
were Richmond tobacco dealers and the publishing house of West & Johnston.
Advertised at $1 by Overall, Campbell, Hughes & Co., the magazine's own
publisher, was *The Punch Song Book*.

The remainder of *Punch*'s space was devoted to comic skits and sketches,
humorous anecdotes, cartoons, and dialect humor. A good example of the latter,
headlined "Not an Uncommon Case," was an account of a Virginian who had
visited in Kentucky, where he taught a local gentleman how to make mint juleps.
On a later visit to Kentucky, the Virginian rode up to his friend's gate and was
met by an elderly Negro man who informed him that his friend had died:

You see, massa stranger, one of dem Virginny gemman come 'long here
las' year, and show'd him *how to eat grass in his liquor*; he like it so well
he done stuck to it 'till it kill him. [1, 12: 5]

A great many brief comic items appeared, such as the following: "A hypo-
critical scoundrel in Athens inscribed over his door, 'Let nothing evil enter here.'
Diogenes wrote under it, 'How does the owner get in?' " (1, 12: 4). Under
"Literary Curiosity" the editor discusses a line written by John Taylor: "Lewd
I Did Live, Evil Did I Dwell," which reads the same when spelled backwards
(1, 12: 5).

Some of Overall's copy was unabashed Confederate "corn": "Why are bar-
keepers like mosquitoes? Because they take their 'nips' free of charge" (1, 12:
7). Some of his better efforts, however, were Southern anecdotes of some charm,
as in this example:

While Governor S——was President of the University of North Carolina, walking on the campus one day, he observed an unlawful assemblage of students. He proceeded toward them with his head down, his eyes fixed on the tip of his toes, as was his wont. In the mean time all but one of the students left, and by the time the Governor reached the place of assembly, were no where to be seen. He lifted his eyes upon the place where the boys *ought to* have been, or rather where they ought *not* to have been, and issued the following *singular* order to the single student left: 'Sir! instantly disperse to your several places of abode!' [1, 12: 7]

Overall exhibited a regrettable anti-Semitism and attributed much of the war-time inflation to Jewish merchants who had come South, he said, to profit from the war. The editor also aimed his shafts at draft dodgers, the civilian militia (of which he was a member), the Confederate Congress, and officers who socialized at the expense of duty. Many of the South's military leaders were accorded good treatment; two who were not were generals Bragg and Wise. The latter must have been anything but pleased by the ''Anecdote of General Wise'' that appeared in volume 1, number 12. During a battle near Richmond, a soldier reported to General Wise that he thought he saw a gun battery being set up on a distant hill. The general rose in his saddle and studied the hill for a considerable period. Then he rode along the line and made:

one of those electrifying little speeches for which he is so celebrated. 'They must be disloged! Right shoulder shift! Over the fence! Give 'em h—ll, G—d d—m 'em!' Over the fence, up the hill, rushed the Brigade. The disappointment can be better imagined than described when the so-thought battery turned out to be a *haystack*!

It is unnecessary to say that there was some tall profanity, over which the recording angel dropped a tear. [1, 12: 7]

Southern Punch also contained some delightful humor verse. Examples worth noting are ''Mrs. Grinoline Abroad'' (1, 5: 3); Overall's own ''Ballad of the Cavaliers'' (1, 9: 6), first published in the *Mobile Tribune*; ''Italian War Song'' (2, 13: 3); and ''Pipes and Cigars'' (1, 12: 3), which celebrates pipe smoking, a habit that intensified greatly in the Civil War South. One of particular delight is a poetic effort contributed by a Confederate soldier who signed himself W.E.M. Addressing his lines to Southern womanhood, he wrote, in part:

Shoeless we meet the well-shod foe,
And bootless him despise;
Sockless we watch, with bleeding toe,
And him Sockdologize!

Perchance our powder giveth out?
We fight them, then with rocks;
With hungry craws we crawfish not,—
But Miss, we miss the socks. . . .

Fair ladies then, if nothing loth,
Bring forth your spinning wheels;
Knit not your brow,—but knit to clothe
In bliss our blistered heels. [1, 14: 6]

Through the difficult months of 1864 the little magazine missed several numbers due to the paper shortage and the calling up of Richmond's militia, yet it survived into early 1865. Editor Overall and his weekly deserve admiration for bringing a measure of mirth to the South during an unimaginably demoralizing period.

Information Sources

BIBLIOGRAPHY:
Linneman, William R. "Southern Punch: A Draught of Confederate Wit." *Southern Folklore Quarterly*, 26 (1962): 131–36.
INDEX SOURCES: None.
LOCATION SOURCES: American Antiquarian Society (Worchester, Massachusetts), Duke University Library, Library of Congress, Newberry Library (Chicago), Princeton University Library, Virginia State Library (Richmond).

Publication History

MAGAZINE TITLE AND TITLE CHANGES: *Southern Punch*.
VOLUME AND ISSUE DATA: Vols. 1–3 (August 15, 1863–1865), weekly.
PUBLISHER AND PLACE OF PUBLICATION: Overall, Campbell, Hughes & Co. Richmond, Virginia.
EDITOR: John W. Overall.
CIRCULATION: Unknown.

THE SOUTHERN QUARTERLY REVIEW

At its birth in January 1842, the *Southern Quarterly Review*'s editor saw his new periodical as filling the void left by Charleston's distinguished *Southern Review*,* edited by Stephen Elliott, Sr., Stephen Elliott, Jr., and Hugh Legaré from 1828 to 1832. In the *Quarterly Review*'s inaugural article, the late *Southern Review* was praised as equal to any periodical of the same kind in Great Britain. The writer claimed that it had attained "a reputation not reached by any American Review during the brief period of its brilliant career" and went on to add that "it existed long enough . . . to prove one thing—that the Southern part of the American confederacy is not destitute of scholars—rare and ripe ones; that it is capable of taking a high and independent literary position before the world'' (1, 1: 39). The *Quarterly Review*'s editor, transplanted Northerner Daniel K. Whitaker, recognized the magnitude of the task before him and set for himself a lofty standard.

In the same article, the progress of the American periodical press is traced from the appearance first of newspapers, then Addisonian essay papers, monthly magazines, and finally quarterly reviews "in which the merits and demerits of authors, in all the departments of science and literature, were examined and pointed out with a fearless spirit, and topics of public interest, embracing political relations, were discussed in a thorough, learned and statesman-like manner" (1, 1: 6). The object of the quarterly review, the writer added, was "to diffuse knowledge, not to foster prejudices; to create, direct and control, not to echo, opinions; to produce beneficial changes upon a large scale, not to perpetuate, or even tolerate, existing abuses. . . . Ably conducted Reviews are the offspring of a high state of civilization, and are the best evidence now-a-days that can be furnished, of intellectual advancement" (1, 1: 42).

Having thus explained his idea of the proper role of his *Review*, the writer, presumably Whitaker, sounds a defensive note, saying:

> the great South and South-West has no organ, through which its voice can be heard, even in a whisper, except piece-meal, so to speak, through the Newspapers and the lighter periodicals. At a moment when fanatical, but powerful writers, unenlightened as to the true merits of the question, and the real state of affairs in this region, are endeavoring to excite a deep, permanent, bitter, living and breathing power of odium and opposition against us, [1, 1: 43]

the region's need for an equally powerful spokesman was great. He also complained that too many of the schoolbooks used in the South came from England or the Northern states ("anti-slavery primers, and spelling books, and catechisms, teeming with sly remarks, covert hints and subtle innuendos against slavery and slave institutions, which make a deep and lasting impression upon the plastic minds of our little ones" [1, 1: 62]. Older Southern children, he said, were too often sent to Northern colleges.

Thus began the periodical that became Charleston's second attempt at a dignified, scholarly, quarterly review, done in solemn one-column format and formidable 300-page length and offered to its public at $5 a year, payable in advance. Its birth did not occur in Charleston, however, but in New Orleans at 166 Royal Street, with Whitaker himself as both editor and publisher. Upon the conclusion of volume 1, the magazine was removed to Charleston, where the firm of Burges and James took over as publisher, the first of several changes in publishers in its fifteen-year life.

From start to finish the *Quarterly Review* espoused slavery and free trade. Its reviews contained comments—many of them voluminous—on a wide variety of issues, encompassing law, economics, history, religion, science, education, philosophy, medicine, poetry and drama, biography, travel, and other subjects. Many of these reviews covered topics of dubious interest to even the readers of a somber quarterly: "State of Education and Learning in Cuba" (1, whole 2: 377–97), "Rhode Island Affairs" (2, whole 1: 232–64), "International Copyright" (4, whole 7: 1–46). Others no doubt enjoyed a wider appeal, as was probably the case with "Woman, Physiologically Considered as to Mind, Morals, Marriage, Matrimonial Slavery, Infidelity and Divorce" (2, whole 4: 279–311) or "Physics and Physicians" (4, whole 7: 192–215; 4, whole 8: 466–98), which contains interesting comments on quackery.

Following the major reviews in each number was a department entitled "Critical Notices," which offered short reviews, typically eight to ten per issue but in some issues more than forty. Early issues contained another department called "Literary Announcements," in which readers were apprised of coming attractions from D. Appleton, S. Colman, Harper & Brothers, Carey & Hart, and other book publishers. In the first number also appeared the ambitious department "Quarterly List of New Publications," in which recent books in a wide array of subject fields were listed. Number 2 listed new books in only history and biography, and this department was then discontinued.

The *Quarterly Review* enjoyed the services as assistant or associate editor of two men who later distinguished themselves in Southern letters. J.D.B. DeBow, who later founded the superb *DeBow's Review** in New Orleans, and George Frederick Holmes,[1] an academic who was to write also for *DeBow's Review* and the *Southern Literary Messenger.**

In running a critical piece entitled "Mr. Calhoun and the Mississippi" (10, whole 20: 441–512) Whitaker bumped into one of South Carolina's sacred cows. For this and other reasons he resigned and was replaced as editor by Milton Clapp, whose first remarks to his readers in April 1847 contained these words:

> For the establishment of slavery in North America, the South is not responsible. It was brought to us and forced upon us by influences beyond our control. . . . We . . . assert that there is no laboring class in any nation, better cared for, better fed, better clothed, better sheltered in old age, enjoying so great a share of personal attention and kindness of his employers, or reaping so large a part of the profits of that capital with which his labor is combined. [11, whole 22: iv, v]

After two years under Clapp, the *Quarterly Review* came under the editorial direction of South Carolina's literary dynamo William Gilmore Simms, whose editorship lasted from 1849 to 1855. During this period Simms showed a great interest in the West, particularly California, the subject of innumerable articles in the *Review*. Also, the number of books reviewed in the "Critical Notices" department was greatly expanded. This editorship was Simms' longest and perhaps his best. It was also his last position as a magazine editor, though after the

Civil War he continued as a contributor, notably to the *Nineteenth Century* and the *Rural Carolinian*. When the war wrought unhappy changes in his personal finances, he turned to a more certain source of income—newspapers.[2]

In July 1853 advertisements began to appear, and by July 1854 ads accounted for many pages per number. Even this additional revenue brought in by the likes of Dr. Valentine's Artificial Guano, Steele's Hat Hall, Stabler's Anodyne Cherry Expectorant, and Stabler's Diarrhoea Cordial were not enough to put the magazine on a paying basis.

In late summer 1854 the *Quarterly Review* was published in Columbia, South Carolina, due to an epidemic in Charleston. Simms' difficulties in running the magazine were compounded in late 1854 by a fire that destroyed, among other things, his list of subscribers.[3] Following disagreements with C. Mortimer, the *Quarterly*'s new owner, Simms resigned, and in 1856 the magazine was moved permanently to Columbia under the Rev. James H. Thornwell.[4] After four Thornwell issues the *Quarterly Review* was laid to rest following the February 1857 number.

Notes

1. For a reasonably complete account of Holmes' accomplishments, see Harvey Wish, "George Frederick Holmes and Southern Periodical Literature of the Mid-Nineteenth Century," *Journal of Southern History*, 7 (February-November 1941): 343–56. Holmes published his first article in the *Quarterly Review* in July 1842—"Whewell on the Inductive Sciences," an essay involving experimental research techniques in social science.

2. Simms wrote for the Charleston *Courier* and the Charleston *Mercury*, edited the *Columbia Phoenix*, returned to Charleston as associate editor of the *Daily South Carolinian*, and later wrote once again for the *Courier*.

3. See "To The Public," which precedes the table of contents to the January 1855 number.

4. Thornwell had been president of South Carolina College and was on the faculty of Columbia's Presbyterian Theological Seminary.

Information Sources

BIBLIOGRAPHY:

Hoole, William Stanley. "William Gilmore Simms's Career as Editor." *Georgia Historical Quarterly*, 19 (March 1935): 47–54.

Mott, Frank Luther. *A History of American Magazines, 1741–1850*. New York, 1930. I:721–27.

Rogers, Edward R. *Four Southern Magazines*. University of Virginia Studies in Southern Literature, 1902. Pp. 61–91.

INDEX SOURCES: Poole's Index to Periodical Literature.

LOCATION SOURCES: American Periodical Series microfilm, University of Michigan Library, University of North Carolina Library (Chapel Hill).

Publication History

MAGAZINE TITLE AND TITLE CHANGES: *The Southern Quarterly Review*.

VOLUME AND ISSUE DATA: Vols. 1–16 (January 1842–January 1850), vols. 17–28

(new series, vols. 1–12, April 1850–October 1855), vols. 29–30 (new series, vols. 1–2, April 1856–February 1857); quarterly.
PUBLISHER AND PLACE OF PUBLICATION: Daniel K. Whitaker (New Orleans, Louisiana, 1842; Charleston, South Carolina, 1843–1847); Burges and James (Charleston, 1847–1850); Walker and Richards (Charleston, 1850–1852); Walker and Burke (Charleston, 1853); C. Mortimer (Charleston, 1854–1855); Edward H. Britton and Company (Columbia, South Carolina, 1856–1857).
EDITORS: Daniel K. Whitaker (1842–1847); Milton Clapp (1847–1849); William Gilmore Simms (1849–1855); J. H. Thornwell (1856–1857).
CIRCULATION: Approximately 2,000.

THE SOUTHERN REVIEW

The first of three important periodicals bearing this title[1] was founded in February of 1828 by an elderly, scholarly Charleston banker, Stephen Elliott,[2] whose main literary contributions to the magazine were in science and history. It is somewhat misleading to speak of the *Southern Review* as a "magazine," which usually implies a fairly general or popular audience. In present-day terms, it was more nearly a scholarly journal. Like most scholarly journals, it was a quarterly, the first number running to 271 pages. Though not directly connected to a college or university or academic association as are most modern journals, some of the *Review*'s most frequent contributors were on the faculty at the College of South Carolina, notably Thomas Cooper, the college's president; Robert Henry; and T. C. Wallace. Other contributors were U.S. Senator Robert Y. Hayne, physician-ethnologist Josiah C. Nott, and South Carolina Attorney General J. L. Petigru. Though several active contributors were politicians, the *Review* was not used for partisan purposes but was held aloof and dedicated to serious scholarship.

One cannot deny that the *Review* took upon itself difficult, if ponderous topics, dividing the contents of its first volume into such sections as "Classical Learning," "Principles of Agriculture," and "Geometry and the Calculus"—topics that have a clearly pedantic ring. Subsequent volumes addressed such weighty topics as "Niebuhr's Roman History," "Roman Literature," Origin of Rhyme," the "Life of Erasmus," "Higgins' Celtic Druids," the "United States Bank," and "Cuvier's Theory of the Globe." This was hardly light reading suitable for a rainy afternoon.

The *Review*'s editors did not shrink from examining works written in other languages. The first such piece was an extensive review of *The Functions of the Brain* by F. J. Gall (Sue les Fonctions du Cerveau: et sur celles de chacune de ses parties: avec des observations sur la possibilité de reconnaitre les instincts, les penchans, les talens, ou les dispositions morales et intellectuelles des Hommes et des Animaux, par la configuration de leur Cerveau et de leur Tete. [1, 1: 134–59]). Other examples are reviews of *Roemische Geschichte*(Roman History) by B. G. Niebuhr (1, 2: 320–41) and *Vita Danielis Wyttenbachii, Literarum hu-*

maniorum nuperrime in Academia Lugduno-Batava Professoris by Gulielmo Leonardo Manhe (1, 2: 410–42).

The lightest materials selected for the *Review* were the editor's comments on travel accounts, such as *Travels in the South of Russia* (Voyage dans la Russie Meridionale, et particulièrement dans les provinces situées au-delà du Caucase) by the Chevalier Gamba (2, 3: 114–52); *Travels through North America during the Years 1825 and 1826* by Bernhard, Duke of Saxe-Weimar Eisenach (3, 5: 192–207); *Travels of the Russian Mission through Mongolia to China, and Residence in Pekin in the years 1820, 1821* by George Timkowski (4, 7: 176–207); and *A Year in Spain* by a young American (8, 15: 154–71).[3]

For a description of this *Southern Review*, surely no one could improve upon that offered by Algernon Tassin, who characterized it as:

> the most perfect example America afforded of that scholarly contempt for popular demand which the English reviews had set native classicists to admiring. The men are not living who have read it throughout, but such as have emerged from its covers come up gasping their surprise that an unsettled and isolated district could have been thought capable of producing in sufficient numbers the savants who would have found such fare palatable. Even the stately *North American* [*Review*] had not ventured to be so exclusively classical or scientific.[4]

Lacking as it was in popular appeal, the *Review* appears to have enjoyed high regard in learned circles elsewhere; some of its contents were translated into other languages and reprinted abroad.[5]

Founding Editor Elliott died in 1830, and his son, Stephen Elliott, Jr., assumed the editorial reins briefly, to be replaced before the end of 1830 by the *Review*'s single most frequent contributor, Charleston lawyer and state legislator Hugh Swinton Legaré, an unabashed classicist, who edited it until its demise early in 1832. Toward the end, its neoclassical leanings diminished somewhat in favor of the coming romanticism, but its oppressive scholarliness continued unabated until Legaré put the periodical to rest in order to assume a consular position in Brussels, Belgium.

One must regard such a periodical with mixed feelings. Such lack of regard for building an audience large enough to ensure continued publication can hardly be admired, yet one can at the same time praise the *Southern Review* for its idealism, as expressed in its prospectus:

> It shall be among our first objects to . . . arrest, if possible, that current which has been directed so steadily against our country generally, and the South in particular; and to offer to our fellow citizens one Journal which they may read without finding themselves the objects of perpetual sarcasm, or of affected commiseration.

Notes

1. The second *Southern Review*, in Baltimore, was founded in January 1867 by lawyer-turned-minister Albert Taylor Bledsoe; this *Review* was published until October of 1879. Third was the *Southern Review* published between 1935 and 1942 at Louisiana State University in Baton Rouge.

2. Elliott was president of the South Carolina State Bank and founding president of the Literary and Philosophical Society of South Carolina.

3. The "young American" was a Lieutenant Slidall of the U.S. Navy.

4. "The Magazine in America," *The Bookman*, April-October 1915, p. 622.

5. See entry for "Southern Review" in Frank McLean, "Periodicals Published in the South before 1880" (Ph.D. diss., University of Virginia, 1928; the page is unnumbered).

Information Sources

BIBLIOGRAPHY:
McLean, Frank. "Periodicals Published in the South before 1880." Ph.D. dissertation, University of Virginia, 1928.
Mott, Frank Luther. *A History of American Magazines, 1741–1850*. New York, 1930. Pp. 573–76.
Rhea, Linda. *Hugh Swinton Legaré: A Charleston Intellectual*. Chapel Hill, N.C., 1934.
Tassin, Algernon. "The Magazine in America," *The Bookman*, 40 (April-October 1915): 622.
Welsh, John R. "An Early Pioneer: Legaré's Southern Review." *Southern Literary Journal*, 3 (Spring 1971): 79–97.
INDEX SOURCES: Poole's Index to Periodical Literature.
LOCATION SOURCES: American Periodical Series microfilm, University of Michigan Library.

Publication History

MAGAZINE TITLE AND TITLE CHANGES: *The Southern Review*.
VOLUME AND ISSUE DATA: Vols. 1–8 (February 1828–February 1832), quarterly.
PUBLISHER AND PLACE OF PUBLICATION: A. E. Miller. Charleston, South Carolina.
EDITORS: Stephen Elliott (1828–1829); Stephen Elliott, Jr. (1830); Hugh Swinton Legaré (1830–1832).
CIRCULATION: Unknown.

THE SOUTHERN ROSE. *See* THE ROSE BUD

SOUTHERN ROSE BUD. *See* THE ROSE BUD

SOUTHERN WORLD

The only magazine brash enough to try competing directly with *Southern Living** as a regional book covering the entire South has been Hilton Head

Island-based *Southern World*. When one wants to go face to face with *Southern Living*, however, the aspiring newcomer is more likely to find himself face to kneecap with them, given their considerable lead and powerful hold on the market. *Southern World*'s brave attempt lasted from the spring of 1979 until the early summer of 1981.

Founding and bankrolling *Southern World* were Ralph Hilton, a retired Foreign Service officer and former co-publisher of the *Savannah Journal-Record*, and retired banker James H. Styers of North Carolina. When the venture began, Styers was listed as publisher, and Hilton, who lived on Hilton Head Island, was editor.

Hilton and Styers had become disenchanted readers of *Southern Living*, largely due to its advertising clutter and the brevity of its feature articles. Also, they disapproved of *Southern Living*'s policy of avoiding controversy in its coverage of the region. Island office space was rented; advertising representatives in Atlanta, New York City, and Chicago were contracted; a number of initial contributors were located; and a small staff was hired. Styers' son Walter was made business manager; other staff were an assistant editor, editorial assistant, research assistant, art editor, photo editor, and travel editor.[1]

The initial issue hit the market bearing an eye-catching cover that featured bearded Hilton Head artist Walter Greer dressed as an Arab sheik and posed beside a Mercedes in the driveway of one of Beaufort, South Carolina's incomparable ante bellum mansions. The cover was a come-on for a story on recent purchases of Southern land and other property by wealthy foreigners (1, 1: 8–11). Other articles in the maiden issue dealt with South Carolina caviar, Hatteras yachts, the wild Oconee River of Tennessee, and the gardens of Mobile, Alabama. An events calendar appeared, as did a bridge column and three sections of brief news items and amusing snippets from the region. One of these three departments was soon replaced by a crossword puzzle.

Also in number 1 was Elizabeth Sendor's article "Are Southern Girls More Desirable," a look at Southern winners of the Miss America Pageant, which she followed up in a later issue with "A Gourmet Guide to Southern Men," a humor piece (1, 4: 25–27). Another Sendor contribution in number 1 asked "Is There a Southern Character?" Southerners want their lives to run smoothly, she wrote. "They don't want to know unhappy truths about themselves or those they love. They are polite. They want to make every guest feel welcome, feel as though he or she has alighted into the world's most sincere and fun-loving family—even though they fear the disruptions that strangers can cause" (1, 1: 4).

A greeting from Editor Hilton on page 1 of the new magazine promised not only fresh views of the region's places and faces but solid reporting on the South's growing pains and on its expanding economic and cultural interests. Hilton kept this promise, giving his magazine a far more journalistic tone than *Southern Living* in articles such as "Profitable Drug Routes of the South" (1, 1: 25–27), "Gasohol from Southern Farms" (1, 2: 10–12), and articles on hazards confronting Southern tugboat operators (2, 5: 26–28, 31–32, 34), oil and gas exploration in the Baton Rouge area (2, 4: 26–28, 31–32), irrigation on Southern farms (2, 5: 38–41), and cancer research in Birmingham (2, 4: 65–69). Beginning with the third number, a financial column by Hilton Head resident John C. Clark became a regular feature. Clark, an authority on bond underwriting and syndicate practices, had been with Wachovia Bank and Trust Company and had served from 1969 to 1976 as director of the Export-Import Bank.

Attention was paid to the region's literary scene. Guy Owen became a *Southern World* regular, writing on Thomas Wolfe (1, 5: 40–41), Erskine Caldwell (2, 3: 64–65), and Eudora Welty (3, 2: 72–75), and making more general observations in "The Pleasures of Southern Speech" (2, 2: 66–67). Bruce Firestone wrote on William Styron, author of *Sophie's Choice* (1, 6: 52–53).

One fiction piece per issue became standard, beginning with the first number of volume 2. Examples of these short stories and excerpts from novels were "Molly" by David Tillinghast, a Clemson University English professor (2, 1: 57–59); "The Blooming of Seth Overly" by Bess Saunders (2, 4: 79–80, 82); and Caroline Goforth's "Mourning" (2, 5: 81–82, 84–85).

In the travel category Sam Riley presented pieces on the South's great resorts (1, 3: 10–16), the Blue Ridge Parkway (1, 2: 34–36, 41), and gem hunting at Franklin, North Carolina (2, 2: 36–38). Randy Johnson contributed an article on cross-country skiing in the South (2, 5: 42–44, 53–55), historian Charles Price did a three-part series, "The South's Finest Golf Holes" (2, 1: 30–34; 2, 2: 50–53; 2, 3: 43–47); and Renee Hopkins did a special section on Alabama (2, 4: A1–A30).

Miscellaneous articles appeared on such standard regional topics as grits, watermellon, kudzu vine, Cajun crawfish, ginseng root, folk remedies, bluegrass music, duelling, bass fishing, and bird hunting. Jerry Simpson's "A Bourbon Biography" informed readers that "the Southern national drink" originated in a still owned by a Lutheran minister and that Jasper Newton Daniels, better known to generations of Southern tipplers as Jack Daniels, was a devout Primitive Baptist (3, 1: 80–84).

Southern World covers were among the most attractive in the business; usually they were reproductions of the work of regional artists: Bob Timberlake, Robert Dance, Walter Greer, Coby Whitmore, Alan Flattmann, Jim Harrison, and others.

The magazine had much to recommend it, yet it also had problems, the worst of which was attracting advertisers. Whereas a city magazine can survive on local hotel, restaurant, and entertainment ads, a new regional book must attract national advertising or the end is near. National advertisers, by and large, demand a track record, having seen many regional magazines come and go, which makes a terribly difficult situation for newcomers of *Southern World*'s geographic reach.

Volume 1, number 1, appeared with a scant 7.25 pages of paid advertising in its 48-page length, plus 3 cover pages of ads. Number 2 had even less. By the sixth number, length had increased to 64 pages, of which 12 pages contained advertisements. Remaining issues varied from 66 to 102 pages, and ad pages numbered 14 to 18, obviously not a satisfactory ad/editorial ratio. Even those who worked for the magazine were unaware of how much money it was losing each month, nor did they ever know, though the amount must have been considerable.

A management change occurred in Summer 1980 when Walter W. "Skip" Styers was named publisher and John F. Blakeslee became editor. James Styers was then listed as chairman and Ralph Hilton as president of the Southern World Publishing Company.

Probably *Southern World* was too journalistic, too significant for its own good given today's readers' expectations for city and regional magazines. Yet even if it had entertained more and informed somewhat less, the meager advertising it secured from resorts, liquors, cigarettes, banks, and insurance companies could not have sustained it. Any new nonspecialized magazine that wants to make its "beat" the entire South should take note of *Southern World*'s experience and proceed with caution.

Note

1. Sam Riley (the author) served as travel editor, having worked earlier for another regional periodical nearby, Savannah's *Coastal Magazine*. This magazine began in 1975 as *Coastal Quarterly* and suffered an early end in 1978 due to the death of its talented young founder, Lee Ashcraft.

Information Sources

BIBLIOGRAPHY:
Riley, Sam G., "Specialized Magazines of the South," *Journalism Quarterly*, 59 (Autumn 1982): 447–50, 455.
————. "The New Money and the New Magazines," *Journal of Regional Cultures*, 1 (Fall/Winter 1981): 107–15.
INDEX SOURCES: None.
LOCATION SOURCES: Clemson University Library, Louisiana State University Library, North Carolina State University Library, Virginia State Library, Wake Forest University Library.

Publication History

MAGAZINE TITLE AND TITLE CHANGES: *Southern World*.
VOLUME AND ISSUE DATA: Vols. 1–3 (March/April 1979–May/June 1981), bimonthly.
PUBLISHER AND PLACE OF PUBLICATION: Southern World Publishing Company: James H. Styers (1979–May/June 1900); Walter W. Styers (July/August 1980–May/June 1981). Hilton Head Island, South Carolina.
EDITORS: Ralph Hilton (1979–May/June 1980); John F. Blakeslee (July/August 1980–May/June 1981).
CIRCULATION: 100,000 press run.

THE SUNNY SOUTH

A long-lived, large-circulation, family magazine of the late 1800s was the *Sunny South* of Atlanta, Georgia. According to Frank Luther Mott[1] and L. Hugh Moore, Jr.,[2] the only Southern magazines to reach 100,000 circulation before 1885 were the *Sunny South* and *Louisville Home and Farm*. For most of its thirty-three years, 1875 to 1907, the Atlanta magazine operated as a weekly; from 1899 to 1901, however, it was published monthly.

The *Sunny South* was newspaper-like in appearance and for most of its run used an unusually large page size. It is a difficult subject for today's researcher, as its sheer bulk has discouraged microfilming, and due to the low-quality paper on which it was printed, many existing issues are now literally falling apart. The file at the Library of Congress is in woeful condition, the sear, brittle leaves crumbling at the gentlest touch.

As Moore pointed out, the *Sunny South* was primarily literary. Its aims were to give Southerners something to read for pleasure and to help rebuild the region's cultural interests. Certainly the culture today's reader sees in its pages was popular culture—the sentimental, moralistic, inspirational product of its era, largely the kind of writing that later made H. L. Mencken wince and wax critical.

The magazine sold for 5¢ an issue or $2 yearly, in advance. On page 1, under an elaborate nameplate, founding editors John H. Seals and William B. Seals further attracted the reader's eye by using large engravings of Southern scenes, which often covered six of the page's seven columns. For today's reader some of the most interesting of these page-one illustrations were a series of portraits run in 1881. Examples are the likenesses of Grand Duke Nicholas of Russia (6, 290), Harriet Beecher Stowe (6, 293), Thomas Alva Edison (6, 295), and Pope Leo XIII (6, 296).

Appearing in the magazine were such varied fare as a chess column, a department called "Southern Agriculture: Home and Farm," a "Boys and Girls Department," the Rev. T. DeWitt Talmage's widely disseminated sermons in a column entitled "Our Pulpit," and "The Household and Woman's Kingdom." Civil War lore was recounted in a department called "The Blue and the Gray: Fagots from the Old Camp Fires," and Lucien Lamar Knight edited "In the Literary World," a books department. "Our Portrait Gallery" was an eye-catching feature that carried small engraved portraits and brief biographical matter on distinguished men and women of the day.

Humor was not neglected. Charles Smith of the *Atlanta Constitution*, who wrote as "Bill Arp," contributed a column called "The Country Philosopher," and Robert J. Burdette did "Burdette's Humor." Idora Plowman Moore wrote yet another regular humor feature, "The Backwoods: Familiar Letters, Betsy Hamilton to Her Cousin Saleny." A long, thin, single column of jokes[3] and short humor verse appeared under the head "Wit and Humor," and material from other well-known humorists was included from time to time, such as "Bill

Nye in High Clover'' (13, 639), on an appearance Nye had made before the Clover Club of Philadelphia.

As promised in the magazine's subtitle, *Devoted to Literature, Romance, the News, and Southern Development*, a limited amount of primarily local news copy appeared. A small portion of this copy was political, but most concerned Atlanta's cultural scene. Obituaries of the prominent appeared, and a personals column consisted of brief notices of individuals' comings and goings. In general, the *Sunny South* was given to printing long single columns of very brief items. Railroad timetables were printed, as well.

According to Moore's reckoning[4] about one-sixth of each issue was filled with advertisements. Like so many other magazines of popular orientation, the largest category was patent medicines. Assailing the reader were the messages of Bile Beans for constipation, Dr. Pierce's Pellets for the liver/stomach/bowels, Ayer's Sarsparilla, Beecham's Pills, and Samaritan Nervine (for nerves, fits, St. Vitus Dance, syphillis, and ugly blood diseases). Ads for Dr. Warner's Celebrated Corsets, Crichton's School of Shorthand, Hotel St. Simons and other resorts, various publishers, Pear's Soap, and Southern railroads also made frequent appearances.

Another important part of the magazine's content was the editorial. The efforts of other magazines' editors were often reprinted, and overall, the *Sunny South*'s editorial offerings tended to the moralistic.

The magazine's *raison d'être*, however, was literature. Favorites of the editors were Shakespeare, Scott, Thomas Hardy, Longfellow, Oliver Wendell Holmes, Poe, Lord Byron, Elizabeth Barrett Browning, Tennyson, and Oscar Wilde.

Serialized novels were a familiar feature; most were of the romantic variety, such as J. H. Prince's *Castle Cursed; or, The Tortures of a Young Bride, A Strange Story of New Orleans*; Robert Buchanan's *The Tryst of Aranamore*; Gage Hempstead's *For Gold: A Story of the Dark Days in South Carolina*; and Fannie May Witt's *The Wheel of Fortune*. Thomas Hardy's *A Laodicean*, which had been serialized earlier in *Harper's*, appeared under the freshly popularized title *Her Two Lovers; or, The Lady and Her Castle*. More moralistic was Bella French Swisher's *Homeless Though at Home; or, The Story of a Woman's Life*.

Joel Chandler Harris did two Uncle Remus stories for the special Thanksgiving issue of 1892 (19, 879), which was printed on slick paper. "Two Dialect Poets," on James Whitcomb Riley and S. W. Foss, appeared in another issue, where also appeared a Charles B. Lewis humor piece typical of the era. The latter was run under a multitiered head that read: "The Limekiln Club/Brother Gardner Makes a Few Remarks about Chickens/Wherein the Conclusion Is Arrived at/ That the Colored Man's Taste for the/Barnyard Denizen Is Still Active/and Untrammaled.''

Poetry appeared in abundance, most of it dripping with inspiration or senti-mentality. In addition to printing the familiar poets already named, and such old Southern favorites as Paul Hamilton Hayne and Father Ryan, the magazine encouraged the work of Southern amateurs.

Though the *Sunny South* can hardly be considered one of the great literary magazines of the region, its popular acceptance and longevity earn it a place as the turn-of-the-century representative of its genre. After passing under the care of a succession of editors, the magazine was put to rest in 1907 and was succeeded by Joel Chandler Harris's even more popular *Uncle Remus's Magazine.**

Notes

1. *A History of American Magazines, 1865–1885* (Cambridge, 1938), III: 46.
2. "The Sunny South and Its Literature," *Georgia Review*, 19 (Spring 1965): 176–85.
3. An example from vol. 13, no. 639, was:

> Minister (dining with the family)—You were a nice little boy in church this morning, Bobby. I noticed you kept very quiet and still. Bobby—Yes, sir; I was afraid of waking pa up.

4. "The Sunny South and Its Literature," p. 177.

Information Sources

BIBLIOGRAPHY:
Moore, L. Hugh, Jr. "The Sunny South and Its Literature." *Georgia Review*, 19 (Spring 1965): 176–85.
Mott, Frank Luther. *A History of American Magazines, 1865–1885*. Cambridge, 1938. III: 46.
INDEX SOURCES: None.
LOCATION SOURCES: Library of Congress, University of Georgia Library.

Publication History

MAGAZINE TITLE AND TITLE CHANGES: *The Sunny South: Devoted to Literature, Romance, the News, and Southern Development.*
VOLUME AND ISSUE DATA: Vols. 1–34 (December 4, 1875–1907); weekly (1875–1899), monthly (1899–1901), weekly (1902–1907).
PUBLISHER AND PLACE OF PUBLICATION: John H. Seals and William B. Seals (December 4, 1875–August 1886); J. H. Seals & Company (September 1886–1891); The Sunny South Publishing Company (1892–1907). Atlanta, Georgia.
EDITORS: J. H. Seals and W. B. Seals (December 4, 1875–August 28, 1886); J. H. Seals (September 18, 1886–December 1891); Wallace P. Reed (January–November 26, 1892); Henry Clay Fairman (December 1892–September 28, 1895); James R. Holliday (November 1895–February 1896); J. R. Holliday and J. H. Seals (March 1896–at least November 1899); no editor listed after November 1899.
CIRCULATION: Approximately 100,000 maximum.

STRICTURES ON THE OMNIUM GATHERUM. *See* OMNIUM GATHERUM

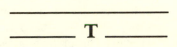

T

TAR HEEL: THE MAGAZINE OF NORTH CAROLINA.
See CAROLINA LIFESTYLE

THE TATLER OF SOCIETY IN FLORIDA

A turn-of-the-century forerunner of today's *Palm Beach Life** was the *Tatler of Society in Florida*, edited and published in St. Augustine from 1892 to 1908 by Anna M. Marcotte. The subscription terms for this magazine were unusual: $1 for "the season" (December 23 to April 8), single copies 10¢. It was sold at various newsstands in St. Augustine, Terminal Station in Jacksonville, Hotel Ormond at Ormond-on-the-Halifax, the Royal Poinciana and Palm Beach Inn in Palm Beach, the Royal Palm in Miami, the Tampa Bay Hotel in Tampa, Key West Hotel in that city, and at the Colonial and Royal Victoria hotels in Nassau. Visitors in St. Augustine were invited to register in the magazine's visitors' book kept in the office at 25 Alcazar Court.

Correspondents at Florida's poshest resorts fed to Anna Marcotte information on hotel facilities and names of guests—their movements, divertisements, golf and tennis scores, and the like. Social events were chronicled, often with photographs included. A personals column allowed the well-to-do a chance to check on their fellow visitors' frequent comings and goings as in these typical examples:

Major and Mrs. Hampden Waldrop of New York City, who during the past several years made St. Augustine their winter's home, are domiciled in the Holly Inn, Pinehurst, N.C., for the season. They will be missed from the gatherings in the hotel palaces by many friends.

Mr. and Mrs. J. Charles Linthicum of Baltimore, Md., and Mr. and Mrs. L. H. Mayott of Springfield, Mass., returned to the Alcazar on Thursday, greatly pleased with their sojourn at the Inn, Palm Beach (9, 5: 13).

A gossip column frequently dealt with social happenings outside Florida, such as notice of a reception at New York's Woman's Press Club in honor of Mrs. J. C. Croly, better known as "Jennie June Croly," on the occasion of her seventieth birthday. The item added that Mrs. Croly's pen name was suggested by a friend who once wrote to her family, saying that she was "the Juniest little girl I ever knew" (9, 4: 7).

A second item in this same column discussed the intention of two Chicago women to publish a sort of bachelors' home companion, a magazine especially for the unmarried male. Editor Marcotte added, however, that these prospective editors "make a serious mistake when they claim it is the first paper ever published in the interests of bachelors. One of the original purposes of *The Tatler* when started eight years ago was to assist bachelors who came to St. Augustine to find wives." Later in the same column appear items on a dinner party given by Mrs. U. S. Grant and the impending arrival of Mrs. Jefferson Davis for a Jacksonville function of the Daughters of the Confederacy.

Many articles on Florida's luxury hotels appeared, with long lists of who was staying where. Most often represented were the Ponce De Leon at St. Augustine, the Royal Poinciana and The Breakers at Palm Beach, and the Royal Victoria in Nassau. Luxurious hostelries in other parts of the country found the *Tatler* a good way to reach potential guests having sufficient wherewithall and the inclination to part with it: The Ebbitt House, the Hotel Grafton, and the Portland in Washington, D.C.; New York City's Hotel Empire; the Kenilworth Inn near Asheville, North Carolina; Pennsylvania's Bedford Springs Hotel; Richmond's marvelous Hotel Jefferson, which advertised Turkish, Russian, and Electric baths; and The Homestead, of Hot Springs, Virginia.

Also advertising in the sixteen-page weekly were Pommery Champagne, Apollinaris bottled water (the Perrier of its day), later Perrier itself, and many other products suited to the tastes of those who frequented "Florida's Riviera."

The little magazine's motto was "Whate'er Men Do, or Say, or Think, or Dream, Our Motley Paper Seizes for Its Theme." Golf rated its own regular column, and articles on miscellaneous topics of interest to the leisure class appeared, such as "Rings, Their Original Meaning" (9, 4: 6). Light verse also made an occasional appearance. An example is "An Angelic Husband," the first and last verses of which appear below:

> There are husbands who are pretty,
>   There are husbands who are witty,
> There are husbands who in public are as smiling as the morn;
>   There are husbands who are healthy,
>   There are husbands who are wealthy,
> But the real angelic husband—well, he's never yet been born.

So the woman who is mated
To a man who is rated
As 'pretty fair' should cherish him for ever and a day;
For the real angelic creature,
Perfect, quite, in every feature—
He has never been discovered, and he won't be, so they say. [9, 3:13]

With volume 9, number 1 (December 23, 1899), the *Tatler*'s page size was increased and the number of issues per season grew from twelve to fifteen with no corresponding increase in subscription price. The editor also announced the establishment of an up-to-date halftone plant in St. Augustine.

Inside the front cover of volume 16, number 6, was bound a good photographic portrait of Florida's most illustrious citizen, Henry M. Flagler; the lead article, "The Work of Henry M. Flagler," recounts how that gentleman developed Florida's east coast.

The *Tatler* fawned over the Flaglers and ran articles that were often thinly veiled puffs for various hotels, but its pages provide something of a record of Florida's invasion by turn-of-the-century society.

Information Sources

INDEX SOURCES: None.
LOCATION SOURCES: Library of Congress, New York Public Library, J. C. Yonge Library (Pensacola, Florida).

Publication History

MAGAZINE TITLE AND TITLE CHANGES: *The Tatler of Society in Florida*.
VOLUME AND ISSUE DATA: Vol. 1–17 (1892–March 14, 1908), weekly during "the season."
PUBLISHER AND PLACE OF PUBLICATION: Anna M. Marcotte. St. Augustine, Florida.
EDITOR: Anna M. Marcotte.
CIRCULATION: Unknown.

THE TAYLOR-TROTWOOD MAGAZINE. *See* BOB TAYLOR'S MAGAZINE

TESTIMONY FROM THE BATTLE-FIELDS. *See* OUR LIVING AND OUR DEAD

TEXAS HOMES

Another Southern house-and-garden magazine with a very, very upscale appeal[1] is Dallas' *Texas Homes*, which came on the scene in March 1977 as a sister periodical of *D Magazine*,* a "city book" that was launched in 1974. *Texas Homes'* founding editor-publisher is Ann Richardson, who assumed this post after having served as *D*'s director of promotion and circulation. Her almost exclusively female staff—only the production manager, advertising director, and one contributing editor are male—gets out this attractive monthly for subscribers whose mean annual income is $146,400,[2] impressive even by Texas standards. Subscribers are 68 percent female; average age is forty-six. From a promotional first issue of 15,000 copies, the magazine has grown to a circulation of 81,150 paid, plus 20,725 nonpaid. Some of the latter are copies sent gratis to all Texas member firms of the American Institute of Architects and to every member of the American Society of Interior Designers in Texas, Arkansas, Oklahoma, Louisiana, and New Mexico.

A second promotional device Richardson has used was a mailing to 275,000 Neiman Marcus credit card holders that invited them to subscribe by billing their Neiman account.[3] *Texas Homes* does not court the middle-income homeowner who wants to know where to find furniture bargains or how to redecorate a kitchen. The appeal is to the more sophisticated and no doubt to some who simply have the money to hire the right decorators to make themselves *appear* sophisticated. In any case, the magazine has little or no interest in do-it-yourself projects.

Asked who her main competitor was,[4] Richardson replied that for furniture and fabric advertising, it was *Architectural Digest*, the same reply given by the publisher of *Southern Accents** in Atlanta. Though *Southern Accents* is the Southern magazine most similar editorially to her own, Richardson said, it had not yet made sufficient inroads in the Texas market to be considered a threat. Her biggest competitor for national advertising, she said, was *Texas Monthly*,* as it, too, sells statewide.

Texas Homes' readers are 35 percent in Dallas-Fort Worth, 25 percent in Houston, and 20 percent in Austin-San Antonio. About 10 percent of its subscribers are outside Texas. The 120 to 168-page monthly's annual subscription rate is $20.00; it sells for $2.50 an issue on newsstands. The ad/editorial mix is roughly 50:50, and though both color and black-and-white photographs are used, about 80 percent are in full color.

Like other slick magazines appealing to the wealthy, *Texas Homes* is heavily laden with ads for Oriental rugs, fine furniture, fabrics and wallcoverings, antiques, and posh condominiums.[5] Occasional cruise, hotel, and luxury auto ads also appear, plus a modest amount of residential real estate advertising.

The houses in the feature spreads are commodious and luxurious and run the gamut of styles from a Norman country house with Baccarat chandeliers and elegant chairs upholstered in Scalamandré and silk brocade, to starkly expensive Bauhaus townhouses, great stucco villas in the Spanish style, North Dallas versions of Connecticut farmhouses, or the more indigenous Western ranch houses with spacious porches that remind one of the wood sidewalks of pioneer days. An unusual pair of recent Texans, the Baron and Baroness François de

Berenx, and their ancestral *objets d'art* were featured in the March number (8, 3: 74–81).

Much of the magazine's editorial space is taken up with roughly twenty regular departments, not all of which appear in every issue. Many of these departments appear in the first fifty to sixty pages of an issue, followed by roughly thirty pages of feature articles, in turn followed by six or seven more departments.

Regular departments usually appearing in the back of the book are "Roommates," four pages of small color photos with brief descriptions of furniture or decorative accessories; "Historic Homes"—four or five per issue; "Travel," for the sophisticated traveler, of course; "Innovators," on varied topics, from ideas for fashionable settings for home computers to a piece on Galveston's Bill Cherry, restorer of more than seventy houses in that city (8, 3: 103–6); "Wine," on Texas Cellars Sanchez Creek Vineyards Cabernet Sauvignon, Wimberly Valley Sauvignon Blanc, and other in-state labels; "Food for Thought," ruminations on life in the well-appointed kitchen, with recipes; "Books," concentrating on design and designers, furniture, decorating, gardens, and flower arranging; and "Appraisals," tips on assessing patina, joinery styles, and so forth to determine the age and value of antiques. An events department lists the state's art and photo exhibits, wine expositions, crafts shows, house and garden tours, and festivals—even the unusual ones, such as Ballinger's annual Antiques and Rattlesnake Show. The final pages of the magazine are devoted to three advertising sections: "Town and Country," two or three pages of ads for fine houses; "Market Place," illustrated ads for furniture and accessories; and a small classified section.

Probably no other Southern state, with the possible exception of Florida, is populous or affluent enough to support an in-state house book so nicely that it could charge $5,075 for a four-color, full-page ad, as *Texas Homes* does. In the same year that *Southern Accents* was born in Atlanta, *Texas Homes'* owners, the Southwest Media Corporation of Dallas, recognized their state as a viable market for a magazine that specialized both by region and by subject matter, and launched their own venture. What has resulted is a most attractive monthly that brings its affluent readers a dreamy world of up-to-the-minute amenities, innovative updates, residences with an unstudied sense of the past, casual ambiance, "ornamental architecture that creates endless surprises," and, as one of the magazine's own writers puts it, "serene country living just beyond the glitter of city lights."

Notes

1. The other Southern "house book" of the same type is Atlanta's *Southern Accents*.* Other Texas competitors are *Houston Home & Garden* and *Dallas-Fort Worth Home/Garden*.

2. Their median income is $69,040.

3. See Henry R. Bernstein, "Local Home Books Blooming in Texas," *Advertising Age*, September 18, 1978, p. 79.

4. Telephone conversation with the author, May 29, 1984.

5. A condo advertiser whose ads are truly outstanding graphically is The Dominion Club of San Antonio, with units that start at $300,000.

Information Sources

BIBLIOGRAPHY:

Bernstein, Henry R. "Local Home Books Blooming in Texas." *Advertising Age*, September 18, 1978, pp. 34, 40, 42, 79.

Neilsen, Bodil W. "Regional Shelter Journals Booming." *New York Times*, April 17, 1980.

INDEX SOURCES: Access: The Supplementary Index to Periodicals.

LOCATION SOURCES: Library of Congress, Southern Methodist University Library, University of Texas Library (Austin).

Publication History

MAGAZINE TITLE AND TITLE CHANGES: *Texas Homes*.

VOLUME AND ISSUE DATA: Vols. 1–8 (March 1977–present); quarterly (August 1977–Winter 1977), bimonthly (March/April 1978–January/February 1980), monthly (March 1980–present).

PUBLISHER AND PLACE OF PUBLICATION: Ann Richardson. Dallas, Texas.

EDITORS: Ann Richardson (March 1977–1980); Mariana Greene (1980–present).

CIRCULATION: 81,150 paid, 20,725 nonpaid (averages for January–December 1983).

THE TEXAS ILLUSTRATED MONTHLY MAGAZINE.
See THE TEXAS MAGAZINE

THE TEXAS MAGAZINE

Probably the boldest nineteenth-century attempt at publishing a quality general-interest magazine in Texas was the *Texas Magazine*, begun in 1896 Austin by Robert E. McCleary. McCleary's magazine was divided into three departments: history and other descriptive matter, political/social/scientific topics of current interest, and fiction/poetry. Certainly the preeminent early feature was a serialized life of Antonio Lopez de Santa Anna,[1] which appeared in the first nine numbers. This biographical piece was the work of Judge C. W. Raines, who was the state librarian of Texas and a regional bibliographer. Raines' account of Santa Anna's accomplishments appears to have been the first in the roughly twenty years since the Mexican leader's death. The cover of volume 1, number 1, featured a photograph of Santa Anna in early middle age supplied by his daughter.[2] By like token, a photo of Sam Houston was contributed by that gentleman's daughter, and one of Sam Austin by Austin's nephew, Col. Guy M. Bryan. When photographs were unobtainable, sketches were used, as was the case with the amateurish William Ford drawing of Davy Crockett that appeared on the cover of volume 1, number 8.

The *Texas Magazine* began with a length of thirty-two pages and sold for $1 yearly, or 10¢ an issue. In June 1897 William G. Scarff of Dallas, president of the wholesale paper firm of Scarff & O'Connor, announced that he had purchased the magazine from McCleary and would move it to Dallas, increasing its page size to that of *Century* and *Harper's* and expanding its length to sixty-four pages. The magazine's new editor was Texas lawyer Dudley G. Wooten, whom Scarff characterized as "one of the ablest writers in the state" (2, 14: unnumbered page inside front cover).

A longer editorial announcement in the following issue alerted readers that most of the intended changes would have to be delayed until September to allow time to secure new type, design a new cover, and make improved arrangements for producing illustrations. Without wishing to be typecast as a historical magazine, wrote Wooten, "we shall always prefer to publish authentic narratives and discussions of historic persons and events, acceptably rendered, to any amount of poor poetry, weak criticism, or frivolous friction" (3, 1: 36). Wooten also expressed his ambition for the monthly ultimately to become less exclusively a Texas vehicle and more of an outlet for the work of quality writers throughout the South and even the "North and East, should they desire to stray so far from the older and better equipped establishments."

While the magazine was still under McCleary's editorship, a department titled "Among Writers and Books" was added, beginning with volume 1, number 4. It was conducted by Austin writer Walfred Wilson and concentrated on reviewing books by Texas or Southern authors. Female readers were wooed with articles of special interest, such as "Austin and Its Women of Note" by Margaret L. Watson, a member of the Texas Women's Press Association (1, 4: 97–100) and later by adding, as of volume 1, number 8, a regular Daughters of the Republic of Texas department under Mrs. Dora Fowler Arthur of Austin.

The *Texas Magazine*'s publishers were also ambitious in that they held to a policy of paying for all the manuscripts they accepted. The Austin *Press Bulletin* praised the magazine for doing so, saying that it was the first periodical in the state—magazine or newspaper—to pay for all the material it printed. The significance of this innovation, they wrote, was that "on the day when *The Texas Magazine* made its announcement that it would operate on the basis that whatever is good enough to print is good enough to pay for, the death knell sounded in this state for all journals that attempt to live on the charity of our writers" (quoted in 1, 9: inside front cover).

A further attempt to corral female readers was a department called "Women's Work" that chronicled the efforts of other clubs and patriotic societies around the state. The department, edited by Kate Scurry Terrell of Dallas, first appeared in the initial number of volume 3.

On a poetry page headlined "Mucho En Poco" appeared a prophetic piece

of verse titled "A Few Years from Now." Its first two verses are indicative of
the whole:

> Oh, the Twentieth Century Girl!
>   What a wonderful thing she will be!
> She'll evolve from a mystical whirl
>   A woman unfettered and free!
> No corsets to crampen her waist,
>   No crimps to encumber her brain;
> Unafraid, bifurcate, unlaced,
>   Like a goddess of old she will reign.
>
> She'll wear bloomers, a matter of course;
>   She will vote, not a question of doubt;
> She will ride like a man on a horse;
>   At the club late at night she'll stay out;
> If she chances to love, she'll propose;
>   To blush will be quite out of date;
> She'll discuss politics with her beaux
>   And outtalk her masculine mate! [3, 2: 99]

On the same page appeared a piece of Negro dialect verse by Mary B. Hill.
Though the genre can only be viewed as regrettable by today's reader, judged
by the standards of her time, Hill's verses show considerable wit and skill. The
poem begins:

> My sistern and bredrin dear,
>   We's sembled on dis cason
> Wid Brudder Jones to wrastle,
>   An ter try by painful suasion
> Ter bring him back into de fole,
>   Frum which he's strayed right fur, I'se tole.

In August 1897 the Texas Magazine Company of Dallas was formed by Scarff
and fellow directors and Dallasites Alvin V. Lane, cashier of the National Exchange Bank; Louis Blaylock, publisher of the *Texas Christian Advocate*; and
Ed. J. Kiest, publisher of the *Daily Times-Herald*. James A. Meeks was business
manager. In a statement appearing at the end of the December 1897 number,
the new management stressed its quality circulation, saying that all subscriptions
are paid in advance with no free list, other than their modest exchange list of
twenty-five. Like modern regional magazines, they put their readers and potential
advertisers on notice that "we appeal to and reach the very best class of people
in this territory." Their magazine, they claimed, had been firmly established,
yet the magazine's fixed costs of $500 an issue appear to have overwhelmed

what was probably a rather modest circulation, and the monthly's death occurred soon after this sanguine claim was made.[3]

The *Texas Magazine* should be remembered as a vehicle for good-quality popular history, virtually all of which was original as opposed to selected. When it folded, the magazine left unpublished a considerable stock of interesting material, including further installments of the "Personnel Recollections of Stephen F. Austin," as recounted by his nephew, Moses Austin Bryan; ex-governor Oran M. Roberts' observations on Texas settlers; a series on the state's government by E. G. Senter; and poetry by Edward McQueen Gray, Elizabeth Lee Murphy, Antoinette Rotan Peterson, Mary Herndon Gray, John P. Sjolander, Nettie Houston Bringhurst, Margery L. Kendall, and others.

Notes

1. Santa Anna was referred to in these times as the "Napoleon of the West."

2. A particularly striking photograph of Santa Anna as a young man appears in vol. 2, no. 14.

3. The *Union List of Serials* lists the magazine's final issue as April 1898. Efforts to locate the issue or the January 1898 number were unsuccessful. The February and March numbers were not published.

Information Sources

BIBLIOGRAPHY:
Mott, Frank Luther. *A History of American Magazines, 1885–1905*. Vol. IV. Cambridge, 1957.
INDEX SOURCES: None.
LOCATION SOURCES: Houston Public Library, Library of Congress, Texas State Library and Historical Commission (Austin), University of Texas Library (Austin).

Publication History

MAGAZINE TITLE AND TITLE CHANGES: *The Texas Magazine* (May–December 1896); *The Texas Magazine: An Illustrated Monthly* (January–April 1897); *The Texas Magazine* (May–June 1897); *The Texas Magazine: Illustrated* (July 1897); *The Texas Illustrated Monthly Magazine* (August 1897–April 1898).
VOLUME AND ISSUE DATA: Vols. 1–4 (May 1896–April 1898), monthly.
PUBLISHER AND PLACE OF PUBLICATION: Robert Emmet McCleary (Austin, Texas, May 1896–May 1897); William G. Scarff (Dallas, Texas, June–July 1897); The Texas Magazine Company (Dallas, Texas, August 1897–January 1898).
EDITORS: R. E. McCleary (May 1896–May 1897); Dudley G. Wooten (June 1897–April 1898).
CIRCULATION: Unknown.

TEXAS MONTHLY

Best of all the state magazines in the nation and a front runner among city and regional periodicals in general is *Texas Monthly*, founded in February 1973 by Dallas-born, University of Texas graduate Michael Levy, then twenty-five years old. The sixties were the decade of the city magazine, the seventies of the regional books founded by publishers who saw the attraction of markets in larger geographical areas: states, groups of states, parts of contiguous states linked by a common geographical feature. An *Advertising Age* poll in early 1982 asked these city and regional magazines' editors to name the five most outstanding periodicals in their field. *Texas Monthly* was overwhelmingly selected as the nation's best, beating out such major-league competitors as *Philadelphia*, which finished a distant second; *Washingtonian*; *Los Angeles*; and *New York*. The only other Southern magazine finishing in the top ten was a Texas competitor, *D Magazine*,* the city magazine for Dallas/Fort Worth.[1]

Texas Monthly's original office above a Guadalupe Street beauty shop in Austin was once described by a newspaper reporter as looking like "the kind of place off-duty sailors go."[2] Now the magazine's staff is housed in a glass-clad suite of offices sixteen floors above downtown Austin's traffic.

From *Texas Monthly*'s inception, publisher Levy's vision for it had been to interpret Texas for Texans—to chronicle the state's progress, as one *Texas Monthly* writer, Rodney Webre, put it, "from the age of the cow chip to the age of the microchip" (12, 5: 167). Its appeal is linked to regional pride, a commodity for which Texans have long been known. Its paying subscribers, 287,000 strong, are considerably affluent, with a mean annual income of $71,700. Content is more journalistic than what one can expect to find in most city magazines, which tend to limit themselves to "all the news that's chic to print." So many magazines of the city and regional genre, as Los Angeles writer Stewart Scott once pointed out, seem to want only to soothe their free-spending, upscale readers with "good-life copy" on the assumption that these readers are "constantly looking for new ways to get it, save it, flaunt it or stash it."[3] *Texas Monthly* includes its share of good-life copy but does far more than the average regional book with investigative and interpretative articles. The editorial efforts of Levy's staff were recognized early; in 1974 *Texas Monthly* received a National Magazine Award for Outstanding Achievement in Specialized Journalism, an awards program sponsored by the American Society of Magazine Editors. This was the first time a magazine only one year old had won this prestigious award. A second National Magazine Award, this one for reporting excellence, came in 1979 for a three-part series by Richard West, "In Search of Rural America" (November 1977, April 1978, September 1978). A third such award followed in 1980, this time in the public service category, for Gene Lyons' "Why Teachers Can't Teach" (September 1979).

Memorable articles in early issues were Bill Brammer's exposé on sex in Texas politics and Terry King's "The Essence of a Redneck," a look at racial prejudice Texas style. A more recent look at race relations in the Lone Star State was "Just Friends," the story of how Dallas' predominantly white justice system gave a young black engineer a life sentence for an armed robbery that someone else had committed, and how another group of whites, his fellow E-Systems engineers, helped free him (12, 5: 184, 186, 188). The Wild West archetype of the lone man and his trusty gun lives on in "Out of Action," on the adventures and misadventures of tough Dallas policeman Dennis Cozby.

A few observers, among them newspaper reporters, who as a group are somewhat prone to confuse the roles of the magazine and the newspaper, have charged that *Texas Monthly* isn't as hard-hitting as it once was. True, the magazine might not be as audacious as in its formative years, but it has maintained a reasonable balance of light feature pieces, such as the droll "Why I Hate Lamaze" (12, 5: 156, 242, 244, 246–48) to the more powerful, insightful "Take Me across the River" in the same issue. The latter article was the first installment of a two-part saga on the illegal entry of Mexican Tianguis Pérez, as translated by Dick J. Reavis, and Pérez's life as an illegal alien in Houston.

Travel copy is used, as in "Funky Riviera: A Complete Guide to the Texas Coast" (June 1983); profiles, such as "The King Ranch: The Last Frontier Empire Confronts the Modern World" (October 1980); and "Dirty Money: How Banks Help Drug Smugglers Launder Money," an exposé piece.

"Bad News" and its companion piece "At the Scene" comprised Gary Cartwright's extensive condemnation of show biz in the Texas news biz (12, 2: 98–100, 168–72; 101–5, 107, 173–81). In the same issue appeared "The Texas Timex," the story of a wristwatch popularly known as the "Rolex President," which became a statewide status symbol when it was prominently displayed as President Lyndon Johnson, never one for subtlety, hiked up his shirt for photographers and pointed at the scar from his gall bladder operation. The watch sold for $1,500 then but has since ticked its way up to $7,950.

Texas Monthly has made a biennial feature of Texas' ten best and ten worst legislators and annually runs its "Bum Steer Awards," modeled after *Esquire*'s "Dubious Achievement Awards," one of the most imitated features in regional magazine journalism. As of 1984 only one legislator named in *Texas Monthly*'s ten best category has been defeated in a subsequent political race.

Regular departments are art, sports, movies (comments by James Wolcott, a razor-sharp reviewer who also reviews books for *Esquire*), architecture, books, business, crime, and theater. "Around the State" is an extensive guide to Texas amusements and events, and "Reporter" is a department in which appear several hard news items per issue—on nuclear waste disposal, politics, oil, game laws, medical controversies—and occasional profiles of interesting Texans. Letters to the editor appear under the standing head "The Roar of the Crowd," and "Touts" tells readers where to buy this and that in Texas—consumer copy labelled as such. Reader involvement is invited in the "Texas Monthly Puzzle," and the magazine's last page is called "State Secrets," Paul Burka's monthly collection of brief, newsy items on politics and vested wealth.

The magazine commands high ad rates; a one-time, full-page, full-color national ad is over $11,000. Even so, *Texas Monthly* is thick with advertisements, sometimes almost 250 pages per issue. Ads beckon the reader to the good life: fashions from Neiman-Marcus, Saks Fifth Avenue, Marshall Field's, Bloomingdales, Frost Bros., The Polo Shop, and Foley's. There are sleek snakeskin belts and purses from Sanger Harris, ostrich bags from Joske's, Bandolino shoes, De Beers diamonds, and high fashion cowboy boots by Larry Mahan and Justin. Texas belles are invited to pamper their faces with Lancôme, Chanel, and Clarins; big spenders of both sexes are tempted by Peugeot automobiles, the Orient Express, Club Med, and New York City's posh Helmsley Palace Hotel. New magazines have found *Texas Monthly* a good place to advertise, including *Vanity Fair* and *FMR: The Magazine of Franco Maria Ricci*, an Italian periodical that immodestly calls itself "the most beautiful magazine in the world." As with most other upscale regional magazines, there are also display ads for liquors, cigarettes, jewelry, watches, banks, and expensive condominium areas, plus a few pages of classifieds.

The *Texas Monthly* story is one of rapid growth and almost overnight recognition. From an initial circulation of 10,000 and 6.5 pages of advertisements in the maiden issue, the magazine grew to 100,000 less than two years later and was identified by the Audit Bureau of Circulations as the fastest growing major magazine in the nation in 1975. A year thereafter circulation had doubled and ad pages passed 1,000 for the year. In 1983 ad pages exceeded 1,600.

In 1977 a *Texas Monthly* offshoot, the Texas Monthly Press, issued its first book, *Lone Stars*, a photo collection. Subsequent volumes have included such varied entries as *Evidence of Love*, the story of an ax murder in suburban Dallas; *The Snakes of Texas*, totaling 106 species and selling for $60; *The Texas Monthly Guidebook*, a $12 state travel guide; *How To Be a Texan*; *Shopping Texas by Mail*; and *Out of the Forties*, a portrait of post-World War II Texas. Levy's company, Mediatex Communication Corp., has resisted the temptation to found other Texas magazines, opting instead for the *New Yorker* approach of doing one magazine well. In 1980, however, Levy gambled that he could do as well with a California statewide regional book as he had in Texas, when he purchased *New West* from Rupert Murdoch, who in turn had bought it from founder Clay Felker.[4] The *Texas Monthly* formula, which *Forbes* writer Toni Mack neatly encapsulated as "urban sophistication overlaid on mythic nostalgia,"[5] failed to work the same magic in the California market, and in August 1983 the magazine, which Levy had rechristened *California*, was sold to the owners of New York's *Savvy Magazine*.

Texas Monthly ended its first decade as the most-read magazine in its state by virtue of good timing and a talented staff, now numbering twenty-seven and headed by Publisher Levy, whose background includes degrees from the Wharton School of Finance and the University of Texas School of Law, plus stints as a UPI reporter and a *Philadelphia* magazine ad salesman. Founding Editor Bill Broyles passed up an offer to edit *Esquire* in order to remain with *Texas Monthly*, later left to edit Levy's *California*, and now edits *Newsweek*. Broyle's wife Sybil, as art director, gave the magazine a lively graphic appearance. Editor Broyles was succeeded at *Texas Monthly* by Gregory Curtis, a talented writer;

and Nicholas Lemann, former managing editor of the *Washington Monthly*, joined *Texas Monthly* in 1983 as associate editor.

Subscribers are fairly evenly split by sex—52 percent male, 48 percent female—and the magazine's renewal rate is high.[6] Roughly 85 percent of sales are by $21 annual subscription and 15 percent on newsstands for $2 a copy. Sales are greatest in the Houston market (roughly 30 percent) and next greatest in Dallas/Fort Worth (25 percent); only 10 percent of sales are outside the state. The Texas market has become a powerhouse, even with oil prices in decline, and this Southern regional magazine, second only in national recognition to *Southern Living*,* is likely to retain its dominant position for some time.

Notes

1. *D Magazine* finished seventh. (*Advertising Age*, April 5, 1982, pp. M26–27.) It is also noteworthy that the only other regional, as opposed to city magazine, of the ten was *California*, Levy's other state magazine, which he acquired in 1980. This magazine had been founded four years earlier by Clay Felker as *New West*.

2. Mike Shropshire, "The Write Stuff," *Dallas Morning News*, February 20, 1983.

3. In "Cheesecake Journalism," *Passages*, May 1980, p. 28.

4. See Stuart Emmrich, "Texas Monthly No California Road Map," *Advertising Age*, May 2, 1983, pp. 4, 44, 46.

5. "Home, Sweet Home?" *Forbes*, April 25, 1983.

6. *Texas Monthly* spokesperson Sally Balcom, in a June 18, 1984, telephone conversation with the author, would not release the figure, as this statistic is not ABC audited, but said renewals were among the highest in the industry.

Information Sources

BIBLIOGRAPHY:
"Cheeky TM." *Time Magazine*, September 27, 1976, p. 65.
Dunn, Si. "Texas Monthly: They Love It in New York." *Dallas Morning News*, October 1, 1983.
Higgins, George V. "Reaching beyond the Region." *Boston Globe*, February 20, 1982.
Mack, Toni. "Home, Sweet Home?" *Forbes*, April 25, 1983.
Marshall, Christy. "Texas Monthly Still Cheeky at 10." *Advertising Age*, May 2, 1983, pp. 4, 42.
Scott, Stewart J. "Cheesecake Journalism." *Passages*, May 1980, pp. 28, 30–33.
Shropshire, Mike. "The Write Stuff: Texas Monthly at 10." *Dallas Morning News*, February 20, 1983.
"Texas Flair Tops 'Em All." *Advertising Age*, April 5, 1982, pp. M26–27.
INDEX SOURCES: Access: The Supplementary Index to Periodicals, New Periodicals Index.
LOCATION SOURCES: Agricultural and Mechanical College of Texas Library, New York Public Library, Rice Institute Library, University of Texas Library (Austin), Yale University Library.

Publication History

MAGAZINE TITLE AND TITLE CHANGES: *Texas Monthly*.
VOLUME AND ISSUE DATA: Vols. 1–11 (February 1973–present), monthly.

PUBLISHER AND PLACE OF PUBLICATION: Michael R. Levy. Austin, Texas.
EDITORS: William D. Broyles (1973–1982); Gregory Curtis (1982–present).
CIRCULATION: 287,100 paid, 15,000 nonpaid.

TEXAS SIFTINGS

Having what must have been the largest circulation of any pre–1900 Texas magazine was *Texas Siftings*, a weekly humor periodical born in 1881 Austin. Presided over by Edwin Sweet and J. Armoy Knox, who listed themselves as "Proprietors, Editors and Sifters," the magazine's copy fell far short of greatness, yet the quality of its cartoon illustrations, its circulation success, and its unusual publishing history earn it a place in this collection.

The material it published was a strange, motley conglomeration. Originally intended as an outlet for Western humor, the content was broadened, became somewhat more sophisticated though not high brow, and allowed the slender weekly to serve as a sort of humor bridge between East and West. Much of its humor was ethnic, the editors supplying laughs at the expense of blacks, Indians, Jews, and both Irish and Italian immigrants.

Both original and selected copy appeared. Though the periodical's title was never explained within its own pages, perhaps the editors' task of culling other magazines and newspapers for content they found humorous would account for the designation *Siftings*.

The earliest issue available (volume 1, number 40) was an eight-page weekly done in six-column tabloid format and abounding in advertisements for patent medicines and other products. Carters' Little Liver Pills for sick headache; Prickly Ash Bitters for the liver, kidney, stomach, and bowel; and St. Jacobs Oil ("the Great German Remedy for Pain") touted their restorative qualities in this space, as did Pond's Extract, which claimed to cure everything from toothache to female complaints. There were nostrums for piles, fits, corns, boils, pimples, and "lost manhood." Ads for humor books appeared occasionally, such as for *Carl Pretzel's Book*,[1] thirty-two pages of sketches and parodies in broken German, selling for 10¢ a copy ("You can read dot pook mit one hant behindt your back").

Originally selling for $2.00 a year, in advance, *Texas Siftings'* price increased to $2.50 in its fourth volume and to $4.00 by 1890. In an effort to bolster circulation in 1896, the price was cut to $2.50, or 5¢ a copy on newsstands, the price level maintained until the magazine's demise after the June 12, 1897, number.

Cartoons in the weekly's first three volumes were in one-column width only. By 1884 two-column cartoons were used regularly, soon to be followed by cartoons three columns wide and eventually full-pagers and even double-page spreads. Foremost among the worthy cartoonists who drew for *Texas Siftings* was Thomas Worth, who poked fun at weather forecasters, gentlemen yachtsmen, census takers, Western inelegance, the ponderous thickness of Sunday newspapers, country editors, and his favorite target, the Negro. Another talented cartoonist was D. M. McCarthy, who in 1893 did a full-page, multipanel cartoon captioned "How the Chivalrous Jim McSnifter, 'the Cavortin' Catachesm of Calaveras Canyon and Long-Ranged Roarer from Devil's River,' Came to Scare a Dude in a New York Boarding House." Sitting in his room, McSnifter hears what he takes to be a man beating his wife. In reality it is the landlady's daughter having her singing lesson in the parlor, while in the kitchen the cook pounds a reluctant cut of meat to tenderize it.

Other cartoonists who contributed to *Siftings* were Charles H. Johnson, C. Howard, and Charles A. David. Still others appeared, but many signed their work in such a flowery manner as to render their own names illegible, a paradoxical defect for one who has the skill to do good-quality cartooning.

First published in Austin, Texas, the magazine listed its places of publication as Austin and New York City beginning in January 1884, expanding to Austin/New York/London in May of the same year. London was dropped from October 1885 until June 1888, and Austin was deleted sometime in 1888.[2] From June 16, 1888, until its final issue on June 12, 1897, the weekly was published in New York and London.[3]

Sweet and Knox were co-publishers until October 1883, when the Texas Siftings Publishing Company was established with Sweet as president and Knox as general manager. Beginning in June 1887 Sweet and A. Miner Griswold were listed as editors, with Knox remaining as manager. Sweet became sole editor in January 1892; T. S. Walling replaced Knox as manager in October 1894. In October 1896 or shortly before, Robert E. Morgan replaced Sweet as editor, and Charles H. Conklin took over as advertising manager. Finally, George W. Yates, Jr., and Conklin became co-publishers with the April 3, 1897, issue.

A staple of *Siftings'* written copy was the Western tale, examples of which are "Tomalo Tommy" (4, 19: 6), written for the magazine by S. H. Jackson; "Poet and Cook" (4, 21: 6) by "Irvonwy"; and a third original piece, F. B. Mott's "Bossie and the Colonel" (4, 26: 6). There was Negro dialect verse, such as Edward Willett's "The Cotton Field Hand" (4, 20: 2; rerun 4, 25: 2), and poetry of higher repute, for example, "Wet Weather Tale" (4, 24: 6) by James Whitcomb Riley and "More in the Man Than in the Land" (4, 21: 2) by Sidney Lanier, which was lifted from the *Southern Cultivator*.* Great quantities of verse were "sifted" from the pages of *Century*, *Life*, and other magazines, and from a wide variety of contemporary newspapers.

It appears that Editor Sweet had a fondness for dubious puns, and thousands of them appeared in these pages, often in long columns of one-liners headed "Chaff" or "Brevities." Examples are "Wheat covers a multitude of bins" and a motto for lynchers: "While there's life, there's rope."

Siftings also printed untold thousands of somewhat longer one-liners and jokes, one of which sounds amazingly current for having been published in 1885: "Gladstone says that the English want peace, but only peace with honor. That is exactly what the Russians want, a piece of Afghanistan with Russians on her"

(5, 3: 1). After departing Austin, the magazine's contents became less firmly Western, and many of its gags took on more of a city air:

> Mrs. Lushly: And there you were, when the policeman found you at three in the morning, hugging a cigar sign. Oh, it's just awful.
>
> Mr. Lushly: My dear, it surely is not possible that you are jealous of a cigar sign. [23, 6: 2]

A longer feature that appeared in serial form in the fifth and sixth volumes was "From the Chaparral to Wall Street," written by someone then working in Wall Street and who preferred to remain anonymous.

The Western newspaper editor was lampooned by Sweet's fictitious character Col. Bill Snort, "the pink of courtesy, the flower of chivalry, and the champion of reform." A marvelous front-page cartoon of Snort appeared on July 17, 1886. Rough, rawboned Texans were epitomized by another character, known variously as "Gen. Lone Star" and "Texas Siftings," who was usually shown getting the better of an effete Eastern dude or bowing with mock gentility to Queen Victoria.

By the late 1880s "Stage" and "Literary" columns had been added. In 1888 *Siftings* advertised its own cartoon contest, to be judged by Thomas Worth, chief of its illustrating department. First prize was $100, second prize $50.

A popular feature in *Siftings'* declining years was the full-page "Snagtown Torchlight" (25, 5: 12; 25, 8: 6; 25, 12: 10), a parody of small weekly newspapers, which editor Morgan borrowed from the *Arkansas Thomas Cat*.[4] Surely the "Torchlight" was one of the most comically awful repositories of mismatched type fonts and garbled thinking ever created by man. A slightly earlier comic feature of a similar kind was "The Plunkville Patriot," which ran in William Sidney Porter's *Rolling Stone** (1894–1895).

Just before *Texas Siftings'* demise, photographs began to appear, the first being an excellent portrait of New York's Oscar Hammerstein (25, 7: 10).

Though much of the humor in *Texas Siftings* was bland and much of the rest in roaring bad taste, it appears to have been the most successful of all pre–1900 Southern humor periodicals, a success that was owed, at least in large part, to its having moved north to the larger New York market.

Notes

1. "Carl Pretzel" was actually Mr. C. H. Harris.
2. Missing issues render impossible the attempt to fix the exact date.
3. Publication addresses in New York and London changed several times. The original New York address, Temple Court Building, later gave way to 240 Broadway. In 1891 the address was 47 John Street; in 1894 it was 114 Nassau Street. The final New York address was 65 West Broadway. First among *Siftings'* London addresses was 40 Charing Cross, second was 4 East Harding Street, and last was 48 Temple Chambers. For a time in 1888 a Chicago office was maintained at 168 Washington Street.

4. *Arkansas Thomas Cat* was published from 1890 to 1948 by J. Davis Orear of Hot Springs, Arkansas.

Information Sources

BIBLIOGRAPHY:
Mott, Frank Luther. *A History of American Magazines, 1865–1885*. Vol. III. Cambridge, 1938.
INDEX SOURCES: None.
LOCATION SOURCES: American Antiquarian Society (Worcester, Massachusetts), Historical and Philosophical Society of Ohio (Cincinnati), Library of Congress, New York Public Library, University of Michigan Library, University of Texas Library (Austin).

Publication History

MAGAZINE TITLE AND TITLE CHANGES: *Texas Siftings*.
VOLUME AND ISSUE DATA: Vols. 1–26 (May 1881–June 12, 1897), weekly.
PUBLISHER AND PLACE OF PUBLICATION: Edwin Sweet and J. Armoy Knox (May 1881–October 10, 1883); Texas Siftings Publishing Company (October 17, 1883–March 18, 1897); George W. Yates, Jr., and Charles H. Conklin (April 3–June 12, 1897). Austin, Texas (May 1881–January 19, 1884); Austin and New York City (January 26, 1884–May 3, 1884); Austin, New York, and London, England (May 10, 1884–October 3, 1885); New York and Austin (October 10, 1885–1888); New York (1888); New York and London (June 16, 1888–June 12, 1897).
EDITORS: Edwin Sweet and J. Armoy Knox (May 1881–May 28, 1887); Edwin Sweet and A. Miner Griswold (June 4, 1887–December 26, 1891); Edwin Sweet (January 2, 1892–October ? 1896); Robert E. Morgan (October ? 1896–June 12, 1897).
CIRCULATION: At least 100,000.

THE TOILET

The South's first magazine intended primarily for women readers was the *Toilet* [pronounced in the French manner]: *A Weekly Collection of Literary Pieces Principally Designed for the Amusement of the Ladies*, printed in Charleston, South Carolina, for several weeks in early 1801. This eight-page weekly was printed by Samuel Etheridge for the editor, who remained anonymous. Whoever the editor was, he had a penchant for commas, as may be seen in the following sentence, in which he announces that actual practice will differ from the magazine's prospectus in that some nonoriginal material will be used: "When selections appropriate, and meritorious can be made, from works, which are rare, or voluminous, the EDITOR conceives they will be quite as acceptable to his readers, as original pieces of equal merit" (1, 1: 8).

In the opening address to readers in number 1, the editor writes of the magazine's birth:

At the opening of an era, like an infant of obscure birth, a new being makes its appearance in 'new dresses and decorations.' And when its intelligent prattle shall catch the distinguishing ear, and its increasing charms captivate the susceptible heart, generosity will anticipate its wants, and forbid a sigh to arise from virtue's bosom. Dedicated to the eye of innocence and purity, it bears in its palm the emblems of morality and refinement.

The haughty look of stupid indifference, the EDITOR hopes never to meet.... He is happy to have lived in an age, when FEMALE EDUCATION is considered with an attention due to its importance . . . and if by his unwearied perserverance in a cause so pleasing and important, he can be in the least instrumental, in promoting the felicity and improvement of his fair patronesses, it will be ranked among the purest pleasures of his life.

Following this address appears a letter to the editor from one Benjamin Lincoln which says, in part: "A publication, which has for its basis, the benevolent design of enriching the young female mind, with that knowledge which will naturally tend to impress on their tender and susceptible hearts . . . lessons of virtue and morality . . . will, as it claims, doubtless receive the most cordial support of the public. I am clearly in opinion, that if mankind are ever made better, we shall be indebted for the reform to female exertions."

Could it be that the *Toilet*'s women readers, even in that era, perceived that the editor and male well-wishers like Mr. Lincoln were talking down to them? Despite excellent intentions and some good editorial judgment—as when the editor asks potential contributors "to compress their compositions within as narrow limits as possible. Brief and sprightly essays are best"—the magazine had a preachy tone that likely hastened its demise, which occurred less than two months after its birth.

Perhaps, on the other hand, we look at yesterday with today's eyes and read too much into the situation. At least one female reader, who signed herself Experience Hanson, appreciated the *Toilet*'s efforts, as expressed in a highly personal letter to the editor printed in number 7 (pp. 53–56). In this letter she offers to serve as a regular correspondent for the magazine, if the editor will pardon her "less than elegant and flowery style."

Most of the *Toilet*'s pages are filled with Addisonian essays on the human condition, some appearing under the standing head "The Censor," others headlined "Hints on Conversation" (no. 2: 9–11) or "The Pleasures of Taste" (no. 5: 34–36). Considerable space was devoted to letters to the editor, and a modest amount of poetry appeared. Some verses were poems of praise to the fair, as in "Edwin on Laura's Excellencies" ("Balmy nectar'd sweets bedew her/Peace enrobes her generous mind," etc., etc.; no. 4: 30–31), and have little enduring value; others are of higher quality, as in the case of "Melancholy" by "Standish."[1]

In number 3 the editor, probably under assault by would-be poets, quotes from Dutton's "The Present State of Literature," noting that these lines "reflect a happy semblence of many of our *tea table orators*, in their present state of oratory'':

> A busy throng, in fashion's livery dight,
> Rife, at a distance, on the Muse's sight
> Loquacious, pert, offensively polite,
> And elegantly dull, from morn to night;
> Who skip about the fair, like dapper elves,
> Lost in attention—to their own dear selves. [No. 3: 24]

The *Toilet* was printed in one-column format; its sales scheme was unusual: payment upon carrier delivery of each number, at the rate of 4¢ a copy.

Other early Southern efforts that took direct aim at the woman reader were the *Charleston Spectator, and Ladies Literary Portfolio* (1806); the *Emerald** of Baltimore, Maryland (1810–1811); the *Masonic Miscellany and Ladies Literary Magazine* of Lexington, Kentucky (1821–1823); the *Ladies' Literary Bouquet* of Baltimore (1823–1824); the *Ladies' Garland* of Harper's Ferry, Virginia (1824–1828); and the *National Magazine; or, Lady's Emporium* (see *National Magazine* [1830]) of Baltimore (1830–1831).

Note

1. An extract reads:

> Retir'd within my solitary room,
> Thoughts dismal swell the tide of sable gloom;
> Reflections painful, sad, foreboding fears,
> With scenes of sorrow crowd life's fleeting years.
> I take my pen, a short relief to gain,
> Divert my sorrow, and assuage my pain
> The labor may awaken pleasure's smile,
> A cheerful tone inspire, or ease beguile;
> A pensive line more cheers a soul like mine,
> Than all the nectar of Madeira's vine. . . . [No. 4: 31]

Information Sources

INDEX SOURCES: None.
LOCATION SOURCES: American Antiquarian Society (Worcester, Massachusetts), American Periodical Series microfilm.

Publication History

MAGAZINE TITLE AND TITLE CHANGES: *The Toilet: A Weekly Collection of Literary Pieces Principally Designed for the Amusement of Ladies*.
VOLUME AND ISSUE DATA: Vol. 1, nos. 1–8 (January 17–March 7, 1801), weekly.
PUBLISHER AND PLACE OF PUBLICATION: Samuel Etheridge, printer. Charlestown, South Carolina.

EDITOR: Unknown.
CIRCULATION: Unknown.

THE TRAITEUR

All hail, SUBSCRIPTION! 'tis to thee we owe
The plenteous fruits, from which invention grow.
Without thy aid, full oft the toiling bard
Wou'd lose, unpitied, his deserved reward,
And genius languish in the cave of night,
Nor once look forward to the dawn of light:
But propt by thee, the poet kens his way
Creeps from his cell, and ventures into day. [February 1, 1796, p. 3]

Thus began "Ode to Subscription," a long unsigned poem in Charleston, South Carolina's first magazine, the *Traiteur* (October 1795–June 1796). Editor-Publisher Henry Jackson's own subscription list, according to Guy Cardwell, began with 106 names—the "cream of Charleston society"[1]—and probably never advanced much beyond that number.

Another verse of this curious poem expresses well the melancholy sentiment felt by many a scribbler over the years:

Severe his lot—his lot severe indeed,
Whose stars compel him in the hour of need
To write for booksellers:—for those he woos,
With awkward suit, the coy, reluctant muse,
For those is doom'd, in strange, affected style,
Or dull narration, hist'ry to compile;
Else in romance, with idle notions fraught,
To tumble round and round the wire of thought,
His joyless time in tedious vigils wears,
His all the drudg'ry—all the profit theirs. [P. 4]

Though Frank Luther Mott[2] refers to the *South Carolina Weekly Museum** (1797–1798) as the first Southern magazine south of Baltimore, and though William Beer missed the *Traiteur* in his 1923 *Checklist of American Periodicals, 1741–1800* compiled for the American Antiquarian Society (Worcester, Massachusetts), Jackson's forty-page monthly appeared roughly a year and a half before the *Weekly Museum* and was the first of several Southern periodicals to be modeled after Joseph Addison's essay papers, the *Tatler* and *Spectator*, so popular in eighteenth-century England.

The *Traiteur* does appear, however, in three often-cited bibliographies compiled during the 1920s and 1930s: Frank McLean's University of Virginia Ph.D.

dissertation, "Periodicals Published in the South before 1880" (1928); Gertrude Gilmer's *Checklist of Southern Periodicals to 1861* (1934)[3]; and William Stanley Hoole's *A Check-List and Finding-List of Charleston Periodicals, 1721–1864* (1936).[4]

The little monthly, which sold for five shillings a number, was printed for the editor by Freneau & Paine,[5] 47 Bay Street, Charleston. According to Cardwell, the first number promised a "happy mixture of entertainment and instruction," true to the tradition of the English essay paper, though Jackson admitted to his readers his doubt that he could match the illustrious *Tatler* and *Spectator*. Politics would be avoided, Jackson went on, nor would he be a publisher "of Intreagues and Cuckoldoms" (October 1, 1795, pp. 5, 7).

The one number examined is (February 1796) done in very plain one-column format without illustration. The aforementioned "Ode to Subscription" fills pages 3–8 and is followed by a fifteen-page article entitled "Caroline: A Novel," which more accurately might be called a moral essay. In it the fair Caroline, the very flower of South Carolina womanhood, is seduced and ruined by the selfish, villainous Frederick and later dies of a broken heart. In the end of this piece of moralistic fiction, the reader is gratified to learn that Frederick is disinherited by his father, who concludes his scathing remarks to his son with "I hereby pronounce you the beggar you deserve to be" (p. 23).

Then follows "Elegy," a six-page poem reflecting dismally on fallen virtue. After an epigram of less than memorable cleverness appears another piece of verse entitled "Character of the Cardinal Fleury," first in the French, then translated as follows:

> By no experience, no reflection taught,
> Dazzled by glory from prospective thought,
> Consigning—blind and faithless of his trust,
> Vice to the throne; and virtue to the dust:
> An upstart pride through rank of station seen,
> Little in grandeur, but *superbly* mean.
> Such outline vices stigmatize the knave,
> Of France the tyrant—and of Rome the slave.
> [Pp. 31–32]

Two letters follow, perhaps by readers, perhaps by the editor himself. The first attacks the Negro justices peculiar to Charleston's legal system, who allegedly profited from the poor of that city. The second took the form of a poem, "A Sprig of Divinity," written in praise of a woman named Claudia. The final page and a half of the number consisted of the editor's chidings to would-be contributors. The originator of a submission signed "Attorney," says Jackson, should consult a spelling book. The unfortunate's spelling errors—*cappital, allmost, suxcess, elce*—are played back for him in painful detail. "Mr. *Whipper-Snapper*," Jackson continues, "might have saved his ink and paper, as such scurrility as his can never have any other effect than to produce contempt" (p. 39). It should be noted that though contributions came to the *Traiteur* signed with whimsical pen names, those that were accepted were run unsigned.

The title of this early monthly is difficult to explain. *The Traiteur*, a mixture of English and French, might well have appeared as *Le Traiteur*. "Traiteur" means "tradesman," a possible reference to the trade of ideas that might be expected to accompany a magazine.

Like so many Charleston magazines that followed it, the *Traiteur* lasted for but a little while. Early references state that its last number was the one for March 1796, but the *Union List of Serials* sets the final date as June 15 of that year.

Notes

1. "The Influence of Addison on Charleston Periodicals, 1795–1860," *Studies in Philology*, 35 (1938): 456–70. Cardwell appears to have located three numbers of the *Traiteur*—those for October, 1795, January 1796, and February 1796—but he fails to mention their locations. The present author has been able to locate only one extant issue— the February 1796 number, held by the Beinecke Library of Yale University.

2. *A History of American Magazines, 1741–1850* (New York, 1930), I: 32.

3. Boston, F. W. Faxon Company.

4. Durham, N.C., Duke University Press.

5. The Freneau here was Peter Freneau, brother of the more famous Philip, who had become known as "The Poet of the Revolution" for "The Prison Ship" and other verse he wrote during the war and for his Anti-Federalist writing while editor of the *National Gazette*.

Information Sources

BIBIOGRAPHY:
Cardwell, Guy A. "The Influence of Addison on Charleston Periodicals, 1795–1860."
    Studies in Philology, 35 (Chapel Hill, 1938): 456–70.
Hoole, William Stanley. *A Check-List and Finding-List of Charleston Periodicals, 1732–
    1864*. Durham, N.C., 1936. P. 17.
INDEX SOURCES: None.
LOCATION SOURCES: Beinecke Library at Yale University.

Publication History

MAGAZINE TITLE AND TITLE CHANGES: *The Traiteur*.
VOLUME AND ISSUE DATA: Vol. 1 (October 1, 1795–June 15, 1796), monthly.
PUBLISHER AND PLACE OF PUBLICATION: Henry Jackson. Charleston, South
    Carolina.
EDITOR: Henry Jackson.
CIRCULATION: 106 in 1795.

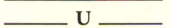

ULTRA MAGAZINE

Outdoing all other Southern magazines in blatant, unabashed, congratulatory appeal to wealth—old or new—is Houston's *Ultra Magazine*, begun in September 1981. A beautifully laid out monthly slick of 120 to 180 pages an issue, *Ultra* goes to an especially affluent readership. Subscribers' mean household income is $212,500, apparently the highest of any Southern magazine. Other items in the magazine's demographic profile show a 61:39 percent split in favor of female subscribers, that 77 percent of subscribers are married, that 90 percent attended college, that 26 percent completed postgraduate studies, and that in 47 percent of subscriber homes the head of the household is on at least one corporate board of directors.

Ultra sells itself to advertisers with the help of an extensive subscriber profile compiled in 1983 by Don Bowdren Associates and neatly packaged in pamphlet form. From it the prospective advertiser will learn that 35 percent of *Ultra* subscribers own two or more homes, that the mean value of their principal residence is $317,500, and that the mean value of their second home is $169,400. Subscribers' mean investment portfolio value is $410,200, and 38 percent purchased wine by the case during the previous twelve months. Within the past year 76 percent had purchased designer clothes; within the last three years 24 percent had taken one or more cruises. The magazine's free-spending "average reader" spends $134 a year on fragrances and within the previous year had taken five air trips for pleasure and five more for business. Subscribers' median age is forty-seven, with a fairly even distribution among age categories.

This kind of monied, globe-hopping readership was not assembled by accident. Like several other recent magazines that center their efforts on the very wealthy, *Ultra* began as a so-called controlled circulation magazine, mailed free to 70,000 wealthy Texans and only later seeking paid subscribers. *Ultra*'s circulation in

1984 was 95,000, of which roughly 50,000 were paid. To be on the controlled, or free list, one's annual income must be at least $100,000. Other magazines that have taken this marketing approach are New York City's *Avenue*, Dallas' *Parkway*, California's *Beverly Hills People*, Chicago's *Avenue M*, and *Washington Dossier Magazine* in D.C. Of these, *Parkway* and *Beverly Hills People* are now defunct.[1]

These new magazines are, in the main, offshoots of the city magazine movement. Their *raison d'être* is identical to that of direct-mail advertising: they provide advertisers, especially retailers of luxury products, a means of reaching the right customers without having to pay for wasted circulation. For a full-page, four-color ad, the one-insertion national rate is $5,145, the state rate $4,630, and the city rate $3,975—good buys for the right advertisers.

Bankrolling *Ultra* is Houston real estate magnate Harold Farb, who according to *Adweek*[2] has invested perhaps $5 million in it since its first issue in September 1981. To run the magazine Farb hired *Forbes* reporter Tedd A. Cohen, who began in November 1981 with the title of managing editor, replacing two earlier editors who had lasted one month each, and is now listed as associate publisher and as president of Farb Publications, Inc. *Ultra* is presently on its fourth editor since Cohen gave up the editorial side for management in April 1982 (seventh editor since the magazine's inception). At this writing the magazine is edited by Barbara L. Dixon.

A look at *Ultra's* highly complementary mix of ad and editorial matter reveals that the magazine isn't for ranchhands. When the *Ultra* reader rides the range, it is probably in a Ferrari, Maserati, Lamborghini, Lotus, Aston Martin, Eagle Excalibur, or Spartan. *Ultra* males get outfitted for the trail at Gerardo's of Dallas and buy their favorite fillies Pam Mahoney furs, baubles from Pacetti-de 'Medici and Linz. When they bed down for the night, it is at such places as The Vineyard in Dallas, The Dominion in San Antonio, and The Huntington of Houston.

Typical of other magazines directed at the wealthy, fashions, fragrances, jewelry, luxury automobiles, and real estate are big advertising categories. In addition to the paid real estate ads, a section called "Ultra Homes" showcases a selection of luxury homes with the black-and-white photos and brief verbal descriptions that have within the last decade come to be so typical of city and regional magazines. Resort and cruise ads appear, and expensive wristwatches are big with Texans. Regional flavor appears in horse ads, such as an eyecatching, full-page reminder of the Texas Select Yearling Sale sponsored by the Texas Thoroughbred Horsemen's Association. The unusual sometimes appears, as in an even more attractive full-page taken out by two Dallas cosmetic dentists who literally sell Texans a smile.

Controversy in editorial matter is forbidden in *Ultra's* pages, where in the apt words of an old cowboy song, "never is heard a discouraging word, and the skies are not cloudy all day." The people pictured in *Ultra* are all smiles, from the well-connected Texas ladies on its covers to the models in its ads to the subjects of its feature articles to the readers who send in photos of themselves for inclusion in two regular society features: "Weddings" and "Around The Towns," where the happy couples are shown and identified by name but not usually commented upon. Additional society tittle-tattle and more small black-and-white photos appear in the "Suzy" column, another monthly feature. Like forerunner *Palm Beach Life,** *Ultra* gives its readers a horoscope page especially written for the rich.

Some of Ultra's most appealing feature articles are profiles of monied Texans, such as a long piece on Texan-gone-to-Venice Evelyn Lambert (3, 8: 49–50, 52–57), spiritual successor to the late Peggy Guggenheim, or a shorter profile of beautiful Dallas philanthropist DeLois Faulkner (3, 9: 66, 68–71). A fashion photo spread appears monthly, and travel features inform the reader about Texas country inns (3, 11: 44, 47–48, 50–53, 55), millionaires' mecca Palm Beach (3, 8: 67–69, 104–7), and luxury canal barge trips in France (3, 8: 78–79, 110–11). Other features tell rich Texans about well-bred investments (3, 10: 46–47, 52), well-bred horses and those who own them (3, 10: 65–70, 88, 90, 93–94), turquoise (3, 11: 95, 142–44), and tequila (3, 11: 131–34).

Ultra is graphically exquisite and can boast the most financially elite readership of any Southern magazine. Still, one might be left with a vague feeling of unease about the magazine, a reaction not experienced while reading and writing about *Palm Beach Life*, for example. Perhaps it is a matter of old money versus new money, with too frequent references by *Ultra* to "smart money." It is almost as though New Yorkers have come to the Sun Belt to instruct the Texans on how to be rich properly.

Notes

1. See "Magazines That Zero In on the Super-Rich," *Business Week*, May 23, 1983, p. 47.
2. Beverly Narum, "Cohen Guides Ultra's Fortunes," *Adweek*, March 26, 1984, p. 24.

Information Sources

BIBLIOGRAPHY:
"Magazines That Zero In on the Super-Rich," *Business Week*, May 23, 1983, p. 47.
Narum, Beverly. "Cohen Guides Ultra's Fortunes," *Adweek*, March 16, 1984, p. 24.
INDEX SOURCES: None.
LOCATION SOURCES: University of Texas Library (Austin).

Publication History

MAGAZINE TITLE AND TITLE CHANGES: *Ultra Magazine*.
VOLUME AND ISSUE DATA: Vols. 1–3 (September 1981–present), monthly.
PUBLISHER AND PLACE OF PUBLICATION: Harold Farb. Houston, Texas.
EDITORS: Carter Rochelle (September 1981); Karl Sternbaum (October 1981); Tedd Cohen (November 1981–April 1982); Judy Lunn (May–June 1982); Wendy Meyer

(July 1982–May 1983); David Bertugli (May 1983–March 1984); Barbara Dixon (April 1984–present).
CIRCULATION: 95,000.

UNCLE REMUS'S MAGAZINE

Of all the Southern magazines launched in the first decade of the 1900s, the largest circulation, around 240,000, was attained by Atlanta's *Uncle Remus's Magazine*, the popularity of which depended in large measure upon the national reputation of Joel Chandler Harris.[1]

Harris' journalistic odyssey began at age thirteen when he left his home in Eatonton, Georgia, to work as a printer's devil for Joseph Addison Turner at Turnwold Plantation. It was in Turner's periodical the *Countryman** that Harris' first literary efforts appeared. After four years at Turnwold, Harris became a typesetter and later a reviewer for the Macon *Telegraph*. Then in 1866 and 1867 he worked for William Evelyn's *Crescent Monthly* (1866–1867), a short-lived New Orleans magazine. From there he returned to Georgia and worked for a weekly newspaper, the *Monroe Advertiser*, in the town of Forsyth. In 1870 he became associate editor of the Savannah *Morning News*, where his daily column "State Affairs," later called "Affairs in Georgia," attracted statewide interest and soon gave him the reputation of being Georgia's premier humorist. A yellow fever epidemic in August of 1876 caused Harris and family to relocate to Atlanta, where he was employed by the Atlanta *Constitution*. Here he remained for more than twenty years, and here he published his Uncle Remus tales, which became so admired and beloved that when selections were made in 1905 for the American Academy of Arts and Letters, Harris was the only Southern writer chosen.

Harris' eldest son, Julian LaRose Harris, also worked for the *Constitution*, first as a reporter and finally as managing editor. The younger Harris resigned in order to plan a new magazine. Financial backing came from Roby Robinson and other Atlanta businessmen who raised a total of $200,000, and $6,000 was provided by philanthropist Andrew Carnegie. The decision was made to buy the *Sunny South*,* a popular Atlanta weekly magazine dating from 1875, published in newsprint by the *Constitution*. Joel Chandler Harris became editor of the new periodical, Don Marquis associate editor, Edwin Camp[2] managing editor, and Julian Harris business manager. Parent corporation and publisher was the Sunny South Publishing Company of Atlanta, of which Robinson, a vice president of the *Constitution*, was president and Robert F. Maddox, an Atlanta banker, was vice president. The title *Uncle Remus's Magazine* was chosen after much debate as a means of capitalizing on the elder Harris' considerable national reputation; the new magazine began in June 1907 with the impressive circulation of 125,000.

In an introductory essay in the initial number, J. C. Harris promised that his magazine would reflect an optimistic, cheerful philosophy and would counsel toleration and social accord. His intention was to promote "neighbor-knowledge," Harris wrote, for "there is a woeful lack of it in the North and East with respect to the South. . . . At the North neighbor-knowledge of the South is confined almost entirely to those who have made commercial explorations of this section" (1, 1: 6). The new magazine was to be generally conservative and would stress fiction, but not neglect nonfiction articles bearing on the progress and development of the New South. The motto Harris adopted was "Typical of the South—National in Scope."

True to his promises, the elder Harris kept the magazine to its "never was heard a discouraging word" format. Looking through the first volume of *Uncle Remus's Magazine*, one is put in mind of the South's most popular magazine of the 1980s, *Southern Living*,* which also eschews controversy and unpleasantness. The reading South is and was the comfortable South and seems to prefer a generous measure of peace and comfort in what it reads. When he wished to be plain-spoken in his editorials, Harris did it via his literary character Billy Saunders, a rustic sage whose ideas were presented in rural Georgia dialect. In this roundabout way, Joel Chandler Harris spoke out gently, but probably effectively against bigotry, lynching, and the evils of greed and monopoly, an interesting approach at a time when muckracking was in full flower in the Northeast. Harris satirized his own gentle techniques by having Billy Saunders offer the magazine some advice:

> You've got to git you some well-hooks an' a drag-net, an' a couple of sticks of dynamite, an' see what you can fetch up from the nasty deep. . . . You've got to whirl in an' show folks that your feet ain't gone to sleep. [1, 1: 7]

Harris also conducted the book review department for volume 1, and since this job sometimes called for negative criticism, the shy editor used a pseudonym for this function, as well. His reviews were written under the name Anne Macfarland. According to biographer Paul Cousins, he even went so far as to try to trick his own staff into thinking that Anne Macfarland, ostensibly a sixty-year-old woman once a resident of Middle Georgia but now living in London, was a real person.[3]

Retiring as he was, Harris was tough-minded enough to insist upon complete control over what went into the magazine. In the first number appeared installment one of his own yet unpublished novel, "The Bishop, the Boogerman, and the Right of Way," which continued through the next four issues, and an Uncle Remus tale, "How Brer Rabbit Saved Brer B'ar's Life." His own work was prominent in all the issues of volume 1.

Don Marquis contributed a column called "A Glance in Passing," the prolific Frank L. Stanton contributed verse, and Richard H. Edmonds wrote about the South. The magazine's first number sold out quickly despite a less than satisfactory job of printing. William F. Mugleston reports that one Augusta, Georgia, subscriber liked the magazine so well that he sent $100 for a 100-year subscription, and that by year's end, *Uncle Remus's* had subscribers in every state, as well as in several foreign countries.[4] The magazine's graphic design improved considerably, and delightful illustrations were obtained from G. P. Haynes, Floy Cowan, R. J. Dean, Lute Pease, A. D. Reed, R. F. James, Charles Bull, and other artists.

The Sunny South Publishing Company bought out the *Home Magazine*, an Indianapolis monthly published by Bobbs-Merrill, in March 1908. Beginning with the May 1908 issue, the two magazines were continued as *Uncle Remus's The Home Magazine*, a title that proved somewhat unwieldy and was altered in August 1909 to *Uncle Remus's Home Magazine*. The combination resulted in a circulation of 200,000 which increased to 240,000 by late Summer 1908.

The gentle Harris, who frequently referred to himself as "The Farmer of Snap-Bean Farm," died of nephritis and cirrhosis of the liver at age fifty-nine on July 2, 1908, little more than a year after the magazine's founding. Some of the company's principals favored ending the magazine with the July issue, but Julian Harris convinced them to continue and became his father's successor as editor. Subsequent issues contained expressions of tribute and condolence over the elder Harris' death. The September number contained a letter from a great admirer of Harris' work, President Theodore Roosevelt (24, 1: 5)[5]; in the same issue, with a nicely illustrated border featuring Brer Rabbit and Brer Fox, was Don Marquis' tribute to his mentor, followed by tributes in verse from Frank Stanton and Grantland Rice, and yet another from Mary E. Bryan (24, 1: 8, 32). Of all these, Rice's seems the most fitting, considering Harris' own style:

> The shadow's on the cotton patch; the light
>   has left the sky;
> A world shall bow in sorrow at his message
>   of good-bye;
> And the gold of all the sunshine in Dixie's
>   turned to gray;
> But the sweetest flowers of the South shall
>   hide his face away.

Under Julian Harris the magazine's graphic appearance changed little, but the fiction content was lessened to make room for more commentary on current affairs, though stories by Jack London and O. Henry were attracted during these years. Joel Harris' abhorrence of mob violence was enlarged upon by his son in a series called "The Menace of the Mask." Some of its installments, one of which was headlined "Tennessee's Tragic Story of Night Riders Who Lynched at Reelfoot Lake," show the serious side of Don Marquis, who today is remembered almost exclusively as a humorist (24, 4: 15–17). A serious Marquis poem, "Reelfoot Lake," appeared more than three years later. (31, 5: 4).

A substantial quantity of theretofore unpublished material from the elder Harris also appeared during the remaining years of the magazine's existence, including

"King Philpo," the last story Harris had written before his death (31, 2: 7, 18). Like so many other Southern magazines of that era, *Uncle Remus's* often used both verse and prose couched in Negro dialect, some of which expanded upon J. C. Harris' own characters, as in G. P. Haynes' "Brer Possum's Luck" (31, 6: 12).[6]

In the midst of all this nostalgic, Old South copy, editor Julian Harris editorialized in favor of a real two-party political system for the "Solid South." Democrats in the region were horrified at such an alien thought, and a few thousand Southern subscribers cancelled their subscriptions.

Despite an impressive circulation, the magazine never became profitable, and Harris backed other "wrong horses" in his editorials. In July 1911 Frederick Fayram, formerly with a Minneapolis woman's magazine, the *Housekeeping Magazine*, became general manager of *Uncle Remus's*, though Julian Harris stayed on as editor until the summer of 1912. Profits failed to improve, and until September 1912 G. P. Haynes was listed as managing editor, while Harris, who had surrendered his financial interest in the company, went to New York City as advertising manager. Edmund Hackett edited the last few numbers, which appeared under the title *Uncle Remus: Dixie's Illustrated Monthly*. The final issue was that of February 1913. The magazine's title and subscription list were purchased by *Pulitzer's Magazine* of New York City, a forty-eight-page monthly published by the Pulitzer Magazine Company, Inc.

There is something vaguely forlorn about the cover of *Uncle Remus's* last issue. It shows a hoopskirted Southern belle of fifty years earlier, sitting as ladies were so often pictured in those days: doing nothing, with hands resting demurely on her lap. A poem, printed on the cover's lower left, portrayed her as remaining constant to her lost Confederate warrior and dreaming of him by the "Trysting Tree."

The melancholy connection between this little poem and its illustration and the magazine in general is that *Uncle Remus's* existed at an awkward time—an era in which homage to the Old South was *de rigueur*, but in which more attention to the region's present and future were needed, yet not necessarily wanted by many readers.

Notes

1. For biographical detail on Harris' life, see Paul Cousins, *Joel Chandler Harris* (Baton Rouge, 1968). Shorter biographical sketches may be found in William Peterfield Trent, *Southern Writers* (London, 1905), p. 423, and in Edwin Mims and Bruce R. Payne, *Southern Prose and Poetry for Schools* (New York, 1910), p. 427.

2. Camp, an Atlanta journalist, was Julian Harris' brother-in-law.

3. See Cousins, *Harris*, p. 211.

4. "The Perils of Southern Publishing: A History of *Uncle Remus's Magazine*," *Journalism Quarterly*, Autumn 1975, p. 516.

5. When *Uncle Remus's Magazine* absorbed the *Home Magazine*, the latter's numbering was adopted.

6. Another example is Frank Stanton's "When Br'er B'ar Stole Honey," 32, 5: 12.

Information Sources

BIBLIOGRAPHY:
Cousins, Paul. *Joel Chandler Harris*. Baton Rouge, 1968.
Harris, Julia Collier. "Joel Chandler Harris." In *Southern Pioneers in Social Interpretations*, edited by Howard W. Odum. Chapel Hill, N.C., 1925. Pp. 143–64.
Mott, Frank Luther. *A History of American Magazines, 1905–1930*.Cambridge, 1968. III: 46n, IV: 361n.
Mugleston, William F. "The Perils of Southern Publishing: A History of *Uncle Remus's Magazine*." *Journalism Quarterly*, Autumn 1975.
INDEX SOURCES: None.
LOCATION SOURCES: Atlanta Public Library, Duke University Library, Library of Congress, New York Public Library, Oberlin College Library, University of Georgia Library.

Publication History

MAGAZINE TITLE AND TITLE CHANGES: *Uncle Remus's Magazine* (June 1907–April 1908); *Uncle Remus's The Home Magazine* (May 1908–July 1909); *Uncle Remus's Home Magazine* (August 1909–October 1912); *Uncle Remus: Dixie's Illustrated Monthly* (November 1912–February 1913).
VOLUME AND ISSUE DATA: Vols. 1–11 (June 1907–April 1908); vols. 23–32 (May 1908–February 1913), monthly.
PUBLISHER AND PLACE OF PUBLICATION: Sunny South Publishing Company. Atlanta, Georgia.
EDITORS: Joel Chandler Harris (June 1907–July 1908); Julian Harris (July 1908–June 1912); G. P. Haynes, managing editor (July 1912–October 1912); Edmund Hackett (November 1912–February 1913).
CIRCULATION: 235,500 paid, 6,000 nonpaid.

UNION STATION TIMES. *See* ARKANSAS TIMES

UNIVERSAL INTELLIGENCER. *See* THE NORTH CAROLINA MAGAZINE

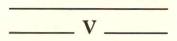

V

VIRGINIA CAVALCADE

In the boxwood gardens of Berkeley Plantation in Virginia's Charles City County stand two ladies dressed in colonial period costume, smiling prettily and holding baskets of spring flowers, which presumably they have just picked— one form of physical work always allowed a Southern lady. This tranquil scene adorns the cover of *Virginia Cavalcade* (5, 4), published since Summer 1951 by the Virginia State Library in Richmond.

The library's purpose in starting the magazine, as expressed in a policy statement[1] drafted in January 1952, was "to present, clearly and simply, through the medium of pictures and text, authentic and interesting episodes of Virginia history." Each issue, the policy statement continued, would include one article consisting mainly of illustrations, one for which text was more important than illustration, and one featuring material from the library's own collection. Each issue was to contain forty-eight pages split into ten or eleven articles, and each was to average two pictures a page. No page was to be without illustration. A managing editor, working with the state librarian, was to assign article topics and supervise the magazine's production and distribution. Articles were to be brief—no more than 2,500 words—and readable. As many color illustrations as possible were to be used, and subject matter would include all eras of the commonwealth's history. Finally, an annual index was to be prepared.

Articles must be related to Virginia history, from the age of exploration to the mid-twentieth century. The magazine's guidelines for writers call for manuscripts that deal with history in such a way as to appeal to a broad readership and may treat social, economic, cultural, political, or military topics of a historical nature. Articles are written in narrative style, and writers are asked to avoid excessive use of quotations. Though articles are not footnoted, contributors must provide the editor source citations and complete bibliography. The style is that of popular history, but certainly respectable popular history. Often authors of longer scholarly historical articles will be asked to provide a shortened version for *Virginia Cavalcade*.

The forty-six-page quarterly is copiously illustrated with a combination of old drawings, paintings, and engravings, many of which are from the library's collection, plus new photos and art. Its illustrations bring new life to material that most scholarly historical journals could not afford to illustrate, even if they wished to do so.

When the magazine was first published, a single copy sold for 35¢, a year's subscription for $1.50. In Winter 1955 rates went up to 50¢ or $2.00 yearly. After further price increases in 1971 and 1975, the present figures are $2.00 a copy or $4.00 a year. Circulation is relatively modest; of the roughly 10,500 copies sold quarterly in 1984, over 7,000 are in-state sales, 1,150 in Richmond alone. The magazine, however, has subscribers in every state, with the next largest circulations in North Carolina (340), Florida (259), Maryland (232), California (216), and Texas (193).

Roughly 75 percent of *Virginia Cavalcade*'s articles are freelanced, and the split between text and illustration is about 60:40. The covers and about 20 percent of the inside illustrations are in color. Twelve men and one woman have edited the magazine, either as editor or managing editor. Deserving much credit for the magazine's development and direction is former state librarian Randolph W. Church, who joined the library staff in 1934, replaced Wilmer L. Hall as state librarian in 1947, and retired from that post in 1972 (see "Randolph Church," 22, 1: 5).

Virginia Cavalcade's lone female editor is the present occupant of this office, Patricia L. Faust, whose personal specialty is Civil War history and who earlier served for four years as editor of *American History Illustrated* and for three years before that as associate editor of *Early American Life*. Article selection is now in the editor's hands entirely; there no longer is an editorial review board for this purpose. Editor Faust has solicited longer manuscripts—up to 4,000 words— to add variety and has made it her policy to use five rather than four articles per issue, to avoid padding articles with marginal art, she says.[2] Due to her own interests, one can expect a reemphasis on Civil War history in the magazine's future issues.

In 1958 appeared the most extensive article the magazine had used to that date—thirty-five pages devoted to an account of a journey down the Appomattox River made in 1796 by English architect/engineer/naturalist/traveler Benjamin Henry Latrobe. The material for this unusual treatment was arranged by librarian Randolph Church and included facsimile reproductions of Latrobe's beautifully illustrated journal (8, 4: 4–38). A second piece on Latrobe appeared six years later as "Latrobe's Proposals for Virginia," again with copious illustration (16, 1: 33–47).

Another issue that owed much to a single writer was a 1955 number (5, 1) for which Robert Leslie Scribner did three biographical pieces on Virginians whose reputations were made primarily in the settling of Texas: Sam Houston (pp. 31–35), Stephen Austin, (pp. 16–19), and William Alexander Anderson Wallace (pp. 40–43), better known as "Bigfoot" Wallace. An earlier piece of note by the same contributor was "The Code Duello in Virginia: The Rise and Decline of a 'Way of Death' " (3, 2: 28–31), in which Scribner names the year of Virginia's first formal duel as 1619, when Captain William Eppes dispatched Captain Edward Stallinge. The practice did not really catch on, however, until the 1770s, according to the writer, and the first Southern "rule book" on dueling did not come out until 1838, when John Lyde Wilson wrote *The Code of Honor*.

As one might expect, considerable attention has been given to the state's favorite sons: Washington, Jefferson, and Lee. Of special interest was an article on George Washington's last hours, accompanied by a nicely illustrated account of the mourning pictures and memorial prints turned out in great number for sale to the grieving public to commemorate the great man's death. One such picture, for example, showed Liberty weeping at Washington's tomb while the angel Gabriel waited to crown him with laurel leaves (33, 3: 136–143). An article on Robert E. Lee that is oh-so-old-line-Virginian was A.G.M. Martin's "Lee's Christmases Far from Home" on his three tours of duty in the Rio Grande Valley border country (7, 3: 28–32).

It should be mentioned that *Virginia Cavalcade* is just as apt to descend from the lofty realms of the Washingtons and the Lees and include pieces on the folkways of humbler Virginians, as in "Hog-Killing Day" by Lamont Pugh (7, 3: 41–46), or on one of the state's first black citizens to gain renown, Bill Robinson, better known as "Bojangles." Robinson was, according to Richmond writer James Meehan, the first black star of a Broadway musical (*Blackbirds*, 1928) and the lead in the first all-Negro talking movie (*Harlem Is Heaven*, 1932) and was earning $5,000 a week in the midst of the Great Depression.[3]

Among other writers worthy of special mention was Elizabeth Dabney Coleman, whose contributions often concerned Virginia women, such as her piece on Mary Johnston, a writer of romantic novels who also wrote *Hagar* to support the women's suffrage movement (6, 3: 8–11), and an article on Grace Sherwood, a Princess Anne County woman charged with witchcraft (6, 1: 28–34). The magazine's first editor, William Edwin Hemphill, also contributed pieces of considerable interest, among them "Hazards of the Highways" on the impediments to travel encountered by illustrator David Hunter Strother ("Porte Crayon") when he toured the commonwealth in 1853 (6, 1: 42–44).

A final contributor to be recognized here was William Harris Gaines, who did "Men against the Swamp" on coastal Virginia's 750-square-mile Great Dismal Swamp (4, 3: 23–29) and "The Fires of Smithfield" on that most excellent of the state's great institutions, the Smithfield ham (4, 3: 14–17).

Virginia Cavalcade has become quite a state institution, bringing an added appreciation of Virginia's history to its readers. Appearing on its title page is the magazine's motto, a quote from Patrick Henry: "I know of no way of judging the future but by the past."

Notes

1. Provided the author in July 1984 by Patricia Faust, editor.
2. In a July 1984 letter to the author.
3. Two articles on Bill "Bojangles" Robinson appeared in vol. 27, no. 3. The first was "The Bill Robinson Statue in Richmond," pp. 100–113, by W. Donald Rhinesmith, then managing editor of *Virginia Cavalcade*; the second was Meehan's article on Robinson's career as a dancer, pp. 118–23.

Information Sources

INDEX SOURCES: Access: The Supplementary Index to Periodicals.
LOCATION SOURCES: Boston Public Library, Duke University Library, Library of Congress, University of North Carolina Library (Chapel Hill), University of Virginia Library, Virginia Tech Library, Yale University Library.

Publication History

MAGAZINE TITLE AND TITLE CHANGES: *Virginia Cavalcade*.
VOLUME AND ISSUE DATA: Vols. 1–33 (Summer 1951–present), quarterly.
PUBLISHER AND PLACE OF PUBLICATION: Virginia State Library. Richmond, Virginia.
EDITORS: W. Edwin Hemphill (1951–Spring 1954); Randolph W. Church (Summer 1954–Autumn 1955); W. E. Hemphill (Winter 1955–Summer 1958); R. W. Church (Autumn–Spring 1959); Ulrich Trobetzkoy (Summer 1959–Summer 1963); Edward F. Heite (Spring 1964–Winter 1968); Benjamin J. Hillman (Spring 1968–Autumn 1969); William Edward Dunstan III (Winter–Autumn 1970); R. W. Church (Winter–Summer 1971); Kent Druyvesteyn (Autumn 1971–Winter 1973); Donald R. Haynes (Spring 1973–Summer 1974); Jon K. Kukla (Autumn 1974–Summer 1976); Christopher M. Beam (Autumn 1976–Spring 1977); W. Donald Rhinesmith (Winter 1978–Winter 1981); Henry G. Ecton (Spring 1981–Winter 1983); Patricia Faust (Winter 1984–present).
CIRCULATION: 10,500 (Summer 1984).

VIRGINIA CONSERVATIONIST. *See* VIRGINIA WILDLIFE

VIRGINIA LITERARY AND EVANGELICAL MAGAZINE. *See* THE LITERARY AND EVANGELICAL MAGAZINE

THE VIRGINIAN

A state magazine with a lively, witty personality is the *Virginian*, which began its life in Fall 1979 as *Shenandoah Valley Magazine*, broadened its coverage area and changed its title accordingly to *Shenandoah/Virginia Town & Country* in Summer 1982, and adopted its less cumbersome present title in late Spring 1984.[1] The handsome bimonthly's sparkle may be attributed to its editor and publisher, Jeffrey Wexler, who had no magazine experience whatever prior to founding *Shenandoah Valley Magazine*. Like many other persons who have entered the regional magazine field, Wexler had his earlier media experience in newspaper work. Besides his newspaper experience on Long Island, New York, Wexler has also worked as a New York City policeman and as a staff member for a New York congressman, not the most likely background for someone publishing a magazine with a predominantly country orientation in Virginia's bucolic Blue Ridge. Wexler, now in his late thirties, first came South as a student at Washington and Lee University and in researching articles for his magazine has probably come to know more about the state than many Virginians whose families have lived here for generations.

Some of the prolific Wexler's best work has been done under the memorable pen name L.Q.C.L. (Lucius Quintus Cincinnatus Lamar) McKittrick IV, whom Wexler first presented to his readers as an eccentric gentleman of leisure whose time was largely spent puttering about the family library. Accompanying a later McKittrick article, "The Perfect Mint Julep," is an editor's note to the effect that in the course of researching the piece, "Col. McKittrick obliged himself to forego the daily pleasures of visiting the Mint Spring Post Office" (2, 3: 24), which Southerners will immediately recognize as an important part of the daily regimen for so many gentlemen of affairs in the small-town South. Other McKittrick articles have involved compendia of the state's ghost legends (3, 3: 28–29) and information on the derivation of Virginia place names. Sweet Chalybeate in Alleghany County, for instance, is named for its springs from which flows water rich in iron salts. Frederick County's Hayfield was named, writes McKittrick, for a meadow in which two or three local farmers were interrupted in 1763. "The Indians who interrupted them," he adds innocently, "massacred them" (1, 2: 20).

Wexler has shown real facility for getting contributions from well-known writers. Conservative newspaper columnist James J. Kilpatrick began writing a column for Wexler in the September/October 1981 issue; the column appears regularly on the magazine's last page. Another Kilpatrick contribution of note was a feature article on his days as a Richmond newspaperman (6, 3: 10–17). The same issue contained the reminiscences of Nobel Prize Laureate William Golding, author of *Lord of the Flies*, about his time as a young writer-in-residence at Hollins College, a prestigious woman's campus outside Roanoke (6, 3: 18–20). Virginia Senator John Warner wrote on his own college experiences at Washington and Lee (1, 1: 11–13), Walter Cronkite did a tribute to General Douglas MacArthur (6, 1: 14–19), William Styron offered a witty piece entitled "If Mr. Jefferson Were Here Today" (6, 1: 23–25, 28–29), Russell Baker contributed an excerpt from his book *Growing Up* (Congdon and Weed, New York, 1982) on his Virginia roots (5, 1: 15–21), and James Dickey wrote "How to Read Poetry" (6, 4: 84–85).

Other articles focus on famous Virginians. An example is a piece on historian/
biographer Douglas Southall Freeman (6, 4: 10–17). Another issue contained
features on sometime-Virginian Eric Sevareid's mountain hideaway between
Marshall and Warrenton (5, 3: 15–16) and on full-fledged Virginian John S.
Mosby, the "Grey Ghost" of Civil War fame (5, 3: 26–28).

The eighty- to ninety-six-page magazine, located at New Hope, Virginia, had
a 1984 paid circulation of just under 25,000, about two-thirds of which are by
subscription and roughly 20 percent of which are out of state. Median household
income is $36,371, mediain age 47.3. The male:female split is 46.3:53.7. Just
over 70 percent of subscribers are married; 27.3 percent are college graduates.

Roughly two-thirds of feature articles are freelanced, though staff-written
features are often longer. The percentage of color to black and white inside the
magazine is increasing and is now about one-third color. Covers are on heavy
stock and feature good photography. Each issue also includes a color photo
spread with fine photographs, some of the most notable of which have been
snowscapes in the Shenandoah and Blue Ridge.

A full page advertisement in color is $1,705 for one insertion. The *Virginian*
was chosen as one of twenty-four magazines nationally in which to advertise
Rolls Royce automobiles, and other prestige advertisers have included Sotheby,
Christie's, The Greenbrier, The Homestead, Palmetto Dunes at Hilton Head
Island, The Hotel Roanoke, and The Boar's Head Inn. Asked what his primary
competitors were, Wexler replied that originally he had competed for advertisers'
dollars with area newspapers, such as those in Winchester and Charlottesville,
but that presently his main competitors are *Southern Living*,* *Southern Accents*,*
and the demographic editions of some national magazines.

The *Virginian* sells for $2.50 a copy or $12.00 a year within Virginia, $14.00
elsewhere, and offers its readers the usual staples of regional magazines: letters
to the editor, an events calendar, a guide to elegant dining, and a section on
fine or historic houses for sale. A department titled "Only Yesterday" runs old
Virginia photos sent in by readers.

Examples of feature articles other than those already cited are "Canoeing the
Shenandoah" written by the commonwealth's outdoor recreation planner (5, 4:
32–35); an interview with Virginia-born movie actor Robert Duvall (5, 4: 39,
42–46); an account of the real people upon whom the popular television series
"The Waltons" was based (2, 3: 16–21); a visit with eighty-year-old fiddler
Pug Allen (4, 2: 11–13); and "The Czarina of Charlottesville," the story of
Mrs. John Manahan, thought by many to have been Anastasia Nickolayevna,
fourth daughter of Tsar Nicholas II of Russia (3, 6: 56–62).

Located as he is in the Shenandoah Valley, Wexler can hardly expect to
generate the advertising revenues of a magazine of comparable quality located
in a major city, yet his location is such a beautiful one that it is at the same time
a real advantage. As was pointed out in an article in the magazine's initial issue
(pp. 8–10), the Shenandoah has a strong romantic appeal, even for those who
have never seen either the river or the valley that bears its name.

Note

1. An earlier Virginia periodical having the same title is the *Virginian* (1963–present), the journal of the Virginia State Society of American Medical Technologists.

Information Sources

BIBLIOGRAPHY:
Click, Carolyn. "Shenandoah Valley's New Yorker Reports Trivia and Triumphs." *Washington Post*, March 25, 1984.
————. "Yankee Magazine Publisher Touts Joys of Shenandoah Valley Living." *Alexandria Gazette*, April 3, 1984.
LeRoux, Margaret. "Valley Scales the Heights." *Advertising Age*, April 5, 1982.
INDEX SOURCES: None.
LOCATION SOURCES: Library of Congress, Virginia Tech Library.

Publication History

MAGAZINE TITLE AND TITLE CHANGES: *Shenandoah Valley Magazine* (1979–May/June 1982); *Shenandoah/Virginia Town & Country* (July/August 1982–March/April 1984); *The Virginian* (May/June 1984–present).
VOLUME AND ISSUE DATA: Vols. 1–6 (Autumn 1979–present), bimonthly.
PUBLISHER AND PLACE OF PUBLICATION: Shenandoah Valley Magazine Corporation; Jeffrey Wexler, publisher. New Hope, Virginia.
EDITOR: Jeffrey Wexler.
CIRCULATION: 25,000 paid (1984).

VIRGINIA WILDLIFE

Oldest of the South's state wildlife magazines is *Virginia Wildlife*, first published in September 1920 as *Virginia Conservationist*, a sixteen-page bimonthly sent free upon request to residents of the state. The dual purpose of its supporting organization, Virginia's Department of Game and Inland Fisheries, was to educate citizens on wildlife conservation and to evolve a more cordial relationship between hunters and game wardens. The *Conservationist* was published in Richmond and in 1922 had a circulation of about 3,000.

In 1922 the little magazine's title was changed to the *Game and Fish Conservationist*, and page size was enlarged from 7″ x 10″ to 9″ x 12″. The magazine remained a bimonthly, and a year's subscription was set at 50¢; a single issue was 10¢. By spring 1923 circulation had advanced to 10,000. In 1924 a three-year subscription was offered for $1 and advertising space sold for 5¢ a word, with lower rates for hunting dog ads; since 1927 the magazine has contained no advertisements.

The magazine was discontinued during the depression era, between November/December 1931 and September 1937. With the September 1937 issue the present title, *Virginia Wildlife*, was adopted. The slender periodical, published at that time in Blacksburg as an eight-page monthly bulletin, sold for 25¢ a year or

50¢ for three years. In the autumn of 1940 *Virginia Wildlife* began being published as a near digest-sized magazine of forty-four-page length. Late in 1941 the magazine was returned to Richmond, where a year later it was suspended for the duration of World War II.

When it resumed publication in July 1946, the monthly again increased page size and set issue length at twenty-two pages, increasing length slightly in subsequent numbers. A year's subscription was $1; a three-years-for-$2 inducement was offered in 1948. Under Editor Joseph Shomon (1948–1961) *Virginia Wildlife*'s recognition was enhanced by being named the nation's best state conservation magazine by the Izaak Walton League of America and by being honored for quality production by the American Association for Conservation Information.[1]

By the early 1960s circulation was up to 38,000; in 1984 the figure was roughly 50,000. The magazine began paying contributors for their work in 1950; the present rate is 7¢ a word, with at least 70 percent of the magazine's articles written by freelancers.

Virginia Wildlife's physical appearance has improved gradually over its many years of publication. Full-color covers were adopted on a regular basis in the early 1960s; earlier covers had alternated between one color and black and white for many years. Today the thirty-five-page monthly is graphically superior and boasts fine nature photography—close-ups of Virginia's birds and animals, landscapes, and nature-related photo essays. The proportion of color versus black-and-white photography is roughly 50:50. Today's *Virginia Wildlife* is infinitely more interesting to a general audience than it was in the 1960s and before. One now sees fewer pictures of grinning fishermen holding up the one that didn't get away, fewer macho shots of a boy and his first buck/bear/wild turkey, and fewer stiffly posed photos of forest rangers or conservation bureaucrats.

One of the longest running regular departments in today's *Virginia Wildlife* is "Bird of the Month," write-ups on the state's many birds, some about which we indoorsmen are apt to know little or nothing: the golden-crowned kinglet, whimbrel, yellow-billed cuckoo, Eastern kingbird, Hudsonian curlew, Eastern wood peewee, or pied-billed grebe. More wildlife information, some of it also about birds, appears in another department entitled "Non-Game Update." Examples are the sparrow hawk, barred owl, pileated woodpecker, brown bat, and black rat snake. Other departments are "Field Notes," "Growing Up Outdoors," and "Personalities," the last named of which profiles wardens and new commissioners and of the several features is dullest, though practically inevitable in a magazine published by an arm of government.

The reader of this magazine's feature articles, many of which are around 1,200 words long, will learn something about a wide variety of the state's living creatures: white-footed deer, freshwater mussels, shrews and moles, whistling swans, turkey vultures, flying squirrels—all creatures great or small. There are articles on hunting and boating safety, how to catch trout in winter, game law information, boat care, skin diving, bow hunting, fish management, outdoor cooking, and endangered species. *Virginia Wildlife*'s editor, Harry Gillam, appears fond of how-to articles: how to fly fish or surf cast, control weeds in farm ponds, skin a deer, build or repair a birdhouse. Recipes for fish, game, or seafoods appear occasionally, as do photo spreads on wildlife art. Profiles of plants are used, for example "Kudzu: The Plant You Love to Hate" (44, 8: 32–33), and profiles of places acquaint the reader with the state's rivers, swamps, and other geographical features. An interesting example of the place profile is "Nathan Cobb's Island," published in 1983 (44, 10: 17–21).

Over the years voluminous attention has been paid the cardinal and the dogwood, the state's official bird and tree. Reminders about the dangers of rabies in wildlife have appeared often, as well. Less frequent are articles with a historical slant; one of this category was "Early Game Legislation," written in the 1950s (15, 3: 16–17) by Dorothy Troubetzkoy, an editorial assistant. Once every few years will come a glimpse of society in the great out-of-doors in such articles as "Cry of the Hounds" (44, 9: 24–27) and "Tally Ho!" (42, 9: 20–22), both of which are on fox hunting. For readers who like "body counts" there is an annual kill summary for deer, bear, and turkey, and from time to time arguments on the pros and cons of hunting will appear, as in Alan Krug's "Sociology of Hunting" in a 1981 issue (42, 2: 16–17).

Of today's 50,000 circulation, all but a few hundred are by subscription, and roughly 10 percent are complimentary copies sent to agency personnel, schools, other magazines, and other government agencies. The magazine has a much larger potential readership, Gillam feels,[2] but is hampered by state regulation as to how it may be advertised.

Notes

1. See Ann E. Pilcher, "A Brief History of Virginia Wildlife Magazine and Its Predecessors," *Virginia Wildlife*, November 1961, pp. 22–23.
2. Telephone conversation with the author, June 25, 1984.

Information Sources

BIBLIOGRAPHY:
Pilcher, Ann E. "A Brief History of Virginia Wildlife Magazine and Its Predecessors." *Virginia Wildlife*, November 1961, pp. 22–23.
INDEX SOURCES: None.
LOCATION SOURCES: Duke University Library, Library of Congress, New York Public Library, University of California at Berkeley Library, University of Virginia Library, Virginia Tech Library.

Publication History

MAGAZINE TITLE AND TITLE CHANGES: *Virginia Conservationist* (September 1920– May 1922); *Game and Fish Conservationist* (May 1922–September 1931); *Virginia Wildlife* (September 1937–present).
VOLUME AND ISSUE DATA: Vols. 1–45 (September 1920–present); bimonthly (1920– 1931), monthly (1937–1940), quarterly (Autumn 1940–1942), monthly (July 1946– present).

PUBLISHER AND PLACE OF PUBLICATION: Department of Game and Inland Fisheries (1920–1931); Commission of Game and Inland Fisheries in cooperation with the Virginia Wildlife Federation (1937–1940); Virginia Commission of Game and Inland Fisheries (1940–present). Richmond, Virginia (1920–1931); Blacksburg, Virginia (1937–1942); Richmond, Virginia (1942–present).

EDITORS: Lewis W. Tyus (1920–1930); Herbert K. Job (1930–1931); Charles O. Handley (1931); C. F. De La Barre (1937–1940); James F. McInteer, Jr. (1940–1942); Henry Mosby (1942); Clyde Patton (1946–1948); Joseph J. Shomon (1948–1961); Rupert M. Cutler (1961–1962); James F. McInteer, Jr. (1962–1973); Henry L. Gillam (1973–present).

CIRCULATION: 40,000 paid, 10,000 nonpaid.

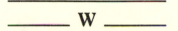

THE WEEKLY MUSEUM

One of the earliest of Baltimore's periodicals was the *Weekly Museum*, published from January to May 1797 by John Smith and Christopher Jackson at No. 67 Market Street. Of these issues, which appeared weekly on Sundays, only two numbers are known to exist. The *Museum* is included in this volume as an example of the early ephemeral periodical in transition between newspaper and magazine. Its subscription price was $2 yearly, half to be paid at time of subscription, the remainder at year's end.

The lead article of the eight-page weekly on February 5, 1797, was headlined "Of Indirect Taxes"; this heavy fare was lightened by a pair of merry feature pieces, the first of which was called "A Paradun":

> To dun—or not to dun? That is the question,
>   Whether 'tis better that the Purse should suffer
> (For lack of cash) by baneful emptiness;
>   Or by a gentle dun to fill it up:
> To dun! to get the money—and be enabled
>   To live—and pay our debts—'tis a consummation
> Devoutly to be wished. To dun—to be deny'd—
>   Deny'd—with "CALL AGAIN"—Ay, there's the rub—
> For in that "call again," what evils come—
>   What disappointment—sore—chagrin—and woe—
> What time is wasted—and what shoes are worn
>   In consequence—must give us pain.
>
>   —It is this—
> That makes so many debts not worth collecting:
> 'Tis this that sickens business to dispair—

And keeps from HONEST LABOUR its reward,
   While thus in language of complaint we speak,
We don't forget our many, many friends;
   To them a debt of gratitude we owe:
To them our gratitude we freely pay.
   Buoy'd by their kindness, still our bark shall sail,
Enjoy the pleasing CALM—nor dread the boist'rous GALE. [No.
   5: 36]

The second verse item came in question-and-answer format:

QUESTION.
Why see we oft that ancient maids
Are peevish and ill natur'd jades?

ANSWER.
Because when young, they were too proud,
To listen to the sparks that vow'd
And, having pass'd their early prime,
Must now lament the loss of time.
By which they might have led their lives
As mothers, friends, and cheerful wives;
For homely sure, the dame must be
That none with eyes of love could see.
And as they more advance in years,
The more for this are shed their tears
And still the more their hopes are crossed,
Of fame and virtue more they boast:
Till finding none to bid them wed,
And love to youthful maidens fled,
Their faces tell the deep regret,
And thus they rail, and pine and fret. [No. 5: 36–37]

Such a large dose of whimsical fare was atypical of the newspapers of the
period. What seems to have been evolving was a perceived need for more
entertainment than the newspaper usually provided. This need was met in weekly
miscellanies that had the appearance of newspapers but a mixture of information-
entertainment content more nearly magazine than newspaper-like.

Also in number 5 appeared a list of the average life spans of a variety of
animals, ranging from the goat and pigeon's 8 years to the raven and eagle's
100 (no. 5: 35).

A brief item lifted from a newspaper informed the *Museum*'s readers that
William Cobbett of Philadelphia intended to publish a paper to be called *Porcupine's Gazette*. His reason, the piece stated, was that there existed so many

"ill conducted papers, calculated to mislead the people, that another is become necessary to undeceive them. Peter will prove a terrible scourge to the patriots" (no. 5: 37).

In the same issue were an account of a fire at the Philadelphia *Gazette* in which the editor's wife, two daughters, one son, and a Negro boy perished, and a statement of antislavery sentiments:

> Humanity blushes and hides her insulted head at the recital of sufferings yesterday detailed in the petition presented to congress by certain persecuted Africans... we trust the time will arrive when every state in the union shall acknowledge
>
> 'The Rights of Man by nature
>   still are due,
> To man of every clime and
>   every hue.' [No. 5: 37]

Number 6, the only other issue still extant, began with a serious essay, "Attempting to Prove Fossil Shells, Bone, Wood, Fish, &c to be the Spoils of the Universal Deluge" (pp. 40–41), followed by a shorter essay on the improvement of worn-out lands. Then appeared a humorous piece called "The Matrimonial Creed," proclaiming the "domain nominal of the husband, and another domain real of the wife." ("The man was not created for the woman, but the woman for the man/Yet the man shall be the slave of the woman, and the woman the tyrant of the man" [p. 43].)

Two poems, "The Wanderer" and "The Complaint" (no. 6: 43–44), are followed by two curious anecdotes, "Of a Vicar and Moses" and "Women Have No Souls" (p. 44), then by a series of newspaper-like notices concerning marriages, the arrival of ships, and news items from abroad brought to port by these ships.

Information Sources

INDEX SOURCES: None.
LOCATION SOURCES: American Periodical Series microfilm, Harvard University Library.

Publication History

MAGAZINE TITLE AND TITLE CHANGES: *The Weekly Museum.*
VOLUME AND ISSUE DATA: Vol. 1, Nos. 1–21 (January 8–May 28, 1797), weekly.
PUBLISHER AND PLACE OF PUBLICATION: John Smith and Christopher Jackson. Baltimore, Maryland.
EDITORS: John Smith and Christopher Jackson.
CIRCULATION: Unknown.

THE WEEKLY REGISTER. *See* NILES' WEEKLY REGISTER

THE WESTERN REVIEW AND MISCELLANEOUS MAGAZINE

Like the *Journal of Belles Lettres** before it, the *Western Review and Miscellaneous Magazine: A Monthly Publication Devoted to Literature and Science* was a quality journal but well ahead of its time on the frontier. It was founded in 1819 by William Gibbes Hunt, an émigré from New England who, with the assistance of faculty from Lexington's Transylvania University and other contributors, hoped to stimulate the cultural attainments in Kentucky. Hunt's two most important writers were Constantine S. Rafinesque, a professor of botany and natural science, and Horace Holley, the university's president. Each contributed both prose and poetry, Holley covering a wide variety of subjects, Rafinesque usually writing on the areas he taught.

The magazine's contents were divided into three departments: review, miscellany, and poetry. The lead article in Hunt's first issue was a long review of a book on the life of Andrew Jackson[1] that began:

> There is a splendor in military greatness, which renders it, to every one, an object of interest. The philosopher, the scholar, the philanthropist, and the statesman, may be approved and respected, but the achievements of the hero dazzle and enchant. The useful application of superior intellect to the purposes of civil and domestic life, will ultimately ensure veneration and gratitude: but what are these, compared with the enthusiastic glow of admiration, which the brilliant exploits of the warrior command! Vain are the efforts of reason to destroy this peculiar charm of military glory.

Among the verse published in the *Western Review*, most of it original, were poems in French, Italian, and Latin; the usual run of precious romanticism ("To a Little Bird," "Lines to a Bird Protected in a Storm," "Ramble by Moonlight"); and more intriguing and unusual efforts ("Apology to Two Ladies" [a tall order] and "To a Wife Returning to the Country"). A reasonable amount of the original amateur verse is pleasing. An example is a tribute to a lady, Miss Anna Clay, written extemporaneously in her album by an admirer:

> 'Tis said that all are made of CLAY:
> If so, how variously hath Heaven,
> Whose will, material shapes obey,
> Deformity, or beauty given!
> Some are as coarse as Charleston (1) ware,
> Made rough and strong for common use,

With scarce a thought, still less a care,
If honour greet them, or abuse:
While some, as *Wedgewood's* (2) art may show,
With service a plain taste combine;
Yet there no rays of beauty glove,
No touch is felt of grace divine.
Some, as in old *Confusius'* school, (3)
In imitation only dare,
From foreign fashions take the rule,
And dazzle with a stupid glare.
In France, the land of brilliant dashes,
Where pure transparent Seve (4) is found,
In pride of porcelain, beauty flashes,
While tea its fragrance spreads around.
But we have far a lovelier mould,
Where heaven's own image loves to play,
Whose magic powers the form unfold
Of Psyche's Vase (5) in ANNA CLAY. [4, 1: 42]

Under "Miscellany" appeared scientific articles ("Botany of Kentucky," "Natural History of Fishes in the Western Waters," "Lightnings Observed in the Western States"); travel copy ("A Ride to the Catskill Mountains," "Scenery at Harper's Ferry"); and an assortment of interesting reading for the thoughtful ("Female Heroism," "Libraries in Europe and in the United States," "New Tales of My Landlord," "Life of Major Zachary Taylor"). One of this magazine's truly outstanding features is the considerable space it devoted to original accounts on the American Indian. The "Miscellany" section of volume 1 contained the following titles: "Adam Poe's Contest with Two Indians," "Adventure With the Indians," "Indian Antiquities," "Conflicts with the Indians," "Indian Antiquities in the Western Country," "Indian Contests" (the last four titles each represent a series of essays), and "Two Men Wounded by Indians."

Nestled among the heavier fare of the February 1820 number is a two-page account that illuminates the frontier mileau in which this periodical was published. Headlined "Severe Encounter with a Wild Cat," the article describes how schoolteacher John McKinney of Bourbon County had been attacked inside his schoolhouse some years earlier by a large wildcat and how he had succeeded in strangling the beast while affecting nonchalance so as not to alarm the women who had come to investigate the commotion (2, 1: 43–44).

In 1820 three of Hunt's regular contributors died, and Prof. Rafinesque split off to begin his own magazine, the *Western Minerva*.[2] These considerations, on top of insufficient subscriptions, led Hunt to fold his *Review* with the July 1821 issue. His "Valedictory" in that number ranks as one of the saddest and most disillusioned of its kind. Excerpts are quoted below:

The present number, which completes the fourth volume of the *Western Review*, terminates also the existence of the work. It is with regret that we announce our determination to discontinue a publication, which we at one time fondly hoped would be a permanent repository of the numerous productions of the intelligence, and taste, and literary acquirements of the citizens of the west. . . . Experience has taught us that our labours, valuable as they might appear to ourselves, were of little importance in the public estimation, and that the literary efforts, which, we are proud to say, have received the favourable notice of distinguished scholars in other parts of our country, were condemned and deemed unworthy of patronage at home. [P. 383]

Notes

1. John Reid and John Henry Eaton, *The Life of Andrew Jackson, Major General in the Service of the United States: Comprising a History of the War in the South, from the Commencement of the Creek Campaign, to the Termination of Hostilities Before New Orleans* (Philadelphia, 1817).

2. Only one number was published (January 1821). The professor later moved to Philadelphia and published another short-lived periodical, the *Atlantic Journal* (1832–33).

Information Sources

BIBLIOGRAPHY:
Edgar, Neal L. *A History and Bibliography of American Magazines, 1810–1820*. Metuchen, N.J., 1975. Pp. 256–57.
Mott, Frank Luther. *A History of American Magazines, 1741–1850*. New York, 1930. I: 311–312.
Rusk, R. L. *The Literature of the Middle Western Frontier*. New York, 1925. Pp. 165–68.
Venable, W. H. *Beginnings of Literary Culture in the Ohio Valley*. Cincinnati, 1891. Pp. 62–66.
INDEX SOURCES: Poole's Index to Periodical Literature.
LOCATION SOURCES: American Antiquarian Society (Worcester, Massachusetts), American Periodical Series microfilm, University of Chicago Library.

Publication History

MAGAZINE TITLE AND TITLE CHANGES: *The Western Review and Miscellaneous Magazine: A Monthly Publication Devoted to Literature and Science*.
VOLUME AND ISSUE DATA: Vols. 1–4, no. 6 (August 1819–July 1821), monthly.
PUBLISHER AND PLACE OF PUBLICATION: William Gibbes Hunt. Lexington, Kentucky.
EDITOR: William Gibbes Hunt.
CIRCULATION: Unknown.

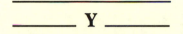

Y

YOUTH'S GAZETTE. *See* THE ROSE BUD

Chronological Listing of Magazines Profiled, by Year Founded

1828   The Southern Literary Gazette
       The Southern Review
1829   American Turf Register and Sporting Magazine
1830   The National Magazine; or, Lady's Emporium
1832   The Rose Bud; or, Youth's Gazette
1834   The Southern Literary Messenger
1835   The Southern Literary Journal, and Monthly Magazine
1836   The Baltimore Monument
1840   The Magnolia; or, Southern Apalachian
1841   The Southern Planter
1842   The Orion
       The Southern Quarterly Review
1843   The Southern Cultivator
1846   DeBow's Review
1857   Russell's Magazine
1860   The Plantation
1861   The Southern Monthly
1862   The Countryman
1863   Southern Punch
1865   Scott's Monthly Magazine
1866   The Land We Love
1873   Our Living and Our Dead
1875   The Sunny South
1881   Texas Siftings
1882   The Arkansaw Traveler
       The Mascot
       The Southern Bivouac
1885   Dixie
1886   The Progressive Farmer
1892   Fetter's Southern Magazine
       The Sewanee Review
       The Tatler of Society in Florida
1894   The Rolling Stone
1895   Reed's Isonomy: A Journal of Justice
1896   The Texas Magazine
1905   Bob Taylor's Magazine
1906   Palm Beach Life
1907   Uncle Remus's Magazine

1920   Miami/South Florida Magazine
       Virginia Wildlife
1921   The Double Dealer
1922   The Fugitive
1923   The Southern Literary Magazine
1928   The Houston Gargoyle
1934   The Southern Magazine
1951   Virginia Cavalcade
1966   New Orleans Magazine
       Southern Living
1967   Antique Monthly
       Foxfire®
1970   The Mother Earth News®
1972   Brown's Guide to Georgia
1973   Delta Scene Magazine
       Southern Exposure
       Texas Monthly
1974   Arkansas Times
       D Magazine
1977   Southern Accents
       Texas Homes
1979   Southern World
       The Virginian
1980   Country Magazine
       Miami Mensual
1981   Ultra Magazine
1982   Carolina Lifestyle

Geographical Location of Magazines Profiled, by State

Alabama

Antique Monthly
The Progressive Farmer[1]
Southern Living

Arkansas

Arkansas Times
The Arkansaw Traveler

Florida

Miami Mensual
Miami/South Florida Magazine
Palm Beach Life
The Tatler of Society in Florida

Georgia

Brown's Guide to Georgia
The Countryman
Dixie
Foxfire®
The Magnolia; or, Southern Apalachian[2]
The Orion[3]
The Plantation: A Southern Quarterly Journal
Scott's Monthly Magazine
Southern Accents
The Southern Cultivator
The Southern Literary Magazine[4]
The Sunny South
Uncle Remus's Magazine

Kentucky

Fetter's Southern Magazine
Journal of Belles Lettres
The Medley; or, Monthly Miscellany
The Southern Bivouac
The Western Review and Miscellaneous Magazine

Louisiana

DeBow's Review[5]
The Double Dealer
The Mascot
New Orleans Magazine

Maryland (prior to the Civil War, only)

The American Farmer[6]
American Turf Register and Sporting Magazine[7]
The Baltimore Monument
The Emerald
The Genius of Universal Emancipation[8]
The Key
Moonshine
The National Magazine; or, Lady's Emporium
Niles' Weekly Register[9]
The Observer
The Portico: A Repository of Science & Literature
The Red Book
The Weekly Museum

Mississippi

Delta Scene Magazine

North Carolina

The Land We Love
The Mother Earth News®
The North Carolina Magazine; or, Universal Intelligencer
Our Living and Our Dead
Southern Exposure

South Carolina

The Monthly Register, Magazine, and Review of the United States
Omnium Botherum
Omnium Gatherum
The Rose Bud; or, Youth's Gazette
Russell's Magazine
South Carolina Weekly Museum and Complete Magazine of Entertainment and
    Intelligence

The Southern Literary Gazette
The Southern Literary Journal, and Monthly Magazine
The Southern Quarterly Review[10]
The Southern Review
Southern World
The Toilet: A Weekly Collection of Literary Pieces Principally Designed for the Amusement of the Ladies
The Traiteur

Tennessee

Bob Taylor's Magazine
The Fugitive
The Sewanee Review
The Southern Monthly[11]

Texas

D Magazine
The Houston Gargoyle
Reed's Isonomy: A Journal of Justice
The Rolling Stone
Texas Homes
The Texas Magazine
Texas Monthly
Texas Siftings
Ultra Magazine

Virginia

The American Gleaner and Virginia Magazine
Carolina Lifestyle
Country Magazine
The Literary and Evangelical Magazine
The Monthly Magazine and Literary Journal
National Magazine
The Southern Literary Messenger
The Southern Magazine
The Southern Planter
Southern Punch
Virginia Cavalcade
The Virginian
Virginia Wildlife

Notes

1. Published in North Carolina, 1886–1911.
2. Published in South Carolina, 1842–43.
3. Published in South Carolina, 1844.
4. Published in Tennessee, 1924.

5. Published in the District of Columbia, 1853–58; South Carolina, 1861–64; Tennessee, 1866–68.

6. Published in the District of Columbia, 1892–97.

7. Published in New York, 1839–44.

8. Published in Ohio, 1821; Tennessee, 1821–24; the District of Columbia, and Maryland, 1830–32; the District of Columbia, 1832–33; Pennsylvania, 1834–39; Illinois, 1839.

9. Published in the District of Columbia, 1836–39; Pennsylvania, 1848–49.

10. Published in Louisiana, 1842.

11. Published in Mississippi, 1862.

Index

About the Author

SAM G. RILEY is Professor of Communication Studies at Virginia Polytechnic Institute and State University. He specializes in mass media history and has written extensively on a variety of academic and popular subjects. His articles have appeared in *Journalism Quarterly, American Journalism,* the *Journal of Popular Culture, Journalism Educator*, and in newspapers throughout the United States.